Front-End Web Development

THE BIG NERD RANCH GUIDE

Chris Aquino & Todd Gandee

Big Nerd
Ranch

Front-End Web Development: The Big Nerd Ranch Guide

by Chris Aquino and Todd Gandee

Big Nerd Ranch, LLC
200 Arizona Ave NE
Atlanta, GA 30307
(770) 817-6373
http://www.bignerdranch.com/
book-comments@bignerdranch.com

The 10-gallon hat with propeller logo is a trademark of Big Nerd Ranch, LLC.

Exclusive worldwide distribution of the English edition of this book by

Pearson Technology Group
800 East 96th Street
Indianapolis, IN 46240 USA
http://www.informit.com

ISBN-10 0134433947
ISBN-13 978-0134433943

First edition, first printing, July 2016

Dedication

To Mom and Dad, for buying us that computer. To Dave and Glenn, for letting your little brother completely hog it. And to Angela, for giving me a life away from the screen.

— C.A.

To my mom and dad, thank you for giving me room to find my own way. To my wife, thank you for loving a nerd.

— T.G.

Acknowledgments

As authors, we can take full credit for typing the words and creating the diagrams. (Yay, us!) But the whole truth is that we would still be staring at a blank page if not for the efforts of an army of contributors, collaborators, and mentors.

- Aaron Hillegass, for believing that the two of us could produce a work worthy of the Big Nerd Ranch name. Thank you for your immeasurable faith and support.

- Matt Mathias, for guiding us through the development of this book, especially during the crucial last mile. You made sure that time that would have been spent watching cat videos or Downton Abbey reruns was instead dedicated to writing.

- Brandy Porter, for the care and (literal) feeding of the authors on numerous occasions. You worked your magic behind the curtain, orchestrating a sequence of events that made finishing this work possible. Thank you.

- Jonathan Martin, our coinstructor and language maven. Thank you for enthusiastically teaching the in-progress course materials on which this book is based and offering thoughtful criticism throughout the many revisions.

- Our proofreaders, technical reviewers, and guinea pigs: Mike Zornek, Jeremy Sherman, Josh Justice, Jason Reece, Garry Smith, Andrew Jones, Stephen Christopher, and Bill Phillips. Thank you for volunteering as tribute.

- Elizabeth Holaday, our infinitely patient and reassuring editor. Thank you for breaking us out of the echo chamber, being the voice of reason, and reminding us always of our readers.

- Ellie Volckhausen, who designed our cover.

- Simone Payment, our proofreader, who kept things consistent.

- Chris Loper at IntelligentEnglish.com, who designed and produced the print and ebook versions of the book. His DocBook toolchain made life much easier, too.

Lastly, thank you to the countless students who have taken the week-long training. Without your curiosity and your questions, none of this matters. This work is a reflection of the insight and inspiration you have given us over the span of those many weeks. We hope the otters made the training a little lighter.

Table of Contents

Introduction

Learning Front-End Web Development

Doing front-end web development may require a shift in perspective, as it is a very different animal from development for other platforms. Here are a few things to keep in mind as you are learning.

The browser is a platform.

Perhaps you have done native development for iOS or Android; written server-side code in Ruby or PHP; or built desktop applications for OS X or Windows. As a front-end developer, your code will target the browser – a platform available on nearly every phone, tablet, and personal computer in the world.

Front-end development runs along a spectrum.

At one end of the spectrum is the look and feel of a web page: rounded corners, shadows, colors, fonts, whitespace, and so on. At the other end of the spectrum is the logic that governs the intricate behaviors of that web page: swapping images in an interactive photo gallery, validating data entered into a form, sending messages across a chat network, etc. You will need to become proficient with the core technologies all along this spectrum, and you will often need to use multiple technologies in synergy to create a good web application.

Web technologies are open.

There is no one company that controls how browsers should work. That means that front-end developers do not get a yearly SDK release that contains all the changes they will need to deal with for the next twelve months. Native platforms are a frozen pond on which you can comfortably skate. The web is a river; it curves, moves quickly, and is rocky in some places – but that is part of its appeal. The web is the most rapidly evolving platform available. Adapting to change is a way of life for a front-end developer.

This book's purpose is to teach you how to develop for the browser. As you follow this guide, you will be taken through the process of building a series of projects. Each project will call for a different mixture of technologies along the front-end spectrum. Because of the sheer number of front-end tools, libraries, and frameworks available, this book will focus on the most essential and portable patterns and techniques.

Prerequisites

This book is not an introduction to programming. It assumes you have experience with the fundamentals of writing code. You are expected to be familiar with basic types, functions, and objects.

That said, it also does not assume you already know JavaScript. It introduces you to JavaScript concepts in context, as you need them.

How This Book Is Organized

This book walks you through writing four different web applications. Each application has its own section of the book. Each chapter in a section adds new features to the application you are building.

Doing the work of building these four applications takes you from one extreme of the front-end spectrum to the other.

Ottergram   In your first project, you will create a web-based photo gallery. Building Ottergram will teach you the fundamentals of programming for the browser using HTML, CSS, and JavaScript. You will build the user interface manually, learning how the browser loads and renders content.

CoffeeRun   Part coffee order form, part checklist, CoffeeRun takes you through a number of JavaScript techniques including writing modular code, taking advantage of closures, and communicating with a remote server using Ajax. Your focus will shift from manually creating the UI to creating and manipulating it programmatically.

Chattrbox   Chattrbox has the shortest section and is the most distinct of the apps. You will use JavaScript to build a chat system, writing a chat server with Node.js as well as a browser-based chat client.

Tracker   Your final project uses Ember.js, one of the most powerful frameworks for front-end development. You will create an application that catalogs sightings of rare, exotic, and mythical creatures. Along the way, you will learn your way around the rich ecosystem that powers the Ember.js framework.

As you work through these applications, you will be introduced to a number of tools, including:

- the Atom text editor and some useful plug-ins for working with code
- documentation resources like the Mozilla Developer Network
- the command line, using the OS X Terminal app or the Windows command prompt
- browser-sync
- Google Chrome's Developer Tools
- normalize.css
- Bootstrap
- jQuery and libraries like crypto-js and moment
- Node.js, the Node package manager (npm), and nodemon
- WebSockets and the wscat module
- Babel, Babelify, Browserify, and Watchify
- Ember.js and addons like Ember CLI, Ember Inspector, Ember CLI Mirage, and Handlebars
- Bower
- Homebrew
- Watchman

How to Use This Book

This book is not a reference book. Its goal is to get you over the initial hump to where you can get the most out of the reference and recipe books available. It is based on our five-day class at Big Nerd Ranch, and, as such, it is meant to be worked through from the beginning. Chapters build on each other, and skipping around would be unproductive.

In our classes, students work through these materials, but they also benefit from the right environment – a dedicated classroom, good food and comfortable board, a group of motivated peers, and an instructor to answer questions.

As a reader, you want your environment to be similar. That means getting a good night's rest and finding a quiet place to work. These things can help, too:

- Start a reading group with your friends or coworkers.

- Arrange to have blocks of focused time to work on chapters.

- Participate in the forum for this book at `forums.bignerdranch.com`, where you can discuss the book and find errata and solutions.

- Find someone who knows front-end web development to help you out.

Challenges

Most chapters in this book end with at least one challenge. Challenges are opportunities to review what you have learned and take your work in the chapter one step further. We recommend that you tackle as many of them as you can to cement your knowledge and move from *learning* JavaScript development from us to *doing* JavaScript development on your own.

Challenges come in three levels of difficulty:

- Bronze challenges typically ask you to do something very similar to what you did in the chapter. These challenges reinforce what you learned in the chapter and force you to type in similar code without having it laid out in front of you. Practice makes perfect.

- Silver challenges require you to do more digging and more thinking. Sometimes you will need to use functions, events, markup, and styles that you have not seen before, but the tasks are still similar to what you did in the chapter.

- Gold challenges are difficult and can take hours to complete. They require you to understand the concepts from the chapter and then do some quality thinking and problem solving on your own. Tackling these challenges will prepare you for the real-world work of JavaScript development.

You should make a copy of your code before you work on the challenges for any chapter. Otherwise, the changes that you make may not be compatible with subsequent exercises.

If you get lost, you can always visit `forums.bignerdranch.com` for some assistance.

For the More Curious

Many chapters also have "For the More Curious" sections. These sections offer deeper explanations or additional information about topics presented in the chapter. The information in these sections is not absolutely essential, but we hope you will find it interesting and useful.

Part I
Core Browser Programming

1

Setting Up Your Development Environment

There are countless tools and resources for front-end development, with more being built all the time. Choosing the best ones is challenging for developers of all skill levels. Throughout the projects in this book, we will guide you in the use of some of our favorites.

To get started, you will need three basic tools: a browser, a text editor, and good reference documentation for the many technologies used in front-end development. Also, there are several extras that – while not essential – will make your development experience smoother and more enjoyable.

For the purposes of this book we recommend that you use the same software we use to get the most benefit from our directions and screenshots. This chapter walks you through installing and configuring the Google Chrome browser, the Atom text editor, Node.js, and a number of plug-ins and extras. You will also find out about good documentation options and get a crash course in using the *command line* on Mac and Windows. In the next chapter, you will put all these resources to use as you begin your first project.

Installing Google Chrome

Your computer should already have a browser installed by default, but the best one to use for front-end development is Google Chrome. If you do not already have the latest version of Chrome, you can get it from www.google.com/chrome/browser/desktop (Figure 1.1).

Figure 1.1 Downloading Google Chrome

Installing and Configuring Atom

Of the many text editor programs out there, one of the best for front-end development is the Atom editor by GitHub. It is a good choice because it is highly configurable, has many plug-ins to help with writing code, and is free to download and use.

You can download Atom for Mac or Windows from atom.io (Figure 1.2).

Figure 1.2 Downloading Atom

Follow the installation instructions for your platform. After Atom is installed, there are several plug-ins you will want to install as well.

Atom plug-ins

The primary things you want out of your text editor are documentation lookup, autocompletion, code formatting, and code linting (more on that in a bit). Atom gives you some of these features by default, but installing a few plug-ins will make it even better.

Open Atom and reveal its Settings screen. On a Mac, this is done by choosing Atom → Preferences... or using the keyboard shortcut Command-, (that is, the Command key plus the comma). On Windows, you can access it via File → Settings or using the keyboard shortcut Ctrl-,.

On the lefthand side of the Settings screen, click + Install (Figure 1.3).

Figure 1.3 Atom's Install Packages screen

Here, you can search for plug-in packages by name. Begin by searching for "emmet."

Writing a lot of HTML can be very tedious and is error-prone. The emmet plug-in (Figure 1.4) lets you write well-formatted HTML using a convenient shorthand. Click the Install button to get emmet.

Figure 1.4 Installing emmet

Next, search for "atom-beautify." The atom-beautify plug-in (Figure 1.5) helps with the indentation of your code, which helps with readability. Again, click Install to get this plug-in.

Figure 1.5 Installing atom-beautify

Search for and install the autocomplete-paths plug-in (Figure 1.6). Very often, your code will need to refer to other files and folders in your project. This plug-in helps by offering filenames in an autocomplete menu as you type.

Figure 1.6 Installing autocomplete-paths

Your next plug-in to install is the api-docs package (Figure 1.7), which lets you look up documentation based on keyword. It displays the documentation in a separate tab in the editor.

Figure 1.7 Installing api-docs

Next, search for and install the linter package (Figure 1.8). A *linter* is a program that checks the syntax and style of your code. Make sure you find and install the package that is just named "linter." This is a base linter that works with language-specific plug-ins. You will need it in order to use the other linter plug-ins below.

Figure 1.8 Installing linter

There are three companions to linter that you will want to install to check your CSS, HTML, and JavaScript code. Start with linter-csslint (Figure 1.9), which ensures that your CSS is syntactically correct and also offers suggestions about writing performant CSS.

Figure 1.9 Installing linter-csslint

The next linter companion plug-in to install is linter-htmlhint (Figure 1.10), which confirms that your HTML is well formed. It will warn you about mismatched HTML tags.

Figure 1.10 Installing linter-htmlhint

The last linter companion plug-in to install is linter-eslint (Figure 1.11). This plug-in checks the syntax of your JavaScript and can be configured to check the style and formatting of your code (for example, how many spaces lines are indented or how many blank lines come before and after comments).

Figure 1.11 Installing linter-eslint

Chrome and Atom are now ready for front-end development. There are just a few more steps to completing your coding environment: accessing documentation, learning command-line basics, and downloading two final tools.

Documentation and Reference Sources

Front-end development is different from programming for platforms like iOS and Android. Aside from the obvious differences, front-end technologies have no official developer documentation other than the technical specifications. This means that you will need to look elsewhere for guidance. We recommend that you familiarize yourself with the resources below and consult them regularly as you work through the book and continue on with front-end development.

The Mozilla Developer Network (MDN) is the best reference for anything to do with HTML, CSS, and JavaScript. One way to access it is devdocs.io, an excellent documentation interface (Figure 1.12). It pulls documentation from MDN for core front-end technologies – and it can work offline, so you can check it even when you do not have an internet connection.

Figure 1.12 Accessing documentation via devdocs.io

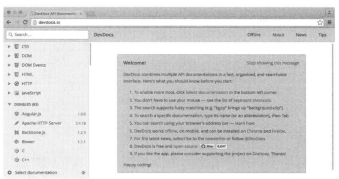

Note that Safari currently does not support the offline caching mechanism used by devdocs.io. You will need to use a different browser, such as Chrome, to access it.

You can also use MDN's website, developer.mozilla.org/en-US (Figure 1.13), or simply add "MDN" as a search engine keyword to find the information you need.

Figure 1.13 The Mozilla Developer Network website

Another site to know about is stackoverflow.com (Figure 1.14). Officially, this is not a source of documentation. It is a place where developers can ask each other about code. The answers vary in quality, but are often very thorough and quite helpful. So it is a useful resource – as long as you bear in mind that the answers are not definitive, due to its crowdsourced nature.

Figure 1.14 The Stack Overflow website

Web technologies are always changing. Support for features and APIs will vary from browser to browser and over time. Two websites that can help you determine which browsers (and which versions of individual browsers) support what features are html5please.com and caniuse.com. When you need information about feature support, we suggest starting with html5please.com to know whether a feature is recommended for use. For more detailed information about which browser versions support a specific feature, go to caniuse.com.

Crash Course in the Command Line

Throughout this book, you will be instructed to use the *command line* or *terminal*. Many of the tools you will be using run exclusively as command-line programs.

To access the command line on a Mac, open Finder and go to the Applications folder, then the Utilities folder. Find and open the program named Terminal (Figure 1.15).

Figure 1.15 Finding the Terminal app on a Mac

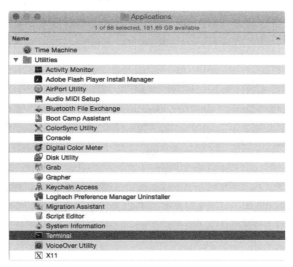

You should see a window that looks like Figure 1.16.

Figure 1.16 Mac command line

To access the command line on Windows, go to the Start menu and search for "cmd." Find and open the program named Command Prompt (Figure 1.17).

Figure 1.17 Finding the Command Prompt program on Windows

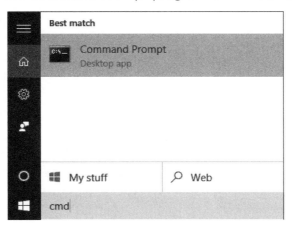

Click it to run the standard Windows command-line interface, which looks like Figure 1.18.

Figure 1.18 Windows command line

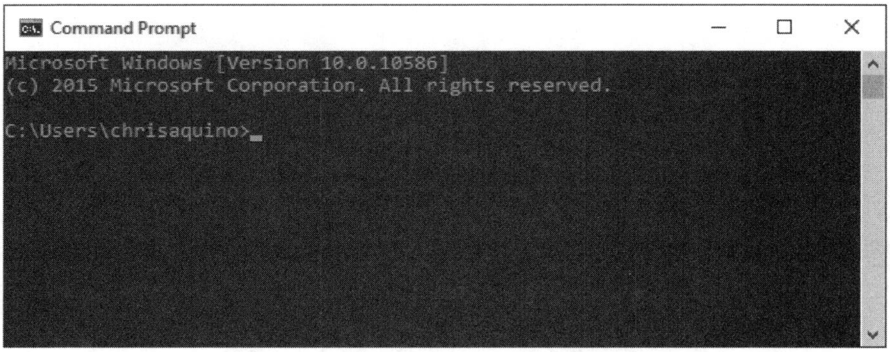

From now on, we will refer to "the terminal" or "the command line" to mean both the Mac Terminal and the Windows Command Prompt. If you are unfamiliar with using the command line, here is a short walkthrough of some common tasks. All commands are entered by typing at the prompt and pressing the Return key.

Finding out what directory you are in

The command line is location based. That means that at any given time it is "in" a particular directory within the file structure, and any commands you enter will be applied within that directory. The command-line prompt shows an abbreviated version of the directory it is in. To see the whole path on a Mac, enter the command pwd (which stands for "print working directory"), as in Figure 1.19.

Figure 1.19 Showing the current path using pwd on a Mac

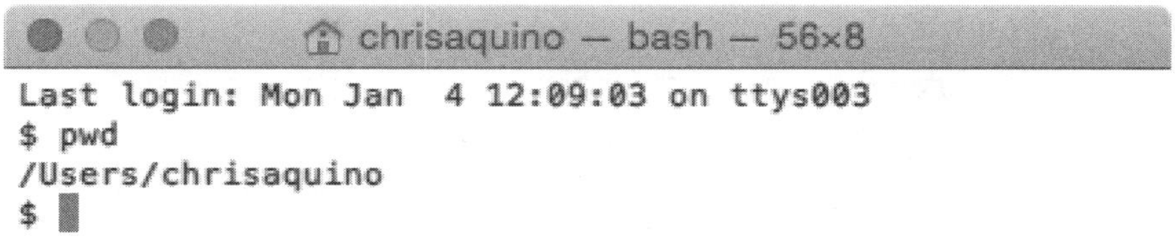

On Windows, use the command echo %cd% to see the path, as in Figure 1.20.

Figure 1.20 Showing the current path using echo %cd% on Windows

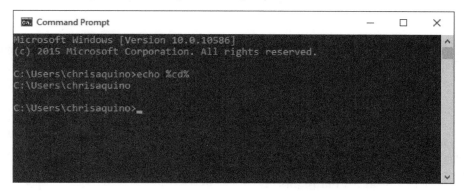

Creating a directory

The directory structure of front-end projects is important. Your projects can grow quickly, and it is best to keep them organized from the beginning. You will create new directories regularly during your development. This is done using the mkdir or "make directory" command followed by the name of the new directory.

To see this command in action, set up a directory for the projects you will build as you work through this book. Enter this command:

```
mkdir front-end-dev-book
```

Next, create a new directory for your first project, Ottergram, which you will begin in the next chapter. You want this new directory to be a subdirectory of the front-end-dev-book directory you just created. You can do this from your home directory by prefacing the new directory name with the name of the projects directory and, on a Mac, a slash:

```
mkdir front-end-dev-book/ottergram
```

On Windows, you use the backslash instead:

```
mkdir front-end-dev-book\ottergram
```

Changing directories

To move around the file structure, you use the command cd, or "change directory," followed by the path of the directory you want to move into.

You do not always need to use the complete directory path in your cd command. For example, to move down into any subdirectory of the directory you are in, you simply use the name of the subdirectory. So when you are in the front-end-dev-book directory, the path of the ottergram folder is just ottergram.

Move into your new project directory:

```
cd front-end-dev-book
```

11

Now, you can move into the ottergram directory:

```
cd ottergram
```

To move up to the parent directory, use the command cd .. (that is, cd followed by a space and two periods). The pair of periods represents the path of the parent directory.

```
cd ..
```

Remember that you can check your current directory by using the pwd command (or echo %cd% on Windows). Figure 1.21 shows the author creating directories, moving between them, and checking the current directory.

Figure 1.21 Changing and checking directories

```
● ◎ ●          front-end-dev-book — bash — 60×15
$ mkdir front-end-dev-book
$ mkdir front-end-dev-book/ottergram
$ pwd
/Users/chrisaquino/Projects
$ cd front-end-dev-book
$ pwd
/Users/chrisaquino/Projects/front-end-dev-book
$ cd ottergram
$ pwd
/Users/chrisaquino/Projects/front-end-dev-book/ottergram
$ cd ..
$ pwd
/Users/chrisaquino/Projects/front-end-dev-book
$ █
```

You are not limited to moving up or down one directory at a time. Let's say that you had a more complex directory structure, like the one shown in Figure 1.22.

Figure 1.22 An example file structure

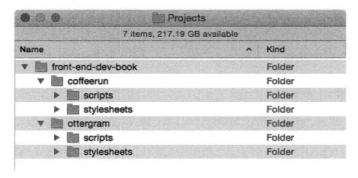

Suppose you are in the ottergram directory and you want to go directly to the stylesheets directory inside of coffeerun. You would do this with cd followed by a path that means "the stylesheets directory inside the coffeerun directory inside the parent directory of where I am now":

```
cd ../coffeerun/stylesheets
```

On Windows, you would use the same command but with backslashes:

```
cd ..\coffeerun\stylesheets
```

Listing files in a directory

You may need to see a list of files in your current directory. On a Mac, you use the `ls` command for that (Figure 1.23). If you want to list the files in another directory, you can supply a path:

```
ls
ls ottergram
```

Figure 1.23 Using `ls` to list files in a directory

By default, `ls` will not print anything if a directory is empty.

On Windows, the command is `dir` (Figure 1.24), which you can optionally give a path:

```
dir
dir ottergram
```

Figure 1.24 Using `dir` to list files in a directory

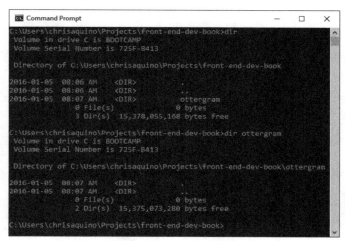

By default, the `dir` command will print information about dates, times, and file sizes.

Getting administrator privileges

On some versions of OS X and Windows, you will need *superuser* or administrator privileges in order to run some commands, such as commands that install software or make changes to protected files.

13

On a Mac, you can give yourself privileges by prefixing a command with sudo. The first time you use sudo on a Mac, it will give you a stern warning, shown in Figure 1.25.

Figure 1.25 sudo warning

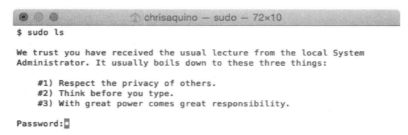

sudo will prompt you for your password before it runs the command as the superuser. As you type, your keystrokes will not be echoed back, so type carefully.

On Windows, if you need to give yourself privileges you do so in the process of opening the command-line interface. Find the command prompt in the Windows Start Menu, right-click it, and choose Run as Administrator (Figure 1.26). Any commands you run in this command prompt will be run as the superuser, so be careful.

Figure 1.26 Opening the command prompt as an administrator

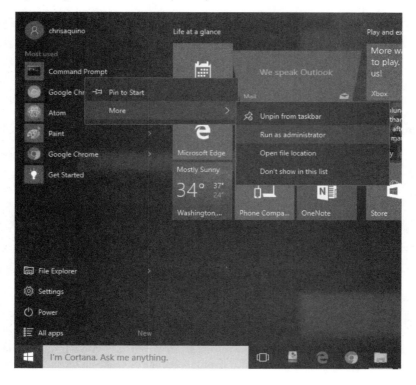

Quitting a program

As you proceed through the book, you will run many apps from the command line. Some of them will do their job and quit automatically, but others will run until you stop them. To quit a command-line program, press Control-C.

Installing Node.js and browser-sync

There is one final set-up step before you begin your first project.

Node.js (or simply "Node") lets you use programs written in JavaScript from the command line. Most front-end development tools are written for use with Node.js. You will learn lots more about Node.js in Chapter 15, but you will begin using one tool that depends on it, browser-sync, right away.

Install Node by downloading the installer from nodejs.org (Figure 1.27). The version of Node.js used in this book is 5.11.1, and you will likely see a different version available for download.

Figure 1.27 Downloading Node.js

Double-click the installer and follow the prompts.

When you install Node, it provides two command-line programs: node and npm. The node program does the work of running programs written in JavaScript. You will not need to use it until Chapter 15. The other program is the Node package manager, npm, which is needed for installing open-source development tools from the internet.

browser-sync is one such tool, and it will be invaluable to you throughout the book. It makes your example code easier to run in the browser and automatically reloads the browser when you save changes to your code.

Install browser-sync using this command at the command line:

```
npm install -g browser-sync
```

(The -g in the command stands for "global." Installing the package globally means that you will be able to run browser-sync from any directory.)

It does not matter what directory you are in when you run this command, but you will probably need superuser privileges. If that is the case, run the command using sudo on a Mac:

```
sudo npm install -g browser-sync
```

If you are on Windows, first open a command prompt as the administrator, as shown above.

When you start browser-sync, as you will in the next chapter, it will run until you press Control-C. It is a good idea to quit browser-sync when you are done working on a project for a while. That means that you will need to start browser-sync each time you begin work on the first two projects in this book (Ottergram and CoffeeRun).

With that, you have the tools you need to get started on your Ottergram project!

For the More Curious: Alternatives to Atom

There are many, many text editors to choose from. If you are not that keen on Atom, when you are done working through the projects in this book you may want to try out one of the following two options. Both are available for free for Mac and Windows, and both have a large number of plug-ins to customize your development experience. Also, like Atom, both are built using HTML, CSS, and JavaScript, but run as desktop applications.

Visual Studio Code is Microsoft's open source text editor, made specifically for developing web applications. It can be downloaded from code.visualstudio.com (Figure 1.28).

Figure 1.28 The Visual Studio Code website

Adobe's Brackets text editor is particularly good for building user interfaces with HTML and CSS. In fact, it provides an extension for helping you work with Adobe's layered PSD image files. Brackets is available from brackets.io (Figure 1.29).

Figure 1.29 The Adobe Brackets website

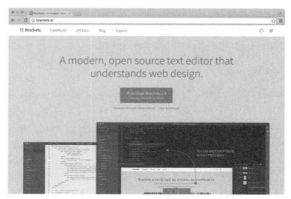

2

Setting Up Your First Project

When you visit a website, your browser has a conversation with a server, another computer on the internet.

Browser: "Hey there! Can I please have the contents of the file named `cat-videos.html`?"

Server: "Certainly. Let me take a look around … here it is!"

Browser: "Ah, it's telling me that I need another file named `styles.css`."

Server: "Sure thing. Let me take a look around … here it is!"

Browser: "OK, that file says that I need another file named `animated-background.gif`."

Server: "No problem. Let me take a look around … here it is!"

That conversation goes on for some time, sometimes lasting thousands of milliseconds (Figure 2.1).

Figure 2.1 The browser sends a request, the server responds

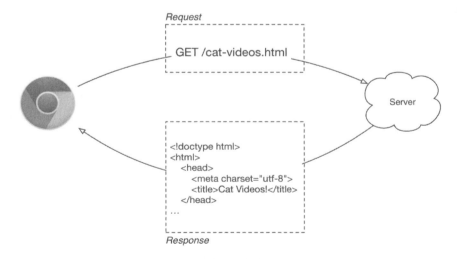

17

It is the browser's job to send requests to the server; interpret the HTML, CSS, and JavaScript it receives in the response from the server; and present the result to the user. Each of these three technologies plays a part in the user's experience of a website. If your app were a living creature, the HTML would be its skeleton and organs (the mechanics), the CSS would be its skin (the visible layer), and the JavaScript would be its personality (how it behaves).

In this chapter, you are going to set up the basic HTML for your first project, Ottergram. In the next chapter, you will set up your CSS, which you will refine in Chapter 4. In Chapter 6, you will begin adding JavaScript.

Setting Up Ottergram

In Chapter 1, you created a folder for the projects in this book as well as a folder for Ottergram. Start your Atom text editor and open the ottergram folder by clicking File → Open (or File → Open Folder... on Windows). In the dialog box, navigate to the front-end-dev-book folder and choose the ottergram folder. Click Open to tell Atom to use this folder (Figure 2.2).

Figure 2.2 Opening your project folder in Atom

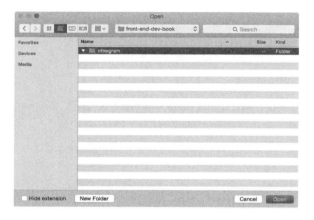

You will see the ottergram folder in the lefthand panel of Atom. This panel is for navigating among the files and folders in your project.

You are going to create some files and folders within the ottergram project folder using Atom. Control-click (right-click) ottergram in the lefthand panel and click New File in the pop-up menu. You will be prompted for a name for the new file. Enter index.html and press the Return key (Figure 2.3).

Figure 2.3 Creating a new file in Atom

You can use the same process to create folders using Atom. Control-click (right-click) ottergram in the lefthand panel again, but this time click New Folder in the pop-up. Enter the name stylesheets in the prompt that appears (Figure 2.4).

Figure 2.4 Creating a new folder in Atom

Finally, create a file named styles.css in the stylesheets folder: Control-click (right-click) stylesheets in the lefthand panel and choose New File. The prompt will pre-fill the text "stylesheets/". After this, enter styles.css and press the Return key (Figure 2.5).

Figure 2.5 Creating a new CSS file in Atom

When you are finished, your project folder should look like Figure 2.6.

Figure 2.6 Initial files and folders for Ottergram

There are no rules about how to structure your files and folders or what to name them. However, Ottergram (like the other projects in this book) follows conventions used by many front-end developers. Your index.html file will hold your HTML code. Naming the main HTML file index.html dates back to the early days of the web, and the convention continues today.

The stylesheets folder, as the name suggests, will hold one or more files with styling information for Ottergram. These will be CSS, or "cascading style sheets," files. Sometimes developers give their CSS files names that describe what part of the page or site they pertain to, such as header.css or blog.css. Ottergram is a simple project and only needs one CSS file, so you have named it styles.css to reflect its global role.

Initial HTML

Time to get coding. Open index.html in Atom and add some basic HTML to get started.

Start by typing html. Atom will offer you an autocomplete option, as shown in Figure 2.7. (If it does not, make sure you installed the emmet plug-in as directed in Chapter 1.)

Figure 2.7 Atom's autocomplete menu

Press the Return key, and Atom will provide bare-bones HTML elements to get you started (Figure 2.8).

Figure 2.8 HTML created using autocomplete

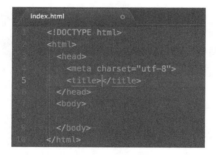

Your cursor is between <title> and </title> – the opening and closing title tags. Type "ottergram" to give the project a name. Now, click to put your cursor in the blank line between the opening and closing body tags. There, type "header" and press the Return key. Atom will convert the text "header" into opening and closing header tags with a blank line between them (Figure 2.9).

Figure 2.9 Header tag created with autocomplete

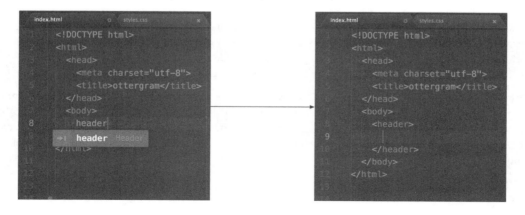

Next, type "h1" and press Return. Again, your text is converted into tags, this time without a blank line. Enter the text "ottergram" again. This will be the heading that will appear on your web page.

Your file should look like this:

```
<!doctype html>
<html>
  <head>
    <meta charset="utf-8">
    <title>ottergram</title>
  </head>
  <body>
    <header>
      <h1>ottergram</h1>
    </header>
  </body>
</html>
```

Atom and emmet have together saved you some typing and helped you build well-formed initial HTML.

Let's examine your code. The first line, `<!doctype html>`, defines the *doctype* – it tells the browser which version of HTML the document is written in. The browser may render, or draw, the page a little differently based the doctype. Here, the doctype specifies HTML5.

Earlier versions of HTML often had long, convoluted, and hard to remember doctypes, such as:

```
<!DOCTYPE html PUBLIC "-//W3C//DTD XHTML 1.0 Transitional//EN"
"http://www.w3.org/TR/xhtml1/DTD/xhtml1-transitional.dtd">
```

Often, folks had to look up the doctype each time they created a new document.

With HTML5, the doctype is short and sweet. It is the one that will be used throughout all of the projects in this book, and you should use it for your apps.

After the doctype is some basic HTML markup consisting of a head and a body.

The head will hold information about the document and how the browser should handle the document. For example, the title of the document, what CSS or JavaScript files the page uses, and when the document was last modified are all included in the head.

Here, the head contains a <meta> tag. <meta> tags provide the browser with information about the document itself, such as the name of the document's author or keywords for search engines. The <meta> tag in Ottergram, <meta charset="utf-8">, specifies that the document is encoded using the UTF-8 character set, which encompasses all Unicode characters. Use this tag in your documents so that the widest range of browsers can interpret them correctly, especially if you expect international traffic.

The body will hold all of the HTML code that represents the content of your page: all the images, links, text, buttons, and videos that will appear on the page.

Most tags enclose some other content. Take a look at the h1 heading you included; its anatomy is shown in Figure 2.10.

Figure 2.10 Anatomy of a simple HTML tag

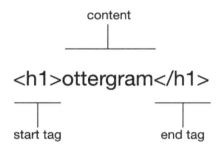

HTML stands for "hypertext markup language." Tags are used to "mark up" your content, designating their purpose – such as headings, list items, and links.

The content enclosed by a set of tags can also include other HTML. Notice, for example, that the <header> tags enclose the <h1> tag shown above (and the <body> tags enclose the <header>!).

There are a lot of tags to choose from – more than 140. To see a list of them, visit MDN's HTML element reference, located at developer.mozilla.org/en-US/docs/Web/HTML/Element. This reference includes a brief description of each element and groups elements by usage (e.g., text content, content sectioning, or multimedia).

Linking a stylesheet

In Chapter 3, you will write styling rules in your stylesheet, styles.css. But remember the conversation between the browser and the server at the beginning of this chapter? The browser only knows to ask for a file from the server if it has been told that the file exists. You have to *link* to your stylesheet so that the browser knows to ask for it. Update the head of index.html with a link to your styles.css file.

```
<!doctype html>
<html>
  <head>
    <meta charset="utf-8">
    <title>ottergram</title>
    <link rel="stylesheet" href="stylesheets/styles.css">
  </head>
  <body>
...
```

The <link> tag is how you attach an external stylesheet to an HTML document. It has two *attributes*, which give the browser more information about the tag's purpose (Figure 2.11). (The order of HTML attributes does not matter.)

Figure 2.11 Anatomy of a tag with attributes

You set the rel (or "relationship") attribute to "stylesheet", which lets the browser know that the linked document provides styling information. The href attribute tells the browser to send a request to the server for the styles.css file located in the stylesheets folder. Note that this file path is *relative* to the current document.

Save index.html before you move on.

Adding content

A web page without content is like a day without coffee. Add a list after your header to give your project a reason for living.

You are going to add an *unordered list* (that is, a bulleted list) using the <ul> tag. In the list, you will include five list items using <li> tags, and in each list item you will include some text surrounded by <span> tags.

The updated index.html is shown below. Note that throughout this book we show new code that you are adding in bold type. Code that you are to delete is shown struck through. Existing code is shown in plain text to help you position your changes within the file.

We encourage you to make use of Atom's autocompletion and autoformatting features. With your cursor in position, type "ul" and press Return. Next, type "li" and press Return twice, then type "span" and press Return once. Enter the name of an otter, then create four more list items and spans in the same way.

```
<!doctype html>
<html>
  <head>
    <meta charset="utf-8">
    <title>ottergram</title>
    <link rel="stylesheet" href="stylesheets/styles.css">
  </head>
  <body>
    <header>
      <h1>ottergram</h1>
    </header>
    <ul>
      <li>
        <span>Barry</span>
      </li>
      <li>
        <span>Robin</span>
      </li>
      <li>
        <span>Maurice</span>
      </li>
      <li>
        <span>Lesley</span>
      </li>
      <li>
        <span>Barbara</span>
      </li>
    </ul>
  </body>
</html>
```

The <span> tags nested inside each <li> tag do not have any special meaning. They are generic containers for other content. You will be using them in Ottergram for styling purposes, and you will see other examples of container elements as you continue through this book.

Next, you will add images of otters to go with the names you have entered.

Adding images

The resource files for all the projects in this book are at www.bignerdranch.com/downloads/front-end-dev-resources.zip. They include five Creative Commons-licensed otter images taken by Michael L. Baird, Joe Robertson, and Agunther that were found on commons.wikimedia.org.

Download and unzip the resources. Inside the ottergram-resources folder, locate the img folder. Copy the img folder to your ottergram/ project directory. (The .zip contains other resources, but for now you will only need the img folder.)

You want your list to include clickable thumbnail images in addition to the titles. You will achieve this by adding anchor and image tags to each item in your ul. We will explain these changes in more detail after you enter them. (If you use autocompletion, note that you will need to move the </a> tags so that they follow the spans.)

```
...
  <ul>
    <li>
      <a href="#">
        <img src="img/otter1.jpg" alt="Barry the Otter">
        <span>Barry</span>
      </a>
    </li>
    <li>
      <a href="#">
        <img src="img/otter2.jpg" alt="Robin the Otter">
        <span>Robin</span>
      </a>
    </li>
    <li>
      <a href="#">
        <img src="img/otter3.jpg" alt="Maurice the Otter">
        <span>Maurice</span>
      </a>
    </li>
    <li>
      <a href="#">
        <img src="img/otter4.jpg" alt="Lesley the Otter">
        <span>Lesley</span>
      </a>
    </li>
    <li>
      <a href="#">
        <img src="img/otter5.jpg" alt="Barbara the Otter">
        <span>Barbara</span>
      </a>
    </li>
  </ul>
...
```

If your lines are not nicely indented, you can take advantage of the atom-beautify plug-in that you installed. Click Packages → Atom Beautify → Beautify and your code will be aligned and indented for you.

Let's look at what you have added.

The <a> tag is the *anchor* tag. Anchor tags make elements on the page clickable, so that they take the user to another page. They are commonly referred to as "links," but beware: They are not like the <link> tag you used earlier.

Anchor tags have an href attribute, which indicates the resource the anchor points to. Usually the value is a web address. Sometimes, though, you do not want a link to go anywhere. That is the case for now, so you assigned the "dummy" value # to the href attributes. This will make the browser scroll to the top of the page when the image is clicked. Later you will use the anchor tags to open a larger copy of an image when the thumbnail is clicked.

Inside the anchor tags you added <img>, or *image*, tags with src attributes indicating filenames in the img directory you added earlier. You also added a descriptive alt attribute to your image tags. alt attributes contain text that replaces the image if it is unable to load. alt text is also what screen readers use to describe an image to a user with a visual impairment.

Image tags are different from most other elements in that they do not wrap other elements, but instead refer to a resource. When the browser encounters an <img> tag, it draws the image to the page. This is known as a *replaced element*. Other replaced elements include embedded documents and applets.

Because they do not wrap content or other elements, <img> tags do not have a corresponding closing tag. This makes them *self-closing* tags (also known as *void* tags). You will sometimes see self-closing tags written with a slash before the right angle-bracket, like <img src="otter.jpg"/>. Whether to include the slash is a matter of preference and does not make a difference to the browser. In this book, self-closing tags are written without the slash.

Save index.html. In a moment, you will see the results of your coding.

Viewing the Web Page in the Browser

To view your web page, you need to be running the browser-sync tool that you installed in Chapter 1.

Open the terminal and change directory to your ottergram folder. Recall from Chapter 1 that you change directory using the cd command followed by the path of the folder you are moving into. One easy way to get the ottergram path is to Control-click (right-click) the ottergram folder in Atom's lefthand panel and choose Copy Full Path (Figure 2.12). Then, at the command line, type cd, paste the path, and press Return.

Figure 2.12 Copying the ottergram folder path from Atom

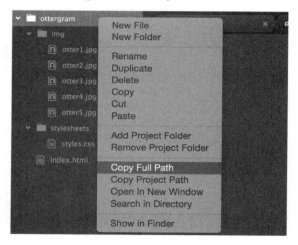

The path you enter might look something like this:

```
cd /Users/chrisaquino/Projects/front-end-dev-book/ottergram
```

Once you are in the ottergram directory, run the following command to open Ottergram in Chrome. (We have broken the command across two lines so that it fits on the page. You should enter it on a single line.)

```
browser-sync start --server --browser "Google Chrome"
                --files "stylesheets/*.css, *.html"
```

If Chrome is your default browser, you can leave out the --browser "Google Chrome" portion of the command:

```
browser-sync start --server --files "stylesheets/*.css, *.html"
```

This command starts browser-sync in server mode, allowing it to send responses when a browser sends a request to get a file, such as the index.html file you created.

The command you entered also tells browser-sync to automatically reload the browser if any HTML or CSS files are changed. This makes the development experience much nicer. Before tools like browser-sync, you had to manually reload the page after every change.

Figure 2.13 shows the result of entering this command on a Mac.

Figure 2.13 Starting browser-sync in the OS X Terminal

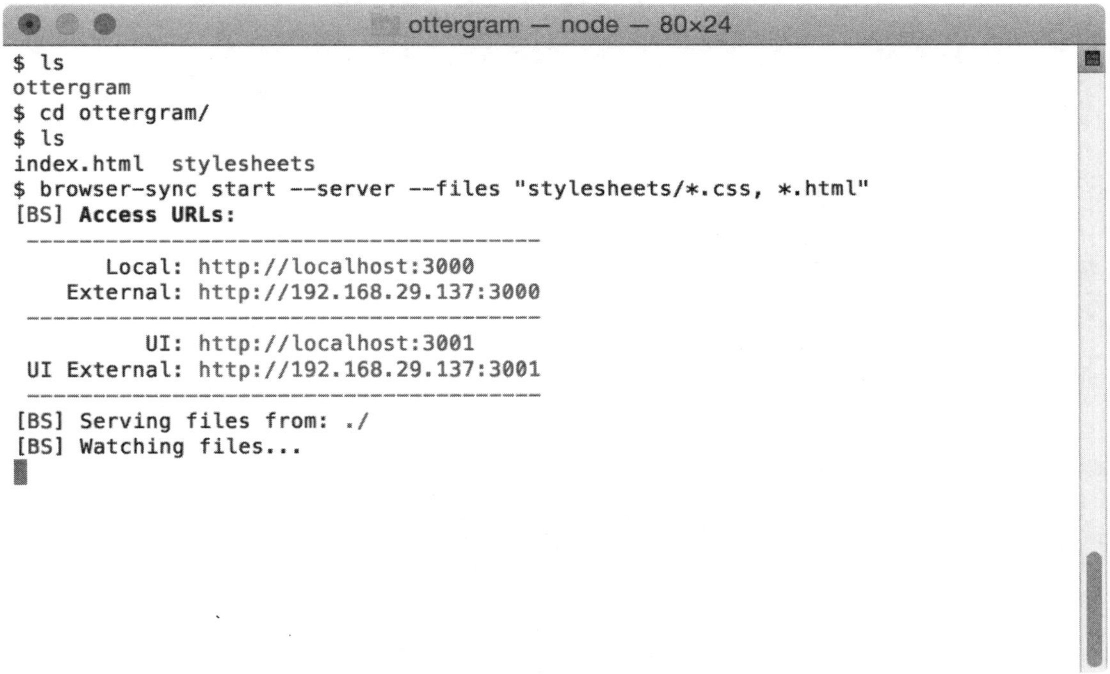

```
● ● ●                    ottergram — node — 80×24
$ ls
ottergram
$ cd ottergram/
$ ls
index.html  stylesheets
$ browser-sync start --server --files "stylesheets/*.css, *.html"
[BS] Access URLs:
   --------------------------------------------
        Local: http://localhost:3000
     External: http://192.168.29.137:3000
   --------------------------------------------
           UI: http://localhost:3001
  UI External: http://192.168.29.137:3001
   --------------------------------------------
[BS] Serving files from: ./
[BS] Watching files...
```

You should see the same output on Windows (Figure 2.14).

Figure 2.14 Starting browser-sync in the Windows Command Prompt

```
Select Command Prompt - browser-sync  start --server --files "stylesheets/*.css, *.html"                    —    □    ×

Microsoft Windows [Version 10.0.10240]
(c) 2015 Microsoft Corporation. All rights reserved.

C:\Users\chrisaquino>cd Projects

C:\Users\chrisaquino\Projects>cd front-end-dev-book

C:\Users\chrisaquino\Projects\front-end-dev-book>dir
 Volume in drive C is BOOTCAMP
 Volume Serial Number is 725F-B413

 Directory of C:\Users\chrisaquino\Projects\front-end-dev-book

2015-10-22  12:05 AM    <DIR>          .
2015-10-22  12:05 AM    <DIR>          ..
2015-10-23  03:21 PM    <DIR>          ottergram
               0 File(s)              0 bytes
               3 Dir(s)   21,512,392,704 bytes free

C:\Users\chrisaquino\Projects\front-end-dev-book>cd ottergram

C:\Users\chrisaquino\Projects\front-end-dev-book\ottergram>browser-sync start --server --files "stylesheets/*.css, *.html"
[   ] Access URLs:
      -----------------------------------
        Local: http://localhost:3000
     External: http://192.168.29.104:3000
      -----------------------------------
           UI: http://localhost:3001
  UI External: http://192.168.29.104:3001
      -----------------------------------
[   ] Serving files from: /
[   ] Watching files...
```

Once the Ottergram page has loaded in Chrome, you should see your page with the "ottergram" heading, "ottergram" as the tab label, and a series of otter photos and names (Figure 2.15).

Figure 2.15 Viewing Ottergram in the browser

The Chrome Developer Tools

Chrome has built-in Developer Tools (commonly known as "DevTools") that are among the best available for testing styles, layouts, and more on the fly. Using the DevTools is much more efficient than trying things out in code. The DevTools are very powerful and will be your constant companion as you do front-end development.

You will start using the DevTools in the next chapter. For now, open the window and familiarize yourself with its major areas.

To open the DevTools, click the ≡ icon to the right of the address bar in Chrome. Next, click More Tools → Developer Tools (Figure 2.16).

Figure 2.16 Opening the Developer Tools

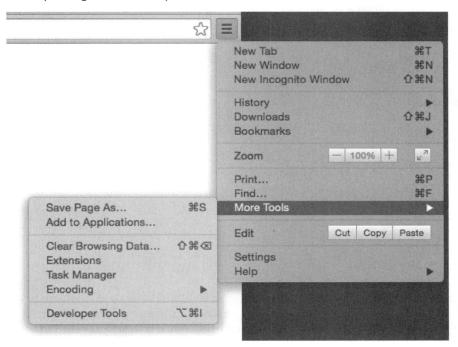

Chrome displays the DevTools to the right by default. Your screen will look something like Figure 2.17.

Figure 2.17 The DevTools showing the elements panel

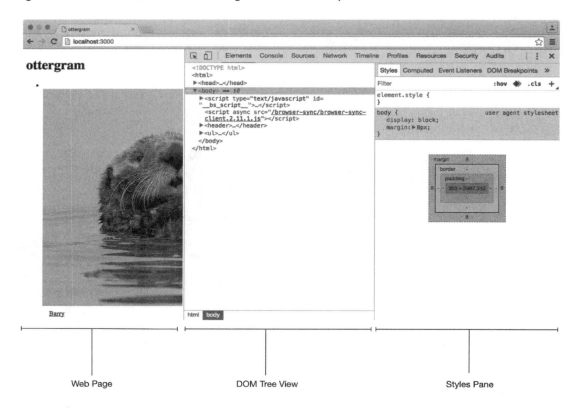

The DevTools show the relationship between the code and the resulting page elements. They let you inspect individual elements' attributes and styles and see immediately how the browser is interpreting your code. Seeing this relationship is critical for both development and debugging.

In Figure 2.17, you can see the DevTools next to the web page, displaying the elements panel. The elements panel is divided into two sections. On the left is the *DOM tree view*. This is a representation of the HTML, interpreted as DOM elements. (You will learn much more about DOM, which stands for "document object model," in upcoming chapters.) On the righthand side of the elements panel is the styles pane. This shows any visual styles applied to individual elements.

Having the DevTools docked on the right side of the screen while you are working is usually convenient. If you want to change the location of the DevTools, you can click the ⋮ button near the upper-right corner. This will show you a menu of options, including buttons for the Dock side, which will change the anchor location of the DevTools (Figure 2.18).

Figure 2.18 Changing the dock side of the DevTools

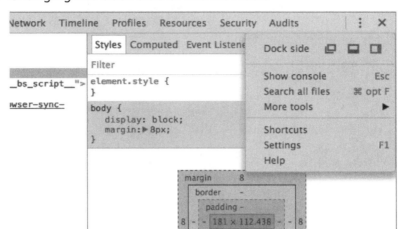

With your otters and markup in place and the DevTools open, you are ready to begin styling your project in the next chapter.

For the More Curious: CSS Versions

The version history of CSS includes standard versions 1, 2, and 2.1. After 2.1, it was decided that the standard needed to be broken up because it was getting too big.

There is no version 3. Instead, CSS3 is a blanket term for a number of modules, each with its own version number.

Table 2.1 CSS versions, real and imagined

Version Number	Release Year	Notable Features
1	1996	Basic font properties (`font-family`, `font-style`), foreground and background colors, text alignment, margin, border, and padding.
2	1998	Absolute, relative, and fixed positioning; new font properties.
2.1	2011	Removed features that were poorly supported by browsers.
"3"	Various	A collection of different specifications, such as media queries, new selectors, semi-transparent colors, `@font-face`.

For the More Curious: The favicon.ico

Have you ever noticed the little icon that appears at the left end of your browser's address bar when you visit most websites? Sometimes they also appear in your browser tab, as in Figure 2.19.

Figure 2.19 The `bignerdranch.com` `favicon.ico`

That is the `favicon.ico` image file. Many sites have one, and browsers request one by default. Because Ottergram does not have one, you may see an error like the one in Figure 2.20 in the DevTools.

Figure 2.20 Error about missing `favicon.ico`

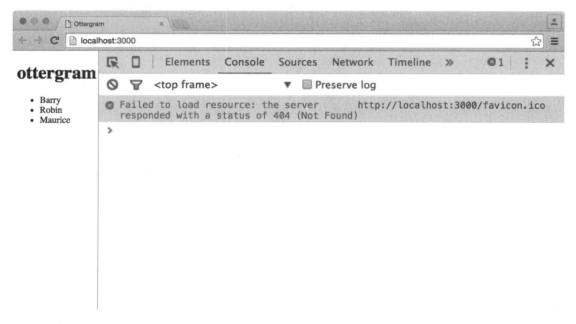

Do not worry about this error if it appears. It will not affect your project. However, you can easily add a `favicon.ico` image – and that is your first challenge.

Silver Challenge: Adding a favicon.ico

You have decided that you like otters more than you like seeing the `favicon.ico` error message. You are going to create a `favicon.ico` file using one of the otter images.

Do a web search for "favicon generator" and you should see a list of websites that will do a file conversion for you. Most will let you upload an image and then provide you with a `favicon.ico` version.

Choose one and upload any one of the otter images.

Save the resulting `favicon.ico` file in the same folder as your `index.html` file. Finally, reload your browser. Your browser tab will look something like Figure 2.21.

Figure 2.21 Ottergram with a `favicon.ico`

3

Styles

In this chapter, you will design a static version of Ottergram. In the chapters that follow, you will make Ottergram interactive.

When you reach the end of this chapter, your website will look like Figure 3.1.

Figure 3.1 Ottergram: stylish

This chapter introduces a number of concepts and examples. Do not worry if you do not feel that you have mastered all of them when you get to the end. You will be encountering them again and again as you progress through this book, and your work in this chapter will provide a solid foundation on which you will build true understanding.

Of course, we can only introduce you to a tiny fraction of all the styles that are available in CSS. You will want to consult the MDN for information about the full set of properties and their values.

Front-end developers have to choose between two approaches to styling a website: start with the overall layout and work down to the smallest details, or start with the smallest details and work up to the overall layout.

Not only does working from detail to big picture produce cleaner, more reusable code, it also has a cool name: *atomic styling*. You will use this approach as you style the otter thumbnails first, then the thumbnail list layout. In the next chapter, you will work on the layout of the site as a whole.

Creating a Styling Baseline

You are going to begin by adding the `normalize.css` file to your project. `normalize.css` helps the CSS you write display consistently across browsers. All browsers come with a set of default styles, but the defaults are different from browser to browser. `normalize.css` gives you a good starting point for developing your own custom CSS for a website or web app.

`normalize.css` is freely available online. You do not need to download it. To add it to Ottergram, you only need to link to it in `index.html`.

To ensure that you are using the most current version of `normalize.css`, you are going to get its address from a content sharing site. Go to `cdnjs.com/libraries/normalize` and find the version of the file ending with `.min.css`. (This version is a smaller download than the others, with the extra whitespace stripped out.) Click the Copy button to copy its address (Figure 3.2).

Figure 3.2 Getting a link to `normalize.css` from `cdnjs.com`

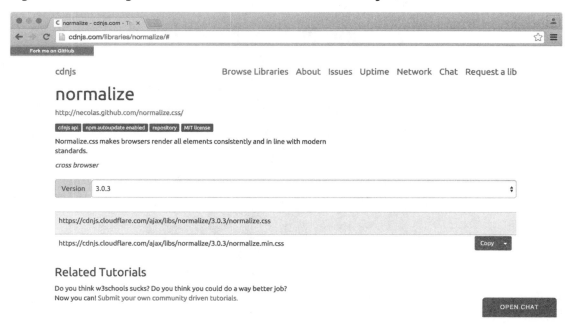

The current version at the time of this writing is 3.0.3, but the version you use may be more recent.

Open your Ottergram folder in Atom, then open index.html. Add a new <link> tag and paste in the address. (In the code below, the <link> has been broken into two lines to fit on the page. You can leave yours on a single line.)

```
<!doctype html>
<html>
  <head>
    <meta charset="utf-8">
    <title>ottergram</title>
    <link rel="stylesheet"
      href="https://cdnjs.cloudflare.com/ajax/libs/normalize/3.0.3/normalize.min.css">
    <link rel="stylesheet" href="stylesheets/styles.css">
  </head>
...
```

Make sure that you add the <link> tag for normalize.css *before* the <link> tag for styles.css. The browser needs to read the styles found in normalize.css before it reads yours.

And, just like that, your project can take advantage of this useful tool. No other setup is required.

You may be wondering why you are linking to an address on a completely different server. In fact, it is not unusual for an HTML file to specify resources located on different servers (Figure 3.3).

Figure 3.3 Requesting resources from different servers

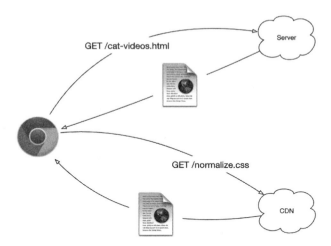

In this case, normalize.css is hosted on cdnjs.com, a public server that is part of a *content delivery network*, or CDN. CDNs have servers all around the world, each with copies of the same files. When users request a file, they receive it from a server nearby, cutting down on the load time for that file. cdnjs.com hosts many versions of popular front-end libraries and frameworks.

Preparing the HTML for Styling

In the last chapter, you created a stylesheet called `styles.css`, and in this chapter you will add a number of CSS *styling rules* to it. But before you get started adding styles, you need to set up your HTML with targets for your styling rules to refer to.

You are going to add `class` attributes identifying the `span` elements with the otters' names as "thumbnail titles." `class` attributes are a way to identify a group of HTML elements, usually for styling. Your "thumbnail title" `class` will allow you to easily style all the names at once.

In `index.html`, add the class name `thumbnail-title` as an attribute of the `spans` inside the `li` elements, as shown:

```
...
    <ul>
      <li>
        <a href="#">
          <img src="img/otter1.jpg" alt="Barry the Otter">
          <span>Barry</span>
          <span class="thumbnail-title">Barry</span>
        </a>
      </li>
      <li>
        <a href="#">
          <img src="img/otter2.jpg" alt="Robin the Otter">
          <span>Robin</span>
          <span class="thumbnail-title">Robin</span>
        </a>
      </li>
      <li>
        <a href="#">
          <img src="img/otter1.jpg" alt="Maurice the Otter">
          <span>Maurice</span>
          <span class="thumbnail-title">Maurice</span>
        </a>
      </li>
      <li>
        <a href="#">
          <img src="img/otter4.jpg" alt="Lesley the Otter">
          <span>Lesley</span>
          <span class="thumbnail-title">Lesley</span>
        </a>
      </li>
      <li>
        <a href="#">
          <img src="img/otter5.jpg" alt="Barbara the Otter">
          <span>Barbara</span>
          <span class="thumbnail-title">Barbara</span>
        </a>
    </ul>
...
```

In a moment, you will use this class name to style all the image titles.

Anatomy of a Style

When you create individual styles, you do so by writing styling rules, which consist of two main parts: *selectors* and *declarations* (Figure 3.4).

Figure 3.4 Anatomy of a styling rule

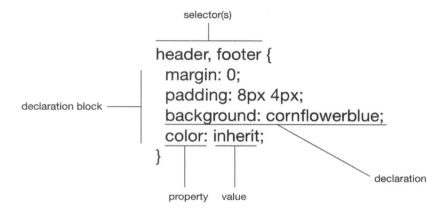

The first part of a styling rule is one or more selectors. Selectors describe the elements that the style should be applied to, like h1, span, or img. But selectors are not limited to tag names. You can write selectors that apply to a more targeted set of elements by increasing the selector's *specificity*.

For example, you can write selectors based on attributes – such as the thumbnail-title class attribute you just added to the <span> tags. Selectors based on attributes are more specific than selectors based on element names.

In addition to making sure that styles are only applied to a limited set of elements (e.g., elements with the class name thumbnail-title versus all <span> elements), specificity also determines the selector's relative priority. If a stylesheet contains multiple styles that could apply to the same element, the styles with a selector of higher specificity will be used instead styles whose selector has a lower specificity. You can read more about specificity in a For the More Curious section at the end of this chapter.

Throughout this chapter, you will be introduced to a number of different kinds of selectors that vary in their specificity. Though there are often many ways to target the same element for styling, understanding specificity is key to choosing the best selector to use so that your styles are maintainable.

The second part of a styling rule is the declaration block, wrapped in curly braces, which defines the styles to be applied. The individual declarations within the block each include a property name and a value for that property.

In your first styling rule, you will use the `class` attribute you just added as a selector to apply styles around the otters' names.

Your First Styling Rule

To use a `class` as a selector in a styling rule, you prefix the class name with a dot (period), as in `.thumbnail-title`. The first styles you are going to add will set the background and foreground colors for the `.thumbnail-title` class.

Open `styles.css` and add your styling rule:

```
.thumbnail-title {
  background: rgb(96, 125, 139);
  color: rgb(202, 238, 255);
}
```

You will learn more about color later in this chapter. For now, just take a look at your changes. Save `styles.css` and make sure `browser-sync` is running. If you need to restart it, the command is:

```
browser-sync start --server --browser "Google Chrome"
                    --files "stylesheets/*.css, *.html"
```

This will open your web page in Chrome (Figure 3.5).

Figure 3.5 A slightly more colorful Ottergram

You can see that you have set the background for the thumbnail titles to a deep gray-blue and the font color to a lighter blue. Nice.

Continue styling the thumbnail titles: Return to `styles.css` and add to your existing styling rule for the `.thumbnail-title` class, as shown:

```
.thumbnail-title {
  display: block;
  margin: 0;
  padding: 4px 10px;

  background: rgb(96, 125, 139);
  color: rgb(202, 238, 255);
}
```

The three declarations you have added all affect an element's *box*. For every HTML tag that has a visual representation, the browser draws a rectangle to the page. The browser uses a scheme called the *standard box model* (or just "box model") to determine the dimensions of that rectangle.

The box model

To understand the box model, you are going to look at its representation in the DevTools. Save `styles.css`, switch to Chrome, and make sure the DevTools are open (Figure 3.6).

Figure 3.6 Exploring the box model

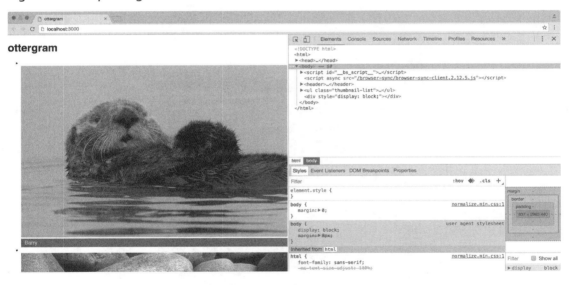

Click the ⌖ button in the upper-left of the elements panel. This is the *Inspect Element* button. Now move your cursor over the word "ottergram" on the web page. As you hover over the word, the DevTools surrounds the heading with a blue- and peach-colored rectangle (Figure 3.7).

Figure 3.7 Hovering over the heading

Click the word "ottergram" on the web page. Although you no longer see the multicolored overlay, the element is now selected and the DOM tree view in the elements panel will expand to show and highlight the corresponding <h1> tag.

The rectangular diagram in the lower-right of the elements panel represents the box model for the h1 element. You can see that the regions of the diagram have some of the same colors as the rectangle you saw overlaying the heading when you inspected it (Figure 3.8).

Figure 3.8 Viewing the box model for an element

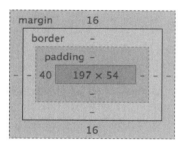

The box model incorporates four aspects of the rectangle drawn for an element (which the DevTools renders in four different colors in the diagram).

content (shown in blue)	the visual content – here, the text
padding (shown in green)	transparent space around the content
border (shown in yellow)	a border, which can be made visible, around the content and padding
margin (shown in peach)	transparent space around the border

The numbers in Figure 3.8 are *pixel* values; a pixel is a unit corresponding to the smallest rectangular area of a computer screen that can display a single color. In the case of the h1 element, the content area has been allocated an area of 197 pixels by 54 pixels (your values may be different, depending on the size of your browser window). There is padding of 40 pixels on the left side. The border is set at 0, and there is a margin of 16 pixels above and below the element.

Where did that margin value come from? Each browser provides a default stylesheet, called the *user agent stylesheet*, in case an HTML file does not specify one. Styles that you specify override the defaults. Because you have not specified values for the h1 element's box, the default styles have been applied.

Now you are ready to understand the styling declarations you added:

```
.thumbnail-title {
  display: block;
  margin: 0;
  padding: 4px 10px;

  background: rgb(96, 125, 139);
  color: rgb(202, 238, 255);
}
```

The `display: block` declaration changes the box for all elements of the class `.thumbnail-title` so that they occupy the entire width allowed by their containing element. (Notice in Figure 3.6 that the background color for the titles now covers a wider area.) Other `display` values, such as the `display: inline` property you will see later, make an element's width fit to its content.

You also set the margin for the thumbnail titles to 0 and the padding to two different values: 4px and 10px (*px* is the abbreviation for "pixels"). This sets the padding to specific pixel values, overriding the default size set by the user agent stylesheet.

Padding, margin, and certain other styles can be written as *shorthand properties*, in which one value is applied to multiple properties. You are taking advantage of this here: When two values are provided for the padding, the first is applied to both vertical values (top and bottom) and the second is applied to both horizontal values (left and right). It is also possible to provide a single value to be applied to all four sides or to specify a separate value for each side.

To sum up, your new declarations say that the box for all elements of the `.thumbnail-title` class will fill the width of its container with no margin and with padding that is 4 pixels at the top and bottom and 10 pixels at the left and right sides.

Style Inheritance

Next, you are going to add styles to change the size and appearance of the text.

Add a new styling rule in `styles.css` to set the font size for the `body` element. To do this, you will use a different type of selector – an *element selector* – by simply using the element's name.

```css
body {
    font-size: 10px;
}

.thumbnail-title {
    display: block;
    margin: 0;
    padding: 4px 10px;

    background: rgb(96, 125, 139);
    color: rgb(202, 238, 255);
}
```

This styling rule sets the body element's `font-size` to `10px`.

You will rarely use element selectors in your stylesheets, because you will not often want to apply the exact same styles to every occurrence of a particular tag. Also, element selectors limit your ability to reuse styles; using them means that you may end up retyping the same declarations throughout your stylesheets. This is not great for maintenance if you need to alter those styles.

But, in this case, targeting the body element is exactly the right amount of specificity. There can be only one <body> element, and you will not be reusing its styles.

Save `styles.css` and check out your web page in Chrome (Figure 3.9).

Figure 3.9 After setting the body font size

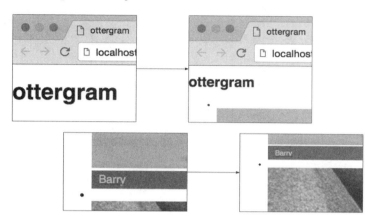

Your headline and thumbnail titles have gotten smaller. You may – or may not – have expected this. While the headline is directly within the body element where you declared the font-size property, the thumbnail titles are not. They are nested several levels deep. However, many styles, including font size, are applied to the elements specified by the styling rule as well as the *descendants* of those elements.

The structure of your document can be described using a tree diagram, as in Figure 3.10. Representing your elements as a tree is a good way to visualize the DOM.

Figure 3.10 Simplified structure of Ottergram

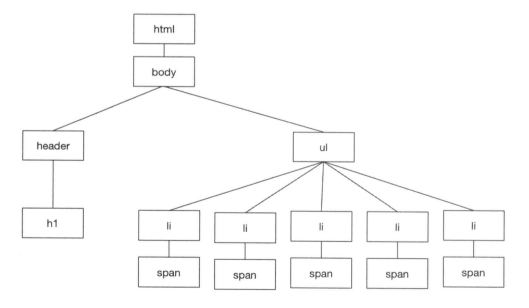

An element contained within another element is said to be its descendent. In this case, your spans are all descendents of the body (as well as the ul and their respective li), so they inherit the body's font-size style.

In the DevTools' DOM tree view, locate and select one of the span elements. In the styles pane, notice the boxes labeled Inherited from a, Inherited from li, and Inherited from ul. These three areas, as indicated, show styles inherited at each level from the user agent stylesheet. Under Inherited from body, you can see that the font-size property has been inherited from the style set for the body element in styles.css (Figure 3.11).

Figure 3.11 Styles inherited from ancestor elements

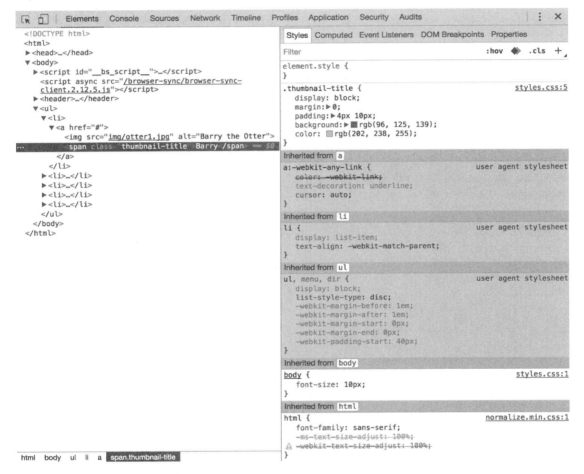

What if a different font size were set at another level, such as the ul? Styles from the closer ancestor take priority, so a font size set in styles.css for the ul would override one set for the body and a font size set for the span element itself would override them both.

To see this, click on the ul element in the DOM tree view. This will allow you to try out styles on the fly. The styles you add here will be immediately reflected in the web page view, but will not be added to your actual project files.

At the top of the styles pane in the elements panel, you will see a section labeled elements.style. Click anywhere in between the curly braces of the elements.style, and the DevTools will give you a prompt (Figure 3.12).

Figure 3.12 Prompting for a style rule

Start typing `font-size`, and the DevTools will suggest possible completions (Figure 3.13).

Figure 3.13 Autocompletion options in styles pane

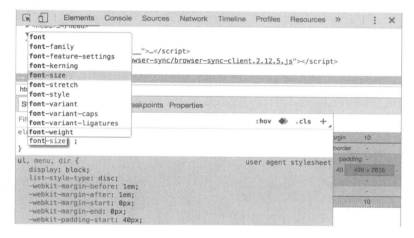

Choose `font-size`, then press the Tab key. Enter a large value, such as `50px`, and press Return. You may need to scroll the page, but you will see that the `ul`'s `font-size` has overridden the `body`'s (Figure 3.14).

Figure 3.14 Giving the `ul` a `font-size` of 50px

Not all style properties are inherited – `border`, for example, is not. To find out whether a property is inherited, refer to the property's MDN reference page.

Back in `styles.css`, update your declaration block for the `.thumbnail-title` class to override the body's `font-size` and use a larger font.

```
body {
    font-size: 10px;
}

.thumbnail-title {
    display: block;
    margin: 0;
    padding: 4px 10px;

    background: rgb(96, 125, 139);
    color: rgb(202, 238, 255);

    font-size: 18px;
}
```

For elements of the class `.thumbnail-title`, you changed the font size to 18 pixels.

Save `styles.css` and admire your thumbnail titles in Chrome (Figure 3.15).

Figure 3.15 Styled thumbnail titles

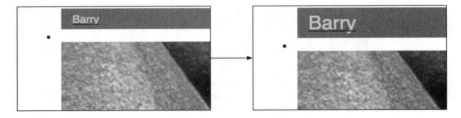

They look good, but the user agent stylesheet is adding underlines to the `.thumbnail-title` elements. This is because you wrapped them (along with the `.thumbnail-image` elements) with an anchor tag, making them inherit the underline style.

You do not need the underlines, so you are going to remove them by changing the `text-decoration` property for the anchor tags in a new styling rule in `styles.css`. What selector should you use for this rule?

If you are confident that you want to remove the underlines from the thumbnail titles *as well as any other anchor elements in Ottergram*, you can simply use an element selector:

```
a {
    /* style declaration */
}
```

(The text between the `/* */` indicators is a CSS *comment*. Code comments are ignored by the browser; they allow the developer to make notes in the code for future reference.)

If you think you might use anchors for another purpose (and will want to style them differently), you can pair the element selector with an *attribute selector*, like this:

```
a[href]{
  /* style declaration */
}
```

This selector would match any anchor element with an href attribute. Of course, anchor elements generally do have href attributes, so that might not be targeted enough to match only the thumbnail images and titles. To make an attribute selector more precise, you can also specify the value of the attribute, like this:

```
a[href="#"]{
  /* style declaration */
}
```

This selector would match only those anchor elements whose href attribute has a value of #.

By the way, you can also use attribute selectors, with or without values, on their own, such as:

```
[href]{
  /* style declaration */
}
```

As it happens, Ottergram is a fairly simple project and you will not, in fact, be using anchor tags for anything other than the thumbnails and their titles. It is therefore safe to use an element selector, and you should do so because it is the most straightforward solution with the right amount of specificity.

Add the new style declaration to styles.css:

```
body {
  font-size: 10px;
}

a {
  text-decoration: none;
}

.thumbnail-title {
  ...
}
```

Save your file and check your browser. The underlines are gone and your thumbnail titles are nicely styled (Figure 3.16).

Figure 3.16 After setting text-decoration to none

Note that you should not remove the underlines from links that are in normal text – text that is not an obvious heading, title, or caption. The underlining of linked text is an important visual indicator that users have come to expect. You did it here because the thumbnails do not require the same visual cues. Users will reasonably expect them to be clickable.

In the rest of the chapter, you will use class selectors to style the thumbnail images, the unordered list of images, the list items (which include the thumbnail images and their titles), and, finally, the header. Go ahead and add class names to the h1, ul, li, and img elements in index.html so they are ready as you need them.

```
...
  </head>
  <body>
    <header>
      <h1>ottergram</h1>
      <h1 class="logo-text">ottergram</h1>
    </header>
    <ul>
    <ul class="thumbnail-list">
      <li>
      <li class="thumbnail-item">
        <a href="#">
          <img src="img/otter1.jpg" alt="Barry the Otter">
          <img class="thumbnail-image" src="img/otter1.jpg" alt="Barry the Otter">
          <span class="thumbnail-title">Barry</span>
        </a>
      </li>
      <li>
      <li class="thumbnail-item">
        <a href="#">
          <img src="img/otter2.jpg" alt="Robin the Otter">
          <img class="thumbnail-image" src="img/otter2.jpg" alt="Robin the Otter">
          <span class="thumbnail-title">Robin</span>
        </a>
      </li>
      <li>
      <li class="thumbnail-item">
        <a href="#">
          <img src="img/otter3.jpg" alt="Maurice the Otter">
          <img class="thumbnail-image" src="img/otter3.jpg" alt="Maurice the Otter">
          <span class="thumbnail-title">Maurice</span>
        </a>
      </li>
      <li>
      <li class="thumbnail-item">
        <a href="#">
          <img src="img/otter4.jpg" alt="Lesley the Otter">
          <img class="thumbnail-image" src="img/otter4.jpg" alt="Lesley the Otter">
          <span class="thumbnail-title">Lesley</span>
        </a>
      </li>
      <li>
      <li class="thumbnail-item">
        <a href="#">
          <img src="img/otter5.jpg" alt="Barbara the Otter">
          <img class="thumbnail-image" src="img/otter5.jpg" alt="Barbara the Otter">
          <span class="thumbnail-title">Barbara</span>
        </a>
      </li>
    </ul>
...
```

By adding class names to these elements, you have given yourself targets for the styles you will be adding.

We favor class selectors over other kinds of selectors, and you should, too. You can write very descriptive class names that make your code easy to develop and maintain. Also, you can add multiple class names to an element, making them a flexible and powerful tool for styling.

Be sure to save index.html before moving on.

Making Images Fit the Window

Following the atomic styling pattern, the images are next in line for styling. They are so large that they are cut off unless the browser window is also large. Add a styling rule for .thumbnail-image in styles.css to make the thumbnails fit in the window:

```
...
a {
  text-decoration: none;
}

.thumbnail-image {
  width: 100%;
}

.thumbnail-title {
  ...
}
```

You set the width to 100%, which constrains it to the width of its container. This means that as you widen the browser window, the images get proportionally larger. Check it out: Save styles.css, switch to your browser, and make your browser window larger and smaller. The images grow and shrink along with the browser window, always keeping their proportions. Figure 3.17 shows Ottergram in one narrow and one wider browser window.

Figure 3.17 Fitting an image by width

If you look closely, the spacing around the `.thumbnail-titles` is off, so that it appears that the titles go with the images below them. Fix that in `styles.css` by setting the `.thumbnail-image`'s `display` property to `block`.

```
...
.thumbnail-image {
  display: block;
  width: 100%;
}
...
```

Now the space between the image and its title is gone (Figure 3.18).

Figure 3.18 After setting `.thumbnail-image` to `display: block`

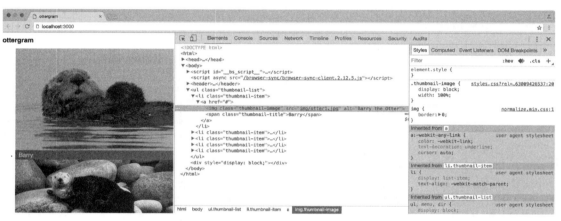

Why does this work? Images are `display: inline` by default. They are subject to similar rendering rules as text. When text is rendered, the letters are drawn along a common baseline. Some characters, such as p, q, and y, have a *descender* - the tail that drops below this baseline. To accommodate them, there is some whitespace included below the baseline.

Setting the `display` property to `block` removes the whitespace because there is no need to accommodate any text (or any other `display: inline` elements that might be rendered alongside the image).

Color

It is time to explore color a little more deeply. Add the following color styles for the body element and the `.thumbnail-item` class in `styles.css`.

```
body {
    font-size: 10px;
    background: rgb(149, 194, 215);
}

a {
    text-decoration: none;
}

.thumbnail-item {
    border: 1px solid rgb(100%, 100%, 100%);
    border: 1px solid rgba(100%, 100%, 100%, 0.8);
}
...
```

You have declared values for the `.thumbnail-item`'s border twice. Why? Notice that the two declarations use slightly different color functions: `rgb` and `rgba`. The `rgba` color function accepts a fourth argument, which is the opacity. However, some browsers do not support `rgba`, so providing both declarations is a technique that provides a *fallback* value.

All browsers will see the first declaration (`rgb`) and register its value for the `border` property. When browsers that do not support `rgba` see the second declaration, they will not understand it and will simply ignore it, using the value from the first declaration. Browsers that *do* support `rgba` will use the value in the second declaration and discard the value from the first declaration.

(Wondering why the body's background color is defined with integers and the `.thumbnail-item`'s border color is defined with percentages? We will come back to that in just a moment.)

Save `styles.css` and switch to your browser (Figure 3.19).

Figure 3.19 Background color and borders

In the DevTools, you can see that Chrome supports rgba. It denotes that the rgb color is not used by striking through the style (Figure 3.20)

Figure 3.20 rgba is used when supported by browser

Now, still in the DevTools, select the body. In the styles pane, notice the declaration for the background color that you just added. To the left of the RGB value is a small square showing you what the color will look like.

Click that square, and a color picker opens (Figure 3.21). The color picker lets you choose a color and will give you the CSS color value in a variety of different formats.

Figure 3.21 The color picker in the styles pane

To see the background color in different color formats, click the up and down arrows to the right of the RGBA values. You can cycle through HSLA, HEX, and RGBA formats.

The HSLA format (which stands for "hue saturation lightness alpha") is used less frequently than the others, partly because some of the most popular design tools do not provide HSLA values that are accurate for CSS. If you are curious about HSLA, visit the HSLA Explorer at css-tricks.com/examples/HSLaExplorer.

Take a look at the HEX value for the background color: #95C2D7. HEX, or hexadecimal, is the oldest color specification format. Each digit represents a value from 0 to 15. (If you are not familiar with hexadecimal numbers, this is done by including the characters A through F as digits.) Each pair of digits, then, can represent a value from 0 to 255. From left to right, the pairs of digits correspond to the intensity of red, green, and blue in the color being specified (Figure 3.22).

Figure 3.22 HEX values correspond to red, green, and blue values

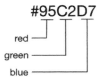

Many find HEX colors unintuitive. A modern alternative is to use RGB (red, green, and blue) values. In this model, each color is also assigned a value from 0 to 255, but the values are represented in more familiar decimal numbers and separated by color. As mentioned earlier, for more capable browsers a fourth value can specify the opacity or transparency of the specified color, from 0.0 (fully transparent) to 1.0 (fully opaque). The opacity is officially known as the *alpha* value – hence the A in RGBA. The RGBA value of the body's background color is (149, 194, 215, 1).

As an alternative to declaring integer values for red, green, and blue, you can also use percentages, as you did for the .thumbnail-item borders. There is no functional difference between the two options. Just do not mix percentages and integers in the same declaration.

By the way, for help selecting pleasing color palettes, Adobe provides a free online tool at color.adobe.com.

Adjusting the Space Between Items

Ottergram now has some nice colors reminiscent of otters' ocean home. But adding the colors has revealed some unwanted whitespace inside the border of the .thumbnail-item elements. Also, those pesky bullets are drawing attention away from the glory of the otters.

To get rid of the bullets, set the `.thumbnail-list`'s `list-style` property to `none` in `styles.css`:

```
...
.thumbnail-item {
  border: 1px solid rgb(100%, 100%, 100%);
  border: 1px solid rgba(100%, 100%, 100%, 0.8);
}

.thumbnail-list {
  list-style: none;
}

.thumbnail-image {
  ...
```

To get rid of the whitespace, you will use the same technique you used with the `.thumbnail-image`. Each `.thumbnail-item` has that whitespace by default to accommodate items in a list, just as the `.thumbnail-image` elements had whitespace to accommodate neighboring text. Add a `display: block` declaration for `.thumbnail-item` to remove it.

```
...
.thumbnail-item {
  display: block;
  border: 1px solid rgb(100%, 100%, 100%);
  border: 1px solid rgba(100%, 100%, 100%, 0.8);
}
...
```

With those additions, the bullets and the excess space above the images disappear, resulting in the more polished layout shown in Figure 3.23.

Figure 3.23 Improved layout

Why use a bullet list if you do not want bullets? It is best to choose HTML tags based on what they are and not how the browser will style them by default. In this case, you want an unordered list of images, so a ul is the way to go. The ul container for your images will let you style them as a scrolling list when you add a detail image to your project in Chapter 4. The fact that the browser represents uls with bullets by default is not important, as they are easily removed.

Next, you are going to adjust the spacing of the items in the list. The individual .thumbnail-item elements currently have no space between them. You are going to add margins between adjacent thumbnails.

However, you do not want to add a margin to *all* of the list items. Why not? Because the heading already has a margin, so the first list does not need one. This means that you cannot use the .thumbnail-item class selector, at least not on its own. Instead, you will use selector syntax that targets elements based on their relationship to other elements.

Relationship selectors

Look again at the diagram of your project in Figure 3.10. It looks much like a family tree, doesn't it? This similarity gives the set of relationship selectors their names: *descendent selectors*, *child selectors*, *sibling selectors*, and *adjacent sibling selectors*.

Relationship selector syntax includes two selectors (like class or element selectors) joined by a symbol called a *combinator* that determines the targeted relationship between them. To understand how relationship selectors work, it is important to keep in mind that the browser reads selector syntax from *right to left*. Let's look at some examples.

A descendent selector targets any element of one specified type that is the descendent of another specified element. For example, to select any span element that is the descendent of the body element, the syntax would be:

```
body span {
  /* style declarations */
}
```

This syntax uses no combinator. Because it is read from right to left, it targets any span descended from a body, which in the current code means the thumbnail titles. It would also affect any spans that might be added within the header or elsewhere within the body.

Note that you can also use a class selector (or attribute selector, or indeed any type of selector) within a relationship selector, so the selector above could also be written as:

```
body .thumbnail-title {
  /* style declarations */
}
```

Child selectors target elements of a specified type that are the immediate children of another specified element. Child selector syntax uses the combinator >. To use child selector syntax to target all the spans currently in Ottergram, the syntax would be:

```
li > span {
  /* style declarations */
}
```

Reading from right to left, this selector targets any span that is the immediate child of a li element – again, the thumbnail titles.

Sibling selector syntax uses the combinator ~. As you might expect, this syntax targets elements with the same parent. However, because of the directional nature of relationship selectors, the results might not be exactly as you expect. Take this example:

```
header ~ ul {
  /* style declarations */
}
```

This selector targets any ul that is *preceded* by a header with the same parent element. This selector would effectively target Ottergram's ul, because it has a sibling header that precedes it in the code. However, reversing the syntax (ul ~ header) would result in no elements being selected, because there is no header preceded by a sibling ul.

The final relationship selector type is the adjacent sibling selector, which targets elements that are *immediately* preceded by a sibling of the specified type. The adjacent sibling combinator is +:

```
li + li {
  /* style declarations */
}
```

This syntax would select all li elements immediately preceded by a sibling li. The result is that the declared styles would be applied to the second through fifth li – but not the first, because it is not immediately preceded by another li. (Note that the general sibling selector and the adjacent sibling selector would work the same way at the moment, due to Ottergram's relatively simple structure.)

Back to the task at hand: adding a margin to the top of each list item except the first. If you used a descendent or child selector to target the .thumbnail-item class or the span or li elements, the margin would be applied to all five thumbnails. Because you want to style all but the first, use the adjacent sibling syntax in styles.css to add a top margin to only those thumbnails that are immediately preceded by another thumbnail.

```
...
a {
  text-decoration: none;
}

.thumbnail-item + .thumbnail-item {
  margin-top: 10px;
}

.thumbnail-item {
  ...
```

Save your file and check out the results in your browser (Figure 3.24).

Figure 3.24 Spacing between adjacent `.thumbnail-item` elements

Note that the DevTools give you an easy way to find out the nesting path of an element, which can help with writing relationship selectors. If you click one of the span elements inside one of the li elements, you can see its path at the bottom of the elements panel (Figure 3.25).

Figure 3.25 Nesting path shown by the elements panel

For one final tweak to the thumbnail list's appearance, return to `styles.css` and override the padding that the ul inherits from the user agent stylesheet so that the images are no longer indented.

```
...
.thumbnail-list {
  list-style: none;
  padding: 0;
}
...
```

As usual, save your file and switch to your browser to see your results (Figure 3.26).

Figure 3.26 ul with padding removed

Ottergram is starting to look polished. With some styling for the header, you will have a nice static web page.

Adding a Font

Earlier, you added the `.logo-text` class to the h1 element. Use that class as the selector for a new styling rule in `styles.css`. Insert it after the styles for the anchor tag. (In general, the order of your styles only matters when you have multiple rule sets for the same selector. In Ottergram, the styles are arranged in roughly the same order as they appear in the code. This is a matter of preference, and you are free to organize your styles as you see fit.)

```
...
a {
  text-decoration: none;
}

.logo-text {
  background: white;

  text-align: center;
  text-transform: uppercase;
  font-size: 37px;
}


.thumbnail-item + .thumbnail-item {
  ...
```

First, you gave the header a white background. Then you centered the text inside the `.logo-text` element and used the `text-transform` property to format it as uppercase. Finally, you set the font size. Your results will look like Figure 3.27.

Figure 3.27 Styling the header

Ottergram looks great. Great... but a little plain for a website with *otters*. To add some pizzazz, you can use a font for the header other than the default provided by the user agent stylesheet.

We included some fonts in the resource files you already downloaded and added to your project directory. To use them, you need to copy the fonts folder into your project. Place it *inside* your stylesheets folder (Figure 3.28).

Figure 3.28 `fonts` folder inside `stylesheets` folder

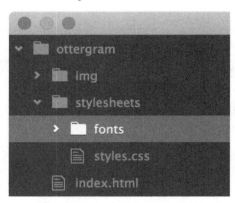

Now you only need to point some styles to those fonts.

The resource files include many formats of each font. As usual, different browser vendors support different kinds of fonts. To support the widest array of browsers, you need to include all of them in your project. Yes, all of them.

To help you out, the *@font-face* syntax lets you give a custom name to a family of fonts that you can then use in the rest of your styles.

An `@font-face` block is a little different from the declaration blocks you have been using. Inside of the `@font-face` block are three main parts:

- First, the `font-family` property, whose value is a string identifying the custom font name you can use throughout your CSS file.

- Next, several `src` declarations specifying different font files. (Take note – the order is important!)

- Last, declarations that modify the font's presentation, such as the `font-weight` and the `font-style`.

Add an @font-face declaration for the lakeshore font family to the top of styles.css and a style declaration to use the new font for the .logo-text class.

```css
@font-face {
    font-family: 'lakeshore';
    src: url('fonts/LAKESHOR-webfont.eot');
    src: url('fonts/LAKESHOR-webfont.eot?#iefix') format('embedded-opentype'),
        url('fonts/LAKESHOR-webfont.woff') format('woff'),
        url('fonts/LAKESHOR-webfont.ttf') format('truetype'),
        url('fonts/LAKESHOR-webfont.svg#lakeshore') format('svg');
    font-weight: normal;
    font-style: normal;
}

body {
  font-size: 10px;
  background: rgb(149, 194, 215);
}

a {
  text-decoration: none;
}

.logo-text {
 background: white;

 text-align: center;
 text-transform: uppercase;
 font-family: lakeshore;
 font-size: 37px;
}
...
```

Admittedly, getting the @font-face declaration just right can be tricky, because the order of the individual url values is important. It is a good idea to keep a copy of the declaration for reference. You can also look into Atom's snippets documentation at flight-manual.atom.io/using-atom/sections/ snippets to see how to create your own code "snippet," or template.

After declaring the custom @font-face, the rest of your CSS has access to the new lakeshore value for the font-family property. In the .logo-text declaration, you set font-family: lakeshore to apply the new font.

Save styles.css, switch to Chrome, and see how good it feels to have a web page as stylish as an otter (Figure 3.29).

Figure 3.29 Applying a custom font to the header

You did a lot of styling work in this chapter, and Ottergram looks great! In the next chapter you will make it even better by adding interactive functionality.

Bronze Challenge: Color Change

Change the background color styles for body. Use the color picker in the DevTools (Figure 3.21) to help you choose one.

For a more sophisticated color palette, go to color.adobe.com and create your own scheme for the body and .thumbnail-title background colors.

For the More Curious: Specificity! When Selectors Collide...

You have already seen how you can override styles. You included the link for `normalize.css` before the one for `styles.css`, for example. This made the browser use `normalize.css`'s styles as a baseline, with your styles taking precedence over the baseline styles.

This is the first basic concept of how the browser chooses which styles to apply to the elements on the page, known to front-end developers as *recency*: As the browser processes CSS rules, they can override rules that were processed earlier. You can control the order in which the browser processes CSS by changing the order of the `<link>` tags.

This is simple enough when the rules have the same selector (for example, if your CSS and `normalize.css` were to declare a different `margin` for the body element). In this case, the browser chooses the more recent declaration. But what about elements that are matched by more than one selector?

Say you had these two rules in your Ottergram CSS:

```
.thumbnail-item {
  background: blue;
  }

li {
  background: red;
}
```

Both of these match your `<li>` elements. What background color will your `<li>` elements have? Even though the `li { background: red; }` rule is more recent, `.thumbnail-item { background: blue; }` will be used. Why? Because it uses a class selector, which is more specific (i.e., assigned a higher specificity value) than the element selector.

Class selectors and attribute selectors have the same degree of specificity, and both have a higher specificity than element selectors. The highest degree of specificity goes to *ID selectors*, which you have not seen yet. If you give an element an `id` attribute, you can write an ID selector that is more specific than any other selector.

ID attributes look like other attributes. For example:

```
<li class="thumbnail-item" id="barry-otter">
```

To use the ID in a selector, you prefix it with #:

```
.thumbnail-item {
  background: blue;
}

#barry-otter {
  background: green;
}

li {
  background: red;
}
```

In this example, the `<li>` is matched by all three selectors, but it will have a green background because the ID selector has the highest specificity. The order of your rulesets makes no difference here, because each has a different specificity.

One note about using ID selectors: It is best to avoid them. ID values must be unique in the document, so you cannot use the `id="barry-otter"` attribute for any other element in your document. Even though ID selectors have the highest specificity, their associated styles cannot be reused, making them a maintenance "worst practice."

To learn more about specificity, go to the MDN page `developer.mozilla.org/en-US/docs/Web/CSS/Specificity`.

The Specificity Calculator at `specificity.keegan.st` is a great tool for comparing the specificty of different selectors. Check it out to get a more precise understanding of how specificity is computed.

4

Responsive Layouts with Flexbox

One of the duties of front-end developers is to provide the best experience to users regardless of what device or browser they are using.

This was not always the prevailing attitude, and the companies that made browsers were partly to blame. In the early days of the web, browser makers were fighting a war. Each would invent new nonstandard features in an attempt to out-do the others. In response, web developers came up with schemes for detecting which browser was requesting a document and what screen size was being used. Based on this information, a different version of the document was served out.

Sadly, this meant that front-end development became weighed down with creating multiple copies of every page on a site, each copy built with the markup and styles that would work for a specific version of a browser running at a particular screen size. Maintaining all of these copies was both time consuming and frustrating.

Thankfully, the Browser Wars are over, and browser makers now strive to conform to the same set of standard features – and modern front-end developers are free to focus on a single codebase for a website. Gone are the days of needing to create browser-specific versions of a page. But that does not mean that developers can no longer provide tailored pages based on different screen sizes or orientations. New technologies – like *flexbox*, which you will learn about in this chapter – allow layouts to adjust to the user's screen size without requiring duplicate documents.

In this chapter, you are going to expand Ottergram from a simple list of images to a proper user interface ready for interactive content. Using flexbox and CSS positioning, you will build a set of interface components that adjust as needed to variations in the size of the browser window while maintaining the overall layout. At the end of the chapter, Ottergram will feature a scrolling list of thumbnail images and an area that displays a large, detailed version of a single image (Figure 4.1).

Figure 4.1 Ottergram with flexible layout

You will do this in two parts. First, you will add the minimal markup and styles necessary to show the large image on the page and to make the thumbnails smaller and scrollable. Then, you will add styles that let parts of the page stretch and shrink as the window changes size or to accommodate screens of different sizes.

Expanding the Interface

Since the introduction of the iPhone, the trend toward accessing the internet via a smartphone, rather than a desktop or laptop, has grown steadily.

For front-end developers, this trend has meant that *mobile-first development* has proven to be the best design approach: designing for small screens first, then building on that design for tablet-size screens, and finally building up to a desktop-sized design.

Ottergram's simple layout is already mobile-friendly. It displays the text and images at a scale that is appropriate for smaller screen sizes. Because of this, you can move right into adding the next level of complexity to your layout.

A vertically scrolling list of otters is fine, but it would be even better if the user could also see a larger version of the images. The plan for Ottergram is to make the thumbnail list scroll horizontally while a larger detail image is featured. For now, the detail image will be below the list. This plan is diagrammed in Figure 4.2.

Figure 4.2 New layout for Ottergram

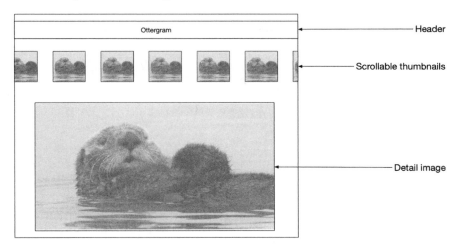

You will begin by adding the detail image.

Adding the detail image

For now, your detail image will be fixed to a single image. In Chapter 6 you will add functionality so that the user can click on a thumbnail to make any image the detail image.

Add a new section of code to create the detail image in index.html:

```
...
    <li class="thumbnail-item">
      <a href="#">
        <img class="thumbnail-image" src="img/otter5.jpg" alt="Barbara the Otter">
        <span class="thumbnail-title">Barbara</span>
      </a>
    </li>
  </ul>

  <div class="detail-image-container">
    <img class="detail-image" src="img/otter1.jpg" alt="">
    <span class="detail-image-title">Stayin' Alive</span>
  </div>

  </body>
</html>
```

You added a <div> with a detail-image-container class. A <div> is a generic container for content – usually for the purpose of applying styling to the enclosed content, which is exactly how you will use it.

Inside the <div> you added an <img> tag to display the large version of the otter image. You also added a <span>, which wraps around the title text for the detail image. You gave the <img> and <span> tags the class names detail-image and detail-image-title, respectively.

Save `index.html`, switch to `styles.css`, and, at the end, constrain the width of your new `.detail-image` class.

```
...
.thumbnail-title {
  ...
}

.detail-image {
  width: 90%;
}
```

Save `styles.css` and start `browser-sync` to open your project in **Chrome** (Figure 4.3). (The command is `browser-sync start --server --browser "Google Chrome" --files "stylesheets/*.css, *.html".`)

Figure 4.3 Initial styling for the detail image

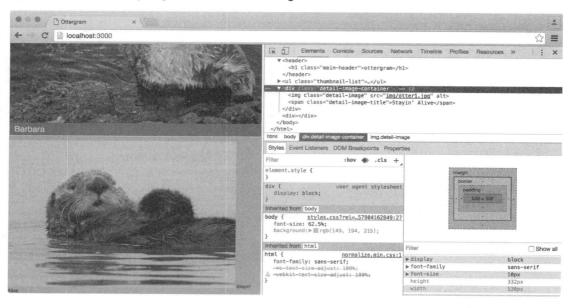

Your `.detail-image` will appear at the bottom of the page, a bit narrower than your thumbnails. By making the detail image 90% of its container's width, you have left a little space next to it. The browser puts the text of the `.detail-image-title` in that space. (You will style that text later in this chapter.)

If you resize the page, you will discover a bug: The detail image may be pushed out of view by the thumbnails as they adjust to the new width. You will address this problem later in this chapter.

Horizontal layout for thumbnails

Next, you will update the `.thumbnail-list` and `.thumbnail-item` classes so that the images scroll horizontally.

To help you test your scrolling, duplicate all five `<li>` elements in `index.html`. This will give you lots of content to scroll through. To do this, simply select all of the lines between `<ul class="thumbnail-list">` and `</ul>`, copy them, and paste the result just above the `</ul>`. You should end up with 10 list items, containing images `otter1.jpg` through `otter5.jpg` twice.

Be sure to save `index.html` when you are done. Duplicating content while you are developing is a good technique for simulating a more robust project. It allows you to see how your code handles real-world situations.

For a horizontally scrolling list of thumbnails, each thumbnail must be constrained to a specific width and the thumbnails should be laid out horizontally on a single line.

The `display: block` property, which you have used several times, will not create the desired effect. It causes the browser to render a line break before and after the element. However, a related style, `display: inline-block`, is perfect for this situation. With `inline-block`, the element's box is drawn as if you declared `display: block`, but without the line breaks – allowing your thumbnails to stay lined up in a row.

Add a `width` declaration and change the `display` declaration for the `.thumbnail-item` class in `styles.css`.

```
...
.thumbnail-item {
  display: block;
  display: inline-block;
  width: 120px;
  border: 1px solid rgb(100%, 100%, 100%, 0.8);
  border: 1px solid rgba(100%, 100%, 100%, 0.8);
}
...
```

(Note that Atom's linter may warn you that "Using width with border can sometimes make elements larger than you expect." This is because the `width` property only applies to the content portion – not the padding or border – of the element's box. You do not need to do anything about this warning.)

With the `.thumbnail-item` element's width set to an absolute value of `120px`, the `.thumbnail-image` is effectively fixed as well, since the `.thumbnail-image` adjusts to its container's width.

Why not just set the `.thumbnail-image` to `width: 120px`? You want the `.thumbnail-image` and the `.thumbnail-title` to be the same width. Instead of setting the `width` property for each of these, you set it on their common parent element. That way, if you need to change the `width`, you only need to change it in one place. Generally, it is a good practice to have inner elements adapt to their containers.

Save `styles.css` and check your page in Chrome. You can see that the `.thumbnail-item` elements line up side by side – but when they fill the width of their container, they wrap around (Figure 4.4).

Figure 4.4 `inline-block` creates rows that wrap

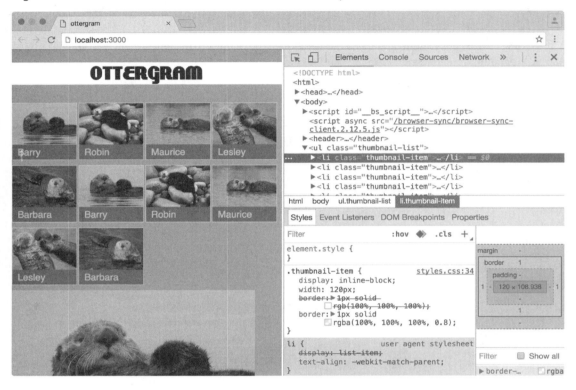

To get the scrolling behavior you want, set `.thumbnail-list` to prevent wrapping and allow scrolling in `styles.css`.

```
...
.thumbnail-list {
  list-style: none;
  padding: 0;

  white-space: nowrap;
  overflow-x: auto;
}
...
```

The `white-space: nowrap` declaration prevents the `.thumbnail-item` elements from wrapping. The `overflow-x: auto` tells the browser that it should add a scrollbar along the horizontal space (the x axis) of the `.thumbnail-list` element to accommodate content that overflows – i.e., does not fit within the `.thumbnail-list`. Without this declaration, you would have to scroll the entire web page to see the additional thumbnails.

Save your file again and take a look at the results in your browser. The thumbnails are now in a single row, and you should be able to scroll through them horizontally (Figure 4.5).

Figure 4.5 Horizontally scrolling thumbnails

This is a good start to the enhanced Ottergram interface. It works just fine for some screen sizes. However, it is not perfect, because it does not adapt well to a wide range of sizes – especially those that are much larger or smaller than the computer you are currently using.

In the next two sections, you will add code that gives Ottergram a more fluid layout and allows its UI - its *user interface* - to shift between different layouts to adapt to ranges of screen sizes.

Flexbox

You have seen `display` styles specifying the properties `block` and `inline`. Inline elements, like the thumbnail items in your newly scrolling list, are laid out next to one another, while block elements occupy their own horizontal line.

Another way to think of this is that block elements *flow* from top to bottom and inline elements flow from left to right (Figure 4.6).

Figure 4.6 Block vs inline elements

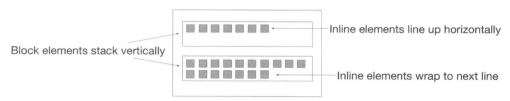

The display property tells the browser how an element should flow in the layout. For blogs or online encyclopedias, the inline and block values work well. But for application-style layouts like web-based email and social media sites, there is a new CSS specification that allows elements to flow more dynamically. This is the *flexible box model*, or flexbox.

Flexbox CSS properties can ensure that thumbnail and detail areas fill the screen and maintain their proportions relative to one another. This is exactly what you need for Ottergram. You can also use flexbox properties to center the contents of the detail area both horizontally and vertically, a task which is notoriously difficult using standard box model properties.

Creating a flex container

Before you add your first flexbox property, set your <html> and <body> elements to height: 100% in styles.css. The <html> element is the root element of your DOM tree, with the <body> as a child element drawn inside of it. Setting the height to 100% for both of them allows the content to fill the browser or device window.

```
@font-face {
  ...
}

html, body {
  height: 100%;
}

body {
  font-size: 10px;
  background: rgb(149, 194, 215);
}
...
```

Notice that you have grouped two selectors, separated by a comma, in this styling rule. Selectors of any type can be combined in this way to set common styles.

Notice also that you now have two styling rules with the body element selector. When the browser sees additional styling declarations for a selector, it simply adds to its existing styling information for that selector. In this case, it first sees that the <body> should have a height of 100% and stores that information. When it reads the next styling rule for the <body>, it stores the background and font-size information along with the height style.

Now you are ready to create your first *flex container*. When an element is a flex container, it can control how its child elements (its *flex items*) are laid out. Inside a flex container, the size and placement of flex items occurs along the *main axis* and the *cross axis* (Figure 4.7).

Figure 4.7 The main and cross axes of a flex container

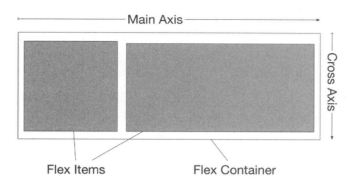

Make your `<body>` element a flex container by adding a `display: flex` declaration to its styling rule in `styles.css`.

```
...
body {
  display: flex;

  font-size: 10px;
  background: rgb(149, 194, 215);
}
...
```

If you saved now, your browser would display a rather sad-looking Ottergram, as in Figure 4.8. This is because the main axis goes from left to right, laying the flex items (all the children of the `<body>`) out in a row.

Figure 4.8 Flex items laid out along the main axis

However, you can see that the individual items shrink to accommodate the space, instead of wrapping. That is the first piece of good news. The second piece of good news is that you can fix the layout with just one style. (Well, almost.)

Changing the flex-direction

To fix the layout, set the <body> element's flex-direction to column in styles.css:

```
...
body {
  display: flex;
  flex-direction: column;

  font-size: 10px;
  background: rgb(149, 194, 215);
}
...
```

This swaps the main and cross axes for the flex container, as illustrated in Figure 4.9.

Figure 4.9 Main and cross axes with flex-direction: column

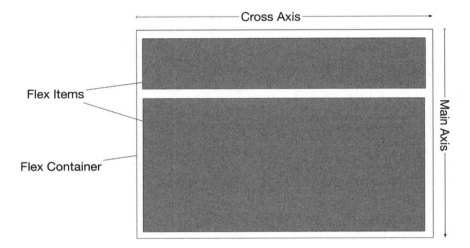

After changing the flex-direction to column, Ottergram is back to normal – almost. There is a visual bug in the layout when the browser window is a lot wider than it is tall, shown in Figure 4.10.

Figure 4.10 Missing thumbnails when the page is stretched wide

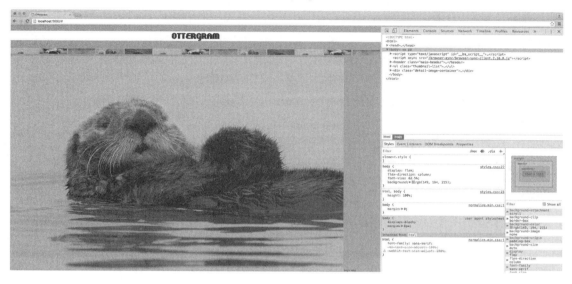

You will remedy this by adding a wrapper element and applying new flexbox properties.

Grouping elements within a flex item

The <body> has three flex items: the <header>, the .thumbnail-list, and the .detail-image-container. No matter what happens during the development (and use) of Ottergram, the <header> is not likely to change much in its layout or complexity. It is going to be at the top of the page, displaying text. That is about it.

On the other hand, as you develop Ottergram the .thumbnail-list and .detail-image-container and their contents may very well change in layout and complexity. Also, changes to one of these items are likely to affect the other.

For these reasons, you are going to group the .thumbnail-list and the .detail-image-container in their own flex container. To do this, you will wrap them in a <main> tag with a class name of .main-content (Figure 4.11).

Figure 4.11 Wrapping the .thumbnail-list and .detail-image-container

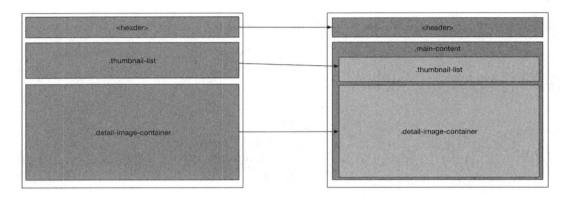

Make it so in index.html: Give the <header> element the class main-header, then wrap the .thumbnail-list (<ul>) and the .detail-image-container (<div>) in a <main> element with the class main-content.

```
...
  <body>
    <header>
    <header class="main-header">
      <h1 class="logo-text">ottergram</h1>
    </header>
    <main class="main-content">
      <ul class="thumbnail-list">
      ...
      </ul>

      <div class="detail-image-container">
        <img class="detail-image" src="img/otter1.jpg" alt="">
        <span class="detail-image-title">Stayin' Alive</span>
      </div>
    </main>
...
```

.main-header and .main-content are now the two flex items inside the <body>.

By wrapping the .thumbnail-list and .detail-image-container in the .main-content element, you are now free to declare a height for the <header>, leaving the rest of the <body>'s vertical space for the .main-content to occupy. That way, the space inside of .main-content can be distributed to .thumbnail-list and .detail-image-container without affecting the header.

Save index.html. Now that you have the markup for the two flex items inside the body, you can set their sizes relative to one another using the flex property.

The flex shorthand property

A flex container distributes its space to the flex items inside of it. If the flex items do not specify their size along the main axis, then the container distributes the space evenly based on the number of flex items, with each flex item getting the same share of space along the main axis. This is the default, illustrated in Figure 4.12.

Figure 4.12 Equal distribution of space between three flex items

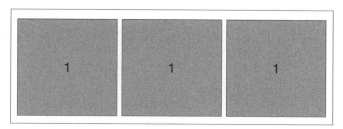

But imagine that one of the three flex items in Figure 4.12 is a bit greedier than the others and claims two shares of the total space. In that case, the flex container divides the space along the main axis into four shares. The greedy item occupies two of them (half the space) and the other items get one share each (Figure 4.13).

Figure 4.13 Unequal distribution of space between three flex items

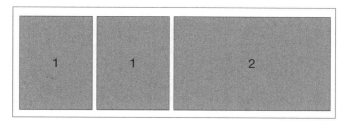

In Ottergram, you want the .main-content element to be the greedy element, taking up as much space along the main axis as possible. The .main-header, on the other hand, should take up as little space as possible.

The flex property lets your flex items specify how much of the available space they will take up. It is a shorthand property, as shown in Figure 4.14.

Figure 4.14 The flex shorthand property and its values

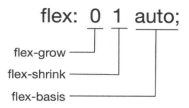

We strongly recommend that you use `flex` instead of the individual properties it represents. It protects you from inadvertently leaving a property out and getting unexpected results.

The first value is the one to focus on right now, as it determines how much the flex item can grow. By default flex items do not grow at all. You want that default behavior for your `.main-header`, but not your `.main-content`.

In `styles.css`, add a declaration block for the `.main-header` class selector, specifying a `flex` shorthand property with default values: `0 1 auto`.

```
...
a {
  text-decoration: none;
}

.main-header {
  flex: 0 1 auto;
}

.logo-text {
  background: white;
  ...
```

The value `0 1 auto` can be read as, "I do not want to grow any larger; I will shrink as needed; please calculate my size for me." The end result will be that the `.main-header` will take up only as much space as it needs, and no more.

Next, add a declaration block for `.main-content`, setting its `flex` to `1 1 auto`.

```
...
.logo-text {
  ...
}

.main-content {
  flex: 1 1 auto;
}

.thumbnail-item + .thumbnail-item {
  ...
```

The first value in `.main-content`'s `flex` declaration corresponds to the `flex-grow` property. A value of 1 tells the container, "I would like to grow as much as possible." Because its only sibling has declared that it will *not* grow, the `.main-content` element will grow to take up all the space not needed for the `.main-header`.

The `<body>`'s two flex items, the `.main-header` and the `.main-content` elements, occupy the flexible space according to their needs. Now it is time to adjust the layout of the `.main-content` element.

Ordering, justifying, and aligning flex items

Flexbox also allows you to subdivide flex items into flex containers. This technique lets you focus on the layers. In a moment, you are going to make your `.main-content` a flex container.

Working with nested flex containers is an exception to the atomic styling approach to creating the look and feel of visual components. Instead of styling the smallest, innermost elements first and then working your way out to the largest elements, when working on a layout with flexbox it is more useful to start with the outermost elements and work your way in.

Here is what you will tackle next. You will change the `.main-content` to a flex container with a vertical main axis. Also, you will specify the `flex` properties for `.main-content`'s flex items so that the `.thumbnail-list` takes the default amount of space and `.detail-image-container` grows to fill the space left over. Finally, you will move the `.thumbnail-list` below the `.detail-image-container` (Figure 4.15).

Figure 4.15 Making `.main-content` a flex container

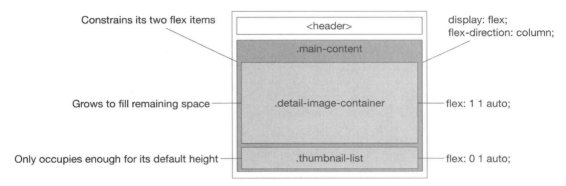

Make these changes in `styles.css` by adding `display: flex` and `flex-direction: column` to `.main-content`'s declaration block, adding `flex` properties to `.thumbnail-list`'s declaration block, and writing a new declaration block for the `.detail-image-container` class.

```
...
.main-content {
  flex: 1 1 auto;
  display: flex;
  flex-direction: column;
}

...

.thumbnail-list {
  flex: 0 1 auto;
  list-style: none;
  padding: 0;

  white-space: nowrap;
  overflow-x: auto;
}

...

.thumbnail-title {
  ...
}

.detail-image-container {
  flex: 1 1 auto;
}

.detail-image {
  ...
```

You might be wondering why you are not defining the heights of the `.thumbnail-list` and `.detail-image-container` boxes with percentages, the way you defined the width of the `.detail-image`. Setting the height of the `.thumbnail-list` at, for example, 25% and the `.detail-image-wrapper` at 75% seems logical – but it would not work the way you intend. The interaction with the `width` property of the `.detail-image` would result in the `.detail-image-container` being much too large, and the `.thumbnail-list` would end up either too small or too large, depending on the window size.

In short, using the `flex` property to set the flex items' sizes in conjunction with the one fixed size you care about – the width of the `.detail-image` – is the way to go.

Now to move the thumbnail list below the detail image. By default, flex items are drawn in the order that they appear in the HTML. This is known as *source order* and is the main way that developers control the order in which elements are drawn.

One option for moving the detail image up would be to cut and paste the markup for the detail image so that it came before the markup for the `.thumbnail-list` – to change the source order. However, it can also be done using a new flexbox property.

To change the order using flexbox, add an `order` declaration to the `.thumbnail-list` selector in `styles.css`.

```
...
.thumbnail-list {
  flex: 0 1 auto;
  order: 2;
  list-style: none;
  padding: 0;

  white-space: nowrap;
  overflow-x: auto;
}
...
```

The `order` property can be assigned any integer value. The default value is `0`, which tells the browser to use the source order. Any other values, including negative numbers, tell the browser to draw a flex item before or after other flex items. Giving `.thumbnail-list` the declaration `order: 2` tells the browser to draw it *after* any of its siblings that have a lower value for `order` – such as `.detail-image-container`, which is using the default.

Save `styles.css` and switch to Chrome. You will see that the thumbnails are rendered along the bottom of the page (Figure 4.16).

Figure 4.16 Changing the order elements are drawn

Next, you will continue to apply display: flex as you work on the layout of the Ottergram UI. So far, you have worked with flex containers that hold only a couple of flex items. Make the .thumbnail-list a flex container so that you can further explore what flexbox can offer you.

```
...
.thumbnail-list {
  flex: 0 1 auto;
  order: 2;
  display: flex;
  list-style: none;
  padding: 0;

  white-space: nowrap;
  overflow-x: auto;
}
...
```

Do not panic if you save your changes and see that the thumbnails are rendered oddly, as in Figure 4.17.

Figure 4.17 Otters, askew

To fix this, replace the .thumbnail-item's width declaration with a pair of declarations, one for min-width and another for max-width. This will remove the variations in size that are causing the strange layout.

You can also remove the declaration block that sets the margin-top for .thumbnail-item + .thumbnail-item elements. It is no longer needed for this layout.

```
...
.thumbnail-item + .thumbnail-item {
  margin-top: 10px;
}

.thumbnail-item {
  display: inline-block;
  width: 120px;
  min-width: 120px;
  max-width: 120px;
  border: 1px solid rgb(100%, 100%, 100%);
  border: 1px solid rgba(100%, 100%, 100%, 0.8);
}
...
```

Next, you will work with the spacing of the flex items inside of .thumbnail-list. In styles.css, add a declaration for justify-content to the .thumbnail-list selector.

```
...
.thumbnail-list {
  flex: 0 1 auto;
  order: 2;
  display: flex;
  justify-content: space-between;
  list-style: none;
  padding: 0;

  white-space: nowrap;
  overflow-x: auto;
}
...
```

The justify-content property lets a flex container control how flex items are drawn on the main axis. You used space-between as the value to make sure there is an even amount of spacing around each individual flex item.

There are five different values you can specify for justify-content. Figure 4.18 illustrates how each of these values works.

Figure 4.18 Values for the `justify-content` property

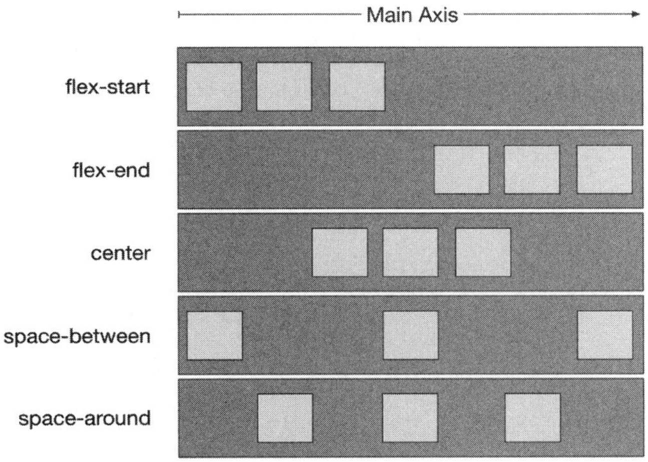

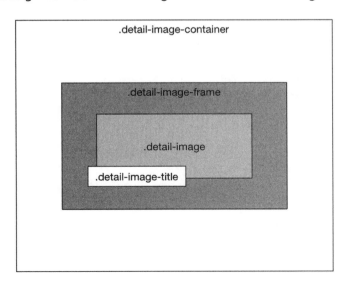

You have tackled the layout of the `.thumbnail-list`. Next, you will work with the `.detail-image-container` and its contents.

Centering the detail image

The detail image should be Ottergram's main focus. It should be front and center to make sure that the user is admiring the majesty of the otter. It should also be adorned with a snazzy title.

To center the detail image, you will first wrap the image and its title in a container, then center the *wrapper* inside the `.detail-image-container`. This idea is illustrated in Figure 4.19.

Figure 4.19 Framing the `.detail-image` and `.detail-image-title`

While you could center the .detail-image itself inside the .detail-image-container, it would be difficult to correctly offset the .detail-image-title, because both the .detail-image and the .detail-image-container are dynamically resizing.

An intermediary wrapper element is a useful technique for this situation. It will constrain the size of the .detail-image and serve as a reference for positioning the .detail-image-title.

In index.html, begin by adding a <div> with the class name detail-image-frame:

```
...
    </ul>

    <div class="detail-image-container">
      <div class="detail-image-frame">
        <img class="detail-image" src="img/otter1.jpg" alt="">
        <span class="detail-image-title">Stayin' Alive</span>
      </div>
    </div>
  </main>
 </body>
</html>
```

Save index.html. Now, in styles.css, add a declaration block for .detail-image-frame with a single style declaration: text-align: center. This is one way to center content without flexbox, but note that it only works horizontally.

```
...
.detail-image-container {
  flex: 1 1 auto;
}

.detail-image-frame {
  text-align: center;
}

.detail-image {
  width: 90%;
}
```

Next, to center the .detail-image-frame inside the .detail-image-container, update styles.css to make .detail-image-container a flex container. Draw its flex items in the center of the main axis (in this case, horizontally – the default) with justify-content: center, and add a new flexbox property, align-items: center, to draw its flex items in the center of the cross axis (vertically).

```
...
.detail-image-container {
  flex: 1 1 auto;
  display: flex;
  justify-content: center;
  align-items: center;
}
...
```

Save your changes and enjoy the proud otter, nobly centered in the `.detail-image-container` (Figure 4.20).

Figure 4.20 After centering `.detail-image-frame` inside `.detail-image-container`

Absolute and Relative Positioning

Sometimes you need to place an element in an exact spot inside of another element. CSS gives you a way to do this using *absolute positioning*.

You will use absolute positioning to place the detail-image-title in the lower left corner of the .detail-image-frame, as shown in Figure 4.21.

Figure 4.21 Absolutely positioned .detail-image-title

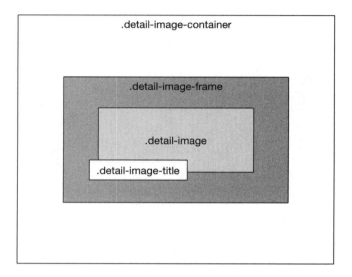

There are three requirements for absolute positioning. The absolutely positioned element must have:

- the property position: absolute, to tell the browser to take it out of the *normal flow* rather than laying it out along with its siblings

- coordinates, provided using one or more of the top, right, bottom, and left properties; absolute lengths (such as pixels) or relative lengths (such as percentages) may be used as values

- an ancestor element with an explicitly declared position property with a value of relative or absolute; this is important – if no ancestor has a declared position property, the absolutely positioned element will be placed relative to the <html> element (the browser window)

A word of warning: It might be tempting to use position: absolute for everything, but it should be used sparingly. A whole layout with absolute positioning is nearly impossible to maintain and will look terrible on any screen size other than the one it was developed for.

When specifying a coordinate, you are really specifying the distance from the edge of the element to the edge of its container, as shown in Figure 4.22.

Figure 4.22 Elements are absolutely positioned based on their edges

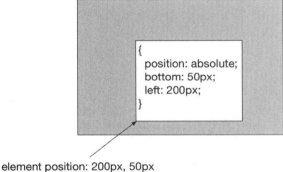

Figure 4.22 has two examples of absolute positioning. In the first one, the element is positioned so that its top edge is 50px from its container's top edge and its left edge is 200px from its container's left edge. The second example shows a variation, where the element is positioned by its bottom and left edges.

To position the .detail-image-title, start by declaring the .detail-image-frame to have position: relative in styles.css. You will position the .detail-image-title relative to it.

```
...
.detail-image-frame {
  position: relative;
  text-align: center;
}
...
```

You used position: relative for .detail-image-frame because you want it to remain in normal flow. You also want it to serve as the container for an absolutely positioned descendant, so its position property must be explicitly defined.

At the end of `styles.css`, add a declaration block for the `.detail-image-title` selector. For now, make the title white and set the font size to be four times the default.

```
...
.detail-image {
  width: 90%;
}

.detail-image-title {
  color: white;
  font-size: 40px;
}
```

So far, so good (Figure 4.23). But so basic.

Figure 4.23 Basic text styling for `.detail-image-title`

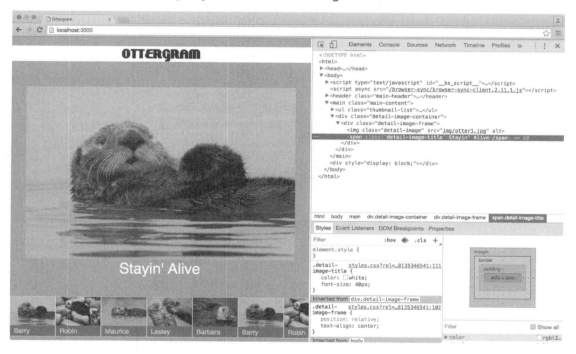

For a touch of style, let's add some text effects to the `.detail-image-title`. When positioning styled text elements, bear in mind that the element's box may change due to the visual characteristics of a custom typeface or other effects. For this example, you will do all of the text styling for `.detail-image-title` before you set its position. Add a `text-shadow` property to `.detail-image-title` in `styles.css`.

```
...
.detail-image-title {
  color: white;
  text-shadow: rgba(0, 0, 0, 0.9) 1px 2px 9px;
  font-size: 40px;
}
```

As the name suggests, the `text-shadow` property adds a shadow to text. It accepts a color for the shadow, a pair of lengths for the *offset* (i.e., whether the shadow falls above or below and to the left or right of the text), and a length for the *blur radius* – an optional part of a `text-shadow` declaration that makes the shadow larger and lighter in color as you make the value higher.

You gave your shadow the color attribute `rgba(0, 0, 0, 0.9)` to make it a slightly transparent black. It is offset, or shifted, `1px` to the right and `2px` below the text (negative values would place it to the left or above the text). The last value of `9px` is the blur radius. Figure 4.24 shows your new shadow.

Figure 4.24 A `text-shadow` for the `.detail-image-title`

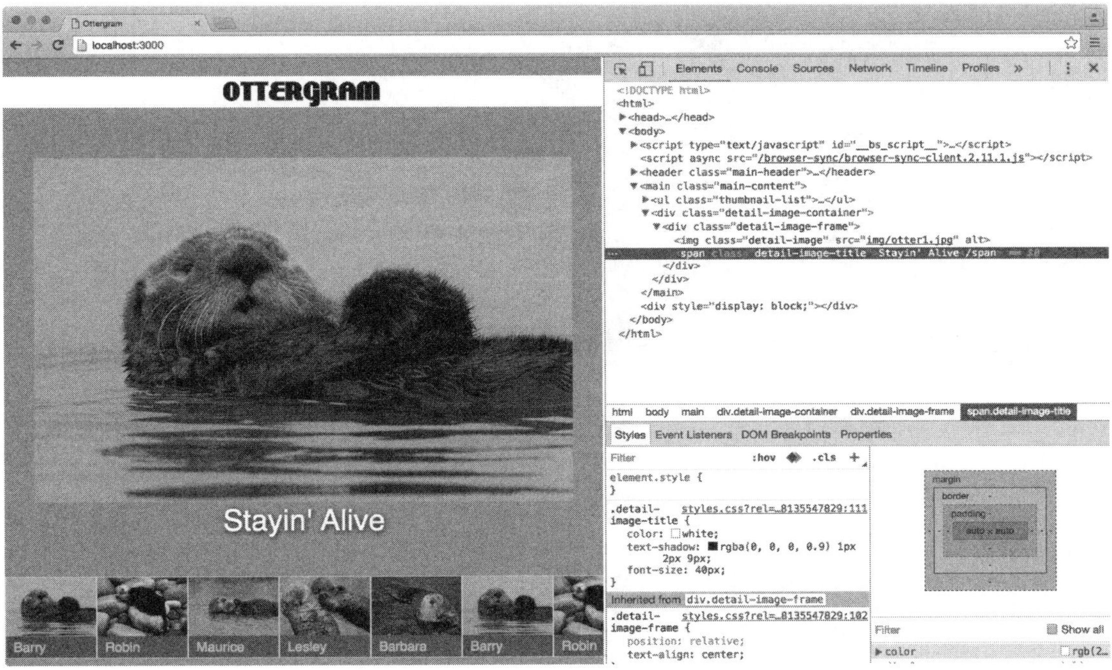

Try adjusting the `text-shadow` values in the styles pane of the DevTool's elements panel to get a feel for how they work (Figure 4.25).

89

Figure 4.25 Exaggerating the text shadow using the DevTools

When you are ready, add one last flourish with a custom font. As you did in Chapter 3, add an @font-face declaration in styles.css to add the Airstream font to your project. Add a font-family: airstreamregular declaration to .detail-image-title to put it to use.

```
@font-face {
    font-family: 'airstreamregular';
    src: url('fonts/Airstream-webfont.eot');
    src: url('fonts/Airstream-webfont.eot?#iefix') format('embedded-opentype'),
        url('fonts/Airstream-webfont.woff') format('woff'),
        url('fonts/Airstream-webfont.ttf') format('truetype'),
        url('fonts/Airstream-webfont.svg#airstreamregular') format('svg');
    font-weight: normal;
    font-style: normal;
}

@font-face {
    font-family: 'lakeshore';
    ...
}

...

.detail-image-title {
  font-family: airstreamregular;
  color: white;
  text-shadow: rgba(0, 0, 0, 0.9) 1px 2px 9px;
  font-size: 40px;
}
```

So far, so stylish (Figure 4.26)!

Figure 4.26 I gotta have more fancy

Now that you have finished the styling of `.detail-image-title`, give it a `position: absolute` declaration so that the browser will place it at a precise location within `.detail-image-frame`. Specify that location with `bottom: -16px` and `left: 4px`, to put it just *below* the bottom edge of `.detail-image-frame` and a little bit inside the left edge of `.detail-image-frame`. (Negative values are fine for the coordinates.)

```
...
.detail-image-title {
  position: absolute;
  bottom: -16px;
  left: 4px;

  font-family: airstreamregular;
  color: white;
  text-shadow: rgba(0, 0, 0, 0.9) 1px 2px 9px;
  font-size: 40px;
}
```

Save `styles.css`, and you will see in the browser that the `.detail-image-title` now sits below and near the left of the otter photo. You now have a positively chic Ottergram in your browser (Figure 4.27).

Figure 4.27 Hello, gorgeous!

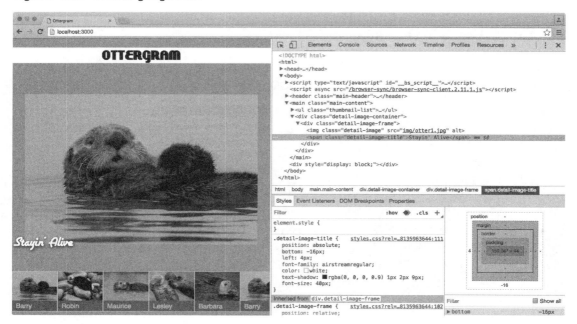

Take a step back to enjoy the fruits of your labor. Ottergram has a dynamic, fluid layout thanks to the addition of flexbox to your styles. In the next chapter you will make the layout adapt to different browser window sizes.

5

Adaptive Layouts with Media Queries

In this chapter, you will explore a technique for turning styles on and off based on the size of the browser window and other characteristics. You will provide an alternate layout for larger screens using a minimal amount of code. The browser will be able to switch between the different layouts in real time, as the browser window changes size – without reloading the page. Figure 5.1 shows the original layout and the alternate layout.

Figure 5.1 Two Ottergram layouts

The industry term for this behavior is *responsive website*. Unfortunately, this term is often a point of confusion. Some think that it means "fast website" or "website with visual animations." We prefer to call it an *adaptive layout*.

There are several ways of including alternate styles to be used based on the current browser conditions. The recommended approach is to write your styles for the smallest screen and then provide override styles in *media queries* that are triggered when the *viewport* – the browser's viewable area – is larger than a set threshold.

On a traditional browser (like the one you are using while developing Ottergram), the viewport is the area shown by the browser window. This is pretty intuitive. On a mobile browser, it gets more complicated. Mobile browsers have multiple viewports, and each one plays a role in how a page is rendered.

Front-end developers need to focus on the *layout viewport* (sometimes called the *actual viewport*). The layout viewport tells the browser, "Pretend that I'm actually 980 pixels wide and then draw the page."

Users are more concerned with a mobile browser's *visual viewport*. This is the thing that they can pinch to zoom in and out on a page (Figure 5.2).

Figure 5.2 Visual viewport vs layout viewport

If you viewed Ottergram on your smartphone right now, you would see something like Figure 5.2, with the browser zoomed in on the upper-left corner of the page. Needless to say, even though a mobile user can zoom out manually, you do not want Ottergram to behave like this by default.

Earlier we mentioned that you are taking a mobile-first approach to developing Ottergram. That was mostly true. Your markup and styles were written in a mobile-friendly way – using a minimal amount of markup and styling the smallest elements first. Now, you just need to give the browser information about the layout viewport it should use.

Resetting the Viewport

In Chapter 3 you added `normalize.css` to Ottergram. This ensured that any browser viewing Ottergram would have the same set of default styles. On top of these defaults, you could confidently add your own CSS, knowing it would work consistently from browser to browser.

You will do something similar for the layout viewport. Just as every browser may have a different user agent stylesheet, every browser may have a different default layout viewport. However, unlike using normalize.css, you are not going to reset the viewport for all browsers to the same value. Instead, you will use a <meta> tag to tell all browsers to display Ottergram at the best size for the device's physical screen.

In index.html, add a <meta> tag that tells the browser that the width of the layout viewport is the same as the device's screen width. Make sure to set the zoom to 100% by setting the initial-scale to 1.

```
<!doctype html>
<html>
  <head>
    <meta charset="utf-8">
    <meta name="viewport" content="width=device-width, initial-scale=1">
    <link rel="stylesheet"
      href="https://cdnjs.cloudflare.com/ajax/libs/normalize/3.0.3/normalize.min.css">
    <link rel="stylesheet" href="stylesheets/styles.css">
    <title>Ottergram</title>
  </head>
...
```

Save your changes. This technique sets the layout viewport to the *ideal viewport*. The ideal viewport is best viewport size for a specific device, as recommended by the browser maker. This varies significantly, since there are many, many different devices and quite a number of different browsers.

Table 5.1 summarizes the different types of viewports.

Table 5.1 Summary of the different viewports

Viewport	Description	Device
viewport	The area equal to the browser's window. It serves as the <html> element's container.	desktop, laptop
layout viewport	A virtual screen, larger than the actual device screen, used for calculating the page layout.	mobile
visual viewport	The zoomable area that a user can see on a device's screen. Zooming has no effect on the page layout.	mobile
ideal viewport	The optimal dimensions for a specific browser on a specific device.	mobile

Start browser-sync and make sure the DevTools are open in Chrome. Look to the left of the Elements menu item and find the Toggle Device Mode button, which looks like this: . It is shown in context in Figure 5.3.

Figure 5.3 Toggle Device Mode button

Click this button to activate *device mode*. You will see that the web page view now shows Ottergram on a simulated smartphone screen. There is a menu for choosing between different screen sizes based on popular devices. You can also click the gray bar below the presets to toggle between small, medium, and large screen sizes. And there is a menu for quickly choosing a screen orientation of landscape or portrait. Figure 5.4 shows a screenshot of the device mode at the time of this writing. Yours may look quite different, as the DevTools undergo regular updates.

Figure 5.4 Using device mode for responsive testing

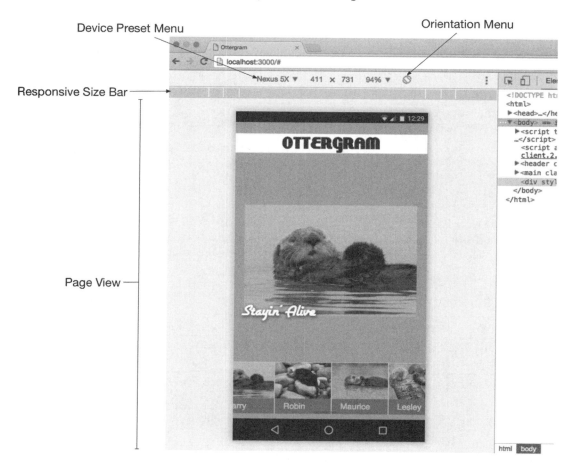

You can see that, thanks to your new `<meta>` element, Ottergram displays well on a small screen, such as a smartphone. For devices with larger screens, such as tablets or laptops, a slightly different layout may be more appropriate. Next, you will apply different layout styles using a combination of flexbox and media queries.

Click the ⬚ button again to deactivate device mode before you continue.

Adding a Media Query

Media queries let you group CSS declaration blocks and specify the conditions under which they should be applied. Those conditions may be something like "if the screen is at least 640 pixels wide" or "if the screen is wider than it is tall and has a high pixel density."

The syntax begins with @media, followed by the conditions to be matched. Next is a set of curly braces that wraps around entire declaration blocks. Let's see what this looks like.

Begin your first media query at the end of `styles.css`. You will create a media query that will activate styles when being viewed on any kind of device when the viewport is at least 768 pixels wide, which is a common device width for tablets.

```
...
.detail-image-title {
  ...
}

@media all and (min-width: 768px) {
  /* Styles will go here */
}
```

`@media` is followed by the *media type* `all`. Media types were originally intended to differentiate between devices, such as smart televisions and handheld devices. Unfortunately, browsers do not implement this accurately, so you should always specify `all`. The only time you might not use `all` is when you want to specify styles for printing, when you can safely use the media type `print`.

After the media type, you write the conditions for applying the styles. Here, you are using the useful condition `min-width`. You can see that conditions look similar to style declarations.

To achieve the effect shown in Figure 5.1, you will need to change the `flex-direction` of the `.main-content` element. This will let the thumbnails and the detail image sit next to one another. You do not want the thumbnails to cause the browser to scroll. Instead, they should continue to scroll independently of the browser window. For that, you will add `overflow: hidden`.

Add those styles to your media query at the end of `styles.css`.

```
...
@media all and (min-width: 768px) {
  /* Styles will go here */
  .main-content {
    flex-direction: row;
    overflow: hidden;
  }
}
```

You would be in for a shock if you saved and then stretched your browser wide enough to trigger your media query. At the moment, your page looks like Figure 5.5. Not to worry. You will fix this with only a few more lines of code.

Figure 5.5 Otters in disarray

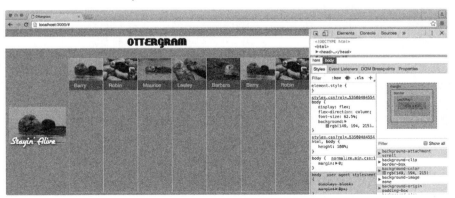

The thumbnails need to be displayed in a column instead of a row. This is easy to do, because you used flexbox for laying them out. Add a declaration block inside the body of the media query in `styles.css` setting `.thumbnail-list`'s `flex-direction` to `column`.

```
...
@media all and (min-width: 768px) {
  .main-content {
    flex-direction: row;
    overflow: hidden;
  }

  .thumbnail-list {
    flex-direction: column;
  }
}
```

Save `styles.css`. That has improved things significantly (Figure 5.6)!

Figure 5.6 After setting `flex-direction` to `column`

According to your design, the thumbnails should go on the left. You can solve this by changing `.thumbnail-list`'s `order`. Earlier, you set it to 2 so that it would be drawn after the `.detail-image-container`. Now, set it to 0 within the media query in `styles.css` so that it follows the source order and is drawn before the `.detail-image-container`.

```
...
@media all and (min-width: 768px) {
  .main-content {
    flex-direction: row;
    overflow: hidden;
  }

  .thumbnail-list {
    flex-direction: column;
    order: 0;
  }
}
```

Save your changes and confirm that the thumbnails are drawn on the left side of the page.

You are almost there! Add a few more styles in styles.css for the .thumbnail-list and .thumbnail-items to make the sizing and spacing a little nicer.

```
...
@media all and (min-width: 768px) {
  .main-content {
    flex-direction: row;
    overflow: hidden;
  }

  .thumbnail-list {
    flex-direction: column;
    order: 0;
    margin-left: 20px;
  }

  .thumbnail-item {
    max-width: 260px;
  }

  .thumbnail-item + .thumbnail-item {
    margin-top: 20px;
  }
}
```

Once again, save styles.css and switch to your browser. Your layout now looks sharp whether the viewport is narrower or wider (Figure 5.7).

Figure 5.7 Responsive otters

Ottergram is making steady progress! You have created a good-looking website with a layout that can adapt to many screen sizes. In the next chapter, you will begin using JavaScript to add a layer of interactivity to Ottergram.

Bronze Challenge: Portrait

Your current media query changes the layout based on the width of the viewport. You could look at this in a different way. One is for viewports that are taller than they are wide, and the other is for viewports that are wider than they are tall. These are two *orientation* modes that your viewport can be in.

Check MDN's documentation for media queries and update your media query so that the layout changes according to orientation and not based on width.

For the More Curious: Common Solutions (and Bugs) with Flexbox Layouts

Philip Walton is a developer who maintains two very important flexbox resources. The first is the Solved by Flexbox site (`philipwalton.github.io/solved-by-flexbox`), which offers demos of common layouts implemented using flexbox and all the information you need to create them yourself. Some of the layouts are very difficult to achieve without flexbox.

The second resource is the Flexbugs page at `github.com/philipwalton/flexbugs`. Flexbox is wonderful, but it is not perfect. Flexbugs provides solutions and workarounds for common problems that developers run into when using flexbox. The information is provided by members of the development community who have encountered these bugs, and the list is well maintained.

Gold Challenge: Holy Grail Layout

Be sure to make a copy of your code before attempting this challenge! It will require significant changes to the markup and styles. Use your copy for working on the challenge and leave the original intact for starting the next chapter.

Using Solved by Flexbox as a reference, implement the Holy Grail layout in Ottergram. Create a second navigation bar with thumbnails, but place it on the other side of the viewport.

Make sure to add a footer element to the bottom of your page. Use the `<footer>` tag and put an `<h1>` inside of it.

6

Handling Events with JavaScript

You know what is cool about otters? Among other things, they hold hands when they sleep so that they do not float away. Keep this image in mind as you learn to work with event callbacks in JavaScript.

JavaScript is a programming language that adds interactivity to websites by manipulating DOM elements and CSS styles on a page. It was originally created for use by people who were not professional programmers. It has grown in power and popularity and is now used for many kinds of application development. When you use sites like Gmail or Netflix, you are interacting with programs written in JavaScript. In fact, the Atom text editor is actually a desktop application written in JavaScript.

Despite its power and widespread use, it has its quirks, like any programming language. As you continue working on Ottergram and the other projects in this book, you will learn to navigate the rough patches of the language and to take advantage of its best parts.

There are several versions of JavaScript, and you will use three of them for the projects in this book. They are all revisions of a standard specification known as ECMAScript (or "ES"). Table 6.1 summarizes them.

Table 6.1 JavaScript versions used in this book

ECMAScript Edition	Release Date	Notes
3	December 1999	Most widely supported version; encompasses most of the language features you will use, such as variables, types, and functions.
5	December 2009	Backward compatible, with opt-in enhancements such as a *strict mode* that prevents the usage of the more error-prone parts of the language.
6	June 2015	Includes new syntax and language features; at the time of this writing, most browsers do not yet support ES6, but ES6 code can be translated into ES5, making it usable by most browsers.

In this chapter, you will use JavaScript to make Ottergram interactive: The detail image and detail title will change when the user clicks or taps one of the thumbnails.

To do this, you are going to write a JavaScript *function* – a set of steps for the browser to follow – that reads the URL for an image and shows it in the detail area. Then you will ensure that this function is run when a thumbnail is clicked. You will also write a separate function that hides the detail area and run that function when the Escape key is pressed.

At the end of the chapter, Ottergram will be able to feature any otter in the detail image (Figure 6.1).

Figure 6.1 Clicking thumbnails changes detail image and title

As you write these functions, you will interact with the page using a set of predefined interfaces built into the browser. There are a large number of them, and the code will only walk you through the ones necessary for the task at hand. If you are curious, you can find more in-depth information about them on the MDN at developer.mozilla.org/en-US/docs/Web/API/Element.

Preparing the Anchor Tags for Duty

Before you start adding interactive features with JavaScript, you need to make a few updates to the markup. Your thumbnail images are wrapped in anchor tags, but those tags do not actually link to any resource. Instead, they use the # value for the href attribute, which tells the browser to stay on the same page. In order to make a click on a thumbnail do anything interesting, you need to fix that.

First, in index.html, remove all but five of the .thumbnail-item elements. You no longer need the duplicates, because your layout is in good shape.

Then, change the anchor tags' href properties to no longer use the dummy value #. Instead, set the values to be the same as each <img> tag's src value.

Atom can help you make these changes, taking the tedium out of working with HTML. Like any text editor, it has a way to find and replace text. Select Find → Find in Buffer or use the keyboard shortcut Command-F (Ctrl-F). This will open the Find in Buffer panel at the bottom of the editor window (Figure 6.2).

Figure 6.2 Using Atom's find-and-replace feature

Enter "#" in the Find in current buffer text box and "img/otter.jpg" in the Replace in current buffer text box. Then click Replace All in the lower right.

This will change all of the <a href="#"> tags to <a href="img/otter.jpg">. Now it is just a matter of manually adding the appropriate number to each one (img/otter1.jpg, img/otter2.jpg, etc.).

Press the Escape key to close the Find in Buffer panel. `index.html` should look like this:

```
...
    <ul class="thumbnail-list">
      <li class="thumbnail-item">
        <a href="#">
        <a href="img/otter1.jpg">
          <img class="thumbnail-image" src="img/otter1.jpg" alt="">
          <span class="thumbnail-title">Barry</span>
        </a>
      </li>
      <li class="thumbnail-item">
        <a href="#">
        <a href="img/otter2.jpg">
          <img class="thumbnail-image" src="img/otter2.jpg" alt="">
          <span class="thumbnail-title">Robin</span>
        </a>
      </li>
      <li class="thumbnail-item">
        <a href="#">
        <a href="img/otter3.jpg">
          <img class="thumbnail-image" src="img/otter3.jpg" alt="">
          <span class="thumbnail-title">Maurice</span>
        </a>
      </li>
      <li class="thumbnail-item">
        <a href="#">
        <a href="img/otter4.jpg">
          <img class="thumbnail-image" src="img/otter4.jpg" alt="">
          <span class="thumbnail-title">Lesley</span>
        </a>
      </li>
      <li class="thumbnail-item">
        <a href="#">
        <a href="img/otter5.jpg">
          <img class="thumbnail-image" src="img/otter5.jpg" alt="">
          <span class="thumbnail-title">Barbara</span>
        </a>
      </li>
    </ul>
...
```

Next, you need to add additional properties to your anchor elements so you can access them using JavaScript. When styling with CSS, you use class name selectors to refer to elements on the page. For JavaScript, you use *data attributes*.

Data attributes are just like the other HTML attributes you have been using except that, unlike attributes such as `src` or `href`, data attributes do not have special meaning to the browser. The only requirement is that the attribute name starts with `data-`. Using custom data attributes lets you designate what HTML elements on the page your JavaScript interacts with.

Technically, in JavaScript, you could access elements on the page using class names. Likewise, you could use data attributes in your selectors for styling. But you really should not. Your code will be much more maintainable if your JavaScript and your CSS do not rely on the same attributes.

Update your anchor tags in `index.html` with data attributes. Note that the line breaks in the code below have been added to make sure that everything fits nicely on the page. You are free to add them or not, as you prefer. They will not make a difference to the browser.

```
...
        <li class="thumbnail-item">
          <a href="img/otter1.jpg" data-image-role="trigger"
                                   data-image-title="Stayin' Alive"
                                   data-image-url="img/otter1.jpg">
            <img class="thumbnail-image" src="img/otter1.jpg" alt="">
            <span class="thumbnail-title">Barry</span>
          </a>
        </li>
          <li class="thumbnail-item">
            <a href="img/otter2.jpg" data-image-role="trigger"
                                     data-image-title="How Deep Is Your Love"
                                     data-image-url="img/otter2.jpg">
              <img class="thumbnail-image" src="img/otter2.jpg" alt="">
              <span class="thumbnail-title">Robin</span>
            </a>
          </li>
        <li class="thumbnail-item">
          <a href="img/otter3.jpg" data-image-role="trigger"
                                   data-image-title="You Should Be Dancing"
                                   data-image-url="img/otter3.jpg">
            <img class="thumbnail-image" src="img/otter3.jpg" alt="">
            <span class="thumbnail-title">Maurice</span>
          </a>
        </li>
        <li class="thumbnail-item">
          <a href="img/otter4.jpg" data-image-role="trigger"
                                   data-image-title="Night Fever"
                                   data-image-url="img/otter4.jpg">
            <img class="thumbnail-image" src="img/otter4.jpg" alt="">
            <span class="thumbnail-title">Lesley</span>
          </a>
        </li>
        <li class="thumbnail-item">
          <a href="img/otter5.jpg" data-image-role="trigger"
                                   data-image-title="To Love Somebody"
                                   data-image-url="img/otter5.jpg">
            <img class="thumbnail-image" src="img/otter5.jpg" alt="">
            <span class="thumbnail-title">Barbara</span>
          </a>
        </li>
...
```

Add data attributes for the detail image, as well:

```
...
    <div class="detail-image-container">
      <div class="detail-image-wrapper">
  <img class="detail-image" data-image-role="target" src="img/otter1.jpg" alt="">
  <span class="detail-image-title" data-image-role="title">Stayin' Alive</span>
      </div>
    </div>
...
```

Your JavaScript code can refer to these data attributes to access specific elements on the page because the browser lets you use JavaScript to make queries about the contents of a web page. For example, you can query for any elements that match a selector, such as data-image-role="trigger". If the query finds matches, it will return *references* to the matching elements.

When you have a reference to an element, you can do all sorts of things with the element. You can read or change the values of its attributes, change the text inside of it, and even get access to the elements around it. When you make changes to an element using a reference, the browser updates the page immediately.

In this chapter, you will write JavaScript code that will get references to the anchor and detail image elements, read the values from the anchor's data attributes, and then change the value of the detail image's src attribute. This is how you will make Ottergram interactive.

You may have noticed that the anchor tags and the detail image's <img> tag all have a data-image-role attribute, but their values are different.

Using the same data attribute names for the anchor and <img> tags is not required, but it is a good practice. It reminds you, the developer, that these elements will be part of the same JavaScript behavior.

One last change is needed in your HTML before you begin work on your JavaScript: You need to tell the HTML to run the JavaScript. Do this by adding a <script> tag in index.html. This <script> tag will refer to the file scripts/main.js, which you will create in just a moment.

```
...
        </div>
      </div>
    </main>
    <script src="scripts/main.js" charset="utf-8"></script>
  </body>
</html>
```

When the browser sees a <script> tag, it begins running the code in the referenced file immediately. JavaScript cannot access an element within your HTML before it has been rendered by the browser, so putting the <script> tag at the bottom of the body ensures that your JavaScript does not run until after all the markup has been parsed.

Your HTML is now ready to connect with the JavaScript you are about to write. Be sure to save index.html before you move on.

Your First Script

Time to create a scripts folder and the main.js file. Recall that you can create folders from within the Atom editor. Control-click (right-click) ottergram in the lefthand panel and click New Folder in the pop-up. Enter the name scripts in the prompt that appears.

Then, Control-click (right-click) scripts in the lefthand panel and choose New File. The prompt will pre-fill the text scripts/. After this, enter main.js and press Return.

Make sure your folder structure looks like Figure 6.3.

Figure 6.3 Ottergram folder structure

The name `main.js` does not have any special significance for the browser, but it is a common convention used by many front-end developers.

One last thing before you dive into JavaScript. You need to start `browser-sync`, and to do so you need to change the command you have been using slightly:

```
browser-sync start --server --browser "Google Chrome"
                --files "*.html, stylesheets/*.css, scripts/*.js"
```

You added the path `scripts/*.js` to the list of files so that `browser-sync` will watch for changes to the JavaScript as well as the HTML and CSS.

Overview of the JavaScript for Ottergram

Before you start coding, it is always good to have a plan. Here is the plain English version of what you need to do with Ottergram.

1. Get all the thumbnails.

2. Listen for a click on each one.

3. If a click occurs, update the detail image with info from that thumbnail.

You can break down #3 into three subparts:

a. Get the image URL from the thumbnail's data attribute.

b. Get the title text from the thumbnail's data attribute.

c. Set the image and title on the detail image.

Here is that same plan expressed as a diagram (Figure 6.4)

Figure 6.4 Plan of attack for Ottergram

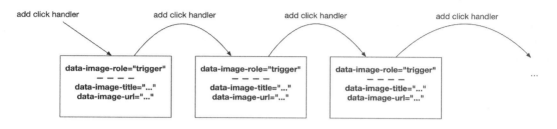

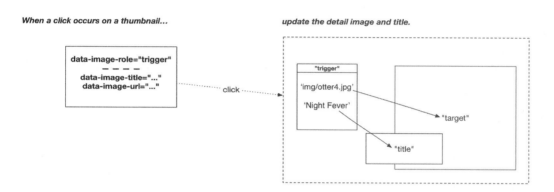

This chapter will walk you through creating the code starting with the last step. This is the "bottom-up" approach, and it works well when writing JavaScript.

Declaring String Variables

Your first JavaScript task is to create string variables for each of the data attributes you added to the markup. (If those are unfamiliar terms, do not worry – we will explain in just a moment.)

At the top of `main.js`, start by adding a variable named `DETAIL_IMAGE_SELECTOR` and assigning it the string `'[data-image-role="target"]'`.

```
var DETAIL_IMAGE_SELECTOR = '[data-image-role="target"]';
```

This might not be much code, but it is worth a closer look. Let's start in the middle, with the = symbol. This is the *assignment operator*. Unlike in mathematics, the = symbol in JavaScript does not mean that two things are equal. Instead, it means "Take the value on the righthand side and give it the name on the lefthand side."

On the righthand side of this particular assignment is a *string* of text: `'[data-image-role="target"]'`. A string is just a sequence of characters representing text, and it is delimited by single quotation marks. The text inside the single quotes happens to be the attribute selector for your detail image. This is a clue that you will use this string to access that element.

On the lefthand side of the assignment is a *variable declaration*. It may be useful to think of a variable as a label that you can use to refer to some value, which could be a numeric value, a string (as in this case), or some other type of value. Using the `var` keyword, you are creating a variable named `DETAIL_IMAGE_SELECTOR`.

Next, declare variables in `main.js` for the detail title selector and the thumbnail anchor selector. Assign the strings for these selectors as well.

```
var DETAIL_IMAGE_SELECTOR = '[data-image-role="target"]';
var DETAIL_TITLE_SELECTOR = '[data-image-role="title"]';
var THUMBNAIL_LINK_SELECTOR = '[data-image-role="trigger"]';
```

As the name *variable* suggests, their values can be reassigned – they can vary. Writing variable names in all capital letters is a convention that developers sometimes use when the values should not change. Other languages have *constants* that serve this purpose. JavaScript is in transition: ES5 does not have constants; ES6 does – but, as we said earlier, it is not yet fully supported. Until constants become well supported, you can follow this convention to label a value that should not change.

As an aside, strings can be delimited by single or double quotes. You are free to use either, but this book will use single quotes as a convention and we suggest that you follow along at least for the projects in this book.

If you want to use double quotes, you have to *escape* any double quotes that are part of the string so that the browser does not incorrectly parse them as part of the code. To escape a character, you precede it with a backslash, like this:

```
var DETAIL_IMAGE_SELECTOR = "[data-image-role=\"target\"]";
```

Using single quotes is not a guarantee that you will not need to escape characters. If a string delimited by single quotes contains single quotes – or apostrophes – you have to escape them.

Save `main.js`. With these variables in hand, let's take them for a spin in Chrome's DevTools.

Working in the Console

One of the most useful parts of the DevTools is the console, which lets you enter JavaScript code and evaluate it immediately. This is especially useful for iteratively developing JavaScript code that makes changes to a page.

In the DevTools, click on the Console tab, to the right of the Elements tab (Figure 6.5).

Figure 6.5 Choosing the console tab

The console has a prompt where you can enter lines of code. Click to the right of the ❯ symbol so that the console is ready for input (Figure 6.6).

Figure 6.6 The console, ready for input

Type the following math expression into the console:

```
137 + 349
```

Press the Return key. The console will print out the result (Figure 6.7).

Figure 6.7 Evaluating a math expression

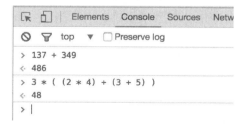

The console's main job is to tell you, in the simplest terms, the value of the code you enter.

As with many things in life, order matters. If you need certain items to be evaluated as a group, you can wrap parentheses around them. (This is much easier than memorizing the order in which JavaScript would do this without the parentheses.) Enter the following expression in the console.

```
3 * ( (2 * 4) + (3 + 5) )
```

Press the Return key, and the console will crunch the numbers in the correct order (Figure 6.8). (By the way, although we have added spaces between the numbers and operators for the sake of readability, you do not need to include them. The console does not care.)

Figure 6.8 Evaluating a more complex math expression

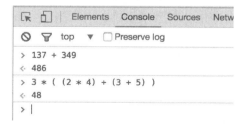

Now, on to using your variables. You can clear the contents of the console by pressing the ⊘ icon in the upper left of the console panel or with the keyboard shortcut Command-K (Ctrl-K).

Start typing DETAIL_IMAGE_SELECTOR. As you type the first few letters, you can see that the console already knows about the variables you created and provides a list of autocomplete suggestions (Figure 6.9).

Figure 6.9 The console's autocomplete menu

Press the Tab key and let the console autocomplete the variable name for you. When you press the Return key, the console reports that the value of DETAIL_IMAGE_SELECTOR is the string "[data-image-role="target"]".

Figure 6.10 The console printing a variable's value

(The console always prints strings with double quotes, even though you actually used single quotes in main.js.)

Strings are one of five *primitive* value types in JavaScript. (Numbers and Booleans are two of the others.) They are "primitive" because they represent simple values. This is in contrast to more complex values in JavaScript, which you will learn about next.

Accessing DOM Elements

You have just seen that the console gives you access to the variables you created. Earlier we said that these variables could be used for accessing elements on the page. You can try that now. Enter the following in the console:

```
document.querySelector(DETAIL_IMAGE_SELECTOR);
```

Press the Return key. It will show you the HTML for the detail image. Hover over this HTML in the console. You will see that the detail image is highlighted on the page, just as if you clicked HTML in the elements panel (Figure 6.11).

110

Figure 6.11 HTML in the console corresponds to an element on the page

In the line of code you wrote on the console, the word document is the variable built into the browser that gives you access to the web page. Its value is not one of the primitive types. It is a complex value, whose type is *object*.

The document object corresponds to the entire page. It gives you access to a number of *methods* for getting references to elements on the page. Methods are a type of function (they are functions with an explicitly designated owner, but you do not need to worry about that detail right now) – a list of steps for the browser to follow. You used the **querySelector** method in the line you entered in the console. The *dot operator* (i.e., the period) in **document.querySelector** is how you access an object's methods.

You asked the document to use its **querySelector** method to find any element matching the string '[data-image-role="target"]'. **querySelector** responded with a reference to the element that it found, the detail image (Figure 6.12).

Figure 6.12 Access to the page provided by `document` and `document.querySelector`

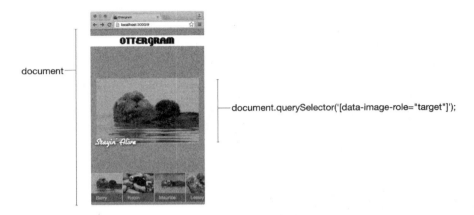

And now, a bit of terminology. You did not really "ask" the page for matching elements. You *called* the document's **querySelector** method and you *passed* it a string. The method *returned* a reference to the detail image element.

When you call a method, you are making it run whatever task it was designed to perform. You will often need to pass it information it needs to do that task, which you place in parentheses after the method's name. Then, in addition to its assigned tasks, the method may return a value that you can use.

Remember that DETAIL_IMAGE_SELECTOR was assigned the value `'[data-image-role="target"]'`, which means that this is what is passed to **querySelector**.

Behind the scenes, **querySelector** uses this string to search for any elements that match that selector. When it searches, the document is not actually searching the page, it is searching the *document object model*, or DOM. The DOM is the browser's internal representation of an HTML document. It builds this representation as it reads through and interprets the HTML.

In JavaScript, you can interact with the DOM using the document object and its methods, such as **querySelector**. For each HTML tag, there is a corresponding element in the DOM, and you can interact with any of these elements using JavaScript. (Generally, when we refer to an "element," we mean a "DOM element.")

In the console, call **document.querySelector** again, passing it DETAIL_IMAGE_SELECTOR to get a reference to the element for the detail image. But this time, assign the reference to a new variable named detailImage:

```
var detailImage = document.querySelector(DETAIL_IMAGE_SELECTOR);
```

Press Return, and the console will print undefined (Figure 6.13). Do not panic! This is not an error.

Figure 6.13 Declaring a variable in the console

The console is just doing its job, telling you that there is no resulting value from declaring a variable. In JavaScript, the absence of a value is represented by the keyword `undefined`.

That does not mean that your `detailImage` variable was not assigned. To check it, just type `detailImage` in the console and press Return. You will see the HTML representation of the detail image, just as you saw when you entered `document.querySelector(DETAIL_IMAGE_SELECTOR)` (Figure 6.14).

Figure 6.14 Checking the value of `detailImage`

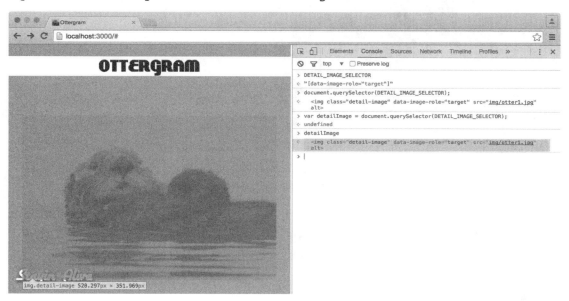

What is the point of all this? By assigning a reference to a variable, you can use the variable name any time you want to refer to the element. Now, instead of having to type `document.querySelector(DETAIL_IMAGE_SELECTOR)` every time, you can just type `detailImage`.

When you have a reference to the detail image, it is easy to change the value of its src attribute. In the console, assign detailImage.src to the string 'img/otter2.jpg'.

```
detailImage.src = 'img/otter2.jpg';
```

Using the dot operator, you accessed the src *property* of the detailImage object. A property is like a variable, but it belongs to a particular object. When you assign (or *set*) src to the string 'img/otter2.jpg', you will see that a different otter occupies the detail image area (Figure 6.15).

Figure 6.15 Setting the src property of the detail image

The src property corresponds to the src attribute of the <img> tag in index.html. Because of this relationship, another way to achieve the same result is to use the detailImage's **setAttribute** method.

Call this method in the console and pass it two strings: the name of the attribute and the new value.

```
detailImage.setAttribute('src', 'img/otter3.jpg');
```

The detail image changes once again (Figure 6.16).

Figure 6.16 Using **setAttribute** to change the image

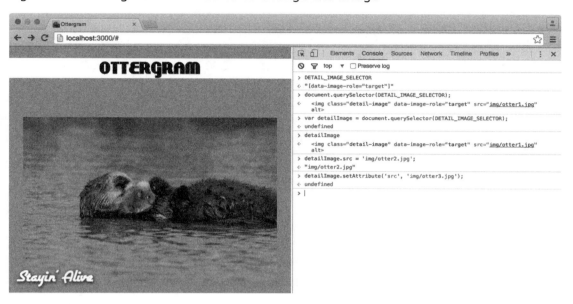

You now have all the pieces you need to create an automated way to change the detail image. Get ready to write your first function!

Writing the setDetails Function

You have been working with methods and have seen that they can be invoked to cause a block of code to run. Functions and methods are really just a list of steps that you would like to use again and again. Calling a function is like saying "Make a sandwich" instead of "Lay out two slices of bread. Put prosciutto, salami, and provolone on one slice. Put the other slice of bread on top."

You will write seven functions for Ottergram in this chapter. Your first function will do two things: change the detail image and the detail image title. Add this *function declaration* to main.js.

```
var DETAIL_IMAGE_SELECTOR = '[data-image-role="target"]';
var DETAIL_TITLE_SELECTOR = '[data-image-role="title"]';
var THUMBNAIL_LINK_SELECTOR = '[data-image-role="trigger"]';

function setDetails() {
  'use strict';
  // Code will go here
}
```

You declared a function named **setDetails** using the function keyword. When declaring a function, the name is always followed by a pair of parentheses. They are not part of the name, however – you will find out what they are for soon.

After the parentheses is a pair of curly braces. Inside the curly braces is the *body* of the function. The body will contain the steps the function needs to perform. These steps are more formally referred to as *statements*.

The first line of your function is the string 'use strict';. You will use this string at the beginning of all your functions to tell the browser that they conform to the most recent standard version of JavaScript. (There is more about strict mode in a For the More Curious section at the end of this chapter.)

The other line in the **setDetails** function is a comment. Like CSS comments, JavaScript comments are ignored by the browser but useful for developers. JavaScript comments that are only one line can be written this way, with //. For comments that span multiple lines, you can use the /* */ style. Both are correct in JavaScript.

In the console, you have already tried out all of the statements needed to change the photo in the detail image. Go back to the console and press the Up arrow key. You will see the most recent statement you entered copied at the prompt. The Up and Down arrows allow you to go backward and forward through your history of statements.

Using the arrow keys, find the statement that gets a reference to the detail image: var detailImage = document.querySelector(DETAIL_IMAGE_SELECTOR);. Copy this line from the console and paste it into main.js in place of the comment. Then, copy and paste the line in the console that calls the detailImage.setAttribute method: detailImage.setAttribute('src', 'img/otter3.jpg');.

Your **setDetails** function in main.js should look like this:

```
...
function setDetails() {
  'use strict';
  // Code will go here
  var detailImage = document.querySelector(DETAIL_IMAGE_SELECTOR);
  detailImage.setAttribute('src', 'img/otter3.jpg');
}
```

Save main.js and go back to the console. Enter the following and press Return to run your **setDetails** function.

```
setDetails();
```

Entering – or calling – the name of a function followed immediately by parentheses makes the function execute all of the code in its body. You should see that img/otter3.jpg is now displayed as the detail image (Figure 6.17).

Figure 6.17 Running **setDetails** to change the image

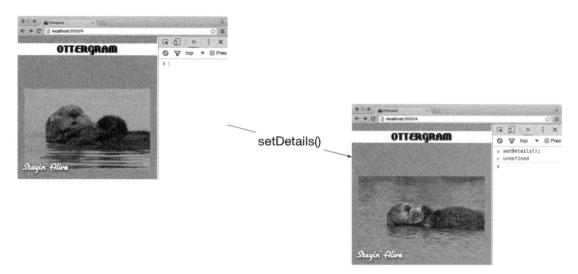

setDetails()

setDetails has changed the detail image, but not the detail image title. You want it to do both. As you did with the detail image, you will add statements to get a reference to the element and to change the element's properties.

In your **setDetails** function in main.js, call **document.querySelector** again, passing it DETAIL_TITLE_SELECTOR. Assign the result to a new variable named detailTitle. Then, set its textContent property to 'You Should Be Dancing'.

```
...
function setDetails() {
  'use strict';
  var detailImage = document.querySelector(DETAIL_IMAGE_SELECTOR);
  detailImage.setAttribute('src', 'img/otter3.jpg');

  var detailTitle = document.querySelector(DETAIL_TITLE_SELECTOR);
  detailTitle.textContent = 'You Should Be Dancing';
}
```

The textContent property is the text (not including HTML tags) inside of an element.

Save your changes and run **setDetails** in the console. Now the image *and* title change (Figure 6.18).

Figure 6.18 Changing the image and title using **setDetails**

Accepting arguments by declaring parameters

setDetails does the work of changing the detail image and title. But every time you run it, it sets the image's src to 'img/otter3.jpg' and the title's textContent to 'You Should Be Dancing'. What if you want to use other images and text?

You need a way to tell **setDetails** *which* image and *what* text to use when you call it.

To achieve this, you need your function to accept *arguments* – values that are passed to the function and that it can work with. And to do that, you have to specify *parameters* in the function declaration.

Add two parameters to **setDetails** in main.js:

```
...
function setDetails(imageUrl, titleText) {
  'use strict';
  var detailImage = document.querySelector(DETAIL_IMAGE_SELECTOR);
  detailImage.setAttribute('src', 'img/otter3.jpg');

  var detailTitle = document.querySelector(DETAIL_TITLE_SELECTOR);
  detailTitle.textContent = 'You Should Be Dancing';
}
```

Now, use those parameters in place of `'img/otter3.jpg'` and `'You should Be Dancing'`:

```
...
function setDetails(imageUrl, titleText) {
  'use strict';
  var detailImage = document.querySelector(DETAIL_IMAGE_SELECTOR);
  detailImage.setAttribute('src', 'img/otter3.jpg');
  detailImage.setAttribute('src', imageUrl);

  var detailTitle = document.querySelector(DETAIL_TITLE_SELECTOR);
  detailTitle.textContent = 'You Should Be Dancing';
  detailTitle.textContent = titleText;
}
```

Your two parameters, `imageUrl` and `titleText`, are used as labels assigned to values passed to **setDetails**. Save `main.js` and try it out in the console to see this working.

Call **setDetails** and pass it the values `'img/otter4.jpg'` and `'Night Fever'`. (Make sure there is a comma between them.)

```
setDetails('img/otter4.jpg', 'Night Fever');
```

You should see the new image and title text, as in Figure 6.19.

Figure 6.19 Passing values to **setDetails**

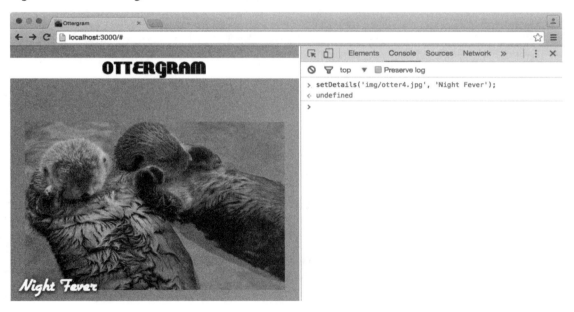

There is an important distinction between arguments and parameters. *Parameters are defined as part of the function.* In JavaScript, parameters are exactly like variables that are declared inside a function body. *Arguments are values you supply to a function when you call it.*

Also, be aware that no matter what variable names you use for your arguments, their values are always mapped to the parameter names so they can be used inside the function body. For example, imagine that you used variables for the image URL and the title text. When you call **setDetails**, you pass in these two variables as arguments.

```
var otterOneImage = 'img/otter1.jpg';
var otterOneTitle = 'Stayin\' Alive';

setDetails(otterOneImage, otterOneTitle);
```

The **setDetails** function accepts the values, labels them with the parameter names `imageUrl` and `titleText`, and then runs the code inside its body. That code uses `imageUrl` and `titleText`, passing them as arguments to **document.querySelector**.

Like variable names, parameter names are just labels for values. You can use whatever parameter names you like, but it is good practice to use descriptive names, as you have done here, to make your code easier to read and maintain.

Returning Values from Functions

You have completed the first (or, rather, last) item on the plan and picked up some JavaScript know-how along the way. Now you will move on to the next two items on the list: getting the image and the title from a thumbnail. For each of these, you will write a new function.

Add a function declaration in `main.js` for **imageFromThumb**. It will accept a single parameter, `thumbnail`, which is a reference to a thumbnail anchor element. It will retrieve and return the value of the `data-image-url` attribute.

```
...
function setDetails(imageUrl, titleText) {
  ...
}

function imageFromThumb(thumbnail) {
  'use strict';
  return thumbnail.getAttribute('data-image-url');
}
```

The **getAttribute** method does the opposite of the **setAttribute** method you used in the **setDetails** function. It only takes a single argument, the name of an attribute.

Unlike **setDetails**, the **imageFromThumb** function uses the `return` keyword. When you call a function that has a `return` statement, it gives you back a value. **querySelector** is an example of this. When you called it, it returned a value that you then assigned to a variable.

Save `main.js` and try out the following in the console, pressing Return between the lines.

```
var firstThumbnail = document.querySelector(THUMBNAIL_LINK_SELECTOR);
imageFromThumb(firstThumbnail);
```

The console reports that the value returned was the string `"img/otter1.jpg"`, because **imageFromThumb** returns the `data-image-url` of the thumbnail.

Figure 6.20 Value returned from **imageFromThumb**

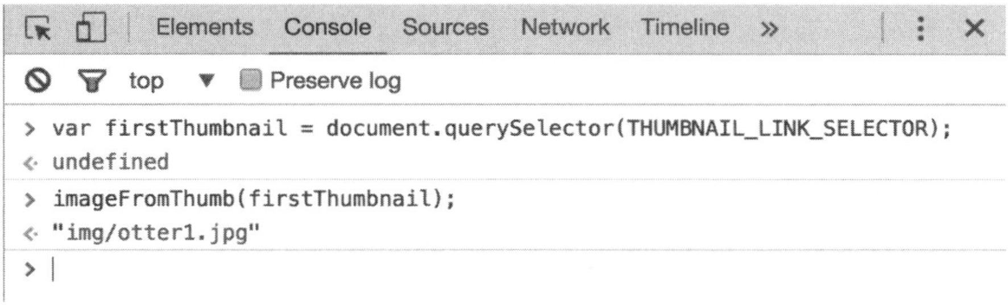

Note that any statements that come after a `return` statement will not be run. A `return` statement effectively stops a running function.

The next function to write is one that will accept a thumbnail element reference and return the title text.

Add a function declaration in `main.js` for **titleFromThumb**, with a `thumbnail` parameter. It will return the value of the `data-image-title` attribute.

```
...
function imageFromThumb(thumbnail) {
  ...
}

function titleFromThumb(thumbnail) {
  'use strict';
  return thumbnail.getAttribute('data-image-title');
}
```

Save `main.js` and try this function out in the console, too:

```
var firstThumbnail = document.querySelector(THUMBNAIL_LINK_SELECTOR);
titleFromThumb(firstThumbnail);
```

Figure 6.21 Value returned from **titleFromThumb**

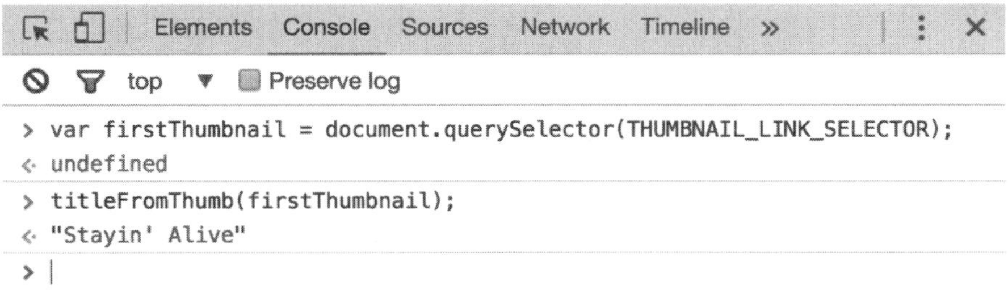

The next function to write brings the three other functions together for convenience, so that you do not need to call them separately. It will accept a reference to a thumbnail element and then call **setDetails**, passing in the values from calling **imageFromThumb** and **titleFromThumb**.

Add **setDetailsFromThumb** in main.js.

```
...
function titleFromThumb(thumbnail) {
  ...
}

function setDetailsFromThumb(thumbnail) {
  'use strict';
  setDetails(imageFromThumb(thumbnail), titleFromThumb(thumbnail));
}
```

Notice that **setDetails** is being called with two arguments – and those arguments are function calls, too. How does this work?

Before **setDetails** is actually called, its arguments are reduced to their simplest values. First, **imageFromThumb(thumbnail)** runs and returns a value. Then, **titleFromThumb(thumbnail)** runs and returns a value. Finally, **setDetails** is called with the values returned by **imageFromThumb(thumbnail)** and **titleFromThumb(thumbnail)**. Figure 6.22 shows this process.

Figure 6.22 Function calls as arguments

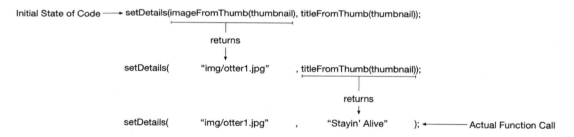

Save main.js. You have completed all the code for retrieving data-attribute values from thumbnails and using those values to update what is shown in the detail image and title.

Moving up from the low-level operations, the next thing to do is write code that will perform your data transfer from thumbnail to detail when the user clicks a thumbnail.

Adding an Event Listener

Browsers are busy pieces of software. Every tap, click, scroll, and keystroke is noticed by the browser. Each of these is an *event* that the browser may respond to. To make websites more dynamic and interactive, you can trigger your own code when one of these events occurs. In this section, you will add *event listeners* to each of your thumbnails.

An event listener is an object that, as the name suggests, "listens" for a particular event, such as a mouse click. When its assigned event occurs, the event listener triggers a function call in response to the event.

(Mouse events, like clicks and double-clicks, and keyboard events like keypresses are among the most common event types. For a complete listing of events, check the event reference in the MDN at developer.mozilla.org/en-US/docs/Web/Events.)

The **addEventListener** method is available on every DOM element, including the document. As before, you will experiment with some code in the console first and then use your tested code to write functions in main.js.

Switch to Chrome and enter the following code in the console. You will need to press Shift-Return to enter the line breaks. Press Return when you have finished typing all the code.

```
document.addEventListener('click', function () {
  console.log('you clicked!');
});
```

The code you entered added an event listener for the document object that is listening for any clicks that occur on the page. When a click happens, the event listener will print "you clicked!" to the console using the built-in **console.log** method (Figure 6.23).

Figure 6.23 Adding a listener for click events

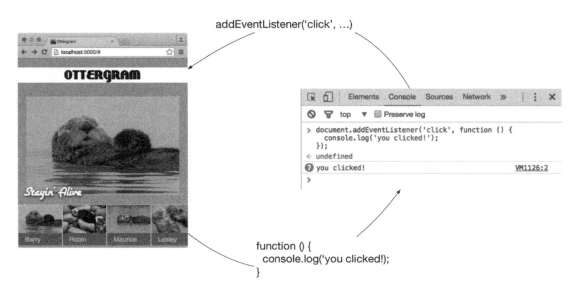

Click on the header, the detail image, or the background. You should see that the text "you clicked!" appears printed in the console. (Do not click the thumbnails – those will take you away from Ottergram's index.html page. When you are not on the index.html page, none of your markup, CSS, or JavaScript will be loaded and running in the browser.)

addEventListener accepts two arguments: a string with the name of the event and a function. This function will be run by addEventListener any time the event occurs for the element. The way this function is written may look a little strange at first. It is an *anonymous function*.

So far, you have worked with *named functions*, like setDetails and titleFromThumb. Named functions have names – no surprise there – and are created using function declarations.

You can also write literal function values, the same way you can write literal number values like 42 and literal string values like "Barry the Otter". Another name for literal function values is *anonymous functions*.

Anonymous functions are frequently used as arguments to other functions, like the one you passed as the second argument to document.addEventListener. This practice of passing a function to another function is quite common in JavaScript and is known as a *callback pattern* because the function you pass in as an argument will get "called back" at some point in the future.

It is perfectly fine to use a named function as a callback, but many front-end developers will use anonymous functions because they can provide more flexibility than named functions. You will see how this works shortly.

Now you will add an event listener for an individual thumbnail. Enter the following in the console. (Remember to use Shift-Return for the line breaks in the call to firstThumbnail.addEventListener.)

```
var firstThumbnail = document.querySelector(THUMBNAIL_LINK_SELECTOR);
firstThumbnail.addEventListener('click', function () {
  console.log('you clicked!');
});
```

If you try clicking the first thumbnail (Barry the Otter, farthest to the left), your browser will take you to the large image of Barry. What happened? Remember that each thumbnail is wrapped in an anchor tag with an href that points to an image, like img/otter1.jpg. This is the normal behavior of a browser when a user clicks a link: It has opened the file indicated by the href attribute.

But you do not want to navigate away from Ottergram when a thumbnail is clicked, and you should not have to change your anchor tags to something else. Luckily, you can handle all of this from your callback function.

Recall from earlier in the chapter that functions carry out their tasks without you having to worry about the details. Usually you only need to know what information to pass as arguments and what information will be returned. When you pass a callback function as an argument, there is one more thing you need to know: what information will be passed to your callback.

When you call addEventListener, you are telling the browser, "When the firstThumbnail is clicked, call this function" – and then the browser diligently waits for that element to be clicked. If a click happens, the browser makes note of all the details about the event (such as the exact position of the mouse, whether it was the left or right mouse button, and whether it was a single or double click). The browser then passes an object with this information to your function. This object is an *event object*.

This relationship is diagrammed in Figure 6.24, using a made-up implementation of **addEventListener**.

Figure 6.24 Passing an anonymous function that expects an argument

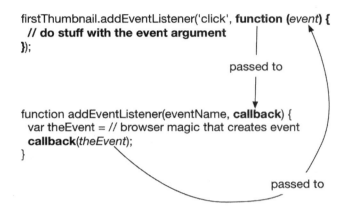

In a moment, you will pass an anonymous function to **addEventListener**, just like before. But, this time, your anonymous function will expect to receive an argument. Make sure Ottergram is on the index.html page and enter the following in the console:

```
var firstThumbnail = document.querySelector(THUMBNAIL_LINK_SELECTOR);
firstThumbnail.addEventListener('click', function (event) {
  event.preventDefault();
  console.log('you clicked!');
  console.log(event);
});
```

The browser will call your anonymous function each time firstThumbnail is clicked, and it will pass your anonymous function the event object. Using this object (which you have labeled event), you call its **preventDefault** method. This method will stop the link from taking the browser to a different page. Finally, you call **console.log** on the event object so that you can inspect it in the DevTools.

Now click on the first thumbnail. Your browser remains on the Ottergram page and the event is logged to the console: MouseEvent {isTrusted: true}. If you click the disclosure arrow next to MouseEvent, you should see quite a bit of information about the event (Figure 6.25), including the mouse coordinates on the page, which mouse button was clicked, and whether any special modifier keys were pressed during the click.

Figure 6.25 Preventing the event default and logging the event object

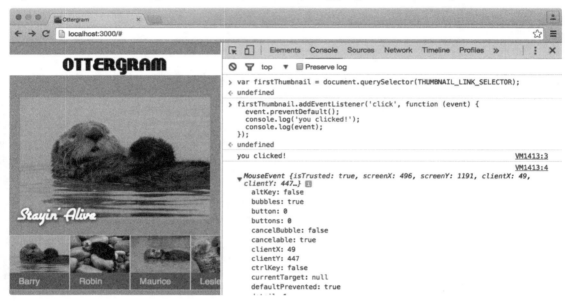

For now, do not focus on the different properties of the event object. Just know that it carries lots of information about the browser event that was triggered.

By the way, it is not required that the callback function's parameter be named event – it will be mapped to the value that is passed in no matter what you name it. You can use whatever parameter names you like, but it is good practice to use descriptive names, as you have done here, to make your code easier to read and maintain.

You now have a function that accepts a thumbnail and adds an event listener. Add a function declaration to main.js for **addThumbClickHandler**. It should define a parameter named thumb.

You can copy your experimental **addEventListener** code from the console and paste it into the body of **addThumbClickHandler**. Modify it so that you are calling **thumb.addEventListener**. For now, you will only need the call to event.preventDefault in the event callback.

```
...
function setDetailsFromThumb(thumbnail) {
  ...
}

function addThumbClickHandler(thumb)
  'use strict';
  thumb.addEventListener('click', function (event) {
    event.preventDefault();
  });
}
```

Inside the event callback, you have access to the `thumb` parameter declared as part of **addThumbClickHandler**. Pass it to a call to **setDetailsFromThumb**.

```
...
function addThumbClickHandler(thumb) {
  'use strict';
  thumb.addEventListener('click', function (event) {
    event.preventDefault();
    setDetailsFromThumb(thumb);
  });
}
```

JavaScript, like many other programming languages, has rules about defining and accessing variables and functions. The anonymous function you passed to **addEventListener** is able to access the **setDetailsFromThumb** function because **setDetailsFromThumb** was declared in the *global scope*. This means that it can be accessed from any other function or from the console. The same is true for variables like DETAIL_IMAGE_SELECTOR, which is also declared in the global scope.

However, the variables detailImage and detailTitle, which you declared *inside* **setDetails**, are only available within the body of **setDetails**. You cannot access them from the console or from other functions. These variables are declared in the *function scope* (or *local scope*) of **setDetails**. A function's parameters work very much like variables declared inside a function. They too are part of that function's scope.

Normally, functions cannot access variables or parameters that are part of another function's scope. **addThumbClickHandler** is interesting because it defines the parameter thumb, which is accessed by another function – the callback function you passed to **addEventListener**. This is possible because the callback function is part of **addThumbClickHandler**'s scope.

You can read more about how all of this works in a For the More Curious section at the end of this chapter.

Accessing All the Thumbnails

In the console, you added an event listener for the first thumbnail. Now you will add an event listener for all of the thumbnails, using a new DOM method.

When you retrieved the detail image and the detail title, you used the **document.querySelector** method to search the DOM for an element that matched the selector passed in. **document.querySelector** will only return a single value, even if you pass in a selector that matches multiple elements.

The **document.querySelectorAll** method, on the other hand, will return a list of all matching elements. Call document.querySelectorAll(THUMBNAIL_LINK_SELECTOR) in the console and examine the results. You should see the list of anchor element results (Figure 6.26).

Figure 6.26 **document.querySelectorAll** returns multiple matching elements

Knowing this, you can test **setDetailsFromThumb** properly. In the console, assign the result of calling document.querySelectorAll(THUMBNAIL_LINK_SELECTOR) to a variable named thumbnails. Use *bracket syntax* to retrieve the fifth element from the thumbnails list, passing it to **setDetailsFromThumb**. Bracket syntax lets you specify an item in the list by its numerical index. The index starts at 0, so the fifth item is at index 4.

Here is your code for the console:

```
var thumbnails = document.querySelectorAll(THUMBNAIL_LINK_SELECTOR);
setDetailsFromThumb(thumbnails[4]);
```

After running this in the console, you can see that an item from the thumbnails list can be passed to **setDetailsFromThumb**, successfully updating the detail image and title (Figure 6.27).

Figure 6.27 Passing an item from **querySelectorAll** to **setDetailsFromThumb**

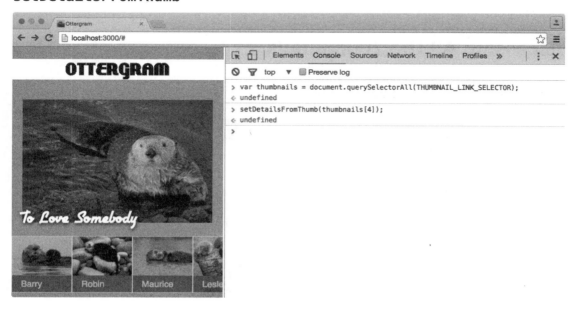

In `main.js`, add a function named **getThumbnailsArray** and paste in the code that retrieves all matching elements for THUMBNAIL_LINK_SELECTOR and assigns the result to a `thumbnails` variable.

```
...
function addThumbClickHandler(thumb) {
  ...
}

function getThumbnailsArray() {
  'use strict';
  var thumbnails = document.querySelectorAll(THUMBNAIL_LINK_SELECTOR);
}
```

Before you go any further, there is a small "gotcha" when working with DOM methods. Methods that return lists of elements do not return *arrays*. Instead, they return *NodeLists*. Both arrays and NodeLists are lists of items, but arrays have a number of powerful methods for working with collections of items, some of which you will want for Ottergram.

You will need to convert the NodeList returned from **querySelectorAll** to an array using an odd-looking bit of JavaScript. Do not worry about this syntax right now. It is a backward-compatible way to convert from a NodeList to an array. Make this change in `main.js`:

```
...
function getThumbnailsArray() {
  'use strict';
  var thumbnails = document.querySelectorAll(THUMBNAIL_LINK_SELECTOR);
  var thumbnailArray = [].slice.call(thumbnails);
  return thumbnailArray;
}
```

Now, armed with all of the otter thumbnails, you can connect them to your event listening code, which will change the detail image and title in response to a click.

Iterating Through the Array of Thumbnails

Connecting the thumbnails to your event handling code will be short and sweet. You will write a function that will be the starting point for all of Ottergram's logic. Other programming languages have a built-in mechanism for starting an application, which JavaScript lacks. But not to worry – it is easy enough to implement by hand.

Begin by adding an **initializeEvents** function at the end of `main.js`. This method will tie together all of the steps for making Ottergram interactive. First, it will get the array of thumbnails. Then, it will iterate over the array, adding the click handler to each one. After you have written the function, you will add a call to **initializeEvents** at the very end of `main.js` to run it.

In the body of your new function, add a call to **getThumbnailsArray** and assign the result (the array of thumbnails) to a variable named `thumbnails`.

```
...
function getThumbnailsArray() {
  ...
}

function initializeEvents() {
  'use strict';
  var thumbnails = getThumbnailsArray();
}
```

Next, you need to go through the array of thumbnails, one item at a time. As you visit each one, you will call **addThumbClickHandler** and pass the thumbnail element to it. That may seem like several steps, but because thumbnails is a proper array, you can do all of this with a single method call.

Add a call to the thumbnails.forEach method in main.js and pass it the **addThumbClickHandler** function as a callback.

```
...
function initializeEvents() {
  'use strict';
  var thumbnails = getThumbnailsArray();
  thumbnails.forEach(addThumbClickHandler);
}
```

Note that you are passing a named function as a callback. As you will read later, this is not always a good choice. However, in this case it works well, because **addThumbClickHandler** only needs information that will be passed to it when **forEach** calls it – an item from the thumbnails array.

Finally, to see everything in action, add a call to **initializeEvents** at the very end of main.js.

```
...
function initializeEvents() {
  'use strict';
  var thumbnails = getThumbnailsArray();
  thumbnails.forEach(addThumbClickHandler);
}

initializeEvents();
```

Remember, as the browser reads through each line of your JavaScript code, it runs the code. For most of main.js, it is only running variable and function declarations. But when it reaches the line initializeEvents();, it will run that function.

Save and return to the browser. Click a few different thumbnails and see the fruits of your labor (Figure 6.28).

Figure 6.28 You should indeed be dancing

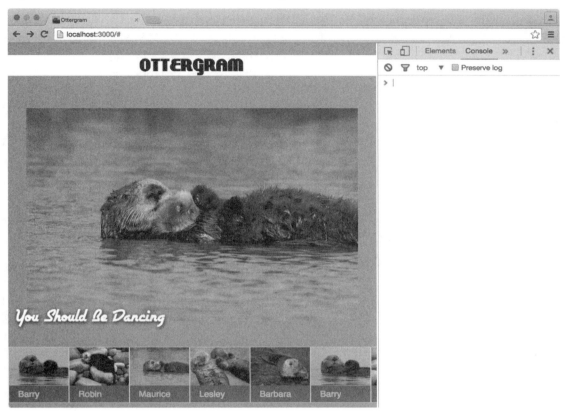

Sit back, relax, and enjoy clicking some otters! There was a lot to work through and absorb while building your site's interactive layer. In the next chapter you will finish Ottergram by adding visual effects for extra pop.

Silver Challenge: Link Hijack

The Chrome DevTools give you a lot of power for toying with pages that you visit. This next challenge is to change all of the links on a search results page so that they do not go anywhere.

Go to your favorite search engine and search for "otters." Open the DevTools to the console. With the functions you wrote in Ottergram as a reference, attach event listeners to all of the links and disable their default click functionality.

Gold Challenge: Random Otters

Write a function that changes the `data-image-url` of a random otter thumbnail so that the detail image no longer matches the thumbnail. Use the URL of an image of your choosing (though a web search for "tacocat" should provide a good one).

For an extra challenge, write a function that resets your otter thumbnails to their original `data-image-url` values and changes another one at random.

For the More Curious: Strict Mode

What is strict mode, and why does it exist? It was created as a cleaner mode of JavaScript, catching certain kinds of coding mistakes (like typos in variable names), steering developers away from some error-prone parts of the language, and disabling some language features that are just plain bad.

Strict mode provides a number of benefits. It:

- enforces the use of the `var` keyword

- does not require `with` statements

- places restrictions on the way the `eval` function can be used

- treats duplicate names in a function's parameters as a syntax error

All this just for adding the `'use strict'` directive to the top of a function. As a bonus, the `'use strict'` directive is ignored by older browsers that do not support it. (These browsers simply see the directive as a string.)

You can read more about strict mode on the MDN at `developer.mozilla.org/en-US/docs/Web/JavaScript/Reference/Strict_mode`.

For the More Curious: Closures

Earlier we mentioned that developers often prefer to use anonymous functions as callbacks instead of named functions. **addThumbClickHandler** illustrates why an anonymous function is a better solution.

Let's say you tried to use a named function, **clickFunction**, for the callback. Inside of that function, you have access to the event object because it will be passed in by **addEventListener**. But the body of **clickFunction** has no access to the thumb object. That parameter is only accessible *inside* the **addThumbClickHandler** function.

```
function clickFunction (event) {
  event.preventDefault();

  setDetailsFromThumb(thumb); // <--- This will cause an error
}

function addThumbClickHandler(thumb) {
  thumb.addEventListener('click', clickFunction);
}
```

On the other hand, using an anonymous function does give it access to the thumb parameter, because it is also inside of **addThumbClickHandler**. When a function is defined inside of another function, it can use any of the variables and parameters of this outer function. In computer science terms, this is known as a *closure*.

When the **addThumbClickHandler** function runs, it calls **addEventListener**, which associates the callback function with the click event. The browser keeps track of these associations, internally holding a reference to the callback function and running the callback when the event occurs.

Technically, when the callback is eventually executed, the variables and parameters of **addThumbClickHandler** no longer exist. They went away when **addThumbClickHandler** finished running. But, the callback "captures" the values of **addThumbClickHandler**'s variables and parameters. The callback uses these captured values when it runs.

For a deeper dive, read up on closures in the MDN.

For the More Curious: NodeLists and HTMLCollections

There are two ways to retrieve lists of elements that live in the DOM. The first
one is **document.querySelectorAll**, which returns a NodeList. The other is
document.getElementsByTagName, which differs from **document.querySelectorAll** in that you can
only pass it a string with a tag name, like "div" or "a", and also in that it returns an *HTMLCollection*.

Neither NodeLists nor HTMLCollections are true arrays, so they lack array methods such as **forEach**,
but they do have some very interesting properties.

HTMLCollections are *live nodes*. This means that when changes are made to the DOM, the contents of
an HTMLCollection can change without you having to call **document.getElementsByTagName** again.

To see how this works, try the following in the console.

```
var thumbnails = document.getElementsByTagName("a");
thumbnails.length;
```

After getting all of the anchor elements as an HTMLCollection, you print the length of that list to the
console.

Now, remove some of the anchor tags from the page using the elements panel in the DevTools:
Control-click (right-click) one of the list items and choose Delete element (Figure 6.29).

Figure 6.29 Deleting a DOM element with the DevTools

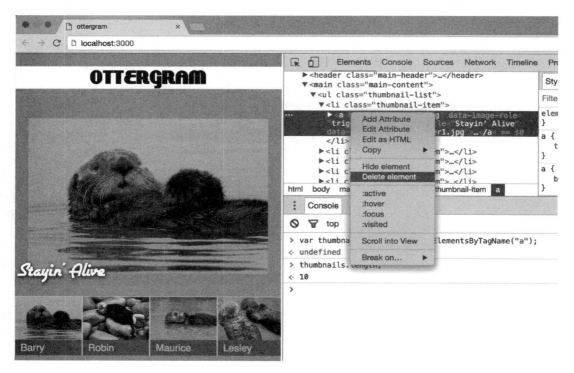

Do this several times, then enter `thumbnails.length` into the console again. You should see that the length is different (Figure 6.30).

Figure 6.30 The length value changes after deleting elements

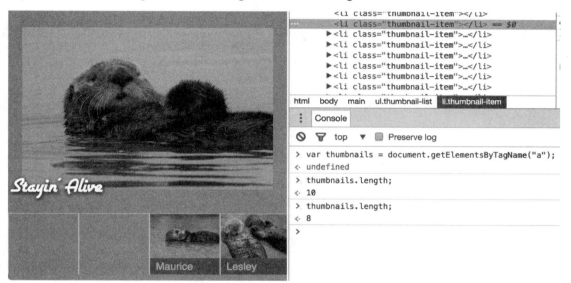

Converting NodeLists and HTMLCollections to arrays not only makes them more convenient to work with via array methods, but you also have the guarantee that the items in the array will not change, even if the DOM is modified.

For the More Curious: JavaScript Types

Throughout the chapter, you created variables so you could refer to some data inside your functions. Early on, we told you that strings, numbers, and Booleans are three of the five *primitive data types*. The other two types are null and undefined.

Table 6.2 summarizes the properties of the five primitive types.

Table 6.2 Primitive data types in JavaScript

Type	Example	Description
string	"And you get $100! And you get $100! And...!"	Letters, numbers, or symbols enclosed in matching quotation marks.
number	42, 3.14159, -1	Whole numbers and decimals.
Boolean	true, false	The keywords true and false, corresponding to logical true and false.
null	null	The value that denotes an invalid value.
undefined	undefined	The value of a variable that has not been assigned to anything.

All other types in JavaScript are considered *compound types* or *complex types*. These include arrays and objects, which can have other types inside of them. For example, you wrote a function that produced an array of thumbnail objects. Arrays also have properties (like length) and methods (such as **forEach**).

You will continue to work with primitive and complex data types throughout this book.

7

Visual Effects with CSS

In the last chapter, you gave Ottergram the ability to respond to user interaction by changing the detail image when the user clicks a thumbnail. You will build on that in this chapter by adding three different visual effects to Ottergram.

The first effect is a simple layout change that involves hiding the detail image and letting the thumbnails take up the width of the page. When the user clicks a thumbnail, you will make the detail image reappear and return the thumbnails to their previous size.

The other two effects will use CSS to create visual animations for the thumbnails and the detail image (Figure 7.1).

Figure 7.1 Ottergram with transition effects

Hiding and Showing the Detail Image

Ottergram's users may want to be able to scroll through the thumbnails without the detail image being on the page (Figure 7.2).

Figure 7.2 Detail image visible and hidden

To make this happen, you need to be able to apply styles to your `.thumbnail-list` and `.detail-image-container` based on a condition that will turn on and off as the website is in use. You could do this by creating new class selectors, like `.thumbnail-list-no-detail` and `.hidden-detail-image-container`, and add those classes to the target elements with JavaScript. The trouble with this approach is that it would be inefficient.

The event that will cause the detail image to hide will *simultaneously* cause the thumbnail list to reposition itself. It is a single event. Adding classes to your <ul> and <div> elements separately does not reflect this.

A better approach is to use JavaScript to add a *single* class selector that affects the layout as a whole. Then, you can target the `.thumbnail-list` and `.detail-image-container` when they are descendents of the new selector.

You are going to dynamically add a class name to the <body> element to hide the detail image and enlarge the thumbnails, and then dynamically remove the class name to return to your current styles (Figure 7.3).

Figure 7.3 Restyling descendants with class change to ancestor

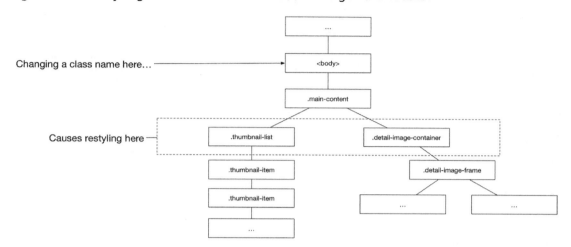

This technique is similar in two ways to the one you used with the media queries.

First, it involves styles that are activated when an ancestor meets a particular condition. With media queries, that ancestor is the viewport and the condition is a minimum width. In this new code, the ancestor will be any element you select that the target elements share, and the condition will be that the ancestor has a particular class name.

The second similarity is that you must place the conditional styles *after* the other declarations for the affected elements in your stylesheet because these conditional styles need to override the previous declarations when they are active.

You will proceed in three steps:

1. In your CSS, define the styles that create the visual effect you are trying to get. Also, test your styles in the DevTools.

2. Write JavaScript functions to add and remove a class name for the <body> element.

3. Add an event listener to trigger your JavaScript function.

Creating styles to hide the detail image

To hide the .detail-image-container, you will add a declaration that sets display: none for this element. display: none tells the browser that the element should not be rendered.

The class you will be adding dynamically to the <body> will be called hidden-detail. Therefore, you only want to apply display: none to .detail-image-container when it is a descendent of .hidden-detail.

Add the style to hide the detail image in styles.css:

```
...
.detail-image-title {
  ...
}

.hidden-detail .detail-image-container {
  display: none;
}

@media all and (min-width: 768px) {
  ...
}
```

Now, give some thought to what your .thumbnail-list will look like. Based on the current styles, it will be a column along the left side of wider screens and a horizontal row at the top of narrower screens. A centered column would be better when the detail image is hidden, regardless of the screen size.

Add styles to the .thumbnail-list and .thumbnail-item in styles.css when they are descendents of .hidden-detail.

```
...
.hidden-detail .detail-image-container {
  display: none;
}

.hidden-detail .thumbnail-list {
  flex-direction: column;
  align-items: center;
}

.hidden-detail .thumbnail-item {
  max-width: 80%;
}

@media all and (min-width: 768px) {
  ...
}
```

Now, the .thumbnail-list will always be displayed as a column while the .detail-image-container is hidden.

You have also added a declaration setting the width of the .thumbnail-item elements to max-width: 80% when the detail image is hidden. This overrides the max-width styles set elsewhere for the .thumbnail-items so that they will become the focus of the page.

When the .detail-image-container, .thumbnail-list, and .thumbnail-item elements are nested anywhere inside of an element with the class hidden-detail, these new styles will be activated.

Note that you added these *before* your media queries. As you already know, the order of your CSS code matters, with styles that appear later in the file overriding those that came before. In general, for the same selector, the browser uses the styles it has seen most recently. In this case, however, your new styles use selectors that are more specific than the ones that appear in your media queries, and specificity trumps recency.

Generally, it is best to keep your media queries at the end of the file. Your media queries will usually reuse the same selectors from existing styles, so putting them at the end makes sure that your media queries overwrite those existing styles. Also, it makes your media queries easier to locate, because they are always at the end of the file.

Save your file. Before you write the JavaScript that depends on the styles you have added, it is wise to test them. Start browser-sync (using `browser-sync start --server --browser "Google Chrome" --files "*.html, stylesheets/*.css, scripts/*.js"`) and open the DevTools. In the elements panel, Control-click (right-click) the <body> element and choose Add Attribute from the menu that appears (Figure 7.4).

Figure 7.4 Choosing the Add Attribute menu item

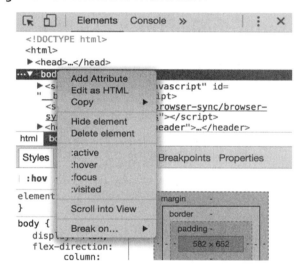

The DevTools provides a space for you to start typing inside the <body> tag. Enter `class="hidden-detail"` and press Return (Figure 7.5).

Figure 7.5 Adding the `hidden-detail` class attribute

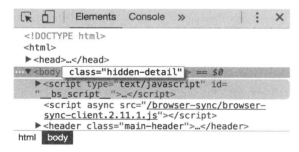

141

After you add the `hidden-detail` class to the `<body>` in the DevTools, the detail image disappears and the thumbnails become much larger – just as you intended (Figure 7.6).

Figure 7.6 Layout change after applying `hidden-detail` class

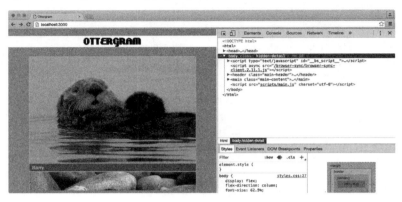

Writing the JavaScript to hide the detail image

Next, you will write the JavaScript that will toggle the `.hidden-detail` class for the `<body>` element.

In `main.js`, add a variable named `HIDDEN_DETAIL_CLASS`.

```
var DETAIL_IMAGE_SELECTOR = '[data-image-role="target"]';
var DETAIL_TITLE_SELECTOR = '[data-image-role="title"]';
var THUMBNAIL_LINK_SELECTOR = '[data-image-role="trigger"]';
var HIDDEN_DETAIL_CLASS = 'hidden-detail';
...
```

Now, write a new function in `main.js` named **hideDetails**. Its job is to add a class name to the `<body>` element. You will use the **classList.add** DOM method to manipulate the class name.

```
...
function getThumbnailsArray() {
  ...
}

function hideDetails() {
  'use strict';
  document.body.classList.add(HIDDEN_DETAIL_CLASS);
}

function initializeEvents() {
  ...
}
...
```

You accessed the `<body>` element using the `document.body` property. This DOM element corresponds to the `<body>` tag in your markup. Like all DOM elements, it gives you a convenient way to manipulate its class names.

You also called the **add** method on `document.body` to add the `hidden-detail` class to the `<body>`.

Listening for the keypress event

Now you need a way to trigger the detail image to hide. As before, you will use an event listener, but this time your event listener will listen for a keypress instead of a click.

We use the term "keypress" generally to mean pressing and releasing a key, but that simple process actually triggers multiple events. When the key is first depressed, the keydown event is sent. If it is a character key (as opposed to a modifier key like Shift) then the keypress event is also sent. When the key is released, the keyup event is sent.

For Ottergram, these differences are minimal. You are going to use the keyup event.

In main.js, add a function named **addKeyPressHandler** that calls **document.body.addEventListener**, passing it the string 'keyup' and an anonymous function that declares a parameter named event. Inside the body of this anonymous function, make sure to **preventDefault** for the event, and then **console.log** the event's keyCode.

```
...
function hideDetails() {
  ...
}

function addKeyPressHandler() {
  'use strict';
  document.body.addEventListener('keyup', function (event) {
    event.preventDefault();
    console.log(event.keyCode);
  });
}

function initializeEvents() {
  ...
}
...
```

All of the keypress events have a property called keyCode that corresponds to the key that triggered the event. The keyCode is an integer, like 13 for Return, 32 for the space bar, and 38 for the up arrow.

Update the **initializeEvents** function in main.js so that it calls **addKeyPressHandler**. You need to do this so that the <body> element can listen for keyboard events when the page loads.

```
...
function initializeEvents() {
  'use strict';
  var thumbnails = getThumbnailsArray();
  thumbnails.forEach(addThumbClickHandler);
  addKeyPressHandler();
}

initializeEvents();
```

Save and switch back to the browser. Make sure the console is visible, then click on the page to make sure that the focus is not on the DevTools – otherwise, the event listener will not be triggered. Now press some keys on your keyboard. You will see numbers printed to the console (Figure 7.7).

Figure 7.7 Logging the keyCode to the console

You want to hide the detail image when the Esc key is pressed, not just any key. If you press the Esc key, you will see that the corresponding event.keyCode value is 27. You will use that to make your event listener more specific.

Add a variable to the top of main.js for the Esc key's value.

```
var DETAIL_IMAGE_SELECTOR = '[data-image-role="target"]';
var DETAIL_TITLE_SELECTOR = '[data-image-role="title"]';
var THUMBNAIL_LINK_SELECTOR = '[data-image-role="trigger"]';
var HIDDEN_DETAIL_CLASS = 'hidden-detail';
var ESC_KEY = 27;
...
```

Now, update your keyup event listener to call **hideDetails** when the value of event.keyCode matches the value of ESC_KEY.

```
...
function addKeyPressHandler() {
  'use strict';
  document.body.addEventListener('keyup', function (event) {
    event.preventDefault();
    console.log(event.keyCode);
    if (event.keyCode === ESC_KEY) {
      hideDetails();
    }
  });
}
...
```

You used the *strict equality operator* (===) to compare the values of event.keyCode and ESC_KEY. When these value are the same, you call **hideDetails**.

You could have used the *loose equality operator* (==) to compare the values instead, but it is usually best to use the strict equality operator. The major difference between the equality operators is that the loose equality operator will automatically convert from one type of value to another. The strict equality operator will not do the conversion. With strict equality, if the types are not the same, then the result of the comparison is always false.

Many front-end developers refer to this automatic type conversion as *type coercion*. It is performed when values need to be compared (when using an equality operator), added together (in the case of numbers), or concatenated (as with strings).

Because of this automatic conversion, there is no syntax error if you try to add the string "27" with the number 42 -- though the result might not be what you expect (Figure 7.8).

Figure 7.8 JavaScript will automatically convert between types

This is very important when working with user-provided data, which you will do in Chapter 10.

Save main.js and test your new functionality in the browser (Figure 7.9).

Figure 7.9 Poof! Pressing Esc hides the detail image and title

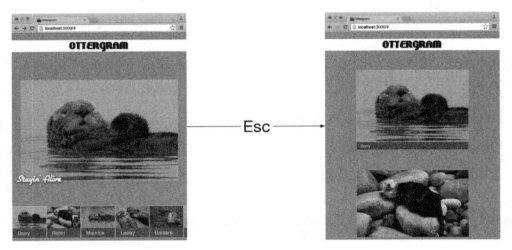

Showing the detail image again

There is one small but important piece to add: making the detail image visible again. This will be triggered when a thumbnail is clicked.

You used **classList.add** to add a class name to the <body> element. You will use **classList.remove** to remove that class name when a thumbnail is clicked. Add a new function named **showDetails** to main.js.

```
...
function hideDetails() {
  ...
}

function showDetails() {
  'use strict';
  document.body.classList.remove(HIDDEN_DETAIL_CLASS);
}

function addKeyPressHandler() {
  ...
}
...
```

Now add a call to **showDetails** in your **addThumbClickHandler** function – no need to add a new event listener.

```
...
function addThumbClickHandler(thumb) {
  'use strict';
  thumb.addEventListener('click', function (event) {
    event.preventDefault();
    setDetailsFromThumb(thumb);
    showDetails();
  });
}
...
```

Save `main.js` and switch to your browser. Try out your new functionality: Hide the detail image, then click on a thumbnail to bring it back (Figure 7.10). The otters look like they approve, don't they?

Figure 7.10 Esc hides details; click shows details

Now, Ottergram can dynamically adapt its layout based on the viewport, using media queries, as well as in response to user input.

At the moment, the layout changes happen abruptly. In the next section, you will smooth that out using CSS transitions.

State Changes with CSS Transitions

CSS transitions create a gradual change from one visual state to another, which is just what you need to make Ottergram's show/hide effect more polished.

When you create a CSS transition, you are telling the browser, "I would like this element's styles to change to these new properties, and I would like for that change to take exactly as long as I tell you."

One common example is the fly-out menu seen on many sites, such as the small-screen version of `bignerdranch.com`. In a browser with a narrow viewport, clicking the menu icon makes the navigation menu appear from the top – but it does not appear all at once. Instead, it slides down from the header, visually animating from the initial state (hidden) to the end state (visible) (Figure 7.11). Clicking the menu icon again causes the navigation menu to slide back up until it is hidden again.

Figure 7.11 Fly-out navigation on `bignerdranch.com`

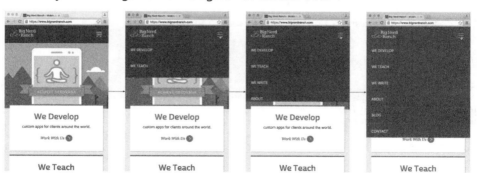

Before you create the transition effect for showing and hiding the detail image, you will build a simpler transition for your thumbnails.

In general, you should create transitions in three steps:

1. Decide what the end state should be. One good approach is to add the CSS declarations for the end state to the target element. This allows you to see them in the browser and make sure that they look the way you intend.

2. Move the declarations from the target element's existing declaration block to a new CSS declaration block. You may want to use a new class for the selector for the new block.

3. Add a `transition` declaration to the target element. The `transition` property tells the browser that it will need to visually animate the changes from the current CSS values to the end-state CSS values and that the transition should take place over a specific period of time.

Working with the transform property

Your first transition will increase the size of a thumbnail when you hover over it with the cursor (Figure 7.12). However, you will not directly change the `width` or `height` styles. You will use the *transform* property, which can alter the shape, size, rotation, and location of an element without interrupting the flow of the elements around it.

Figure 7.12 A thumbnail with zoom effect

The target element for this transition is the `.thumbnail-item`. You will begin by adding a `transform` declaration directly to the `.thumbnail-item` element.

After you have tested it and determined that it is working the way you want, you will move the transformation to a new `.thumbnail-item:hover` declaration block. Finally, you will add a `transition` declaration to `.thumbnail-item`.

In `styles.css`, begin by adding a `transform` declaration to `.thumbnail-item`.

```
...
.thumbnail-item {
  display: inline-block;
  min-width: 120px;
  max-width: 120px;
  border: 1px solid rgb(100%, 100%, 100%);
  border: 1px solid rgba(100%, 100%, 100%, 0.8);

  transform: scale(2.2);
}
...
```

`transform: scale(2.2)` tells the browser that the element should be drawn at 220% of its original size. There are many values that can be used with `transform`, including advanced 3D effects. The MDN has good coverage of them at `developer.mozilla.org/en-US/docs/Web/CSS/transform`.

Save and view the changes in your browser (Figure 7.13).

Figure 7.13 Dramatically large otter thumbnails

You can see that the thumbnails are now much larger than before. In fact, they are too large. Change the value so that they are only a little bit larger:

```
...
.thumbnail-item {
  display: inline-block;
  min-width: 120px;
  max-width: 120px;
  border: 1px solid rgb(100%, 100%, 100%);
  border: 1px solid rgba(100%, 100%, 100%, 0.8);

  transform: scale(2.2);
  transform: scale(1.2);
}
...
```

After you save, you should see that the otter thumbnails are only slightly larger than their original size (Figure 7.14).

Figure 7.14 Reasonably large otter thumbnails

This scale for the thumbnails looks good, so you can move on to the next step.

Adding a CSS transition

Now it is time to move the end-state style to a new style declaration and set up the transition for the `.thumbnail-item` element.

When the user hovers the mouse cursor over a thumbnail, that thumbnail should increase its `scale` by 120%. Add a declaration block to `styles.css` that uses the modifier `:hover` to designate styles that should only be applied when the user hovers over the element.

```
...
.thumbnail-item {
  display: inline-block;
  min-width: 120px;
  max-width: 120px;
  border: 1px solid rgb(100%, 100%, 100%);
  border: 1px solid rgba(100%, 100%, 100%, 0.8);

  transform: scale(1.2);
}

.thumbnail-item:hover {
  transform: scale(1.2);
}
...
```

The proper name for this modifier is *pseudo-class*. The psuedo-class `:hover` matches an element when the user holds the mouse cursor over it. There are a number of pseudo-class keywords that describe the various states an element can be in. You will encounter some when you work with forms later in this book, and you can search the MDN to learn more.

Next, make this change happen as a transition by adding a `transition` declaration to `.thumbnail-item` in `styles.css`. You need to specify the property to animate and how long the animation should take.

```
...
.thumbnail-item {
  display: inline-block;
  min-width: 120px;
  max-width: 120px;
  border: 1px solid rgb(100%, 100%, 100%);
  border: 1px solid rgba(100%, 100%, 100%, 0.8);

  transition: transform 133ms;
}

.thumbnail-item:hover {
  transform: scale(1.2);
}
...
```

You set a `transition` for the `transform` property. This tells the browser that it will need to animate the change, but only for the `transform` property. You also specified that the transition should take place over a period of 133 milliseconds.

Save and give your new transition a try. You should see that each thumbnail enlarges when you hover over it. When you move your mouse away, the transition runs in reverse, and the thumbnail returns to its original size (Figure 7.15).

Figure 7.15 Transition occurs when hovering, reverses on mouse out

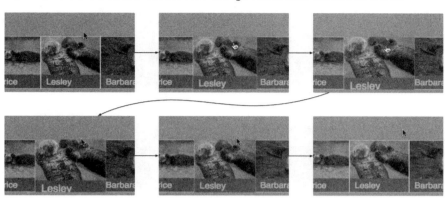

The DevTools give you a handy way to test pseudo-class states. Go to the elements panel and expand the tags until one of the `<li>` tags is displayed. Click the tag so that it is highlighted and you will see an ellipsis to the left. Click the ellipsis, and in the contextual menu that is revealed choose `:hover` from the list of pseudo-classes (Figure 7.16).

Figure 7.16 Toggling a pseudo-class in the elements panel

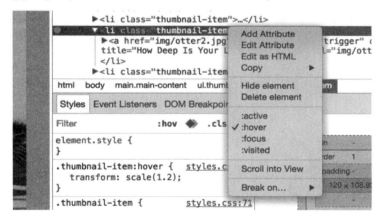

An orange circle appears to the left of the `<li>` tag in the elements panel, telling you that one of the pseudo-classes has been activated via the DevTools. The corresponding thumbnail will remain in the `:hover` state, even if you mouse over it and then mouse away from it.

Open the contextual menu again, by clicking the orange circle, and disable the `:hover` state before you continue.

Your transition is nice, but there is a small bug. Currently, the hover effect causes parts of the thumbnail to be cut off. This is because the transform applied to the .thumbnail-item does not cause its parent to adjust *its* size. The solution is to add a bit of padding to the .thumbnail-list. Change the vertical padding for .thumbnail-list in styles.css.

```
...
.thumbnail-list {
  flex: 0 1 auto;
  order: 2;
  display: flex;
  justify-content: space-between;
  list-style: none;
  padding: 0;
  padding: 20px 0;

  white-space: nowrap;
  overflow-x: auto;
}
...
```

You used the shorthand for the padding property. The first value, 20px, applies to the top and bottom padding, while the second value applies to the left and right padding. Make a similar adjustment inside your @media query, but add an extra padding of 35px to the left and right.

```
...
@media all and (min-width: 768px) {
  .main-content {
  ...
  }

  .thumbnail-list {
    flex-direction: column;
    order: 0;
    margin-left: 20px;

    padding: 0 35px;
  }
  ...
```

Save and check the results in your browser. This produces a nicer effect for the thumbnails (Figure 7.17).

Figure 7.17 Extra room for the hover effect in portrait and landscape

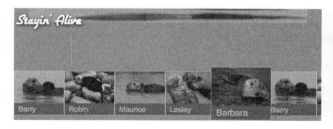

Using a timing function

Your hover effect is looking good! But it lacks that visual *pop* that would make it really special. With CSS transitions, you can not only specify how much time a transition should take, but also make it transition at different speeds during that time.

There are several timing functions that you can use with transitions. By default, the *linear* timing function is used, which makes the transition animate at a single, constant rate. The others are more interesting, and give the transition the feeling of speeding up or slowing down.

Update your transition in `styles.css` so that it uses the `ease-in-out` timing function. This will make the rate of the transition slower at the beginning and end and faster in the middle.

```
...
.thumbnail-item {
  display: inline-block;
  min-width: 120px;
  max-width: 120px;
  border: 1px solid rgb(100%, 100%, 100%);
  border: 1px solid rgba(100%, 100%, 100%, 0.8);

  transition: transform 133ms ease-in-out;
}
...
```

Save and then hover over one of your thumbnails. The effect is subtle, but noticeable.

There are a number of timing functions available. See the list on the MDN at
`developer.mozilla.org/en-US/docs/Web/CSS/transition-timing-function`.

Your `transition` uses the same duration value and timing function for both the transition *to* the end state and the transition *from* the end state. That does not have to be the case – you can use different values depending on the direction of the transition. If you specify a `transition` property on both the beginning-state declaration and the end-state declaration, the browser uses the value of the declaration it is moving toward.

It might be easier to see this in action. For a quick demonstration, add a `transition` declaration to `.thumbnail-item:hover` in `styles.css`. (You will delete it after trying it out in the browser.)

```
...
.thumbnail-item:hover {
  transform: scale(1.2);
  transition: transform 1000ms ease-in;
}
...
```

Save and again hover over one of the thumbnails in the browser. The scaling effect will be very slow, taking a full second to complete. This is because it is using the value declared for `.thumbnail-item:hover`. Now, move your mouse off of the thumbnail. This time, the transition takes 133 milliseconds, the value declared for `.thumbnail-item`.

Remove the `transition` declaration from `.thumbnail-item:hover` before you continue.

```
...
.thumbnail-item:hover {
  transform: scale(1.2);
  transition: transform 1000ms ease-in;
}
...
```

Transition on class change

Your second transition will make the `.detail-image-frame` look like it is zooming in from very far away.

Instead of using a pseudo-class selector to trigger a transition, this time you will add and remove class names with JavaScript to trigger a transition. Why? Because there is no pseudo-class that corresponds to a click event. Using JavaScript gives you much more control over how and when these UI changes are triggered.

Also, you will set different duration times for the beginning and end of the transition. The end result will be that when you click a thumbnail the corresponding otter image will be used for the detail image. It will immediately be sized down to a tiny dot in the center of the detail area, then it will transition to its full size (Figure 7.18).

Figure 7.18 Clicking a thumbnail scales it from very small to full size

Start by adding a style declaration for a new class named `is-tiny` in `styles.css`.

```
...
.detail-image-frame {
  ...
}

.is-tiny {
  transform: scale(0.001);
  transition: transform 0ms;
}

.detail-image {
  ...
```

You added two styles for `.is-tiny`. The first `scales` the element down to a small fraction of its original size. The second specifies that any `transition` for the `transform` property should last 0 milliseconds, applying the style change immediately. Put another way, going toward the `.is-tiny` class styles, the detail image will effectively have no transition. Because it lasts for 0 milliseconds, there is no need to specify a timing function.

Next, you will add another `transition` declaration with a 333 millisecond duration. This value will be used when transitioning away from the `.is-tiny` class, making the detail image grow to normal size over a period of a third of a second. Add this `transition` declaration to the `.detail-image-frame` in `styles.css`.

```
...
.detail-image-frame {
  position: relative;
  text-align: center;

  transition: transform 333ms;
}
...
```

Save `styles.css` before you move on.

Triggering transitions with JavaScript

Now that your transition styles are in place, you need to trigger them with JavaScript. To give your JavaScript a hook, add a data attribute to the `.detail-image-frame` element in `index.html`.

```
...
      <div class="detail-image-container">
        <div class="detail-image-frame" data-image-role="frame">
    <img class="detail-image" data-image-role="target" src="img/otter1.jpg" alt="">
    <span class="detail-image-title" data-image-role="title">Stayin' Alive</span>
        </div>
      </div>
...
```

Save `index.html`. Now, in `main.js`, you just need to add variables for your `.is-tiny` class and `data-image-role="frame"` selector, and then you will update **showDetails** to perform the class name changes to that trigger the transition.

Begin with the variables. Add a `DETAIL_FRAME_SELECTOR` variable for a selector string `'[data-image-role="frame"]'`. Also, add a `TINY_EFFECT_CLASS` variable for the `is-tiny` class name.

```
var DETAIL_IMAGE_SELECTOR = '[data-image-role="target"]';
var DETAIL_TITLE_SELECTOR = '[data-image-role="title"]';
var DETAIL_FRAME_SELECTOR = '[data-image-role="frame"]';
var THUMBNAIL_LINK_SELECTOR = '[data-image-role="trigger"]';
var HIDDEN_DETAIL_CLASS = 'hidden-detail';
var TINY_EFFECT_CLASS = 'is-tiny';
var ESC_KEY = 27;
...
```

It is not required that you put your variables in this order. (It makes no difference to the browser.) But it is a good idea to keep them organized. In `main.js`, all of the selector variables are grouped together, followed by the class variables, followed by the numeric code for the Escape key.

Now, update **showDetails** in main.js so that it gets a reference to the [data-image-role="frame"] element. To trigger the transition, you will need to add the TINY_EFFECT_CLASS and remove it.

```
...
function showDetails() {
  'use strict';
  var frame = document.querySelector(DETAIL_FRAME_SELECTOR);
  document.body.classList.remove(HIDDEN_DETAIL_CLASS);
  frame.classList.add(TINY_EFFECT_CLASS);
  frame.classList.remove(TINY_EFFECT_CLASS);
}
...
```

If you saved this and tried it in the browser, you would not see a transition take place. Why not? Because the TINY_EFFECT_CLASS is added and then immediately removed. The net result is that there is no actual class change to render. This is an optimization on the part of the browser.

You need to add a small delay before removing the TINY_EFFECT_CLASS. JavaScript, however, does not have a built-in delay or sleep function, as some other languages do. Time for a workaround!

You are going to use the **setTimeout** method, which takes a function and a delay (specified in milliseconds). After the delay, the function is queued for execution by the browser.

Add a call to **setTimeout** after calling **frame.classList.add** in main.js. Pass it two arguments: a function with a list of steps to perform and the number of milliseconds to wait before invoking that function argument. There is only one step to perform, and that is to remove TINY_EFFECT_CLASS.

```
...
function showDetails() {
  'use strict';
  var frame = document.querySelector(DETAIL_FRAME_SELECTOR);
  document.body.classList.remove(HIDDEN_DETAIL_CLASS);
  frame.classList.add(TINY_EFFECT_CLASS);
  setTimeout(function () {
    frame.classList.remove(TINY_EFFECT_CLASS);
  }, 50);
}
...
```

Let's take a closer look at what this code does. First, it adds the .is-tiny class to the frame element. This applies your transform: scale(0.001).

Then, the browser is told to wait 50 milliseconds, after which it will add an anonymous function to its execution queue. The **showDetails** function finishes. Fifty milliseconds later, the anonymous function is queued for execution. (Basically, it gets in line for the CPU, waiting behind any other functions that were already in line.)

When this anonymous function runs, it removes the TINY_EFFECT_CLASS from the frame's class list. This causes the transform transition to run over a period of 333 milliseconds, making the frame grow to its normal size.

Save your changes and admire the results. Click the thumbnails and enjoy those wacky otters zooming into view.

Custom Timing Functions

Now, for some icing on your Ottergram cake: You can create custom timing functions for your transitions instead of being limited to the built-in ones.

Timing functions can be graphed to show the transition's progress over time. Graphs of the built-in timing functions (from the site `cubic-bezier.com`) are shown in Figure 7.19.

Figure 7.19 Built-in timing functions

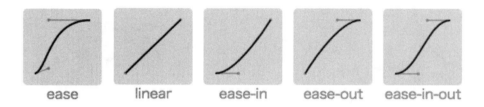

The shapes in these graphs are known as *cubic Bezier curves*. The lines in the graphs describe the behavior of the animation over time. They are defined by four points. You can create custom transitions by specifying the four points that define a curve. Try the following `cubic-bezier` as part of your transition declaration for `.detail-image-frame` in `styles.css`.

```
...
.detail-image-frame {
  position: relative;
  text-align: center;

  transition: transform 333m cubic-bezier(1,.06,.28,1);
}
...
```

Save it and click on some thumbnails in the browser to see the difference in the transition.

Thanks to developer Lea Verou and her site `cubic-bezier.com`, creating custom timing functions is painless (Figure 7.20).

Figure 7.20 Creating a custom timing function with `cubic-bezier.com`

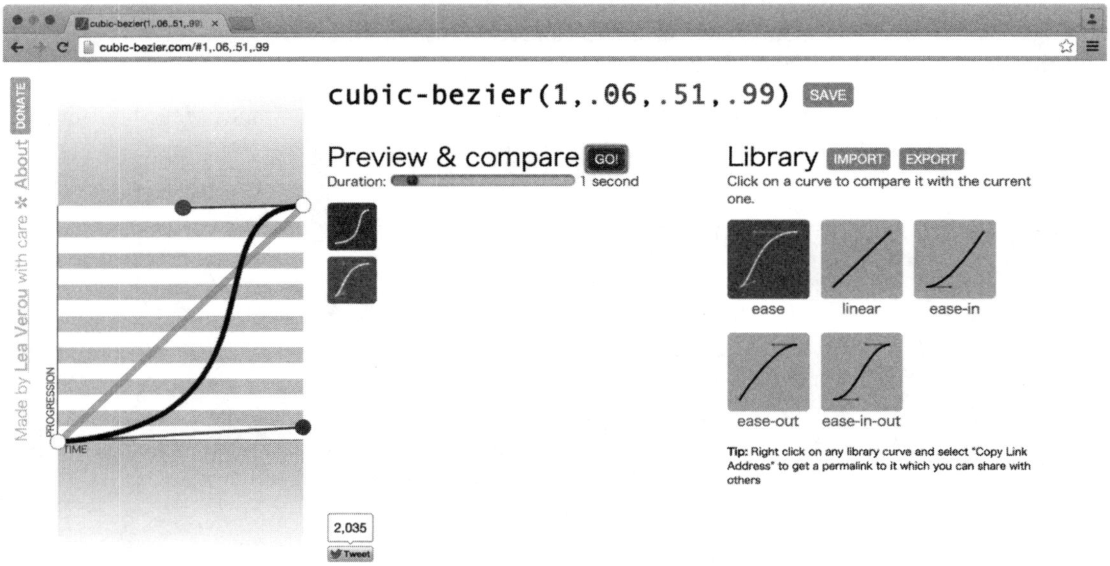

On the left side is a curve with red and blue drag handles. The curve is a graph of how much of the transition has occurred over the duration. Click and drag the handles to change the curve. As it changes, the decimal values at the top of the page change, too.

On the right side are the built-in timing functions: ease, linear, ease-in, ease-out, and ease-in-out. Click on one, then on the GO! button next to Preview & compare. The icons representing the two timing functions – the custom cubic-bezier and the built-in function – will animate, allowing you to see your custom timing in action and compare it to a built-in option.

Create a custom timing function and, when you are happy with it, copy and paste the values from the website to your code in `styles.css`:

```
...
.detail-image-frame {
  position: relative;
  text-align: center;

  transition: transform 333m cubic-bezier(your values here);
}
...
```

Congratulations! Ottergram is feature-complete! Save your file and admire your finished product. You have taken Ottergram from a simple, static web page to an interactive, responsive page with animated visual effects.

You have come a long way, and hopefully you have enjoyed learning about the basics of front-end development. It is time to wave goodbye to the otters, because you will be starting a new project in the next chapter.

For the More Curious: Rules for Type Coercion

As mentioned in Chapter 6, JavaScript was originally created so that folks who were not professional programmers could add interactivity to web pages. It was thought that these "regular humans" should not need to worry about whether a value was a number, an object, or a banana. (Just kidding – there is no banana type in JavaScript.)

One of the ways this is achieved is through type coercion. With type coercion, you can compare two values, regardless of their types, using the == operator and concatenate two values using the + operator. When you do, JavaScript will figure out a way to make that work – even if it has to do something a little weird, like changing the string "2" to the number 2.

This has mystified programmers and nonprogrammers alike. Most programmers agree that it is best to use strict comparison using the === operator. However, the rules for type coercion are very well defined in the language, and they are worth knowing about.

Let's say you are trying to compare two variables: x == y. If they are the same type and have the same value, the comparison results in a Boolean true. The only exception to this is: If either x or y have the value NaN (the language constant meaning "not a number"), then the result is false.

However, if x and y are different types, things get a bit tricky. Here are some of the rules JavaScript applies:

- These comparisons result in true: null == undefined and undefined == null.

- When comparing a string and a number, first convert the string to its numerical equivalent. This means that "3" == 3 is true, and "dog" == 20 is false.

- When comparing a Boolean to another type, first convert the Boolean to a number: true to the number 1, and false to the number 0. This means that false == 0 is true, and true == 1 is also true.

- Finally, if you compare a string or a number to an object, first try to convert the object to a primitive value. If that conversion does not work, then try converting the object to a string.

For even more information, check out the MDN's discussion at developer.mozilla.org/en-US/docs/Web/JavaScript/Equality_comparisons_and_sameness.

Part II
Modules, Objects, and Forms

8

Modules, Objects, and Methods

Over the next seven chapters, you will build a shopping-cart style application called CoffeeRun to manage coffee orders for a food truck. You will create CoffeeRun in three layers of code: the UI, the internal logic, and the server communication.

In this chapter, you will create the internal logic and interact with it through the DevTools console, as shown in Figure 8.1.

Figure 8.1 CoffeeRun, under the hood

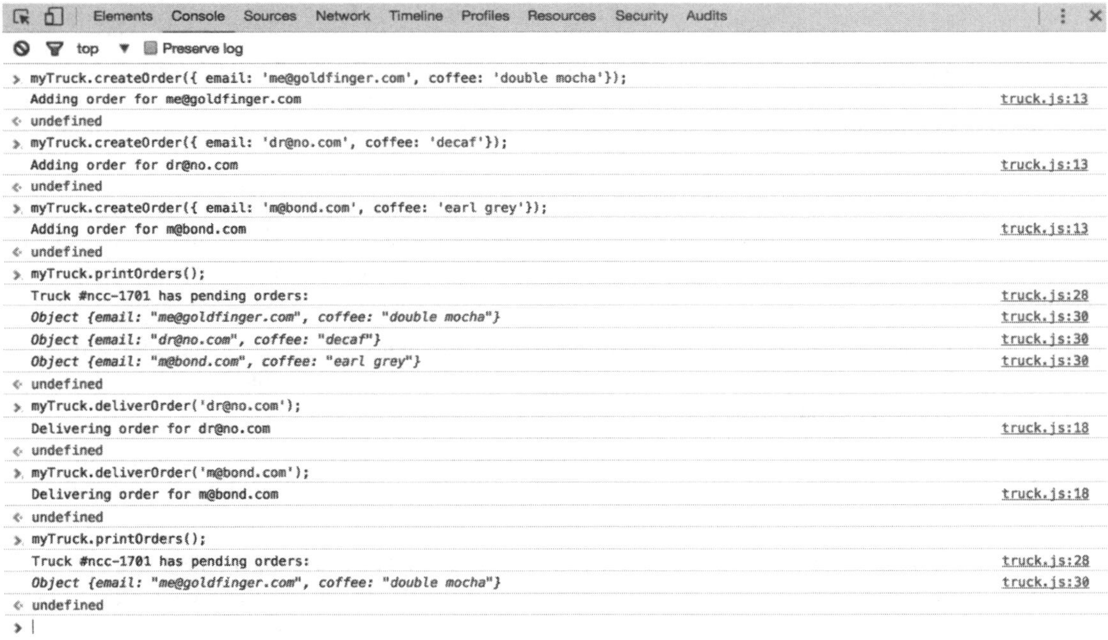

Modules

CoffeeRun is more complex than Ottergram, so it is important to organize your code to make it easier to debug and to extend. CoffeeRun will be structured in components, which are diagrammed in Figure 8.2.

Figure 8.2 Overview of components and interactions in CoffeeRun

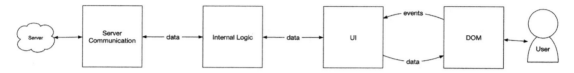

Each part of the application will focus on one area of responsibility. The code for your application's internal logic will manage the data. The UI code will handle events and DOM manipulation (much like the code for Ottergram). The server communication code will talk to a remote server, saving and retrieving data over the network.

JavaScript was created for writing very small scripts that add tiny bits of interactivity, not for writing complex applications. CoffeeRun is not extremely complex, but it breaks the threshold for what should be accomplished in a single script file.

To keep your code neatly separated, you will create three JavaScript files for the subsets of functionality within your application. You will have different files for your internal logic, your UI, and your server communication code. You will achieve this separation by writing your code in separate units, or *modules*.

How to group code into modules is entirely up to the developer. Most often, code is grouped around concepts, like "inventory" or "food menu." In terms of code, modules group related functions together. Some of the functions will be available externally, while others will only be used internally by the module.

Think about a restaurant. The kitchen has lots of tools and ingredients that are available internally, but the customers only see a menu with a few items. That menu is the customer's interface to the food-making module called the kitchen.

Likewise, if the restaurant has a bar, the drink-making tools and ingredients are internal; the customer can only access the items on the drink list, which is their interface to the drink-making module called the bar.

As a customer, you cannot borrow the butcher's knife from the kitchen or use the blender from the bar. You cannot grab an extra pat of butter from the refrigerator or pour an extra shot in your cocktail. You are restricted to the interfaces provided by the kitchen and bar modules.

Similarly, each of CoffeeRun's modules will keep some of its functionality private. Only a portion of its functionality will be made publicly accessible, so that other modules can interact with it.

For CoffeeRun, you will continue to work in ES5, which is the best-supported version of JavaScript as of this writing. (Your next project, Chattrbox, will use the most recent version, ES6). ES5 does not have a formal way to organize code into self-contained modules, but you can get the same kind of organization by putting related code (variables and functions) inside the body of a function.

The module pattern

Code can be organized using functions, but it is a common practice to use a variation of a regular function for this purpose. Before you get started with your new project, let's take a brief look at the *module pattern* for organizing code, examining how a function from Ottergram could be rewritten as a module.

Here is the code for a basic module:

```
(function () {
  'use strict';
  // Code will go here
})();
```

If this is the first time you have seen this pattern, it probably looks rather odd. This is known as an *immediately invoked function expression* (or IIFE), and it is best to examine it from the inside out.

The main part of it is the anonymous function:

```
function () {
  'use strict';
  // Code will go here
}
```

You worked with anonymous functions in Ottergram, so this should be familiar.

Here, however, the anonymous function is enclosed in parentheses:

```
(function () {
  'use strict';
  // Code will go here
})
```

These enclosing parentheses are very important because they tell the browser, "Please do not interpret this code as a function declaration."

The browser sees the parentheses and says, "Ah. OK. I get that I am looking at an anonymous function. I will hold off from doing anything with it."

Most of the time, you use an anonymous function by passing it as an argument. In this case, you are calling it immediately. This is done with the empty pair of parentheses:

```
(function () {
  'use strict';
  // Code will go here
})()
```

When the browser sees the empty parentheses, it realizes that you want it to invoke whatever comes before them, and says, "Oh! I see that I've got an anonymous function that I can run!"

You may be thinking, "This is both crazy and useless." Actually, you have already written code that works similarly. Recall Ottergram's **initializeEvents** function. After you declared it, you called it immediately and never called it again. Here is that code for reference.

```
function initializeEvents() {                  // Function declared
  'use strict';
  var thumbnails = getThumbnailsArray();
  thumbnails.forEach(addThumbClickHandler);

  addKeyPressHandler();
}

initializeEvents();                            // Function called
```

The purpose of this function was to bundle some steps together and run them when the page loads. Here is that same code, rewritten as an IIFE. (You do not need to change your Ottergram code; this is just to illustrate the concept.)

```
function initializeEvents() {
(function () {
  'use strict';
  var thumbnails = getThumbnailsArray();
  thumbnails.forEach(addThumbClickHandler);

  addKeyPressHandler();
}
})();

initializeEvents();
```

IIFEs are useful when you want to run some code once without creating any extra global variables or functions. To understand why this is important, consider the variables and functions you wrote for Ottergram.

In Ottergram, you built up a collection of useful functions and then called them as needed. These functions had names like **getThumbnailsArray** and **addKeyPressHandler**. Luckily, these names were unique. If you had tried to define two functions with the same name, the first one would have simply been replaced by the second one.

When you define functions or variables, they are added to the *global namespace* by default. This is the browser's registry of all of the function and variable names for your JavaScript program, along with any built-in functions and variables. More generally, a *namespace* is the means by which code is organized: Code is organized in namespaces the same way files on your computer are organized in folders.

In CoffeeRun, you may have functions that could reasonably have the same name, like **add** or **addClickHandler**. Instead of adding them to the global namespace, where they could be accidentally overwritten, you can declare them inside of a function. This protects them from being accessed or overwritten by code outside of the function.

As you group code together in a module, you will want to make some, but not all, of the functionality accessible to the world outside of the module. To do this, you will take advantage of the fact that IIFEs, like any function, can accept arguments.

Modifying an object with an IIFE

IIFEs are not only good for running set-up code, like Ottergram's **initializeEvents**. They are also good for running code that augments an object, which is usually passed in as an argument. To illustrate how this works, our friend **initializeEvents** will be used once again.

Here is a version of **initializeEvents** whose job is to modify the thumbnails by adding a click handler. (To simplify things, the **addKeyPressHandler** call has been removed.)

```
function initializeEvents() {
  'use strict';
  var thumbnails = getThumbnailsArray();
  thumbnails.forEach(addThumbClickHandler);
}

initializeEvents();
```

In this form, **initializeEvents** modifies an array of thumbnails using **addThumbClickHandler**. But it could also receive the array as an argument. To do that, you would declare a parameter as part of the function definition. Then, when you call it, you would pass in the array, like this:

```
function initializeEvents(thumbnails) {
  'use strict';
  var thumbnails = getThumbnailsArray();
  thumbnails.forEach(addThumbClickHandler);
}

var thumbnails = getThumbnailsArray();
initializeEvents(thumbnails);
```

To rewrite this as an IIFE, you would remove the function name, wrap the function in parentheses, and add a pair of empty parentheses to invoke the function:

```
(function initializeEvents(thumbnails) {
  'use strict';
  thumbnails.forEach(addThumbClickHandler);
})();

var thumbnails = getThumbnailsArray();
initializeEvents(thumbnails);
```

However, you would still need to pass in the array of thumbnails as an argument. You can do this by moving the call to **getThumbnailsArray**. Instead of assigning the result to a variable, you would pass the result to your IIFE:

```
(function (thumbnails) {
  'use strict';
  thumbnails.forEach(addThumbClickHandler);
})(getThumbnailsArray());

var thumbnails = getThumbnailsArray();
```

In this version of the code, an array (resulting from calling **getThumbnailsArray**) is passed in to the IIFE. The IIFE receives this array and places the label thumbnails on it. Inside the body of the IIFE, the event listeners are attached to each item in the array (Figure 8.3).

Figure 8.3 IIFE modifying its arguments

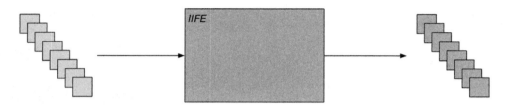

Array of thumbnails   *Array of thumbnails with event listeners*

Anything can be passed to an IIFE for modification. Your CoffeeRun IIFEs will be passed the window object. But instead of attaching their module code directly to the global namespace, they will attach code to a single App property *within* the global namespace. Every CoffeeRun module will be contained in its own file and loaded into the browser by an individual <script> tag. An overview of this process is shown in Figure 8.4.

Figure 8.4 <script> tags load modules, which modify window.App

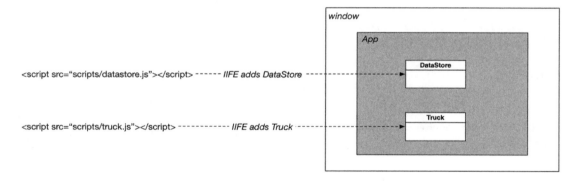

Setting Up CoffeeRun

Enough theory – let's get to work. Because this is a new project, start by creating a new directory. Open Atom and choose File → Add Project Folder.... Select your front-end-dev-book directory and click New Folder. Name the new folder coffeerun and click Open.

Next, Control-click (right-click) your new coffeerun folder in Atom's navigation panel. Choose New File and enter index.html for the filename. Control-click (right-click) on coffeerun again and choose New Folder. Name the folder scripts.

In your front-end-dev-book folder, you should now have a folder for each of your projects, ottergram and coffeerun, with similar file structures (Figure 8.5).

Figure 8.5 Creating files and folders for CoffeeRun

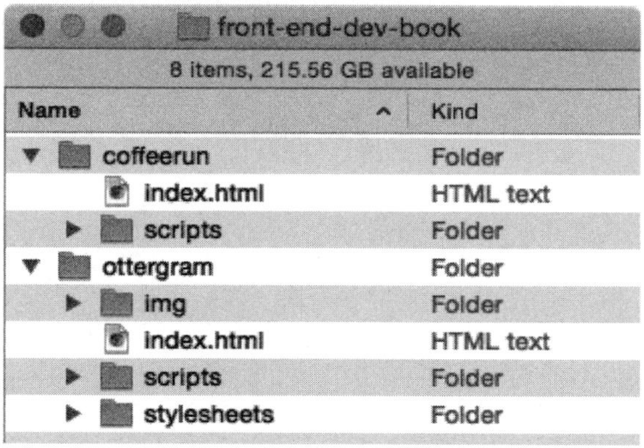

If you already have a terminal session open and running browser-sync, close browser-sync using Control-C. If you do not, open a new terminal window. Either way, change to your new coffeerun directory (refer to the commands in Chapter 1 if you are not sure about how to do this) and start browser-sync again. As a reminder, the command to start it is browser-sync start --server --files "stylesheets/*.css, scripts/*.js, *.html".

In index.html add the basic skeleton of your document. (Remember, Atom's autocomplete will do most of this for you; just start typing "html.")

```html
<!doctype html>
<html>
  <head>
    <meta charset="utf-8">
    <title>coffeerun</title>
  </head>
  <body>

  </body>
</html>
```

You are now ready to create your first module!

Creating the DataStore Module

The first module you will write will store coffee order information in a simple database, not unlike writing down the orders by hand. Each order will be stored by the customer's email address. To get started, you will only keep track of a text description of the order, like "quadruple espresso" (Figure 8.6).

Figure 8.6 Initial structure of CoffeeRun's database

email	order
caquino@bignerdranch.com	quadruple espresso
tgandee@bignerdranch.com	black coffee
jreece@bignerdranch.com	grayish brown smoothie

Later, you will also keep track of the size, flavor, and caffeine strength of each coffee order. The customer's email address will serve as the unique identifier for the entire order, so all of the order details will be associated with a single email address. (Sorry, coffee addicts! Only one order per customer.)

Create a new file called `scripts/datastore.js`. Next, in `index.html`, add the `<script>` tag to include the new file in your project.

```
<!doctype html>
<html>
  <head>
    <meta charset="utf-8">
    <title>coffeerun</title>
  </head>
  <body>
    <script src="scripts/datastore.js" charset="utf-8"></script>
  </body>
</html>
```

Save `index.html`. In `scripts/datastore.js`, begin with the basic IIFE for your module structure:

```
(function (window) {
  'use strict';
  // Code will go here
})(window);
```

Now that the skeleton of your module exists and has a corresponding `<script>` tag, it is time to attach it to the namespace for your application.

Adding Modules to a Namespace

Many other programming languages have special syntax for creating modules and packaging them together. ES5 does not. Instead, you can get the same kind of organization using objects.

You can use objects to associate any kind of data with a key name. In fact, this is precisely how you will organize your modules. Specifically, you will use a single object as the namespace for your CoffeeRun application. This namespace is where individual modules register themselves, which makes them available for use by your other application code.

There are three steps to using IIFEs to register modules in a namespace:

1. Get a reference to the namespace, if it exists.

2. Create the module code.

3. Attach your module code to the namespace.

Let's see what that looks like in practice. Update your IIFE in `datastore.js` as shown. We will explain the code after you enter it.

```javascript
(function (window) {
  'use strict';
  // Code will go here
  var App = window.App || {};

  function DataStore() {
    console.log('running the DataStore function');
  }

  App.DataStore = DataStore;
  window.App = App;
})(window);
```

In the body of the IIFE, you declared a local variable named `App`. If there is already an `App` property of the `window`, you assign the local `App` to it. If not, the label `App` will refer to a new, empty object, represented by `{}`. The `||` is the *default operator*, otherwise known as the *logical or operator*. It can be used to provide a valid value (in this case, `{}`) if the first choice (`window.App`) has not yet been created.

Each of your modules will do this same check. It is like saying "Whoever gets there first: Go ahead and start a new object. Everyone else will use that object."

Next, you declared a function named **DataStore**. You will add more code to this function shortly.

Finally, you attached **DataStore** to the `App` object and reassigned the global `App` property to your newly modified `App`. (If it did not already exist and you had to create it as an empty object, you must attach it.)

Save your files and switch over to the browser. Open the DevTools, click on the tab for the console, and call your **DataStore** function with the following code:

```javascript
App.DataStore();
```

DataStore runs and prints some text to the console (Figure 8.7).

Figure 8.7 Running the **App.DataStore** function

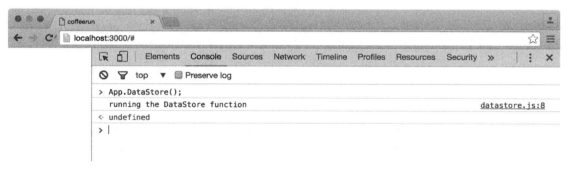

Notice that you did not need to write `window.App.DataStore();`. This is because the `window` object is the global namespace. All of its properties are available to any JavaScript code you write, including in the console.

Constructors

IIFEs let you take advantage of function scope to create namespaces to organize large pieces of your code. There is another use of functions that makes them act like factories for objects that all have similar properties and methods. In other languages, you might use a class for this kind of organization. Strictly speaking, JavaScript does not have classes, but it does give you a way to create custom types.

You have already started to create the **DataStore** type. Now you will customize it in two steps. In the first step, you will give it a property that will be used internally for storing data. In the second step, you will give it a set of methods for interacting with that data. You do not need to give other objects direct access to that data, so this type will provide an external interface through a set of methods.

Object factory functions are called *constructors* in JavaScript.

Add the following code to the body of the **DataStore** function in datastore.js.

```
(function (window) {
  'use strict';
  var App = window.App || {};

  function DataStore() {
    console.log('running the DataStore function');
    this.data = {};
  }

  App.DataStore = DataStore;
  window.App = App;
})(window);
```

The job of a constructor is to create and customize a new object. Inside the body of the constructor, you can refer to that new object with the keyword this. You used the dot operator to create a property named data on your new object and assigned an empty object to data.

You may have noticed that you capitalized the first letter of **DataStore**. This is a convention in JavaScript when naming constructors. It is not necessary, but it is a good practice as a way to tell other developers that the function should be used as a constructor.

To differentiate a constructor from a regular function, you use the keyword new when you call it. This tells JavaScript to create a new object, set up the reference from this to that new object, and to *implicitly* return that object. That means it will return the object without an explicit return statement in the constructor.

Save and return to the console. To learn how to use a constructor, you are going to create two **DataStore** objects (or *instances*) and add values to them. Begin by creating the instances.

```
var dsOne = new App.DataStore();
var dsTwo = new App.DataStore();
```

You created these **DataStore** instances by calling the **DataStore** constructor. At this point, each has an empty data property. Add some values to them:

```
dsOne.data['email'] = 'james@bond.com';
dsOne.data['order'] = 'black coffee';
dsTwo.data['email'] = 'moneypenny@bond.com';
dsTwo.data['order'] = 'chai tea';
```

Then inspect the values:

```
dsOne.data;
dsTwo.data;
```

The results tell you that each instance holds different information (Figure 8.8).

Figure 8.8 Saving values to instances of the **DataStore** constructor

A constructor's prototype

Using a **DataStore** instance, you can manually store and retrieve data. But, in its current form, **DataStore** is just a roundabout way of creating an object literal, and any module that will use a **DataStore** instance has to be coded to use the data property directly.

This is not good software design. It would be better if **DataStore** provided a public interface for adding, removing, and retrieving data – all while keeping the details of how it works a secret.

The second part of creating your custom **DataStore** type is to provide these methods for interacting with the data. The goal is for these methods to serve as the interface that other modules use when they interact with a **DataStore** instance. To accomplish this, you will make use of a very cool feature of JavaScript functions, the *prototype* property.

Functions in JavaScript are also objects. This means that they can have properties. In JavaScript, all instances created by a constructor have access to a shared storehouse of properties and methods: the prototype property of the constructor.

To create these instances, you used the new keyword when you called the constructor. The new keyword not only creates your instance and returns it but also creates a special link from the instance to the constructor's prototype property. This link exists for any instance created when the constructor is created with the new keyword.

When you add a property to the `prototype` and assign it a function, every instance you create with the constructor will have access to that function. You can use the keyword `this` inside of the function body, and it will refer to the instance.

To see this in action, create the **add** function in `datastore.js` as a property of the prototype. You can also delete the call to `console.log`.

```
(function (window) {
  'use strict';
  var App = window.App || {};

  function DataStore() {
    console.log('running the DataStore function');
    this.data = {};
  }

  DataStore.prototype.add = function (key, val) {
    this.data[key] = val;
  };

  App.DataStore = DataStore;
  window.App = App;
})(window);
```

You gave `DataStore.prototype` the property **add** and you assigned a function to it. That function takes two arguments, `key` and `val`. Inside the function body, you used those arguments to make changes to the instance's `data` property.

In terms of how **DataStore** works with coffee orders, it will store the order information (the `val`), using the customer's email address (the `key`).

You are not setting up a true database, but **DataStore** works well enough for CoffeeRun. It is able to save some information, `val`, under the unique identifier specified by `key`. Because you are using a JavaScript object for storage, each `key` is guaranteed to be a unique entry in the database. (In a JavaScript object, a property name is always unique, like function names within a namespace. If you tried to store different values using the same key, you would just overwrite any previous values for that key.)

This aspect of JavaScript objects fulfills the one major requirement of any database: keeping the individual pieces of data separate.

Save your code and switch back to the browser. Create an instance of **DataStore** in the console and use its **add** method to store some information.

```
var ds = new App.DataStore();
ds.add('email', 'q@bond.com');
ds.add('order', 'triple espresso');
ds.data;
```

Inspect the `data` property to confirm that it works (Figure 8.9).

Figure 8.9 Calling a prototype method

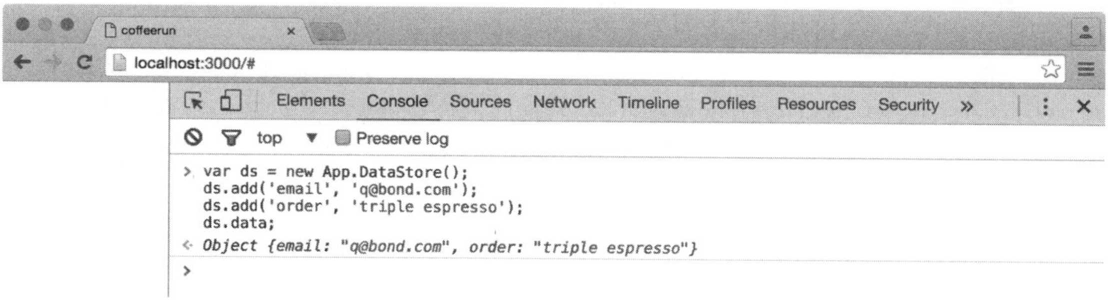

Adding methods to the constructor

The next thing to do is to create methods for accessing the data. In `datastore.js`, add a method to look up a value based on a given key and one to look up all keys and values.

```
...
  DataStore.prototype.add = function (key, val) {
    this.data[key] = val;
  };

  DataStore.prototype.get = function (key) {
    return this.data[key];
  };

  DataStore.prototype.getAll = function () {
    return this.data;
  };

  App.DataStore = DataStore;
  window.App = App;
})(window);
```

You created a **get** method that accepts a key, looks up the value for it in the instance's `data` property, and `returns` it. You also created a **getAll** method. It is almost the same, but instead of looking up the value for a single key, it returns a reference to the `data` property.

You can now add and retrieve information from a **DataStore** instance. To complete the cycle, you need to add a method for removing information. Add that to `datastore.js` now.

```
...
  DataStore.prototype.getAll = function () {
    return this.data;
  };

  DataStore.prototype.remove = function (key) {
    delete this.data[key];
  };

  App.DataStore = DataStore;
  window.App = App;
})(window);
```

The `delete` operator removes a key/value pair from an object when your new **remove** method is called.

175

With that, you have completed the **DataStore** module, which provides the most important part of the CoffeeRun application. It can store data, provide stored data in response to queries, and delete unnecessary data on command.

To see all of your methods in action, save your code and go to the console after browser-sync has reloaded your browser. Enter the following code, which exercises all of the methods of **DataStore**:

```
var ds = new App.DataStore();
ds.add('m@bond.com', 'tea');
ds.add('james@bond.com', 'eshpressho');
ds.getAll();
ds.remove('james@bond.com');
ds.getAll();
ds.get('m@bond.com');
ds.get('james@bond.com');
```

As shown in Figure 8.10, **DataStore**'s instance methods should now work as expected. These methods are exactly the way that other modules will interact with your application's database.

Figure 8.10 Working with **DataStore** using only its prototype methods

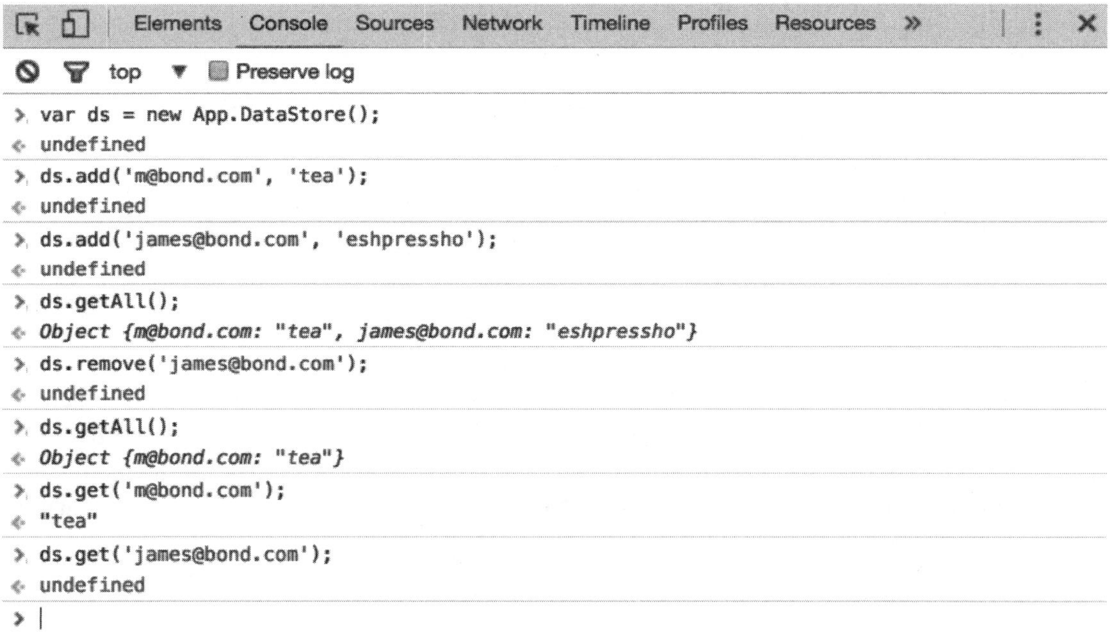

Your next module will use the same structure: an IIFE with a parameter for the namespace to modify. But it will provide completely different functionality from **DataStore**.

Creating the Truck Module

The next module you will write is the **Truck** module, which will provide all of the functionality for managing the food truck. It will have methods for creating and delivering orders and for printing a list of pending orders. Figure 8.11 shows how the **Truck** module will work with the **DataStore** module.

Figure 8.11 **Truck** module interacting with **DataStore** module

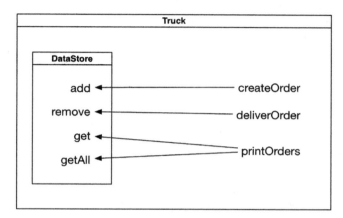

When a **Truck** instance is created, it is given a **DataStore** object. A **Truck** has methods for working with coffee orders, but it should not need to worry about how to store and manage that information. Instead, the **Truck** just passes those duties to the **DataStore**. For example, when you call the **Truck**'s **createOrder** method, it calls the **DataStore**'s **add** method.

Create the scripts/truck.js file and add a <script> tag for it to index.html.

```
<!doctype html>
<html>
  <head>
    <meta charset="utf-8">
    <title>coffeerun</title>
  </head>
  <body>
    <script src="scripts/datastore.js" charset="utf-8"></script>
    <script src="scripts/truck.js" charset="utf-8"></script>
  </body>
</html>
```

Save index.html. In truck.js, set up your module with an IIFE and a constructor for the **Truck** type.

```
(function (window) {
  'use strict';
  var App = window.App || {};

  function Truck() {
  }

  App.Truck = Truck;
  window.App = App;

})(window);
```

Next, you will add parameters to your constructor so that each instance will have a unique identifier and its own **DataStore** instance. The identifier is just a name for differentiating one **Truck** instance from another. The **DataStore** instance will play a much more important role.

Add the new parameters in `truck.js`.

```
(function (window) {
  'use strict';
  var App = window.App || {};

  function Truck(truckId, db) {
    this.truckId = truckId;
    this.db = db;
  }

  App.Truck = Truck;
  window.App = App;

})(window);
```

You declared parameters for the `truckId` and the `db`, then you assigned each of them as properties to the newly constructed instance.

The **Truck** instances will need methods for managing coffee orders, and you will add those next. Order data will include an email address and a drink specification.

Adding orders

The first method to add is **createOrder**. When this method is called, the **Truck** instance will interact with its db property through the **DataStore** methods you declared earlier. Specifically, you will call **DataStore**'s **add** method to store a coffee order, using the email address associated with the order.

Declare this new prototype method in `truck.js`.

```
...
  function Truck(truckId, db) {
    this.truckId = truckId;
    this.db = db;
  }

  Truck.prototype.createOrder = function (order) {
    console.log('Adding order for ' + order.emailAddress);
    this.db.add(order.emailAddress, order);
  };

  App.Truck = Truck;
  window.App = App;

})(window);
```

You log a message to the console in **createOrder**, then you store the order information using db's **add** method.

Using the **add** method was as simple as referring to the **Truck**'s db instance variable and calling **add**. You did not need to specify the **App.DataStore** namespace or mention the **DataStore** constructor anywhere in this module. Instances of **Truck** are designed to work with anything that has the same method names as a **DataStore**. There is no need for **Truck** to know any details beyond that.

Save your file and test **createOrder** in the console using the following entries:

```
var myTruck = new App.Truck('007', new App.DataStore());
myTruck.createOrder({ emailAddress: 'dr@no.com', coffee: 'decaf'});
myTruck.createOrder({ emailAddress: 'me@goldfinger.com', coffee: 'double mocha'});
myTruck.createOrder({ emailAddress: 'm@bond.com', coffee: 'earl grey'});
myTruck.db;
```

Your results should look like Figure 8.12.

Figure 8.12 Taking **Truck.prototype.createOrder** for a test drive

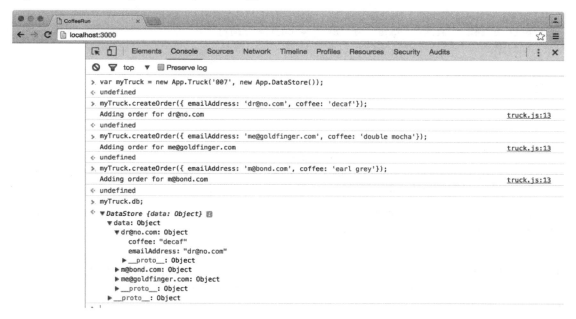

When the console prints the value of myTruck.db, you will need to click the ▶ icon so that you can see the nested properties (such as the dr@no.com property inside the data object).

Removing orders

When an order is delivered, the **Truck** instance should remove the order from its database. Add a new **deliverOrder** method to the Truck.prototype object in truck.js.

```
...
  Truck.prototype.createOrder = function (order) {
    console.log('Adding order for ' + data.emailAddress);
    this.db.add(data.emailAddress, order);
  };

  Truck.prototype.deliverOrder = function (customerId) {
    console.log('Delivering order for ' + customerId);
    this.db.remove(customerId);
  };

  App.Truck = Truck;
  window.App = App;

})(window);
```

You assigned a function expression to **Truck.prototype.deliverOrder**. This function accepts a customerId argument, which it then passes to **this.db.remove**. The value of customerId should be the email address associated with an order.

Just like **createOrder**, **deliverOrder** is only interested in calling the **remove** method of this.db. It does not need any details about how **remove** actually works.

Save and switch to the console. Create a **Truck** instance, add a few orders with **createOrder**, and then make sure that **deliverOrder** removes them from the instance's db. (You can press Return or Shift-Return after each call to **createOrder** and **deliverOrder**, but make sure you press Return after each myTruck.db entry.)

```
var myTruck = new App.Truck('007', new App.DataStore());
myTruck.createOrder({ emailAddress: 'm@bond.com', coffee: 'earl grey'});
myTruck.createOrder({ emailAddress: 'dr@no.com', coffee: 'decaf'});
myTruck.createOrder({ emailAddress: 'me@goldfinger.com', coffee: 'double mocha'});
myTruck.db;
myTruck.deliverOrder('m@bond.com');
myTruck.deliverOrder('dr@no.com');
myTruck.db;
```

As you enter these test commands, you will see that the order information in myTruck.db changes after you call **deliverOrder** (Figure 8.13).

Figure 8.13 Removing order data with **Truck.prototype.deliverOrder**

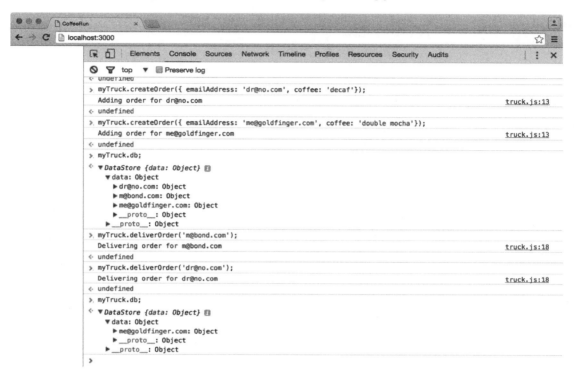

Note that the console shows you the state of the data *at the time* you click the ▶ icon. If you do not inspect the values in myTruck.db until after calling **deliverOrder**, it will seem as though the data was never added (Figure 8.14).

Figure 8.14 Console shows values at time of clicking arrow icon

The console shows the state of objects at the time you click the disclosure arrow, not at the time they are printed.

Debugging

Your last method to add to the `Truck.prototype` object is **printOrders**. This method will get an array of all of the customer email addresses, iterate through the array, and **console.log** the order information.

The code for this method is very similar to other functions and methods you have already written. But it will start out with a bug, which you will find using Chrome's debugging tools.

Let's take this step by step. Start by creating the basic version of **printOrders** in `truck.js`. In the body, you will retrieve all the coffee orders from the db object. Then you will use the **Object.keys** method to get an array containing the email addresses for the orders. Finally, you will iterate through the email address array and run a callback function for each element in the array.

```
...
  Truck.prototype.deliverOrder = function (customerId) {
    console.log('Delivering order for ' + customerId);
    this.db.remove(customerId);
  };

  Truck.prototype.printOrders = function () {
    var customerIdArray = Object.keys(this.db.getAll());

    console.log('Truck #' + this.truckId + ' has pending orders:');
    customerIdArray.forEach(function (id) {
      console.log(this.db.get(id));
    });
  };

  App.Truck = Truck;
  window.App = App;

})(window);
```

Inside the new **printOrders** method, you call **this.db.getAll** to retrieve all the orders as key/value pairs and pass them to **Object.keys**, which returns an array containing only the keys. You assign this array to the variable `customerIdArray`.

When you iterate through this array, you pass a callback to **forEach**. In the body of that callback, you try to **get** the order associated with an id (the customer email address).

Save and return to the console. Create a new instance of `Truck` and add some coffee orders. Then try your new **printOrders** method.

```
var myTruck = new App.Truck('007', new App.DataStore());
myTruck.createOrder({ emailAddress: 'm@bond.com', coffee: 'earl grey'});
myTruck.createOrder({ emailAddress: 'dr@no.com', coffee: 'decaf'});
myTruck.createOrder({ emailAddress: 'me@goldfinger.com', coffee: 'double mocha'});
myTruck.printOrders();
```

Instead of a list of the coffee orders, you will see the error `Uncaught TypeError: Cannot read property 'db' of undefined` (Figure 8.15).

Figure 8.15 Error when **printOrders** is run

This is one of the most common errors that you will see when writing JavaScript. Many developers find it especially frustrating because it can be hard to pinpoint the cause. Knowing how to use the debugger, as you are about to do, is key to locating the problem.

Locating bugs with the DevTools

Debugging requires you to reproduce the error as you progressively isolate the buggy code. The Chrome debugger makes this process (almost) enjoyable.

When an error occurs, the console shows you the filename and the line number of the code that caused the error. (In Figure 8.15, the reference is to truck.js:30; your line number might be different.) Click that text to open the offending line of code in the debugging tools (Figure 8.16).

Figure 8.16 Viewing the error in the debugging tools

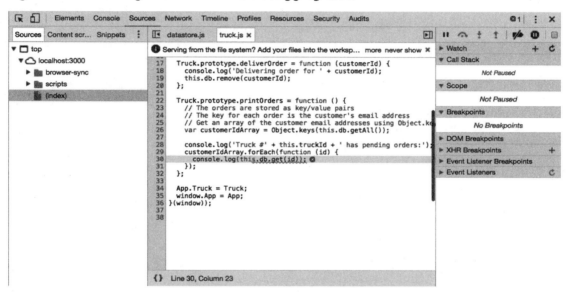

You are now viewing the sources panel of the DevTools. Click the red icon in the problem line to see the error information (Figure 8.17).

Figure 8.17 Error line called out in the sources panel

```
// Get an array of the customer email addresses using Object.ke
var customerIdArray = Object.keys(this.db.getAll());

console.log('Truck #' + this.    ● Uncaught TypeError: Cannot read property 'db' of undefined
customerIdArray.forEach(funct
    console.log(this.db.get(id)); ●
});
};
```

This error message indicates that the browser thinks you are trying to read a property named db, but that the object it belongs to does not exist.

The next step is to run the code just up to the line that is causing the error and then check the value of that object. In the sources panel, click the line number to the left of the line with the error flag. This sets a *breakpoint* for the debugger, telling the browser to pause just before it tries to run this line. When you set a breakpoint, the line number on the left turns blue and an entry is added to the breakpoints panel on the right (Figure 8.18).

Figure 8.18 Setting a breakpoint

```
22   Truck.prototype.printOrders = function () {
23       // The orders are stored as key/value pairs
24       // The key for each order is the customer's email address
25       // Get an array of the customer email addresses using Object.ke
26       var customerIdArray = Object.keys(this.db.getAll());
27
28       console.log('Truck #' + this.truckId + ' has pending orders:');
29       customerIdArray.forEach(function (id) {
30           console.log(this.db.get(id)); ⊘
31       });
```

Not Paused

▼ Breakpoints
☑ truck.js:30
    console.log(this.db.get(id))..

▶ DOM Breakpoints
▶ XHR Breakpoints   +

Press the Escape key to show the console at the bottom of the sources panel (Figure 8.19). This is also known as the *drawer*. You will need to be able to see the code in the sources panel and interact with the console at the same time.

Figure 8.19 Showing the console drawer

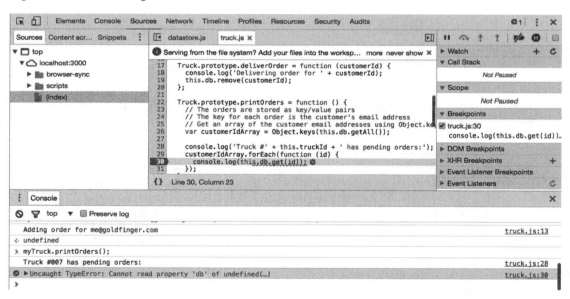

Run `myTruck.printOrders();` again in the console. The browser will activate the debugger, and your code will pause at the breakpoint (Figure 8.20).

Figure 8.20 Debugger paused at breakpoint

When the debugger pauses, you have access to all of the variables that are available at that point. Using the console, you can check the values of the variables, looking for signs of trouble.

Try to reproduce the error by evaluating parts of the line of code with the error flag. Start with the code that is nested furthest inside of any parentheses. In this case, that is the id variable. When you enter that on the console, it reports that the value is m@bond.com (Figure 8.21).

Figure 8.21 Inspecting the innermost value

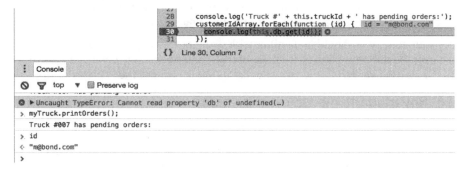

Because that did not reproduce the error, try the code just outside that set of parentheses, this.db.get(id). Evaluate it on the console. You should see that the error is reported (Figure 8.22).

Figure 8.22 Reproducing the error

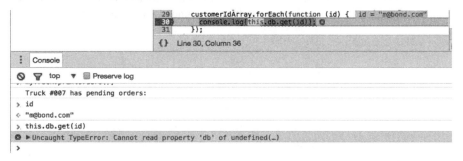

Now you can further isolate the cause. Begin evaluating that same piece of code, but remove parts of it, starting from the right. You will do this until the error is no longer printed. Start with `this.db.get`. After that, enter `this.db`. The console continues to report the error (Figure 8.23).

Figure 8.23 The search continues

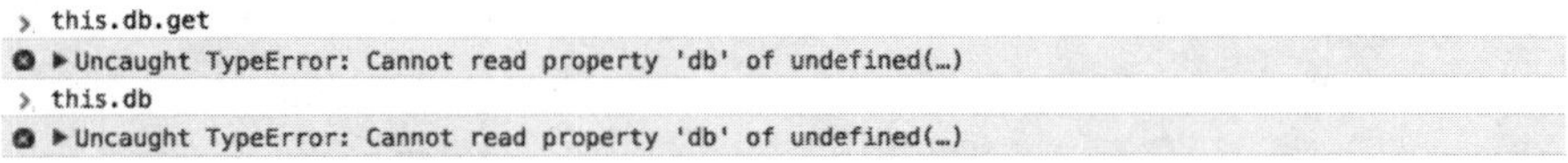

```
> this.db.get
⊘ ▶ Uncaught TypeError: Cannot read property 'db' of undefined(…)
> this.db
⊘ ▶ Uncaught TypeError: Cannot read property 'db' of undefined(…)
```

Finally, enter `this`. You are now at the point where the error is not happening (Figure 8.24).

Figure 8.24 Trimming down the code to find the cause of the error

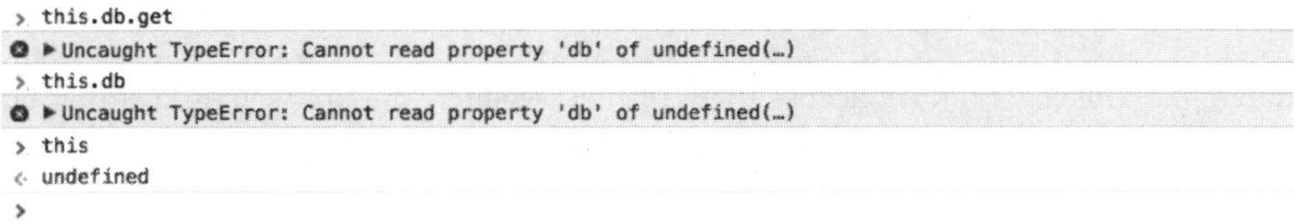

```
> this.db.get
⊘ ▶ Uncaught TypeError: Cannot read property 'db' of undefined(…)
> this.db
⊘ ▶ Uncaught TypeError: Cannot read property 'db' of undefined(…)
> this
⟨· undefined
>
```

Why does `this` have the value `undefined` inside of your callback? Inside of a callback function, `this` is not assigned to an object. You need to explicitly assign one.

This situation is different from your **Truck.prototype** methods, where `this` refers to the instance of **Truck**. Even though the callback is inside of **Truck.prototype.printOrder**, it has its own `this` variable, which is *not* assigned to a value and is therefore `undefined`.

Before fixing your code, you should be familiar with two other ways you could have located the bug. If you mouse over the different parts of the code in the sources panel, the debugger will show you their values. With the mouse over `this`, it shows you that its value is `undefined` (Figure 8.25).

Figure 8.25 Hovering the mouse reveals values

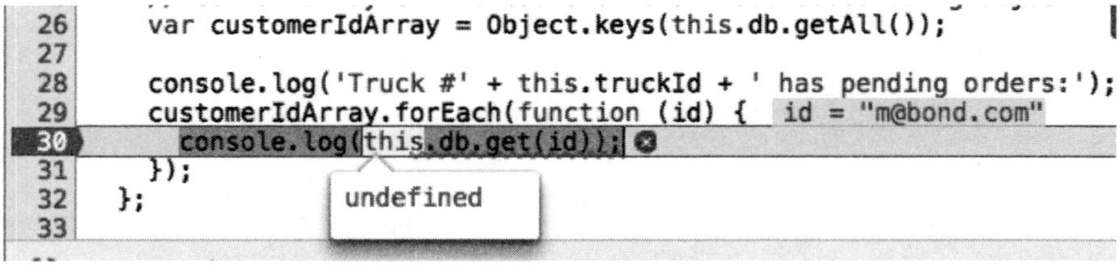

```
26      var customerIdArray = Object.keys(this.db.getAll());
27
28      console.log('Truck #' + this.truckId + ' has pending orders:');
29      customerIdArray.forEach(function (id) {    id = "m@bond.com"
30          console.log(this.db.get(id)); ⊘
31      });
32  };
33
```
undefined

To the right of the code is the scope panel, which contains a list of variables available. You can see that values for `id` and `this` are shown – and, again, that `this` is `undefined` (Figure 8.26).

Figure 8.26 Variable values shown in scope panel

```
▼ Scope
▼ Local
     id: "m@bond.com"
     this: undefined
 ▶ Global                    Window
```

Click the blue ▐▶ button at the top of the right hand panel (Figure 8.27). This unpauses your code, allowing it to resume execution.

Figure 8.27 Debugger control panel

Before moving on, remove the breakpoint by clicking the blue line number again. The blue indicator will disappear (Figure 8.28).

Figure 8.28 Click the line number to toggle a breakpoint

Now, it is time to fix that pesky bug!

Setting the value of this with bind

In JavaScript, the keyword `this` inside of a function is automatically assigned a value when you call that function. For constructor functions and for prototype methods, the value of `this` is the instance object. The instance is called the *owner* of the function call. Using the keyword `this` gives you access to the properties of the owner.

As we said earlier, for callback functions `this` is not automatically assigned to an object. You can manually specify what object should be the owner by using a function's **bind** method. (Remember that JavaScript functions are actually objects and can have their own properties and methods, such as **bind**.)

The **bind** method accepts an object argument and returns a new version of the function. When you call the new version, it will use the object argument passed in to **bind** as the value of `this` inside of the function's body.

Inside the **forEach** callback, `this` is undefined because the callback has no owner. Fix that by calling **bind** and passing it a reference to the **Truck** instance.

Add the call to **bind** in truck.js.

```
...
  Truck.prototype.printOrders = function () {
    var customerIdArray = Object.keys(this.db.getAll());

    console.log('Truck #' + this.truckId + ' has pending orders:');
    customerIdArray.forEach(function (id) {
      console.log(this.db.get(id));
    }.bind(this));
  };
...
```

Outside the body of the **forEach** callback, the keyword this refers to the **Truck** instance. By adding `.bind(this)` immediately after the anonymous function – but inside the parentheses for the **forEach** call – you are passing **forEach** a modified version of the anonymous function. This modified version uses the **Truck** instance as its owner.

Save and confirm that the orders are printed correctly. You will need to re-declare myTruck and run **createOrder** again.

Your output should look like Figure 8.29.

Figure 8.29 **printOrders** works after using **bind(this)**

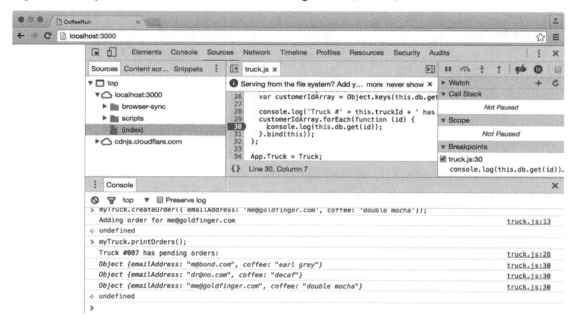

Initializing CoffeeRun on Page Load

Your **DataStore** and **Truck** modules work correctly. You have been able to instantiate a new **Truck** on the console, supplying it a new **DataStore** as part of its creation.

Now you are going to create a module that performs these same steps when the page loads. Create a scripts/main.js file and add a <script> tag to index.html.

```html
<!doctype html>
<html>
  <head>
    <meta charset="utf-8">
    <title>coffeerun</title>
  </head>
  <body>
    <script src="scripts/datastore.js" charset="utf-8"></script>>
    <script src="scripts/truck.js" charset="utf-8"></script>>
    <script src="scripts/main.js" charset="utf-8"></script>
  </body>
</html>
```

Save `index.html`. You are going to add an IIFE to `main.js`, as you have done with the other modules, but this time you will not need to export any new properties to `window.App`. Set up `main.js` as shown:

```
(function (window) {
  'use strict';
  var App = window.App;
  var Truck = App.Truck;
  var DataStore = App.DataStore;
})(window);
```

The job of this module is to receive the `window` object for use inside the function body. It also retrieves the constructors you defined as part of the `window.App` namespace.

Technically, you can just write all of your code with the full names (e.g., `App.Truck` and `App.DataStore`), but your code is more readable when you have shorter names.

Creating the Truck instance

Now, just as you did on the console, you will create an instance of **Truck**, providing it an `id` and an instance of **DataStore**.

Call the **Truck** constructor in `main.js`, passing it an `id` of `ncc-1701` and a new instance of **DataStore**.

```
(function (window) {
  'use strict';
  var App = window.App;
  var Truck = App.Truck;
  var DataStore = App.DataStore;
  var myTruck = new Truck('ncc-1701', new DataStore());
})(window);
```

This is nearly the same as the code you entered in the console earlier, but you do not need to prefix **Truck** or **DataStore** with `App`, because you created local variables that point to `App.Truck` and `App.DataStore`.

At this point, your application code is nearly complete. However, you still cannot interact with the instance of **Truck**. Why not? The variable is declared inside of a function, the `main` module. Functions protect their variables from being accessed by code outside of the function, including code you write on the console.

So that you can interact with the instance of **Truck**, export it to the global namespace in `main.js`.

```
(function (window) {
  'use strict';
  var App = window.App;
  var Truck = App.Truck;
  var DataStore = App.DataStore;
  var myTruck = new Truck('ncc-1701', new DataStore());
  window.myTruck = myTruck;
})(window);
```

Save your work and go back to the console. Reload the page manually to make sure that any prior work you did in the console has been cleared out.

Start typing `myTruck` and you should see that the console is trying to autocomplete it (Figure 8.30). That means that it found the `myTruck` variable that you exported as a property of the `window` object.

Figure 8.30 The console finds myTruck in the global namespace

Call **myTruck.createOrder** a few times, providing it some test data. You can do this easily by letting the console autocomplete your previous calls to **createOrder** (Figure 8.31).

Figure 8.31 Console autocompleting previous calls to **createOrder**

Alternatively, enter the following code to confirm that everything functions as expected.

```
myTruck.createOrder({ emailAddress: 'me@goldfinger.com', coffee: 'double mocha'});
myTruck.createOrder({ emailAddress: 'dr@no.com', coffee: 'decaf'});
myTruck.createOrder({ emailAddress: 'm@bond.com', coffee: 'earl grey'});
myTruck.printOrders();
myTruck.deliverOrder('dr@no.com');
myTruck.deliverOrder('m@bond.com');
myTruck.printOrders();
```

After exercising the methods **createOrder**, **printOrders**, and **deliverOrder**, you should see something like Figure 8.32.

Figure 8.32 One busy coffee truck

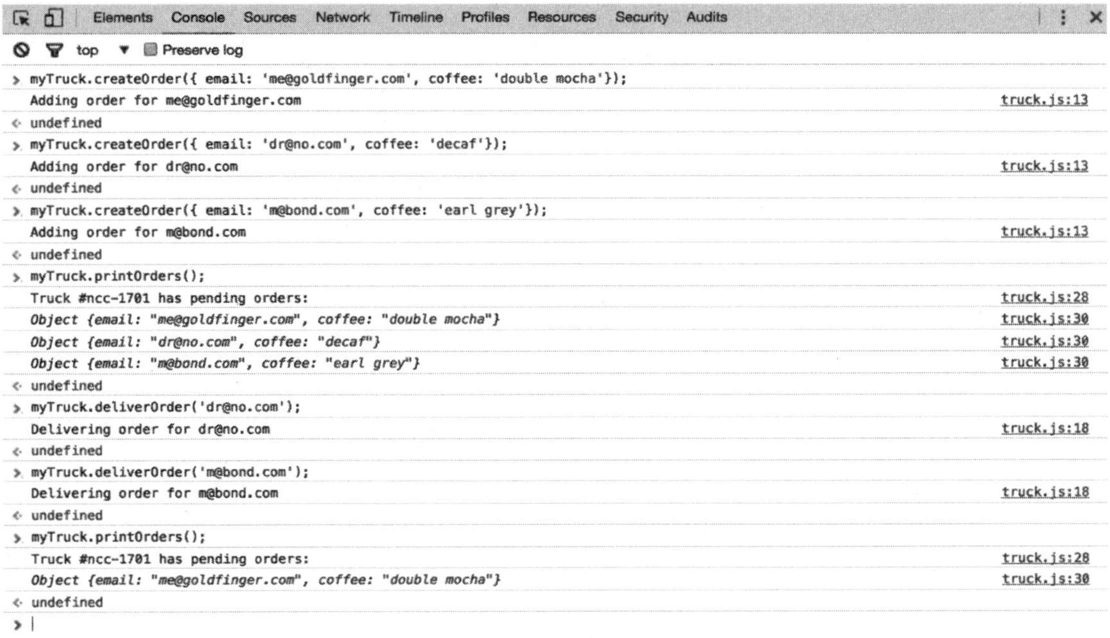

Congratulations! You have completed the foundation of CoffeeRun. It does not have a UI yet, but you will add that in upcoming chapters. And you will not need to make changes to the core, because the UI will simply call the `Truck.prototype` methods you have already written and tested.

This is the advantage of the modular approach: You can work on your application in layers, knowing that each new layer is built on working code in the underlying modules.

Bronze Challenge: Truck ID for Non-Trekkies

In main.js, pass in a different string for the truckId.

(Some good options include "Serenity," "KITT," or "Galactica." "HAL" is probably a bad idea.)

For the More Curious: Private Module Data

Inside a module, your constructors and prototype methods have access to any variables declared inside the IIFE. As an alternative to adding properties to the prototype, this is a way to share data between instances but make it hidden from any code outside the module. It looks like this:

```
(function (window) {
  'use strict';
  var App = window.App || {};
  var launchCount = 0;

  function Spaceship() {
    // Initialization code goes here
  }

  Spaceship.prototype.blastoff = function () {
    // Closure scope allows access to the launchCount variable
    launchCount++;
    console.log('Spaceship launched!')
  }

  Spaceship.prototype.reportLaunchCount = function () {
    console.log('Total number of launches: ' + launchCount);
  }

  App.Spaceship = Spaceship
  window.App = App;
})(window);
```

Other languages provide a way to declare a variable as *private*, but JavaScript does not. You can take advantage of closure scope (a function using variables declared in the outer scope) to simulate private variables.

Silver Challenge: Making data Private

Update your **DataStore** module so that the data property is private to the module.

Are there any reasons you would *not* want to do this? What happens if you declare multiple instances of **DataStore**?

For the More Curious: Setting this in forEach's Callback

We told a small fib earlier. Using **bind** is not the *only* way to set the value of this for the callback to **forEach**.

Look at the documentation for **Array.prototype.forEach** on MDN (developer.mozilla.org/en-US/docs/Web/JavaScript/Reference/Global_Objects/Array/forEach). You can see that **forEach** takes an optional second argument, which it will use as the value of this in the callback.

That means that you could have also written the **printOrders** method like so:

```
...
Truck.prototype.printOrders = function () {
  var customerIdArray = Object.keys(this.db.getAll());

  console.log('Truck #' + this.truckId + ' has pending orders:');
  customerIdArray.forEach(function (id) {
    console.log(this.db.get(id));
  }, this);
};
...
```

bind, however, is a useful method that you will see again in the coming chapters. **Truck.prototype.printOrders** provided a good opportunity to introduce you to the syntax.

9

Introduction to Bootstrap

In this chapter, you will create the HTML markup for your UI. You will use the styles provided by the popular Bootstrap CSS framework to give your UI a bit of polish without having to create the CSS yourself. This way, you can focus on the application logic in JavaScript, which you will do in Chapter 10.

You will be creating the UI for the CoffeeRun app in two parts. The first consists of a form into which a user can enter a coffee order with all of its details (Figure 9.1). In the second part, the existing coffee orders will be displayed in a checklist. Each of these parts will have a corresponding JavaScript module to handle user interaction.

Figure 9.1 CoffeeRun styled with Bootstrap

Adding Bootstrap

The Bootstrap CSS library provides a collection of styles that you can use for your sites and applications. Because of its popularity, you may not want to use Bootstrap for your user-facing production site without making some customizations. Otherwise, your site may end up looking like everyone else's. However, Bootstrap is great for quickly creating good-looking prototypes.

As you did with normalize.css in Ottergram, you will get Bootstrap by loading it from cdnjs.com. Use version 3.3.6 of Bootstrap, which is at cdnjs.com/libraries/twitter-bootstrap/3.3.6. (To find the most current version for your own projects, search cdnjs.com for "twitter bootstrap.")

Make sure to get the link for bootstrap.min.css (Figure 9.2), not one for the theme or fonts.

Figure 9.2 cdnjs.com page for twitter-bootstrap

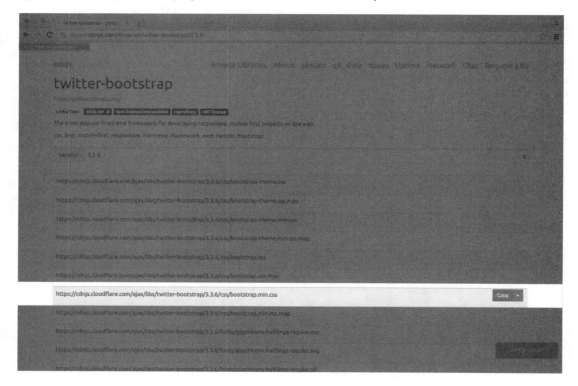

After you have copied the link, open index.html and add a <link> tag with the URL. (Although we had to wrap the href attribute around to a second line to fit on this page, you should enter it on one line.)

```
...
  <head>
    <meta charset="utf-8">
    <title>coffeerun</title>
    <link rel="stylesheet" href="https://cdnjs.cloudflare.com/ajax/libs/twitter-bootst
rap/3.3.6/css/bootstrap.min.css">
  </head>
...
```

How Bootstrap works

Bootstrap can provide out-of-the-box responsive styling for your website or web app. Most of the time, you will just need to include the CSS file and then add classes to your markup. One of the main classes you will use is the container class.

Add the container class to your <body> element in index.html. While you are there, add a header to your page as well.

```
...
    <title>coffeerun</title>
    <link rel="stylesheet" href="https://cdnjs.cloudflare.com/ajax/libs/twitter-bootst
rap/3.3.6/css/bootstrap.min.css">
  </head>
  <body>
  <body class="container">
    <header>
      <h1>CoffeeRun</h1>
    </header>
    <script src="scripts/datastore.js" charset="utf-8"></script>
    <script src="scripts/truck.js" charset="utf-8"></script>
    <script src="scripts/main.js" charset="utf-8"></script>
  </body>
</html>
```

The container class acts as a wrapper for all the content that needs to adapt to the size of the viewport. This provides basic responsive behavior to the layout.

Save index.html, make sure browser-sync is running, and view your page. It should resemble Figure 9.3.

Figure 9.3 Header styled with Bootstrap

Although there is not much to your page yet, notice that there is already a comfortable amount of padding around your header and that it has a font style applied to it.

Bootstrap has styles for a huge number of different visual elements. CoffeeRun will just scratch the surface, but you will get a chance to explore more styles in a later chapter. For now, it is time to add the markup for the order form.

Creating the Order Form

Add a `<section>` tag, two `<div>`s, and a `<form>` to `index.html`, below the `<header>` element you just created.

```
...
    <header>
      <h1>CoffeeRun</h1>
    </header>
    <section>
      <div class="panel panel-default">
        <div class="panel-body">
          <form data-coffee-order="form">
            <!-- Input elements will go here -->
          </form>
        </div>
      </div>
    </section>
    <script src="scripts/datastore.js" charset="utf-8"></script>
...
```

The `<form>` tag is going to be where all the important stuff happens. You gave it a `data-coffee-order` attribute with the value `form`. In CoffeeRun, you will use data attributes for accessing DOM elements from JavaScript, just as you did in Ottergram.

For layout, you added two `<div>` tags. It is not important that you use `<div>` tags, specifically. What is important is that you are applying the `panel`, `panel-default`, and `panel-body` classes to them. These are Bootstrap classes that will trigger styles for you.

Remember, `<div>`s are just general-purpose block-level containers for other markup. They take up as much horizontal space as provided by their containing parent element. They will be used often in CoffeeRun, and you will see them throughout the examples in the Bootstrap documentation.

You may be wondering why the `<section>` tag wraps around your `<div>` and `<form>` tags. `<div>`s have no semantic meaning. `<section>`s do: they logically group other markup. This one will house the UI for the form. You could easily have another `<section>` of the page that is for some other piece of the UI.

Adding text input fields

The main piece of information that you care about is the coffee order itself. If you have been in a coffee shop in the last decade, you know how complicated orders can get. For now, you will use a single-line text field to represent an order. Later you will add more fields to capture more information about the order.

When you use Bootstrap for your forms, you add extra `<div>` elements that are solely for applying styles defined in the Bootstrap library.

Add another `<div>` to `index.html` with the class `form-group`. The `form-group` Bootstrap class provides consistent vertical spacing for form elements. Then add `<label>` and `<input>` elements.

```
...
      <div class="panel panel-default">
        <div class="panel-body">
          <form data-coffee-order="form">
            <!-- Input elements will go here -->
            <div class="form-group">
              <label>Coffee Order</label>
              <input class="form-control" name="coffee">
            </div>
          </form>
        </div>
      </div>
...
```

The `form-control` class is another one defined by Bootstrap. It provides layout and typography styling for your form elements.

Save `index.html` and check the results in the browser (Figure 9.4).

Figure 9.4 Input field for a coffee order

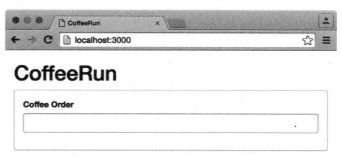

Your `<input>` element defaults to a single-line text field. Other than its `form-control` class, it has one attribute: `name`. When a form is submitted, the data will be sent to a server, and the `name` attribute will be sent with that data. If you think about form data as a key/value pair, then the `name` attribute is the key and the data that the user types in the field is the value.

Linking a label and a form element

`<label>` tags are important usability enhancements for your form elements. You tell a `<label>` what form element it is labeling by setting its `for` attribute to match the `id` attribute of the form element.

In `index.html`, add `for` and `id` attributes to your `<label>` and `<input>` form elements, respectively. Give both attributes the same `coffeeOrder` value.

```
...
      <div class="panel panel-default">
        <div class="panel-body">
          <form data-coffee-order="form">
            <div class="form-group">
              <label for="coffeeOrder">Coffee Order</label>
              <input class="form-control" name="coffee" id="coffeeOrder">
            </div>
          </form>
        </div>
      </div>
...
```

When a `<label>` is linked to a form element, you can click the `<label>`'s text on the page and it will make the linked form element active. You should always link your `<label>`s to their form elements.

To see this in action, save `index.html`, switch to the browser, and click the **Coffee Order** label text. The `<input>` should gain focus, ready for you to start typing (Figure 9.5).

Figure 9.5 Clicking the linked label causes the input to gain focus

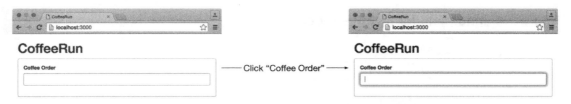

Adding autofocus

Because this is the first field on the screen, you want the user to be able to enter text in it as soon as the page loads, instead of having to click.

To achieve this, add an `autofocus` attribute to the `<input>` in `index.html`.

```
...
          <div class="form-group">
            <label for="coffeeOrder">Coffee Order</label>
            <input class="form-control" name="coffee" id="coffeeOrder" autofocus>
          </div>
...
```

Save your changes to index.html and return to the browser. You will see that the text input field has a cursor and a highlight as soon as the page loads (Figure 9.6).

Figure 9.6 Input field with autofocus on page load

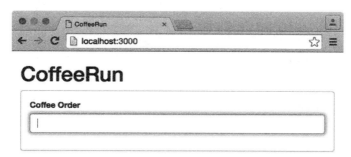

Notice that the autofocus attribute does not have a value. It does not need one. The mere presence of the autofocus attribute in an <input> tag tells the browser to activate that field. The autofocus attribute is a *Boolean* attribute, which means that its only possible values are true and false. You only need to add the attribute name to the tag in order to set its value. When it is present, it has the value true. When it is not present, the attribute is considered false.

Adding an email input field

When you created your Truck and DataStore modules, you tracked orders by the customer's email address. Now you will capture that information using another <input> element.

Add another .form-group element to index.html with a <label> and an <input>. For the <input> element, set the type as email, the name to emailAddress, and the id to emailInput. Also, add a value attribute, set to an empty string. This ensures that this field is blank when the page loads. Finally, link the <input> and the <label> using the id.

```
...
        <form data-coffee-order="form">
          <div class="form-group">
            <label for="coffeeOrder">Coffee Order</label>
            <input class="form-control" name="coffee" id="coffeeOrder" autofocus>
          </div>
          <div class="form-group">
            <label for="emailInput">Email</label>
            <input class="form-control" type="email" name="emailAddress"
              id="emailInput" value="">
          </div>
        </form>
...
```

Save index.html and check the browser to see your new form field (Figure 9.7).

Figure 9.7 Input field for an email address

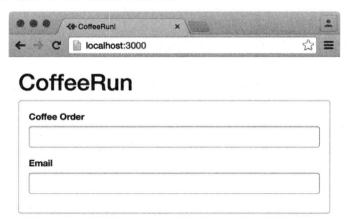

Showing example input with placeholder text

Sometimes users appreciate a suggestion about what they should enter into a text field. To create example text, use the `placeholder` attribute.

Add a `placeholder` attribute to your new `<input>` element in `index.html`.

```
...
        <div class="form-group">
          <label for="emailInput">Email</label>
          <input class="form-control" type="email" name="emailAddress"
            id="emailInput" value="" placeholder="dr@who.com">
        </div>
...
```

Save your file. The result will look like Figure 9.8.

Figure 9.8 Placeholder text in the email input

The value of the `placeholder` attribute appears in the text field until the user enters some text, at which point it disappears. If the user deletes all of the text in the field, the placeholder text appears again.

Offering choices with radio buttons

Next, you want the user to be able to specify the size of their coffee drink. They should be able to choose between short, tall, and grande – and they should not be able to choose more than one size. For this kind of data input, you can use `<input>` fields whose `type` attribute is set to `radio`.

The markup for your radio buttons will be different from your other `<input>` fields. Each radio button will have an `<input>` field, *wrapped* by a `<label>` element. The `<label>` will be wrapped in a `<div>` whose `class` is *also* `radio`.

The `<label>` elements will not need the `for` attribute that you added to the `<label>`s for the coffee order and email. Because the `<input>` is wrapped with the `<label>`, they are automatically linked.

In case you are wondering why the HTML is different for radio buttons, it is because Bootstrap styles them differently from the other form elements.

When writing your own code, you can choose to wrap an `<input>` element in a `<label>` or to use the `for` attribute – both are correct. But, when you use Bootstrap, you must follow its patterns and conventions for the styles to work as expected. Refer to the Bootstrap documentation for examples of how to structure your HTML (`getbootstrap.com/css/#forms`).

In `index.html`, add the markup for your radio buttons just after the email `<input>`.

```
...
        <div class="form-group">
          <label for="emailInput">Email</label>
          <input class="form-control" type="email" name="emailAddress"
            id="emailInput" value="" placeholder="dr@who.com">
        </div>
        <div class="radio">
          <label>
            <input type="radio" name="size" value="short">
            Short
          </label>
        </div>
        <div class="radio">
          <label>
            <input type="radio" name="size" value="tall" checked>
            Tall
          </label>
        </div>
        <div class="radio">
          <label>
            <input type="radio" name="size" value="grande">
            Grande
          </label>
        </div>
      </form>
...
```

You gave all three of your radio inputs the same value for the `name` attribute (`size`). This tells the browser that only one of them can be selected (or "checked") at a time. You gave the Tall radio button a Boolean attribute named `checked`. This works the same way that `autofocus` does: When it is present, the value of the attribute is `true` and when it is absent it is `false`.

Save `index.html` and take a look at your new radio buttons (Figure 9.9).

Figure 9.9 Radio buttons for coffee sizes

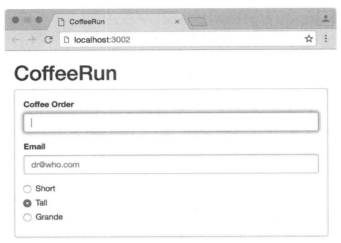

Try clicking either a radio button or the text next to it. Either way, that radio button should indicate that it was selected.

Adding a dropdown menu

Some folks are crazy for flavored coffee. You want to give them the option to choose from a few different flavors. By default, no flavor shot will be added.

You could use a set of radio buttons for this, but you might add many more flavors to the list. To make sure that the flavor choices do not clutter up the UI, you will use a dropdown menu.

To create a dropdown menu styled with Bootstrap, add a <div> to index.html with the class form-group. Create a <select> element with the class form-control. Bootstrap will style this element as a dropdown. Link it to its <label> with the id flavorShot. Inside of the <select>, add an <option> element for each of the menu items you want to display, giving each of them a matching value.

```
...
            <div class="radio">
              <label>
                <input type="radio" name="size" value="grande">
                Grande
              </label>
            </div>
            <div class="form-group">
              <label for="flavorShot">Flavor Shot</label>
              <select id="flavorShot" class="form-control" name="flavor">
                <option value="">None</option>
                <option value="caramel">Caramel</option>
                <option value="almond">Almond</option>
                <option value="mocha">Mocha</option>
              </select>
            </div>
          </form>
        </div>
      </div>
...
```

Each of the <option> elements provides one of the possible values, while the <select> element specifies the name.

Save index.html and check that your dropdown is displayed with all of the options you added (Figure 9.10).

Figure 9.10 Coffee flavor dropdown

By default, the first <option> element is selected. You can also add the selected Boolean attribute to an option element, if you want one other than the first to be selected automatically.

You set the value attribute to an empty string for the first dropdown item. If you left off the value attribute completely, the browser would have used the string "None" as the value. It is best to set the value attribute, as you should never assume that browsers will do what you expect.

Adding a range slider

Not everyone wants a killer coffee buzz. You want to let users choose a value between 0 and 100 for the strength of their coffee. On the other hand, you do not want them to have to type in an exact value.

For this, add an <input> element in index.html whose type is range. This creates a *range slider*. The <input> and <label> should be linked and wrapped in a <div> with the form-group class. Go easy on your coffee customers and provide a default value of 30.

```
...
            <option value="mocha">Mocha</option>
          </select>
        </div>
        <div class="form-group">
          <label for="strengthLevel">Caffeine Rating</label>
          <input name="strength" id="strengthLevel" type="range" value="30">
        </div>
      </form>
...
```

Save `index.html` and try out your new slider in the browser. It will look like Figure 9.11.

Figure 9.11 Slider for caffeine strength

Adding Submit and Reset buttons

The last thing to do in the markup is to add a Submit button. As a usability convenience, you should also add a Reset button to clear the form, in case the user wants to start over.

Normally, Submit buttons are just an <input> element whose type is submit. Likewise, Reset buttons are <input> elements whose type is reset. However, to take advantage of Bootstrap's CSS, you will use a <button> element instead.

In `index.html`, add two <button> elements with the class names btn btn-default. Set the type of the first one to submit, and set the type of the second one to reset. In between the opening and closing tags, put Submit and Reset as descriptive text.

```
...
        <div class="form-group">
          <label for="strengthLevel">Caffeine Rating</label>
          <input name="strength" id="strengthLevel" type="range" value="30">
        </div>
        <button type="submit" class="btn btn-default">Submit</button>
        <button type="reset" class="btn btn-default">Reset</button>
      </form>
...
```

When you save your changes, your browser will add the buttons at the bottom of the form (Figure 9.12).

Figure 9.12 Submit and Reset buttons

Your Submit button will not do anything yet. That is coming in the next chapter. However, your Reset button will reset the values to their defaults.

These buttons have a pair of classes that might seem redundant. This is a convention of Bootstrap and is purely for styling. The `btn` class provides all of the standard visual properties of a Bootstrap button. This includes rounded corners and padding. The `btn-default` class adds a white background color.

You have used the Bootstrap UI framework to style your CoffeeRun app. By applying Bootstrap's pattern of markup and class names, your app will have a consistent look and feel for a variety of screen sizes and browser versions.

To learn more about what Bootstrap has to offer, look through the excellent documentation at `getbootstrap.com/css`.

Bootstrap is particularly good for quickly styling an app while you focus on the application logic. In the next chapters, you will do just that.

10

Processing Forms with JavaScript

CoffeeRun is off to a good start. It has two JavaScript modules that handle its internal logic and an HTML form styled with **Bootstrap**. In this chapter, you will write a more complex module that connects the form to the logic, allowing you to use the form to enter coffee orders.

Recall from Chapter 2 that browsers communicate with servers by sending requests for information for a particular URL. Specifically, for every file that the browser needs to load, it sends a GET request to the server for that file.

When the browser needs to send information *to* a server, such as when a user fills out and submits a form, the browser takes the form data and puts it in a POST request. The server receives the request, processes the data, and then sends back a response (Figure 10.1).

Figure 10.1 Traditional server-side form processing

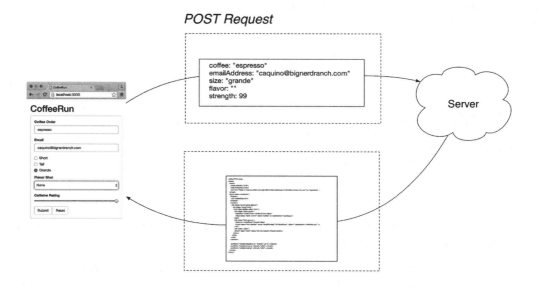

In CoffeeRun, you will not need to send the form data to a server for processing. Your **Truck** and **DataStore** modules serve the same purpose as traditional server-side code. Their job is to handle the business logic and data storage for your application.

Because this code lives in the browser and not on a server, you need to capture the data from the form before it goes out. In this chapter you will create a new module called **FormHandler** to do just that. In addition, you will add the jQuery library to CoffeeRun to help you with your work. As you build out CoffeeRun over the next few chapters, you will use more of jQuery's powerful features.

Creating the FormHandler Module

The **FormHandler** module will prevent the browser from trying to send form data to a server. Instead, it will read the values from the form when the user clicks the Submit button. Then it will send that data to a **Truck** instance, using the **createOrder** method you wrote in Chapter 8 (Figure 10.2).

Figure 10.2 Application architecture of CoffeeRun with **App.FormHandler**

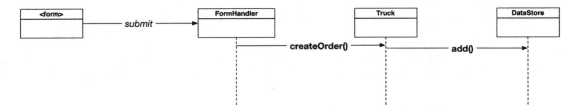

Create a new file called formhandler.js in your scripts folder and add a <script> tag for it in index.html.

```
...
        </form>
      </div>
    </div>
  </section>
  <script src="scripts/formhandler.js" charset="utf-8"></script>
  <script src="scripts/datastore.js" charset="utf-8"></script>
  <script src="scripts/truck.js" charset="utf-8"></script>
  <script src="scripts/main.js" charset="utf-8"></script>
  </body>
</html>
```

Like your other modules, **FormHandler** will use an IIFE to encapsulate the code and attach a constructor to the window.App property.

Open scripts/formhandler.js and create an IIFE. Inside the IIFE, create an App variable. Assign it the existing value of window.App. If window.App does not exist yet, assign it an empty object literal. Declare a **FormHandler** constructor function, and export it to the window.App property.

```
(function (window) {
  'use strict';
  var App = window.App || {};

  function FormHandler() {
    // Code will go here
  }

  App.FormHandler = FormHandler;
  window.App = App;

})(window);
```

So far, this code follows the familiar pattern you used in your **Truck** and **DataStore** modules. It will be different soon, though, in that it will import and use jQuery to do its work.

Introduction to jQuery

The jQuery library was created by John Resig in 2006. It is one of the most popular general-purpose open-source JavaScript libraries. Among other things, it provides convenient shorthands for DOM manipulation, element creation, server communication, and event handling.

It is useful to be familiar with jQuery, because there is so much code that has been written using it. Also, many libraries have copied jQuery's conventions. In fact, jQuery has directly influenced the standard DOM API (document.querySelector and document.querySelectorAll are two examples of this influence).

jQuery will not be covered in depth right now. Instead, aspects of it will be introduced as needed to help you build more complex parts of CoffeeRun. Should you want to explore jQuery further, check out the documentation at jquery.com.

As you did with Bootstrap, you will add a copy of jQuery to your project from cdnjs.com. Go to cdnjs.com/libraries/jquery to find version 2.1.4 and copy its address. (There may be a more recent version available, but you should use 2.1.4 for CoffeeRun to avoid any compatibility issues.)

Add jQuery in a <script> tag in index.html.

```
...
    </div>
  </section>
  <script src="https://cdnjs.cloudflare.com/ajax/libs/jquery/2.1.4/jquery.min.js"
    charset="utf-8"></script>
  <script src="scripts/formhandler.js" charset="utf-8"></script>
  <script src="scripts/datastore.js" charset="utf-8"></script>
  <script src="scripts/truck.js" charset="utf-8"></script>
  <script src="scripts/main.js" charset="utf-8"></script>
...
```

Save index.html.

Importing jQuery

FormHandler will import jQuery the same way that it is importing App. The reason for doing this is to make it explicit that your module is using code that is defined elsewhere. This is a best practice for coordinating with team members and for future maintenance.

In formhandler.js, create a local variable named $ and then assign it the value window.jQuery.

```
(function (window) {
  'use strict';
  var App = window.App || {};
  var $ = window.jQuery;

  function FormHandler() {
    // Code will go here
  }

  App.FormHandler = FormHandler;
  window.App = App;

})(window);
```

When you added the jQuery `<script>` tag, it created a function named **jQuery** as well as a variable, named $, pointing to the function. Most developers prefer to use $ in their code. In keeping with that practice, you are importing window.jQuery and assigning it to the local variable $.

Wondering why $ is used for the variable name? JavaScript variable names can contain letters, numbers, the underscore (_), or the dollar sign ($). (They can only *start* with letters, underscores, or dollar signs, though – not numbers.) The creator of jQuery chose the $ variable name because it is short and unlikely to be used by any other code in a project.

Configuring instances of FormHandler with a selector

Your **FormHandler** module should be usable with any `<form>` element. To achieve this, the **FormHandler** constructor will be passed a selector matching the `<form>` element in index.html.

Update formhandler.js to add a parameter called selector to the **FormHandler** constructor. Throw an **Error** if it is not passed in.

```
(function (window) {
  'use strict';
  var App = window.App || {};
  var $ = window.jQuery;

  function FormHandler(selector) {
    // Code will go here
    if (!selector) {
      throw new Error('No selector provided');
    }
  }

  App.FormHandler = FormHandler;
  window.App = App;

})(window);
```

Error is a built-in type that lets you formally signal that there is an unexpected value or condition in your code. For now, your **Error** instance will simply print out your message on the console.

Save and try instantiating a new **FormHandler** object without passing it an argument (Figure 10.3). (Remember to start browser-sync, if it is not already running.)

Figure 10.3 Instantiating a **FormHandler** object without passing arguments

This is the first step in making **FormHandler** more reusable. In Ottergram, you created variables for the selectors you used in your DOM code. You will not be doing that with the **FormHandler** module. Instead, you will use the selector that was passed in to the constructor and use jQuery to find the matching elements.

jQuery is most often used for finding elements in the DOM. To do that, you call the jQuery **$** function and pass it a selector as a string. In fact, you use it the same way you have been using **document.querySelectorAll** (although jQuery works differently under the hood, as we will explain in a moment). It is common to refer to this as "selecting elements from the DOM" with jQuery.

Declare an instance variable named $formElement in formhandler.js. Then find a matching element in the DOM using that selector and assign the result to this.$formElement.

```
(function (window) {
  'use strict';
  var App = window.App || {};
  var $ = window.jQuery;

  function FormHandler(selector) {
    if (!selector) {
      throw new Error('No selector provided');
    }

    this.$formElement = $(selector);
  }

  App.FormHandler = FormHandler;
  window.App = App;

})(window);
```

Prefixing a variable with $ is a sign that the variable refers to elements selected using jQuery. This prefix is not a requirement when using jQuery, but it is a common convention used by many front-end developers.

When you use jQuery's **$** function to select elements, it does not return references to DOM elements, the way that **document.querySelectorAll** does. Instead, it returns a single object, and the *object* contains references to the selected elements. The object also has special methods for manipulating the collection of references. This object is called a "jQuery-wrapped selection" or "jQuery-wrapped collection."

Next, you want to make sure that the selection successfully retrieved an element from the DOM. jQuery will return an empty selection if it does not find anything – it will not throw an error if the selector does not match anything. You will need to check manually, because **FormHandler** cannot do its work without an element.

The `length` property of a jQuery-wrapped selection tells you how many elements were matched. Update `formhandler.js` to check the `length` property of `this.$formElement`. If it is 0, throw an `Error`.

```
(function (window) {
  'use strict';
  var App = window.App || {};
  var $ = window.jQuery;

  function FormHandler(selector) {
    if (!selector) {
      throw new Error('No selector provided');
    }

    this.$formElement = $(selector);
    if (this.$formElement.length === 0) {
      throw new Error('Could not find element with selector: ' + selector);
    }
  }

  App.FormHandler = FormHandler;
  window.App = App;

})(window);
```

Your **FormHandler** constructor can be configured to work with any <form> element based on the selector passed in. Also, it keeps a reference to that <form> element as an instance variable. This ensures that your code will not make make unnecessary trips to the DOM. This is a performance best practice. (The alternative is to call **$** over and over, which re-selects the same elements each time.)

Adding the submit Handler

The next step is for **FormHandler** to listen for the `submit` event on the <form> element and run a callback when it occurs.

To make the **FormHandler** module more reusable, you will not hardcode the `submit` handler code. You will instead write a method that accepts a function argument, adds the `submit` listener, and then calls the function argument inside that listener.

First, add a prototype method called **addSubmitHandler** to `formhandler.js`.

```
...
    if (this.$formElement.length === 0) {
      throw new Error('Could not find element with selector: ' + selector);
    }
  }

  FormHandler.prototype.addSubmitHandler = function () {
    console.log('Setting submit handler for form');
    // More code will go here
  };

  App.FormHandler = FormHandler;
...
```

Instead of using the **addEventListener** method as you did with Ottergram, you will use jQuery's **on** method. It is similar to **addEventListener** but provides added conveniences. For now, though, you will use it the same way you would use **addEventListener**. (You will take advantage of some of the extra conveniences in the next chapter.)

```
...
  if (this.$formElement.length === 0) {
    throw new Error('Could not find element with selector: ' + selector);
  }
}

FormHandler.prototype.addSubmitHandler = function () {
  console.log('Setting submit handler for form');
  // More code will go here
  this.$formElement.on('submit', function (event) {
    event.preventDefault();
  });
};
...
```

The **on** method accepts the name of the event and a callback to run when the event is triggered. Its callback should expect to receive the event object. You called **event.preventDefault** to ensure that submitting the form does not take the user away from the CoffeeRun page. (You did the same thing with the thumbnail links in Ottergram.)

Extracting the data

When the form is submitted, your code should read the user input from the form, then *do* something with that data. In the submit handler in formhandler.js, create a new variable named data. Assign it an object literal. It will hold the value of each element of the form.

```
...
  FormHandler.prototype.addSubmitHandler = function () {
    console.log('Setting submit handler for form');
    this.$formElement.on('submit', function (event) {
      event.preventDefault();

      var data = $(this).serializeArray();
      console.log(data);

    });
  };
...
```

Inside your submit handler callback, the this object is a reference to the form element. jQuery provides a convenience method (**serializeArray**) for getting the values from the form. In order to use **serializeArray**, you need to "wrap" the form using jQuery. Calling $(this) gives you a wrapped object, which has access to the **serializeArray** method.

serializeArray returns the form data as an array of objects. You are assigning that to a temporary variable named data and logging it to the console. To get an idea of what **serializeArray** looks like, save your file and run the following code in the console:

```
var fh = new App.FormHandler('[data-coffee-order="form"]');
fh.addSubmitHandler();
```

Next, fill out the form with some test data and click the Submit button. You should see the array printed to the console. Click the ▶ next to a couple of the Object items in the array. You should see something like Figure 10.4.

Figure 10.4 **serializeArray** returns form data as an array of objects

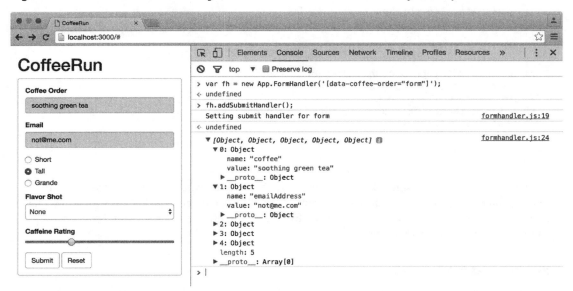

You can see that each object in the array has a key that corresponds to the name attribute of a <form> element and the user-supplied value for that element.

Now you can iterate through the array and copy the values from each element. Add a call to the **forEach** method to **serializeArray** in formhandler.js and pass it a callback. As the callback is run for each object in the array, it will use the object's name and value to create a new property on the data object.

```
...
  FormHandler.prototype.addSubmitHandler = function () {
    console.log('Setting submit handler for form');
    this.$formElement.on('submit', function (event) {
      event.preventDefault();

      var data = $(this).serializeArray(); {};
      $(this).serializeArray().forEach(function (item) {
        data[item.name] = item.value;
        console.log(item.name + ' is ' + item.value);
      });
      console.log(data);

    });
  };
...
```

To see this in action, save your changes and run your test code again in the console before filling out the form:

```
var fh = new App.FormHandler('[data-coffee-order="form"]');
fh.addSubmitHandler();
```

When you fill out the form and click the Submit button, you should see that the information you entered is copied to the data object and logged to the console (Figure 10.5).

Figure 10.5 Form data is copied in the iterator callback

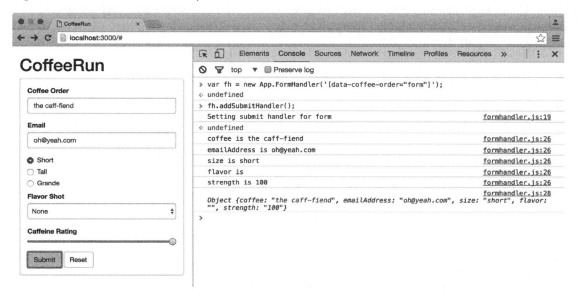

Accepting and calling a callback

Now that you have the form data as a single object, you need to pass that object to your **Truck** instance's **createOrder** method. But **FormHandler** has no access to the **Truck** instance. (And it would do no good to create a new **Truck** instance here.)

You can solve this by making **addSubmitHandler** accept a function parameter, which it can call inside the event handler.

In formhandler.js, add a parameter called fn.

```
...
  FormHandler.prototype.addSubmitHandler = function (fn) {
    console.log('Setting submit handler for form');
    this.$formElement.on('submit', function (event) {
      event.preventDefault();
...
```

The submit handler callback will be called any time the form's submit event is triggered in the browser. When that happens, you want the fn function to be called.

Call fn inside the submit handler callback in formhandler.js and pass it the data object that contains the user input.

```
...
  FormHandler.prototype.addSubmitHandler = function (fn) {
    ...
      console.log(data);
      fn(data);
    });
  };
...
```

Now, when a **FormHandler** instance is created, any callback can be passed to **addSubmitHandler**. From then on, when the form is submitted, the callback will be invoked and will be passed whatever data the user entered into the form.

Using FormHandler

In main.js, you need to instantiate a **FormHandler** instance and pass it the selector for the <form> element: [data-coffee-order="form"]. Create a variable at the top of main.js for this selector so that it can be reused if needed.

```
(function (window) {
  'use strict';
  var FORM_SELECTOR = '[data-coffee-order="form"]';
  var App = window.App;
...
```

Next, create a local variable called **FormHandler** and assign it to App.FormHandler.

```
(function (window) {
  'use strict';
  var FORM_SELECTOR = '[data-coffee-order="form"]';
  var App = window.App;
  var Truck = App.Truck;
  var DataStore = App.DataStore;
  var FormHandler = App.FormHandler;
  var myTruck = new Truck('ncc-1701', new DataStore());
  ...
```

At the end of the main.js module, call the **FormHandler** constructor and pass it the FORM_SELECTOR variable. This will make sure that the instance of **FormHandler** will work with the DOM element matching that selector. Assign the instance to a new variable called **FormHandler**.

```
...
  var Truck = App.Truck;
  var DataStore = App.DataStore;
  var FormHandler = App.FormHandler;
  var myTruck = new Truck('ncc-1701', new DataStore());
  window.myTruck = myTruck;
  var formHandler = new FormHandler(FORM_SELECTOR);

  formHandler.addSubmitHandler();
  console.log(formHandler);
})(window);
```

When you save your code and return to the browser, the console should report Setting submit handler for form, showing that **addSubmitHandler** was called when the page loaded. However, if you fill out and submit the form, you will get an error (Figure 10.6).

Figure 10.6 Calling **addSubmitHandler** on page load

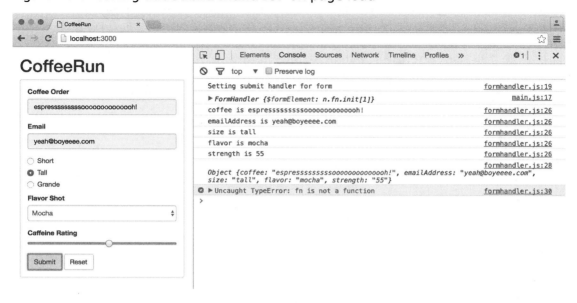

This is because you did not pass anything to **addSubmitHandler**. You will correct that in the next section.

Registering createOrder as a submit handler

You want **createOrder** to be called each time a submit event occurs. But you cannot just pass a reference to **createOrder** to **formHandler.addSubmitHandler**. This is because createOrder's *owner* changes when it is invoked inside of the event handling callback. With a different owner, the value of this inside the body of createOrder will not be the **Truck** instance, thus causing an error when createOrder runs.

Instead, you will pass a *bound reference* to **myTruck.createOrder** to **formHandler.addSubmitHandler**.

Update formhandler.js with this change. Make sure to **bind** the method reference so that its owner is guaranteed to be myTruck.

```
...
  window.myTruck = myTruck;
  var formHandler = new FormHandler(FORM_SELECTOR);

  formHandler.addSubmitHandler(myTruck.createOrder.bind(myTruck));
  console.log(formHandler);
})(window);
```

Could you have added **bind** to the definition of the original prototype method? When defining prototype methods, you have access to the instance, but only *inside* the method body. **bind** requires you to have a reference to the intended owner of the invocation – a reference that must be available outside of the method body. As you have no way of referencing the instance from outside the method body, you cannot **bind** the original prototype method.

Save and fill out your form. After you submit, you should be able to call `myTruck.printOrders` and see that the data you entered into the form has been added to the list of pending orders, as shown in Figure 10.7.

Figure 10.7 **createOrder** is called when the form is submitted

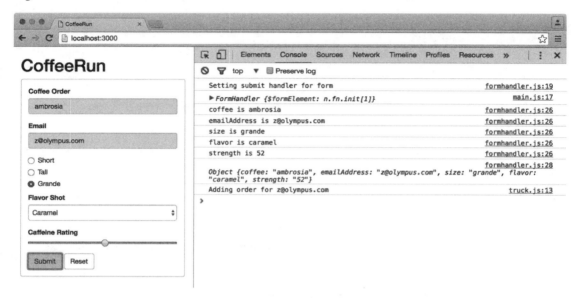

UI Enhancements

It would be nice if the form were cleared of its old data after it was submitted, so that the user could immediately start entering the next order. Resetting the form is as simple as calling the `<form>` element's **reset** method.

Find the `FormHandler.prototype.addSubmitHandler` method in `formhandler.js`. At the end of the `this.$formElement.on('submit'...)` callback, add a call to the form's **reset** method:

```
...
  FormHandler.prototype.addSubmitHandler = function (fn) {
    console.log('Setting submit handler for form');
    this.$formElement.on('submit', function (event) {
      event.preventDefault();

      var data = {};
      $(this).serializeArray().forEach(function (item) {
        data[item.name] = item.value;
        console.log(item.name + ' is ' + item.value);
      });
      console.log(data);
      fn(data);
      this.reset();
    });
  };
...
```

Save and enter some data into the form. When you submit the form, you should see that the data is cleared out.

Finally, add one last tweak to the UI. When a form field is ready for input, it has focus, as you saw in the last chapter. To set the focus on a specific form field, you can call its **focus** method. (The autofocus attribute you added to the coffee order field only takes effect when the page first loads.)

You can conveniently access the individual form fields via the form's elements property. The elements property is an array of the form's fields, which you can refer to by their indices, starting with 0.

In formhandler.js, right after the call to **this.reset** in the submit handler callback, invoke the **focus** method on the first field.

```
...
  FormHandler.prototype.addSubmitHandler = function (fn) {
    console.log('Setting submit handler for form');
    this.$formElement.on('submit', function (event) {
      event.preventDefault();

      var data = {};
      $(this).serializeArray().forEach(function (item) {
        data[item.name] = item.value;
        console.log(item.name + ' is ' + item.value);
      });
      console.log(data);
      fn(data);
      this.reset();
      this.elements[0].focus();
    });
  };
...
```

CoffeeRun is now jQuery-powered and can accept user input! You have bridged the gap between your HTML and your JavaScript modules. In the next chapter, you will complete the picture by creating interactive DOM elements based on the data captured from the form.

Bronze Challenge: Supersize It

Add another size option for coffee orders – one with an inspiringly large-sounding name, such as "Coffee-zilla."

Add a new order using this extra-large size and check your application data in the console to make sure it is being saved correctly.

Silver Challenge: Showing the Value as the Slider Changes

Create a handler for the slider's change event. As the value of the slider changes, show the number next to the label for the slider.

As an extra challenge, change the color of the number (or the label) to reflect the intensity of the caffeine strength. Use green for weaker coffee, yellow for regular strength coffee, and red for very strong coffee.

Gold Challenge: Adding Achievements

When users submit an order for the largest, strongest coffee with a flavor shot, unlock an achievement: Bring up a Bootstrap modal to inform them of their amazing intensity and commitment to flavor. Ask them if they would like to use their achievement, and, if so, add an additional form field that is only visible when their email address is entered in the email field. It should let them choose one or more power-up options for their coffee, like time travel, mind reading, or bug-free code.

Refer to the documentation at getbootstrap.com/javascript for information on how to include and trigger Bootstrap's modal behaviors. (You will need to add a <script> tag from cdnjs.com for Bootstrap's JavaScript code.)

11

From Data to DOM

In the last chapter, you built the **FormHandler** module. It serves as a bridge between the form that the user interacts with and the rest of your code. By intercepting its submit event, you supply the user's input to your **Truck** module, which saves it to its **DataStore** instance.

In this chapter, you will build the other piece of UI code, the **CheckList** module. Like the **Truck** module, it will receive data from the **FormHandler**, but its job is to add a checklist of pending orders to the page. When a checklist item is clicked, the **CheckList** will remove it from the page and signal the **Truck** to remove it from the **DataStore**. Figure 11.1 shows CoffeeRun equipped with its checklist of pending orders.

Figure 11.1 Keep those orders coming!

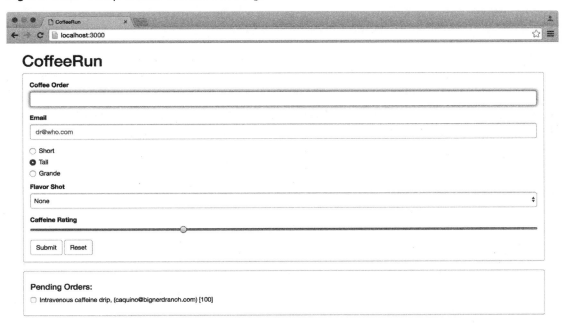

Setting Up the Checklist

You will continue to use Bootstrap classes for styling your form elements. Begin in index.html by adding a pair of <div> elements with the Bootstrap class names panel, panel-default, and panel-body, as you did for your coffee order form. Inside of them, add a header and another <div> that will hold the actual checklist items. This markup should be added after the <div>s that hold your form.

```
...
    <header>
      <h1>CoffeeRun</h1>
    </header>
    <section>
      <div class="panel panel-default">
        <div class="panel-body">
          <form data-coffee-order="form">
            ...
          </form>
        </div>
      </div>

      <div class="panel panel-default">
        <div class="panel-body">
          <h4>Pending Orders:</h4>
          <div data-coffee-order="checklist">
          </div>
        </div>
      </div>
    </section>
...
```

As before, you added <div>s to carry the styling provided by Bootstrap. The main part of your checklist is the [data-coffee-order="checklist"] element. It will be the target for the JavaScript that creates an individual coffee order checklist item and adds it to the DOM.

Save index.html, start browser-sync, and make sure CoffeeRun shows an empty Pending Orders area (Figure 11.2).

Figure 11.2 After adding the markup for the checklist items

Now you are ready to dive back into the JavaScript.

Creating the CheckList Module

Create a new file in your `scripts` folder called `checklist.js` and add a link to it in `index.html`:

```
...
    <script src="https://cdnjs.cloudflare.com/ajax/libs/jquery/2.1.4/jquery.js"
      charset="utf-8"></script>
    <script src="scripts/checklist.js" charset="utf-8"></script>
    <script src="scripts/formhandler.js" charset="utf-8"></script>
    <script src="scripts/datastore.js" charset="utf-8"></script>
    <script src="scripts/truck.js" charset="utf-8"></script>
    <script src="scripts/main.js" charset="utf-8"></script>
...
```

Save `index.html`. In `checklist.js`, add the standard module code using an IIFE. Import the App namespace and jQuery, assigning each to a local variable. Create a constructor for **CheckList**, making sure to confirm that there is a selector passed in and that the selector matches at least one element in the DOM. At the end of the IIFE, export the **CheckList** constructor as part of the App namespace.

```
(function (window) {
  'use strict';

  var App = window.App || {};
  var $ = window.jQuery;

  function CheckList(selector) {
    if (!selector) {
      throw new Error('No selector provided');
    }

    this.$element = $(selector);
    if (this.$element.length === 0) {
      throw new Error('Could not find element with selector: ' + selector);
    }
  }

  App.CheckList = CheckList;
  window.App = App;
})(window);
```

The **CheckList** module will need three methods to do its work. One will create a checklist item, including the checkbox and the text description. Think of this group of elements as a row in a table.

Another method will remove a row from the table. The third method will add a listener for `click` events, so that your code knows *when* to remove a row.

The first method you will tackle is the one to create a row for a new order. Figure 11.3 shows how **CheckList** will add checklist items to the page when the order form is submitted.

Figure 11.3 Order of events when the order form is submitted

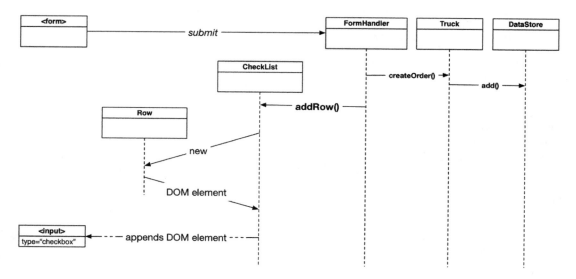

Creating the Row Constructor

You cannot create the markup in index.html for the checklist items, because they need to be added after the page has already been rendered, in response to form submissions. Instead, you will add a **Row** constructor to the **CheckList** module.

The **Row** constructor will be in charge of creating all the DOM elements necessary to represent a single coffee order, including the checkbox and text description. But the **Row** constructor will not be exported to the App namespace. It will only be used internally by one of the CheckList.prototype methods.

Add the **Row** constructor in checklist.js, just before the App.CheckList = CheckList; statement. It should accept an argument called coffeeOrder that will be the same data that is sent to **Truck.prototype.createOrder**.

```
...
    this.$element = $(selector);
    if (this.$element.length === 0) {
      throw new Error('Could not find element with selector: ' + selector);
    }
  }

  function Row(coffeeOrder) {
    // Constructor code will go here
  }

  App.CheckList = CheckList;
  window.App = App;
})(window);
```

Creating DOM elements with jQuery

Your **Row** constructor will use jQuery to build DOM elements. You will declare variables for the individual elements that make up a checklist item. Then the constructor will append them together into a *subtree* of DOM elements, as shown in Figure 11.4. The **CheckList** will take that subtree and attach it to the page's DOM tree as a child of the [data-coffee-order="checklist"] element.

Figure 11.4 **CheckList** creates a row and appends its DOM elements

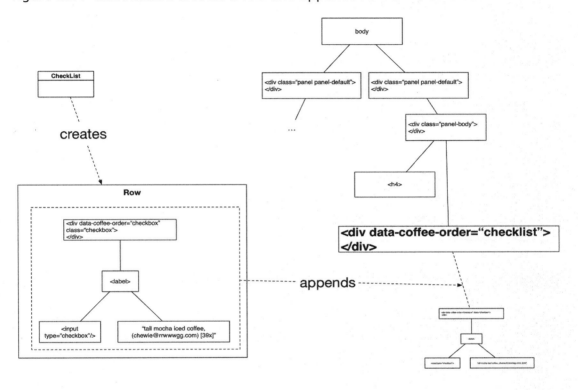

(The "[39x]" in the order description represents the caffeine strength.)

The DOM subtree created by the **Row** constructor in Figure 11.4 is the equivalent of the following markup:

```
<div data-coffee-order="checkbox" class="checkbox">
  <label>
    <input type="checkbox" value="chewie@rrwwwgg.com">
    tall mocha iced coffee, (chewie@rrwwwgg.com) [39x]
  </label>
</div>
```

A <div> with a checkbox class is used to house your <label> and an <input> element. The checkbox class will apply the appropriate Bootstrap styles to the <div>. The data-coffee-order attribute will be used in your JavaScript when you need to trigger the click action on the checkbox.

Note that the type attribute of your <input> is also checkbox. This tells the browser to draw the input as a checkbox form element. A plain text description of the order comes right after the <input>. The <label> wraps both the checkbox input and the plain text description. This turns the text and the input into a click target for the checkbox.

You will create the <label>, <div>, and <input> elements one at a time. Then you will manually place the elements inside of one another to create a DOM subtree that you will attach to the live DOM (the DOM tree currently shown on the page). You will also create a string that holds the text description of the order, like "tall mocha iced coffee, (chewie@rrwwwgg.com) [39x]."

To create these elements, you will use jQuery's **$** function. Up to now, you only used the **$** function to select elements from the DOM, but it can also be used to create them.

First, you are going to create the <div> by calling the **$** function in the **Row** constructor in checklist.js. Pass it two arguments describing the DOM element you want it to create. Make the first argument a string with the HTML tag of the DOM element, in this case '<div></div>'. Make the second argument an object that specifies the attributes that jQuery should add to the <div>. The key/value pairs of the object literal are translated into the attributes of the new element.

The result is a DOM element created by jQuery that you will assign to a new variable called $div. This will not be an instance variable (that is, it is just $div and not this.$div). It is prefixed with the $ to denote that it is not a plain DOM element, but one that jQuery created a reference to.

Make it so in checklist.js.

```
...
  function Row(coffeeOrder) {
    // Constructor code will go here
    var $div = $('<div></div>', {
      'data-coffee-order': 'checkbox',
      'class': 'checkbox'
    });
  }
...
```

Notice that your two property names are in single quotation marks. You might assume from this that you should always use single quotes around property names when creating a DOM element using jQuery, but actually that is not the case. Property names that have special characters (like the dash) need to be in quotes, otherwise it is considered a syntax error. Valid characters that can be used in a property name (or a variable name) without single quotes are the letters of the alphabet, numerical digits, the underscore (_), and the dollar sign ($).

'class' is in single quotes because "class" is a JavaScript-reserved word, so single quotes are needed to prevent the browser from reading it as JavaScript (which would also result in a syntax error).

Next, create the <label> element in checklist.js with the **$** function but without an object argument. It does not need any extra attributes.

```
...
  function Row(coffeeOrder) {
    var $div = $('<div></div>', {
      'data-coffee-order': 'checkbox',
      'class': 'checkbox'
    });

    var $label = $('<label></label>');
  }
...
```

Now, create the `<input>` element for the checkbox by calling the **$** function and passing it the HTML for an `<input>` tag. For the second argument, specify that the type should be a `checkbox` and that the `value` should be the email address of the customer. Because none of these property names use special characters, you do not need to put them in single quotes.

```
...
  function Row(coffeeOrder) {
    var $div = $('<div></div>', {
      'data-coffee-order': 'checkbox',
      'class': 'checkbox'
    });

    var $label = $('<label></label>');

    var $checkbox = $('<input></input>', {
      type: 'checkbox',
      value: coffeeOrder.emailAddress
    });
  }
...
```

By setting the `value` to the customer's email address, you are associating the checkbox with the customer's coffee order. Later, when you add the `click` handler, you can identify which coffee order was clicked based on the email address in the `value` attribute.

The last thing to create is the text description that will be displayed next to the checkbox. You will build a string for this by concatenating the pieces using the += operator.

Create a variable called `description` in `checklist.js`. Set it to the `size` property of the order, then add a comma and a space. If a flavor was provided, concatenate it using +=. Then concatenate the `coffee`, `emailAddress`, and `strength` values. The `emailAddress` should be wrapped in parentheses and the `strength` should be in brackets and followed by the letter "x." (The parentheses and brackets are not for syntactic purposes, just for formatting the text.)

```
...
  function Row(coffeeOrder) {
    ...

    var $checkbox = $('<input></input>', {
      type: 'checkbox',
      value: coffeeOrder.emailAddress
    });

    var description = coffeeOrder.size + ' ';
    if (coffeeOrder.flavor) {
      description += coffeeOrder.flavor + ' ';
    }

    description += coffeeOrder.coffee + ', ';
    description += ' (' + coffeeOrder.emailAddress + ')';
    description += ' [' + coffeeOrder.strength + 'x]';
  }
...
```

The += concatenation operator does addition and assignment in one step. That means that the following two lines of code are equivalent:

```
description += coffeeOrder.flavor + ' ';
description = description + coffeeOrder.flavor + ' ';
```

You now have all the individual parts of the checklist item and are ready to append them to one another (Figure 11.5).

Figure 11.5 Assembling the individual DOM elements into a subtree

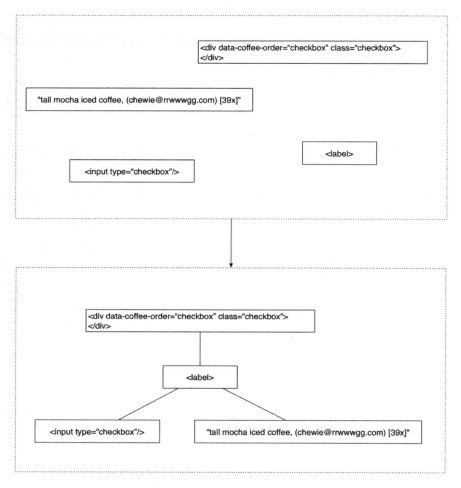

You will do this in three steps:

1. Append the $checkbox to the $label

2. Append the description to the $label

3. Append the $label to the $div

More generally, you will build the subtree by working from left to right, bottom to top. This approach is similar to how you developed your CSS for Ottergram in Chapter 3, by beginning with the smallest, innermost elements and working your way up.

In checklist.js, use the jQuery **append** method to connect the elements together. This method accepts either a DOM element or a jQuery-wrapped collection and adds it as a child element.

```
...
  function Row(coffeeOrder) {
    ...
    description += coffeeOrder.coffee + ', ';
    description += ' (' + coffeeOrder.emailAddress + ')';
    description += ' [' + coffeeOrder.strength + 'x]';

    $label.append($checkbox);
    $label.append(description);
    $div.append($label);
  }
...
```

Your **Row** constructor can now create and assemble the subtree of elements using the coffee order data passed in. However, because **Row** will be used as a constructor and not as a regular function, it cannot simply return this subtree. (In fact, constructors should *never* have a return statement; JavaScript automatically returns a value for you when you use the keyword new with a constructor.)

Instead, make the subtree available as a property of the instance by assigning it to this.$element in checklist.js. (This name was chosen just to follow the convention used with your other constructors; it does not have any special meaning by itself.)

```
...
  function Row(coffeeOrder) {
    ...
    $label.append($checkbox);
    $label.append(description);
    $div.append($label);

    this.$element = $div;
  }
...
```

The **Row** constructor is ready for work. It can build up the DOM subtree necessary to represent an individual coffee order with a checkbox. It holds on to that DOM representation in an instance variable.

Creating CheckList Rows on Submit

Next, you will add a method to **CheckList** that will use the **Row** constructor to create **Row** instances. It will append each **Row** instance's $element to the live DOM on the page.

In checklist.js, add a method to CheckList.prototype called **addRow**. It should accept an argument called coffeeOrder, which will be an object that contains all of the data for a single coffee order.

In this new method, create a new **Row** instance by calling the **Row** constructor and passing it the coffeeOrder object. Assign the new instance to the variable rowElement. Then, append the rowElement's $element property (which contains the DOM subtree) to the **CheckList** instance's $element property (which is a reference to the container for the checklist items).

```
...
  function CheckList(selector) {
    ...
  }

  CheckList.prototype.addRow = function (coffeeOrder) {
    // Create a new instance of a row, using the coffee order info
    var rowElement = new Row(coffeeOrder);

    // Add the new row instance's $element property to the checklist
    this.$element.append(rowElement.$element);
  };

  function Row(coffeeOrder) {
    ...
```

This is all you need to do to add the **Row**'s DOM subtree to the page. Save checklist.js.

In main.js, add a variable for the selector that matches the entire checklist area, [data-coffee-order="checklist"]. Then, import the **CheckList** module from the App namespace to a local variable, CHECKLIST_SELECTOR.

```
(function (window) {
  'use strict';
  var FORM_SELECTOR = '[data-coffee-order="form"]';
  var CHECKLIST_SELECTOR = '[data-coffee-order="checklist"]';
  var App = window.App;
  var Truck = App.Truck;
  var DataStore = App.DataStore;
  var FormHandler = App.FormHandler;
  var CheckList = App.CheckList;
  var myTruck = new Truck('ncc-1701', new DataStore());
...
```

Now you can instantiate a **CheckList** instance to add checklist items.

You might be tempted to just add another call to **formHandler.addSubmitHandler**, but this would not work the way you might expect. Why not? Each time you call **addSubmitHandler**, it registers a new callback that resets the form (by calling **this.reset**).

Consider the following code:

```
...
// Instantiate a new CheckList
var checkList = new CheckList(CHECKLIST_SELECTOR);

var formHandler = new FormHandler(FORM_SELECTOR);
formHandler.addSubmitHandler(myTruck.createOrder.bind(myTruck));

// This will not do what you want!
formHandler.addSubmitHandler(checkList.addRow.bind(checkList));
...
```

This code registers two callbacks that will run when the form is submitted. After the first submit handler (**myTruck.createOrder**) is called, the form gets reset. When the second submit handler (**checkList.addRow**) is called, there is no information left in the form. The result is that the data is added to the **DataStore**, but a checklist item does not get added to the page.

To get around this, you need to pass a single anonymous function to **formHandler.addSubmitHandler** and have that anonymous function call both **myTruck.createOrder** and **checkList.addRow**.

Also, each of these methods needs to be bound to a specific instance (meaning its this keyword needs to be set). You have been using **bind** to set the value of this, but you will use a different technique here.

Manipulating this with call

The **call** method works similarly to **bind** to set the value of this. The difference between the two is that while **bind** returns a new version of the function or method, it does not invoke it. **call** actually invokes the function or method and allows you to pass in the value of this as the first argument. (If you need to pass any other arguments to the function, you just add them to the argument list.) **call** runs the body of the function and returns any value that would normally be returned.

You need to use **call** instead of **bind** here because you need to invoke **myTruck.createOrder** and **checkList.addRow** in addition to setting the value of this.

In `main.js`, remove the existing invocation of **`formHandler.addSubmitHandler`**. Add a new call to **`formHandler.addSubmitHandler`** and pass it an anonymous function that expects a single argument, `data`. Inside the anonymous function, use the **`call`** methods of **`myTruck.createOrder`** and **`checkList.addRow`** to set the value of `this`, passing the `data` object as the second argument.

```
...
  var myTruck = new Truck('ncc-1701', new DataStore());
  window.myTruck = myTruck;
  var checkList = new CheckList(CHECKLIST_SELECTOR);
  var formHandler = new FormHandler(FORM_SELECTOR);

  formHandler.addSubmitHandler(myTruck.createOrder.bind(myTruck));
                              function (data) {
    console.log(formHandler);
    myTruck.createOrder.call(myTruck, data);
    checkList.addRow.call(checkList, data);
  });
})(window);
```

You have created a single `submit` handler function that invokes both **`createOrder`** and **`addRow`**. When it invokes them, it passes the correct value of `this` and the `data` from the form.

Save your changes and try out your checklist functionality in the browser by entering some data and submitting the form. When you submit each order, you will see it added to the Pending Orders checklist, as in Figure 11.6.

Figure 11.6 Submitting the form adds an item to the checklist

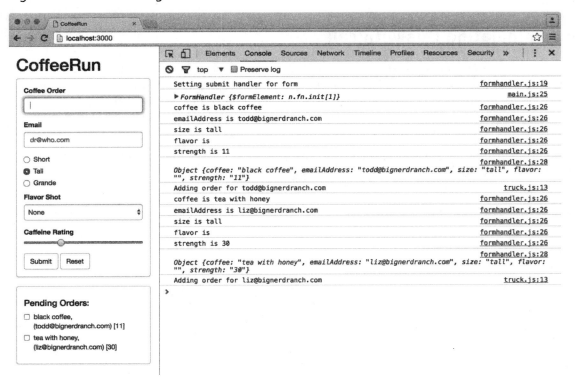

Delivering an Order by Clicking a Row

You are almost there! CoffeeRun's users can fill out the form to add orders. When they submit the form, it adds the order information to the application's database and draws a checklist item for the order.

Next, users should be able to check off the checklist items. When a checklist item is clicked, meaning that the order has been delivered, the order information should be deleted from the database and the checklist item should be removed from the page. Figure 11.7 shows this process.

Figure 11.7 Sequence diagram: clicking a checklist item

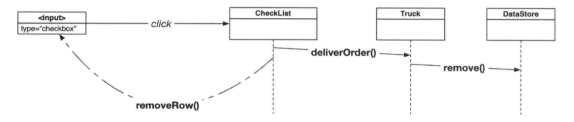

First, you will create the functionality for removing the checklist item from the page.

Creating the CheckList.prototype.removeRow method

When you create a **Row**, the value of the <input> is set to the customer's email address. **removeRow** will use the email address argument to find the right **CheckList** item to remove from the UI. It will do that by creating an attribute selector to find the <input> whose value attribute matches the email address.

When it has found the matching element, it will move up the DOM until it finds the [data-coffee-order="checkbox"].

This is the <div> that wraps around all of the elements that are part of a row. Finally, with that <div> selected using jQuery, its .**remove** method can be called, removing the element from the DOM and also cleaning up any event listeners that were attached to any element in that DOM subtree.

Add the **removeRow** method in checklist.js and specify an emailAddress parameter. Use the $element instance property to search for any descendant elements whose value attribute matches the email parameter. From that matching element, add a call to **closest** to search for an ancestor whose data-coffee-order attribute is equal to "checkbox". Finally, call **remove** on that element. (You will notice some new syntax in this code, which we will explain after you enter it.)

```
...
  CheckList.prototype.addRow = function (coffeeOrder) {
    ...
  };

  CheckList.prototype.removeRow = function (email) {
    this.$element
      .find('[value="' + email + '"]')
      .closest('[data-coffee-order="checkbox"]')
      .remove();
  };

  function Row(coffeeOrder) {
    ...
```

Here, you have *chained* several method calls together. jQuery is designed so that you can write multiple method calls for an object like a list of steps. You only include the semicolon at the end of the very last method call.

The requirement for chaining is that a method must return a jQuery-wrapped selection in order to have another method call chained to it. **find** returns a jQuery-wrapped selection, as does **closest**. This allows you to chain the three method calls together.

Notice that you used **this.$element.find**. This does a *scoped* selection: Instead of searching the entire DOM, it only searches the descendants of the checklist, which you have a reference to with this.$element.

Removing overwritten entries

Save your file and switch to the browser. Using your form, enter two orders for the same email address. Make the `coffee` for the first "order 1" and for the second "order 2." After submitting both orders, call **myTruck.printOrders** in the console. Figure 11.8 shows the result.

Figure 11.8 Orders for same email address remain in UI

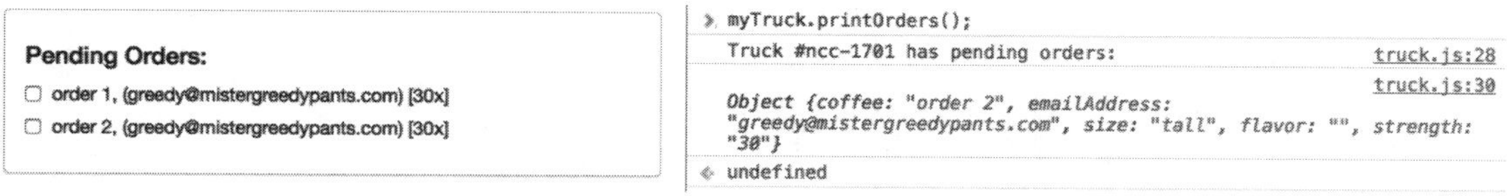

You decided early on to allow only one open order per customer. Because you are using a simple key/value store for your data, any subsequent orders for the same customer email address overwrite the existing one. So, as the console shows, "order 2" is the only pending order. "Order 1" has been overwritten.

But the checklist does not reflect this – it still shows rows for both "order 1" and "order 2." When you add a row for an order, you need to make sure that any existing rows associated with the same customer email address are removed.

Now that you can remove rows based on the customer's email address, this is straightforward. In `checklist.js`, update the **addRow** prototype method so that the first thing it does is call **removeRow**, passing in the email address of the customer.

```
...
CheckList.prototype.addRow = function (coffeeOrder) {
  // Remove any existing rows that match the email address
  this.removeRow(coffeeOrder.emailAddress);

  // Create a new instance of a row, using the coffee order info
  var rowElement = new Row(coffeeOrder);

  // Add the new row instance's $element property to the checklist
  this.$element.append(rowElement.$element);
};
...
```

Save `checklist.js` and verify in the browser that the first order's checklist item is removed when a second order with the same email is submitted.

Now that you can remove a checklist row from the UI, turn your attention to handling the checklist `click` event.

Writing the addClickHandler method

To handle clicks to the checklist, you will use the same event handler registration technique that you used with **FormHandler**.

FormHandler.prototype.addSubmitHandler accepts a function argument, fn, and then registers an anonymous function to handle the submit event of this.$formElement. Inside of that anonymous function, fn is invoked. Here is that method definition for reference:

```
FormHandler.prototype.addSubmitHandler = function (fn) {

  console.log('Setting submit handler for form');
  this.$formElement.on('submit', function (event) {
    event.preventDefault();

    var data = {};
    $(this).serializeArray().forEach(function (item) {
      data[item.name] = item.value;
      console.log(item.name + ' is ' + item.value);
    });
    console.log(data);

    fn(data);
    this.reset();
    this.elements[0].focus();
  });
};
```

This makes **FormHandler.prototype.addSubmitHandler** flexible, because it can be passed any function that needs to run when the form is submitted. This way, **FormHandler.prototype.addSubmitHandler** does not need to know the details of that function or what steps it takes.

You will add a prototype method to **CheckList** called **addClickHandler** that will work the same way as **FormHandler**'s **addSubmitHandler**. That is, it will:

1. Accept a function argument.

2. Register an event handler callback.

3. Invoke the function argument inside the event handler callback.

CheckList.prototype.addClickHandler differs from **FormHandler.prototype.addSubmitHandler** in that it will listen for a click event and **bind** the callback to the **CheckList** instance.

In checklist.js, add the **addClickHandler** method and specify a parameter named fn. Listen for a click event using jQuery's **on** method.

Inside the event handler function, declare a local variable named email and assign it event.target.value, which is the customer's email address. Then call **removeRow**, passing it email. After that, invoke fn and pass it email also. Make sure to use **bind(this)** to set the context object of the event handler function.

```
...
  function CheckList(selector) {
    ...
  }

  CheckList.prototype.addClickHandler = function (fn) {
    this.$element.on('click', 'input', function (event) {
      var email = event.target.value;
      this.removeRow(email);
      fn(email);
    }.bind(this));
  };

  CheckList.prototype.addRow = function (coffeeOrder) {
    ...
```

When you registered the event handler callback with this.$element.on, you specified click as the event name. But you also passed in a *filtering selector* as the second argument. The filtering selector tells the event handler to run the callback function *only* if the event was triggered by an <input> element.

This is a pattern called *event delegation*. It works because some events, like clicks and keypresses, *propagate* through the DOM, meaning each ancestor element is informed about the event.

Any time you need to listen for an event on elements that are dynamically created and removed, such as the checklist items, you should use event delegation. It is easier and more performant to add a single listener to the dynamic elements' container and then run the handler function based on what element triggered the event.

Notice that you do *not* call event.preventDefault inside the event handler. Why not? If you called event.preventDefault, the checkbox would not actually change its visual state to show a checkmark in the box.

Also, notice that you **bind** the event handler callback to this, which refers to the instance of **CheckList**.

Calling addClickHandler

addClickHandler needs to be connected to **deliverOrder**. Go to main.js to make that connection. Pass a bound version of **deliverOrder** to **checkList.addClickHandler**.

```
...
  var myTruck = new Truck('ncc-1701', new DataStore());
  window.myTruck = myTruck;
  var checkList = new CheckList(CHECKLIST_SELECTOR);
  checkList.addClickHandler(myTruck.deliverOrder.bind(myTruck));
  var formHandler = new FormHandler(FORM_SELECTOR);
...
```

Save your changes and add some coffee orders in the form. Click either the checkbox or the text of one of the checklist items, and it will be removed (Figure 11.9)!

Figure 11.9 Clicking a checklist item removes it

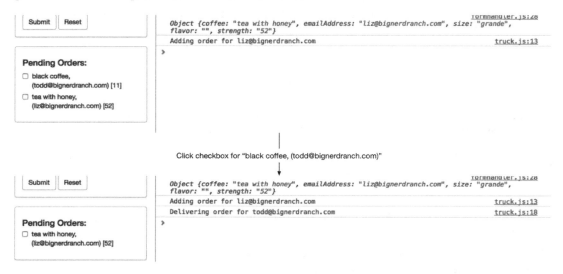

You have learned how to create dynamic form elements and work with the events they generate. You were able to associate each one with a specific coffee order by using the email address as an identifier.

Using these techniques, you completed the modules that manage the UI, turning what was a console-only application into one that could be used for a real-world task.

You have completed two of the three major parts of CoffeeRun. The internal logic governs the data within the application. The form elements, **FormHandler**, and **CheckList** provide the interactive UI. The next chapters deal with preparing and exchanging data with a remote server.

Bronze Challenge: Adding the Strength to the Description

You have decided that the strength of the coffee is a more important piece of information and should be the first part of the description.

Change the way you are writing the order descriptions so that the coffee strength is at the beginning of the description text.

Silver Challenge: Color Coding by Flavor Shot

Color code your orders based on the flavor shot. Based on the options chosen for each coffee, display the row in the checklist with a different background color.

Make sure that the text has enough contrast with the background color.

Gold Challenge: Allowing Order Editing

Allow existing orders to be edited. You will need to change the way the checklist works.

If the user double-clicks an order, load it back into the form for editing. If the user only clicks once, gray out the row. After a few seconds, treat the item as if it were delivered and remove it from the checklist and from the application's data.

As an extra bonus, make sure that after the user finishes editing the existing row is updated in place, not removed and replaced with a new row.

12

Validating Forms

CoffeeRun is humming along! Users can enter coffee orders in the form, and the order information is processed and stored. But what would happen to your app – and your coffee truck – if someone submitted an order with missing or unusable information?

Not to worry. You can easily handle these scenarios with a little bit of code to make sure the data is OK for your application to use. In fact, this is an essential step if you ever send data back to a server. Almost every modern browser is prepared to validate form data when it is submitted. All you need to do is provide the rules.

In this chapter, you are going to learn two techniques for form validation. The first technique is to add validation attributes to the HTML, allowing the browser's built-in validation mechanisms to take effect. The second is to write your own validation code in JavaScript, using the Constraint Validation API.

The required Attribute

The most basic form of validation is to check whether a field has a value and is not completely empty. This kind of check does not make sense for fields with default values, like your size, flavor, and strength fields. But it is just what you need for your order and email fields – you definitely do not want orders to be submitted with those fields left blank.

In `index.html`, add the `required` Boolean attribute to the order and email fields.

```
...
        <div class="form-group">
          <label for="coffeeOrder">Order</label>
          <input class="form-control" name="coffee" id="coffeeOrder"
            autofocus required />
        </div>

        <div class="form-group">
          <label for="emailInput">Email</label>
          <input class="form-control" type="email" name="emailAddress"
          id="emailInput" value="" placeholder="dr@who.com"
            required />
        </div>
...
```

Remember that a Boolean attribute should not be assigned a value. If you make the mistake of writing something like `required="false"`, the value will be `true` and the field will be required! The browser only cares about the *existence* of the attribute and ignores any value assigned.

That point bears repeating: If a Boolean attribute exists for an element, the browser considers the value to be true, regardless of the value you set for it.

Save index.html, make sure browser-sync is running, and load CoffeeRun in the browser. Try submitting the form without filling out either or both of the required fields. You will see a warning, as in Figure 12.1.

Figure 12.1 Errors when required fields are blank

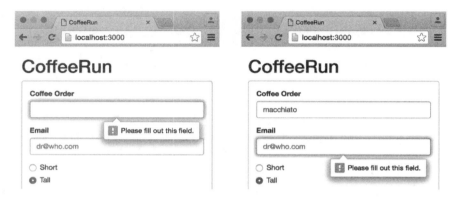

Also, notice that there are no console messages from your submit handlers. The submit event only fires *after* the browser validates your form (Figure 12.2).

Figure 12.2 Two possible sequences of events when a form is validated

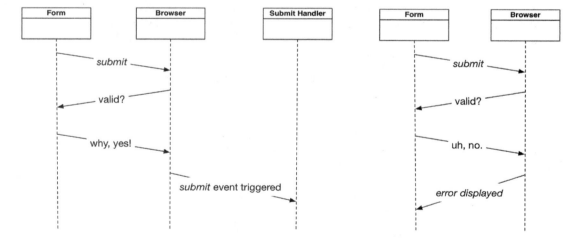

Validating with Regular Expressions

Making a field `required` is an easy way to ensure that the user does not leave the field blank. But what if you want to be specific about what should go into a field? This kind of validation calls for the `pattern` attribute.

After the `required` attribute on your order `<input>`, add a `pattern` attribute. Assign it a specially formatted string called a *regular expression*, which we will explain in a moment.

```
...
        <div class="form-group">
          <label for="coffeeOrder">Order</label>
          <input class="form-control" name="coffee" id="coffeeOrder"
            autofocus required pattern="[a-zA-Z\s]+" />
        </div>
...
```

A regular expression is a sequence of characters for pattern matching. The regular expression `[a-zA-Z\s]+` matches any character from the set consisting of lowercase letters (a–z), uppercase letters (A–Z), and whitespace characters (\s), repeated one or more times (+).

In short, when you submit the form this field will only be valid if it contains letters or spaces.

Save and reload. See what happens if you put symbols or numbers into the order field and try to submit the form.

Constraint Validation API

The most robust way to validate a form field in the browser is to write a validation function. You can use validation functions in conjunction with the Constraint Validation API to trigger built-in validation behavior.

But there is a catch, and it is not a small one: The Constraint Validation API has poor support in Apple's Safari browser.

Despite this oversight, it is important to write code that targets standard behavior and then add a JavaScript library that adds support for noncompliant browsers. (You can read more about this in the section called *For the More Curious: The Webshims Library* at the end of this chapter.)

Suppose your coffee truck is only for employees of your company, so you want to make sure that the customer is an employee. One way to do this would be to ensure that the email address that is submitted is from your company's domain.

You *could* use a `pattern` attribute for your `emailAddress` field. But this problem is a good one for learning the Constraint Validation API. (Also, after you work through the next chapter, you could expand beyond a simple email domain check and query a remote server to find out whether the email address actually exists.)

Create a new file, `scripts/validation.js`, to hold your validation functions. Add a `<script>` tag in `index.html` for your new module.

```
...
    </div>
  </section>
  <script src="https://cdnjs.cloudflare.com/ajax/libs/jquery/2.1.4/jquery.js"
    charset="utf-8"></script>
  <script src="scripts/validation.js" charset="utf-8"></script>
  <script src="scripts/checklist.js" charset="utf-8"></script>
  <script src="scripts/formhandler.js" charset="utf-8"></script>
  <script src="scripts/datastore.js" charset="utf-8"></script>
  <script src="scripts/truck.js" charset="utf-8"></script>
  <script src="scripts/main.js" charset="utf-8"></script>
  </body>
</html>
```

Save `index.html`. In `validation.js`, add an IIFE module that creates an empty object literal, assigns it to a variable named `Validation`, and then exports that variable to the `App` namespace.

```
(function (window) {
  'use strict';
  var App = window.App || {};

  var Validation = {

  };

  App.Validation = Validation;
  window.App = App;
})(window);
```

Your new `Validation` module will only be used for organizing functions, so it does not need to be a constructor.

Add a method called **isCompanyEmail**. This method will test an email address against a regular expression and return `true` or `false`. (Feel free to change the email domain specified.)

```
(function () {
  'use strict';
  var App = window.App || {};

  var Validation = {
    isCompanyEmail: function (email) {
      return /.+@bignerdranch\.com$/.test(email);
    }
  };

  App.Validation = Validation;
  window.App = App;
})(window);
```

You created a literal regular expression by putting a pattern between the forward slashes, `//`. Inside the slashes, you specify a string that consists of one or more characters (`.+`), followed by "@bignerdranch.com" – you also used a backslash to indicate that the period in `bignerdranch.com` should be treated as a literal period. (Normally, a period in a regular expression is a wildcard that matches any character.) The "$" at the end of regular expression means that "@bignerdranch.com" should be at the end of the string – there should be no more characters that appear after it.

This regular expression is an object and has a **test** method. You can pass a string to the **test** method, and it will return a Boolean – true if the regular expression matches the string and false if not. (For a list of other regular expression methods, see developer.mozilla.org/en-US/docs/Web/JavaScript/Reference/Global_Objects/RegExp.)

Test your **App.Validation.isCompanyEmail** function on the console (Figure 12.3).

Figure 12.3 Testing **App.Validation.isCompanyEmail** on the console

You now have a function that can check for valid email addresses. The next thing to do is to connect it to the form.

Listening for the input event

When should you use this function? There are several events that the input field could trigger while a user is filling out the form. One occurs as the user types each character. Another is when the user removes focus from the field. Or you could run the function when the form is submitted.

The Constraint Validation API requires that invalid fields be marked prior to submission. If any fields are invalid, the browser stops short of triggering the submit event. So doing the check on submit is too late.

The event triggered when the user removes focus from a field is known as a *blur* event. It is not a good choice for validation, either. Suppose the user's cursor is in the email input, so that field has focus. If the user then presses the Return key, this would trigger form submission, but the blur event would not be triggered and any validation tied to it would not be performed.

So the validation check will need to happen as the user enters each character. Update the **FormHandler** module in formhandler.js with an **addInputHandler** prototype method. It should add a listener for the input event of the form. Like the **addSubmitHandler** method, it should accept a function argument.

```
...
  FormHandler.prototype.addSubmitHandler = function (fn) {
    ...
  };

  FormHandler.prototype.addInputHandler = function (fn) {
    console.log('Setting input handler for form');
  };

  App.FormHandler = FormHandler;
  window.App = App;
...
```

Attach the listener for the input event using jQuery's **on** method. Make sure to use the event delegation pattern to filter out events created by anything but the [name="emailAddress"] field.

```
...
  FormHandler.prototype.addInputHandler = function (fn) {
    console.log('Setting input handler for form');
    this.$formElement.on('input', '[name="emailAddress"]', function (event) {
      // Event handler code will go here
    });
  };

  App.FormHandler = FormHandler;
  window.App = App;
...
```

Inside the event handler, extract the value of the email field from the event.target object. Then console.log the result of running **addInputHandler**'s function argument fn and passing it the value of the email field.

```
...
  FormHandler.prototype.addInputHandler = function (fn) {
    console.log('Setting input handler for form');
    this.$formElement.on('input', '[name="emailAddress"]', function (event) {
      // Event handler code will go here
      var emailAddress = event.target.value;
      console.log(fn(emailAddress));
    });
  };

  App.FormHandler = FormHandler;
  window.App = App;
...
```

Save formhandler.js.

Associating the validation check with the input event

In main.js, import **Validation** from the App namespace and assign it to a local variable.

```
...
  var Truck = App.Truck;
  var DataStore = App.DataStore;
  var FormHandler = App.FormHandler;
  var Validation = App.Validation;
  var CheckList = App.CheckList;
  var myTruck = new Truck('ncc-1701', new DataStore());
...
```

With the **Validation** object imported, you can connect it to **FormHandler**'s new **addInputHandler** method.

At the end of main.js, pass **Validation.isCompanyEmail** to the **addInputHandler** method of the formHandler instance:

```
...
  formHandler.addSubmitHandler(function (data) {
    myTruck.createOrder.call(myTruck, data);
    checkList.addRow.call(checkList, data);
  });

  formHandler.addInputHandler(Validation.isCompanyEmail);

})(window);
```

Save and reload. Fill out the email field and see what appears on the console. As you type a valid email address, the console will show a number of false results, printed by the console.log(fn(emailAddress)); line in **FormHandler.prototype.addInputHandler**. When you have finished typing a valid email address, you will see true printed in the console (Figure 12.4).

Figure 12.4 Logging the email validation check

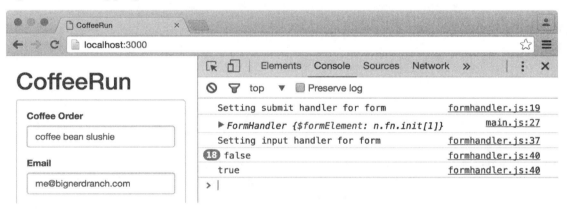

Your validation function is run each time a character is entered (or removed) from the email field. When you have confirmed that it is correctly checking your input, you can use it to show a custom error message.

Triggering the validity check

Now that you can reliably test that the email address is from your company's domain, you should notify the user if the validation fails. You will use the **setCustomValidity** method for the event.target to mark it as invalid.

In formhandler.js, remove the console.log statement and replace it with a variable for a warning message and an if/else clause. If the fn(emailAddress) call returns true, clear the custom validity of the field. If it returns false, assign the message variable to a string with the warning message and set the custom validity to message.

```
...
  FormHandler.prototype.addInputHandler = function (fn) {
    console.log('Setting input handler for form');
    this.$formElement.on('input', '[name="emailAddress"]', function (event) {
      var emailAddress = event.target.value;
      console.log(fn(emailAddress));
      var message = '';
      if (fn(emailAddress)) {
        event.target.setCustomValidity('');
      } else {
        message = emailAddress + ' is not an authorized email address!'
        event.target.setCustomValidity(message);
      }
    });
  };
...
```

You passed in the error message that should be shown to the user. If there is no error, you still have to call **setCustomValidity**, but with an empty string as the argument. This has the effect of marking the field as valid.

The validation check that occurs as you type only marks the field as valid or invalid. It does not display the error message. When you press the Submit button, the browser checks for invalid fields and displays the validation message if it finds any.

To try it out, submit the form after entering an email address that does not match the domain. Right after you press the Submit button, you should see your custom validation message appear as a warning next to the field (Figure 12.5).

Figure 12.5 Only valid email addresses allowed!

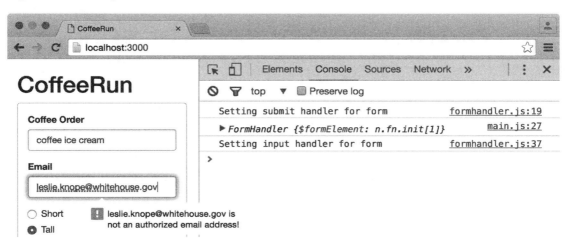

Styling Valid and Invalid Elements

CoffeeRun now validates both the order field and the email address. Now it is time to enhance the UI by visually marking invalid fields. For this very short piece of CSS, you will add one ruleset in a `<style>` tag to the `<head>` in index.html.

```
...
  <head>
    <meta charset="utf-8">
    <title>coffeerun</title>
    <link rel="stylesheet" href="https://cdnjs.cloudflare.com/ajax/libs/twitter-bootst
rap/3.3.6/css/bootstrap.min.css">
    <style>
      form :invalid {
        border-color: #a94442;
      }
    </style>
  </head>
...
```

This adds a border to any field inside your form that has the pseudo-class `:invalid`. This pseudo-class is automatically added by the browser when the form runs its validation checks.

Save and return to the browser. Press the Tab key a few times (or click outside of the text-entry fields) to focus on a form element other than the order or email fields. The two required fields will have a reddish border color (Figure 12.6).

Figure 12.6 Trust us: These borders are red

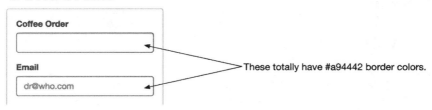

It would be more appropriate for the border to only appear on an invalid field that is required and has focus. Add two more pseudo-classes to your selector in index.html:

```
<head>
  <meta charset="utf-8">
  <title>coffeerun</title>
  <link rel="stylesheet" href="https://cdnjs.cloudflare.com/ajax/libs/twitter-bootst
rap/3.3.6/css/bootstrap.min.css">
  <style>
    form :focus:required:invalid {
      border-color: #a94442;
    }
  </style>
</head>
...
```

You have specified that fields that have the three pseudo-classes :focus, :required, and :invalid will get the new border color (Figure 12.7).

Figure 12.7 :invalid border color only for field with focus

CoffeeRun is developing into a fully featured web app. In the next two chapters, you will sync the data to a remote server using Ajax.

Silver Challenge: Custom Validation for Decaf

Add another function to your Validation module. It should accept two arguments: a string and an integer. If the string contains the word "decaf" and the integer is greater than 20, the function should return false.

Add listeners for the coffee order text field and for the caffeine strength slider. Trigger the custom validation for whichever field is currently being edited and caused the validation failure.

For the More Curious: The Webshims Library

As mentioned earlier, one notable browser that does not support the Constraint Validation API is Apple's Safari browser. Should you need to support Safari, you can use a library, or *polyfill*, that simulates the API for browsers that do not implement it.

One library that will provide Constraint Validation in Safari is the Webshims Lib, which you can download from github.com/aFarkas/webshim.

Actually, the Webshims library can act as a polyfill for many, many features. Setting it up and using it is straightforward. (However, it does do a lot of different things, and it is easy to get lost in the documentation.)

Here is how you use it with CoffeeRun so that Safari works with your **Validation** module. First, download a zip file from the project page: github.com/aFarkas/webshim/releases/latest. Unzip the file and put the js-webshim/webshim folder in your coffeerun directory (next to index.html and your scripts folder).

Add a <script> tag in index.html for the webshim/polyfiller.js file.

```
...
    </div>
  </section>
  <script src="https://cdnjs.cloudflare.com/ajax/libs/jquery/2.1.4/jquery.js"
    charset="utf-8"></script>
  <script src="webshim/polyfiller.js" charset="utf-8"></script>
  <script src="scripts/validation.js" charset="utf-8"></script>
  <script src="scripts/checklist.js" charset="utf-8"></script>
  <script src="scripts/formhandler.js" charset="utf-8"></script>
  <script src="scripts/datastore.js" charset="utf-8"></script>
  <script src="scripts/truck.js" charset="utf-8"></script>
  <script src="scripts/main.js" charset="utf-8"></script>
  </body>
</html>
```

Then, add these lines to main.js:

```
...
  var Validation = App.Validation;
  var CheckList = App.CheckList;
  var webshim = window.webshim;
  var myTruck = new Truck('ncc-1701', new DataStore());

  ...

  formHandler.addInputHandler(Validation.isCompanyEmail);

  webshim.polyfill('forms forms-ext');
  webshim.setOptions('forms', { addValidators: true, lazyCustomMessages: true });

}(window));
```

This imports the webshim library and then configures it for use with forms.

Finally, there is one quirk with the library that you need to know. Anywhere you use **setCustomValidity**, you must wrap the objects with jQuery. For CoffeeRun, you need to wrap the event.target objects of the **addInputHandler** function in formhandler.js:

```
...
  FormHandler.prototype.addInputHandler = function (fn) {
    console.log('Setting input handler for form');
    this.$formElement.on('input', '[name="emailAddress"]', function (event) {
      var emailAddress = event.target.value;
      var message = '';
      if (fn(emailAddress)) {
        $(event.target).setCustomValidity('');
      } else {
        message = emailAddress + ' is not an authorized email address!'
        $(event.target).setCustomValidity(message);
      }
    });
  };
...
```

The authors of Webshim chose to implement the polyfill functionality entirely as an extension of jQuery. Other than this wrapping, you do not need to modify your code.

After you save your changes, you can test your validation in Safari. You should see that it also reports an issue if you forget to fill out the coffee order or if you enter an invalid email address (Figure 12.8).

Figure 12.8 Using Webshim as a Safari polyfill

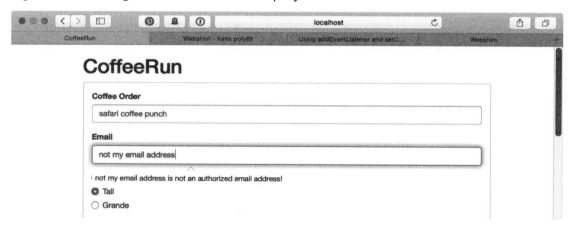

Webshim goes well beyond providing form validation. You should browse through the documentation to see what else it can do for you on your projects.

13

Ajax

In the last chapter, you used the browser's built-in validation to ensure that the user entered data that fit CoffeeRun's parameters. After doing those checks, you can feel confident about sending that data to the server.

At the moment, the **FormHandler.prototype.addSubmitHandler** method calls the event object's **preventDefault** method to keep the browser from sending a request to the server. Normally, the server sends back a response that causes the page to reload. Instead, you are extracting the data that the user enters into the form and updating the form and the checklist with JavaScript.

In this chapter, you will create a **RemoteDataStore** module that sends a request to the server and handles the response (Figure 13.1). But it will do this in the background using *Ajax*, without causing the browser to reload.

Figure 13.1 CoffeeRun at the end of the chapter

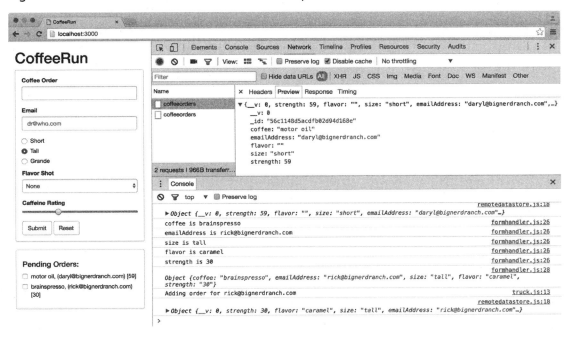

Ajax is a technique for communicating with a remote server via JavaScript. The JavaScript usually changes the contents of a web page using data returned by the server without reloading the browser. This can improve the experience of using a web application.

Originally, the term "Ajax" was an acronym for "asynchronous JavaScript and XML," but it is now used generically for this style of asynchronous data communication, regardless of what technologies are actually involved. (Asynchronous communication means that the app, having sent a request, does not have to wait for a response from the server before continuing with other tasks.) Ajax is now the standard mechanism for sending and receiving data in the background.

XMLHttpRequest Objects

At the core of Ajax is the XMLHttpRequest API. In modern browsers, you can instantiate new XMLHttpRequest objects, which allow you to send requests to servers without causing a page reload. They perform their work in the background.

Using XMLHttpRequest objects, you can attach callbacks to different stages of the request/response cycle, much in the same way that you listen to events on DOM objects. You can also inspect the XMLHttpRequest object's properties to access information about the status of the request/response cycle. Two useful properties are response and status, which are updated as soon as any changes occur. The response property contains the data (such as HTML, XML, JSON, or another format) sent back by the server. The status is a numeric code that tells you whether the HTTP response was successful or not. These are officially known as *HTTP Status Codes*.

Status codes are grouped in ranges, and these ranges have basic meanings. For example, the status codes in the 200-299 range are success codes, while status codes in the 500-599 range mean that there was a server error. You will often see these ranges referred to generically, as in "2xx" or "3xx" statuses.

Table 13.1 shows some of the more common codes.

Table 13.1 Common HTTP status codes

Status Code	Status Text	Description
200	OK	The request was successful.
400	Bad Request	The server did not understand the request.
404	Not Found	The resource could not be found, often because the file or path name did not match anything on the server.
500	Internal Server Error	The server encountered an error, such as an unhandled exception in the server-side code.
503	Service Unavailable	The server could not handle the request, often because it is overloaded or down for maintenance.

jQuery has a number of methods that create and manage XMLHttpRequest objects and provide a concise, backward-compatible, cross-browser API. It is not the only library available for managing Ajax requests, but many other libraries simply follow jQuery's lead. You will be using jQuery's **get** and **post** methods to work with Ajax GET and POST requests and the jQuery **ajax** method to handle DELETE requests.

RESTful Web Services

You are going to enhance CoffeeRun by using a remote web service to store your application data. The server you will use has been created specifically for this book.

The CoffeeRun server provides a RESTful web service. "REST" stands for "representational state transfer," which is a style of web service that relies on HTTP verbs (GET, POST, PUT, DELETE) and URLs that identify resources on the server.

Frequently, the URL path (the part that comes after the server name) will refer either to a collection of things (such as /coffeeorders) or to individual things, specified by an ID (such as /coffeeorders/ [customer email]).

This difference affects how the HTTP verbs apply. For example, when working with a collection, a GET request retrieves a list of all items in the collection. With an individual item, a GET request retrieves all of the details for that item.

The URL and HTTP verb patterns are summarized in Table 13.2.

Table 13.2 Example of RESTful URL and HTTP verb patterns

URL Path	GET	POST	PUT	DELETE
/coffeeorders	list all records	create one record	-	delete all records
/coffeeorders/a@b.com	get the record	-	update the record	delete the record

The RemoteDataStore Module

In a moment, you will create a new module called **RemoteDataStore**. The job of **RemoteDataStore** will be to talk to a server on behalf of the rest of the application. It will have all the same methods as **DataStore** – **add**, **get**, **getAll**, and **remove** – which it will use to communicate with the server (Figure 13.2).

Figure 13.2 **DataStore** vs **RemoteDataStore**

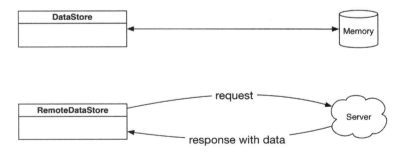

You will be able to use an instance of **RemoteDataStore** in place of **DataStore** without having to change your **Truck**, **FormHandler**, or **CheckList** modules. (You will not be deleting your **DataStore** module, though. You might want to create a future enhancement allowing CoffeeRun to switch between the two storage modules based on whether the app is running online or offline.)

RemoteDataStore's methods will communicate asynchronously with the server by sending a network request in the background. When the browser receives the response from the server, it has an opportunity to invoke a callback.

Each of **RemoteDataStore**'s methods will accept a function argument that will be invoked after the response arrives with any data from the server.

Create a new `scripts/remotedatastore.js` file and add a `<script>` tag for it in `index.html`.

```
...
    <script src="scripts/validation.js" charset="utf-8"></script>
    <script src="scripts/checklist.js" charset="utf-8"></script>
    <script src="scripts/formhandler.js" charset="utf-8"></script>
    <script src="scripts/remotedatastore.js" charset="utf-8"></script>
    <script src="scripts/datastore.js" charset="utf-8"></script>
    <script src="scripts/truck.js" charset="utf-8"></script>
    <script src="scripts/main.js" charset="utf-8"></script>
  </body>
</html>
```

Save `index.html`. In remotedatastore.js, import the App namespace and jQuery, then create an IIFE module with a constructor named **RemoteDataStore**. The constructor should accept an argument for a remote server URL and throw an error if a URL is not passed in. At the end of the module definition, export the **RemoteDataStore** to the App namespace:

```
(function (window) {
  'use strict';
  var App = window.App || {};
  var $ = window.jQuery;

  function RemoteDataStore(url) {
    if (!url) {
      throw new Error('No remote URL supplied.');
    }

    this.serverUrl = url;
  }

  App.RemoteDataStore = RemoteDataStore;
  window.App = App;

})(window);
```

Sending Data to the Server

The first method you will create is the **add** method to store customer order data on the remote web service.

Add a prototype method to **RemoteDataStore**. Like **DataStore**'s **add** method, it will accept arguments called key and val. Note that it is not required for you to use the same parameter names, but it is good practice to keep them consistent.

```
...
  function RemoteDataStore(url) {
    ...
  }

  RemoteDataStore.prototype.add = function (key, val) {
    // Code will go here
  };

  App.RemoteDataStore = RemoteDataStore;
  window.App = App;
...
```

Using jQuery's $.post method

Inside the `RemoteDataStore` module, you will use jQuery's `$.post` method. This method sends a POST request in the background as an XMLHttpRequest object (Figure 13.3).

Figure 13.3 **RemoteDataStore** uses jQuery for Ajax

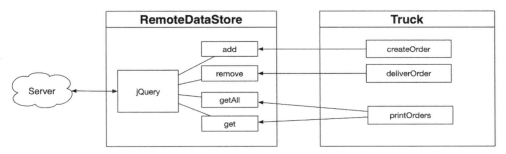

The `$.post` method only requires two pieces of information: the URL of the server to send the request to and what data to include.

In `remotedatastore.js`, update the body of the **add** method so that it calls `$.post`, passing it `this.serverUrl` and the `val`.

```
...
  RemoteDataStore.prototype.add = function (key, val) {
    // Code will go here
    $.post(this.serverUrl, val);
  };

  App.RemoteDataStore = RemoteDataStore;
  window.App = App;
...
```

Notice that the key argument is not used. It is kept as part of the method declaration so that the **add** method of **RemoteDataStore** is identical to the **add** method of **DataStore**. Both take the coffee order information as the second argument. For the **RemoteDataStore**, this is the crucial part.

Adding a callback

Like many jQuery methods, `$.post` can accept additional, optional arguments. You are going to pass it a callback function as a third argument. When the response arrives from the server, this function will be called and the data in the response will be passed to it.

261

This is similar to the event handling code you have written – you register a function to run at some point in the future. When handling events, this point is something like a mouse click or a form submission. When handling remote data, it is the the arrival of a response from the server.

Add an anonymous function as the third argument to **$.post**. This anonymous function should expect an argument, which you will label serverResponse. Print this serverResponse to the console using **console.log**.

```
...
  RemoteDataStore.prototype.add = function (key, val) {
    $.post(this.serverUrl, val, function (serverResponse) {
      console.log(serverResponse);
    });
  };

  App.RemoteDataStore = RemoteDataStore;
  window.App = App;
...
```

Now **$.post** knows three things: who to talk to, what to say, and what to do with the information it gets back in the response.

After you save these changes to remotedatastore.js, start browser-sync and open the console in your browser. Instantiate a **RemoteDataStore** object with the URL shown below, which is the address of the test server created for this book. (Once again, this line is broken in order to fit on the page; enter it on one line.)

```
var remoteDS = new App.RemoteDataStore
    ("http://coffeerun-v2-rest-api.herokuapp.com/api/coffeeorders");
```

Now invoke its **add** method, passing it some test data:

```
remoteDS.add('a@b.com', {emailAddress: 'a@b.com', coffee: 'espresso'});
```

In the console, look at what was printed from your **console.log** statement (Figure 13.4).

Figure 13.4 Console showing result of calling **RemoteDataStore.add**

```
> var remoteDS = new App.RemoteDataStore("http://coffeerun-v2-rest-api.herokuapp.com/api/coffeeorders");
< undefined
> remoteDS.add('a@b.com', {emailAddress: 'a@b.com', coffee: 'espresso'});
< undefined
                                                         remotedatastore.js:17
  Object {__v: 0, coffee: "espresso", emailAddress: "a@b.com", _id: "5712c496e36db403007d087c"}
>
```

The object in the console's log statement contains some information sent back by the server in its response: the coffee and emailAddress information, in addition to some bookkeeping data that will vary from server to server.

Inspecting the Ajax request and response

In the DevTools, open the network panel by clicking Network in the menu at the top (between Sources and Timeline). This panel shows a list of requests that your browser has made and lets you inspect each of them for more information (Figure 13.5).

Figure 13.5 Viewing Ajax requests in the network panel

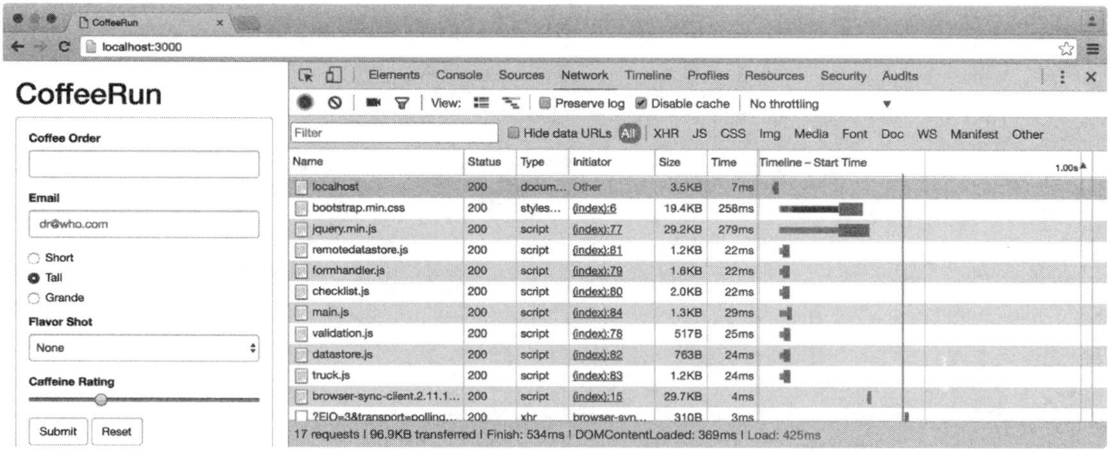

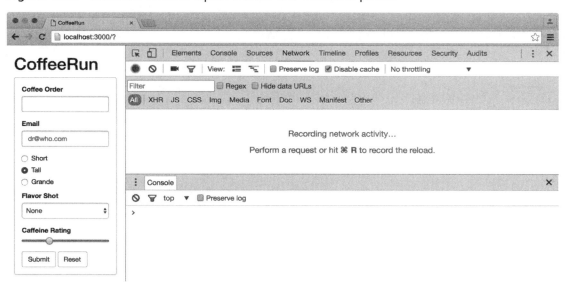

Your network panel will likely have many network requests in the list. Clear it out by clicking the ⊘ icon near the upper left of the DevTools. Then activate the console drawer at the bottom so you can see the console as well as the network panel. You can do this by pressing the Escape key on your keyboard or by clicking the ⋮ icon in the upper right. This will open a menu with the option Show console.

The console drawer will appear at the bottom of the DevTools (Figure 13.6).

Figure 13.6 Console drawer open below the network panel

In the console, enter the following:

```
var remoteDS = new App.RemoteDataStore
    ("http://coffeerun-v2-rest-api.herokuapp.com/api/coffeeorders");
remoteDS.add('a@b.com', {emailAddress: 'a@b.com', coffee: 'espresso'});
```

You will see a new entry in the network panel (Figure 13.7).

Figure 13.7 Ajax request in network panel

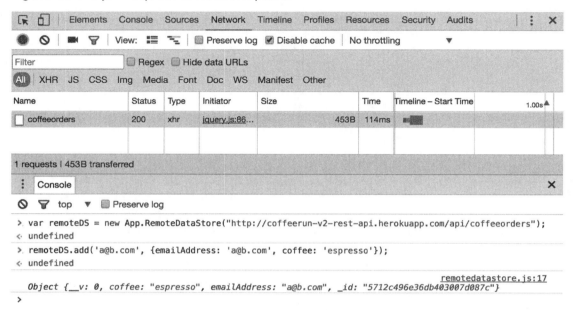

To find out more about the request, click on its entry (Figure 13.8). You may find it easier to view the details if you hide the console drawer.

Figure 13.8 Request details

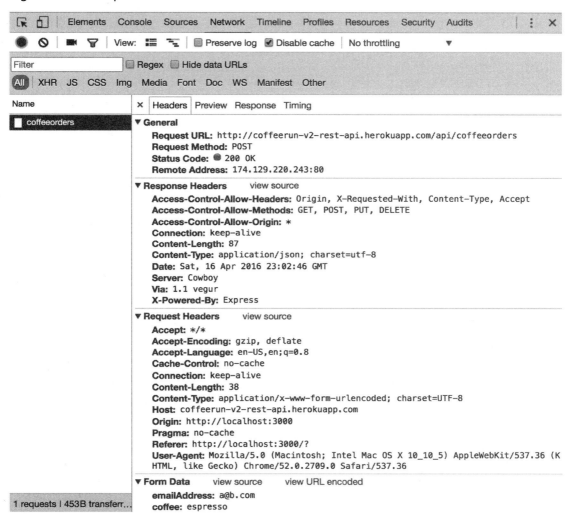

The details include some general information about the request at the top and the form data at the bottom. In the middle are panes that show the request and response *headers*. Headers are metadata and options that have been specified for the request and response.

Of all this data, the status code (in the General pane) and the Form Data pane are usually the most useful while developing and debugging Ajax requests.

Retrieving Data from the Server

Your **RemoteDataStore** module can save individual coffee orders to the server. The next thing to do is add a **getAll** prototype method so that it can retrieve all orders from the server. Get it started in remotedatastore.js:

```
...
  RemoteDataStore.prototype.add = function (key, val) {
    ...
  };

  RemoteDataStore.prototype.getAll = function () {
    // Code will go here
  };

  App.RemoteDataStore = RemoteDataStore;
  window.App = App;
...
```

Next you will add a call to jQuery's **$.get** method. Like **$.post**, you will pass it the server URL. But you will not pass it any data, because you are retrieving information instead of saving information. You will need to pass it a function argument so that it knows what to do with the data when it comes back from the server.

Call **$.get** in **RemoteDataStore.prototype.getAll**.

```
...
  RemoteDataStore.prototype.getAll = function () {
    // Code will go here
    $.get(this.serverUrl, function (serverResponse) {
      console.log(serverResponse);
    });
  };

  App.RemoteDataStore = RemoteDataStore;
  window.App = App;
...
```

Save and return to the DevTools in the browser.

Inspecting the response data

In the console, instantiate a **RemoteDataStore** with the same URL as before. (Pro tip: Instead of re-typing the very long line with the URL, you can use the up and down arrow keys to cycle through statements you have entered into the console.) Then call its **getAll** method:

```
var remoteDS = new App.RemoteDataStore
    ("http://coffeerun-v2-rest-api.herokuapp.com/api/coffeeorders");
remoteDS.getAll();
```

In the network panel of the DevTools, you will see that the GET request went out. It should return within a few dozen milliseconds. Some coffee order info (from data preloaded on the server) will appear in the console (Figure 13.9).

Figure 13.9 Inspecting the response from **getAll**

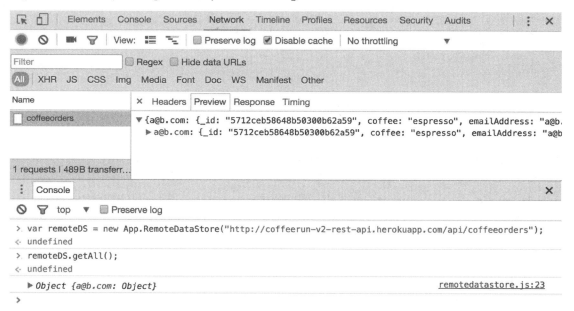

You may see slightly different results, depending on what has been added to the server. However, getting any result shows that you are successfully retrieving data from the server.

Adding a callback argument

You can retrieve the data from the server, but you cannot return it from **getAll**. This is because **getAll** only makes the initial Ajax request; it does not handle the response.

Instead, you pass a response handling callback to **$.get**. Your response handling callback will work like the event handling callbacks you have written – in both cases, the callback should expect to receive an argument. This means that the response data is only available inside the body of the callback. How will you access it outside of that callback?

If you pass **getAll** a function argument, you can call that function *inside* the **$.get** callback. There, you have access to both the function argument *and* the server response.

Add the function argument and call in remotedatastore.js:

```
...
  RemoteDataStore.prototype.getAll = function (cb) {
    $.get(this.serverUrl, function (serverResponse) {
      console.log(serverResponse);
      cb(serverResponse);
    });
  };

  App.RemoteDataStore = RemoteDataStore;
  window.App = App;
...
```

The **getAll** method retrieves all the coffee orders on the remote server and passes them to the callback **cb** function that is passed in.

You also need to implement the **get** method, which retrieves a single coffee order by the customer email address. Like **getAll**, it will accept a function argument, which it will call and pass the retrieved coffee order.

Add this implementation of **get** to remotedatastore.js:

```
...
  RemoteDataStore.prototype.getAll = function (cb) {
    ...
  };

  RemoteDataStore.prototype.get = function (key, cb) {
    $.get(this.serverUrl + '/' + key, function (serverResponse) {
      console.log(serverResponse);
      cb(serverResponse);
    });
  };

  App.RemoteDataStore = RemoteDataStore;
  window.App = App;
...
```

Save your changes to remotedatastore.js. Enter the following code in the console, passing an empty anonymous function to **remoteDS.get**. (It is expecting a function argument, but you only want to take it for a quick test.)

```
var remoteDS = new App.RemoteDataStore
    ("http://coffeerun-v2-rest-api.herokuapp.com/api/coffeeorders");
remoteDS.get('a@b.com', function () {});
```

Your console will look something like Figure 13.10.

Figure 13.10 Testing **RemoteDataStore.prototype.get**

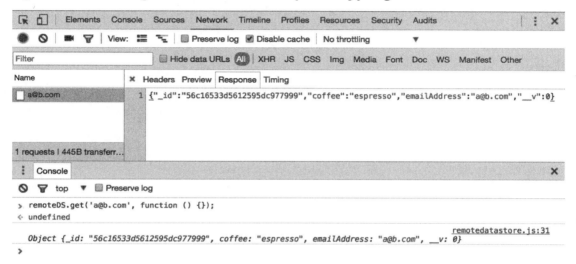

Deleting Data from the Server

Using Ajax, you can now save orders to the server and retrieve orders from the server. The last thing to do is to delete orders from the server when they are delivered.

To do this, you will send an HTTP request to the URL for an individual order. As you did with **RemoteDataStore.prototype.get**, you will use the server URL, but you will append a slash and the customer's email address.

You will be sending the server a DELETE request. DELETE is one of the HTTP verbs. The server knows to remove the data associated with that customer's email address if it receives a DELETE request at that URL.

Using jQuery's $.ajax method

jQuery provides the **$.get** and **$.post** methods as a convenience because these are the two most common HTTP verbs used. For example, a GET request is used whenever the browser asks for an HTML, CSS, JavaScript, or image file (among others). A POST request is used most often when a form is submitted.

jQuery does not provide a convenience method for sending DELETE requests via Ajax. Instead, you will need to use the **$.ajax** method. (**$.get** and **$.post** actually call **$.ajax** for you, specifying GET and POST as the HTTP verbs.)

In remotedatastore.js, add the **remove** prototype method. In it, call the **$.ajax** method, passing it two arguments. The first argument is an individual coffee order's URL, made up of the server URL, a slash, and the key (the customer's email address). The second argument is an object that contains the options, or settings, for the Ajax request. The only option you need to specify for the **remove** method is that the type is DELETE.

```
...
  RemoteDataStore.prototype.get = function (key, cb) {
    ...
  };

  RemoteDataStore.prototype.remove = function (key) {
    $.ajax(this.serverUrl + '/' + key, {
      type: 'DELETE'
    });
  };

  App.RemoteDataStore = RemoteDataStore;
  window.App = App;
...
```

(There are many options available for Ajax requests, which you can read about at api.jquery.com/ jquery.ajax.)

Save and return to the console. Instantiate a new **RemoteDataStore** and invoke the **remove** method. Pass it the email address for the test orders you have created. Finally, call **getAll** to confirm that it is no longer included in the orders returned from the server.

```
var remoteDS = new App.RemoteDataStore
    ("http://coffeerun-v2-rest-api.herokuapp.com/api/coffeeorders");
remoteDS.remove('a@b.com');
remoteDS.getAll();
```

If you inspect the response from the server for the DELETE request, you can see that the server sends back information about what it did (Figure 13.11). (As we mentioned earlier, other servers may provide different information in the response.)

Figure 13.11 Inspecting the response from a DELETE request

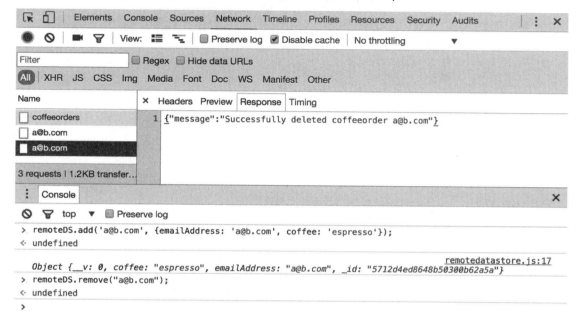

Replacing DataStore with RemoteDataStore

Your **RemoteDataStore** module is complete. It is time to replace your **DataStore** instance with a **RemoteDataStore** instance.

Open main.js. Begin by importing **RemoteDataStore** from the App namespace.

```
(function (window) {
  'use strict';
  var FORM_SELECTOR = '[data-coffee-order="form"]';
  var CHECKLIST_SELECTOR = '[data-coffee-order="checklist"]';
  var App = window.App;
  var Truck = App.Truck;
  var DataStore = App.DataStore;
  var RemoteDataStore = App.RemoteDataStore;
  var FormHandler = App.FormHandler;
...
```

Also, add a new variable called SERVER_URL and assign it a string with the URL of the CoffeeRun test server.

```
(function (window) {
  'use strict';
  var FORM_SELECTOR = '[data-coffee-order="form"]';
  var CHECKLIST_SELECTOR = '[data-coffee-order="checklist"]';
  var SERVER_URL = 'http://coffeerun-v2-rest-api.herokuapp.com/api/coffeeorders';
  var App = window.App;
  var Truck = App.Truck;
  var DataStore = App.DataStore;
  var RemoteDataStore = App.RemoteDataStore;
...
```

Next, create a new instance of **RemoteDataStore**, passing it SERVER_URL.

```
...
  var RemoteDataStore = App.RemoteDataStore;
  var FormHandler = App.FormHandler;
  var Validation = App.Validation;
  var CheckList = App.CheckList;
  var remoteDS = new RemoteDataStore(SERVER_URL);
  var webshim = window.webshim;
  var myTruck = new Truck('ncc-1701', new DataStore());
  window.myTruck = myTruck;
...
```

Finally, instead of passing the **Truck** constructor a new instance of **DataStore**, pass it remoteDS. Because **DataStore** and **RemoteDataStore** have methods with the same names and take (mostly) the same arguments, this change will work seamlessly.

```
...
  var RemoteDataStore = App.RemoteDataStore;
  var FormHandler = App.FormHandler;
  var Validation = App.Validation;
  var CheckList = App.CheckList;
  var remoteDS = new RemoteDataStore(SERVER_URL);
  var webshim = window.webshim;
  var myTruck = new Truck('ncc-1701', new DataStore()); remoteDS);
  window.myTruck = myTruck;
...
```

Save your changes and go back to the browser. Enter some coffee order information and submit the form. Keep the network panel open while you do so. You should see network transactions for every coffee order you add through the form or deliver via the checklist (Figure 13.12).

Figure 13.12 Saving coffee orders to the remote server

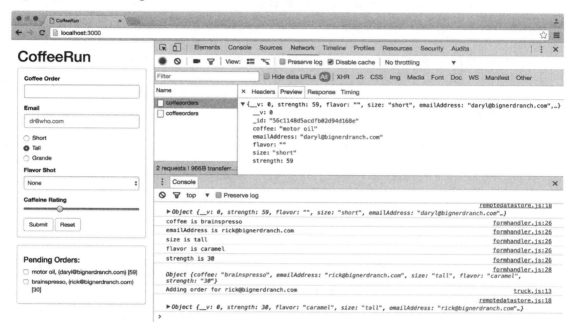

Congratulations! CoffeeRun is fully functional and is integrated with a remote web service.

The next chapter is the final one for CoffeeRun. It does not add any new features. Instead, it focuses on refactoring your existing code so you can learn a new pattern for working with asynchronous code.

Silver Challenge: Validating Against the Remote Server

Your validation code currently does a simple domain check. Update your validation code so that it also checks whether an email address has already been used for an order that exists on the server. Prevent the form from being submitted if that address has been used and provide an appropriate validation warning.

You may want to open a second browser window for CoffeeRun and enter different coffee orders in the two windows.

Pay attention to how often a request is sent to the server when doing this validation check. (You can see these in the DevTools network panel.) Can you find a good way to minimize the number of requests?

For the More Curious: Postman

One of the best tools for sending test requests to a server is Postman, a free plug-in for Chrome. It lets you build HTTP requests and specify the HTTP verbs, form data, headers, and user credentials (Figure 13.13).

Figure 13.13 The Postman

Postman is an indispensable tool for exploring an API before you write your server communication code. Download it from the Chrome web store, chrome.google.com/webstore. (Search for "Postman" to find it.)

14

Deferreds and Promises

In CoffeeRun, your modular code has helped you avoid the dreaded "spaghetti code" that can easily happen when you mix event-handling (UI) code with your application's internal logic.

Your modules interact via function arguments, also known as callbacks. Callbacks are a fine solution for situations in which you have code that only depends on a single, asynchronous step. Figure 14.1 shows a simplified version of one asynchronous flow from CoffeeRun.

Figure 14.1 Asynchronous flow for adding a coffee order

What happens when you have many dependent asynchronous steps? One option is to nest lots of callbacks, but this quickly becomes unwieldy and dangerous. With a simplified version of your submit handler code that does extra error checking, that approach might look like this:

```
formHandler.addSubmitHandler(function (data) {
  try {
    myTruck.createOrder(function (error) {
      if (error) {
        throw new Exception(error)
      } else {
        try {
          saveOnServer(function (error) {
            if (error) {
              throw new Exception({message: 'server error'});
            } else {
              try {
                checkList.addRow();
              } catch (e2) {
                handleDomError(e2);
              }
            }
          })
        } catch (e) {
          handleServerError(e, function () {
            // Try adding the row again
            try {
              checkList.addRow();
            } catch (e3) {
              handleDomError(e3);
            }
          });
        }
      }
    });
  } catch (e) {
    alert('Something bad happened.');
  }
});
```

Promises, which you will learn about in this chapter, are a better solution. That same series of steps might be expressed as a *chain* of Promises like this:

```
formHandler.addSubmitHandler()
  .then(myTruck.createOrder)
  .then(saveOnServer)
  .catch(handleServerError)
  .then(checkList.addRow)
  .catch(handleDomError);
```

Promises provide a way to architect very complex asynchronous code in a manageable way, and in this chapter you will use them to simplify the architecture of CoffeeRun. Promises are a relatively new feature, but they are well supported in recent browsers, including Chrome.

In CoffeeRun, you are mainly interested in performing the next step if the current one succeeds without errors. Promises make this simple. Instead of relying on callback arguments, you will return Promise objects, which will let you decouple your modules even further.

Promises and Deferreds

Promise objects are always in one of three states: *pending*, *fulfilled*, or *rejected* (Figure 14.2).

Figure 14.2 Three states of a Promise object

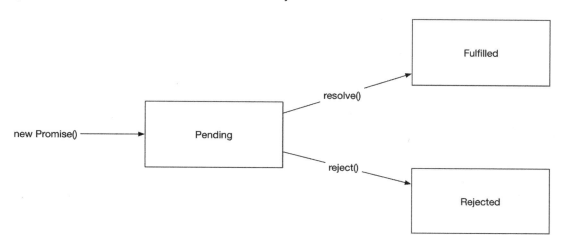

Every Promise object has a **then** method that is triggered when the Promise becomes fulfilled. You can call **then** and pass it a callback; when the Promise is fulfilled, the callback is invoked and passed whatever value the Promise received when doing its asynchronous work.

You can also chain multiple **then** calls together. Instead of writing functions that accept and then invoke callbacks, it is better to return Promise objects and let the caller chain a **then** off of that Promise.

You are going to start with jQuery's Deferred object, which works similarly to a Promise for simple use cases.

jQuery's **$.ajax** methods (including **$.post** and **$.get)** return a Deferred. Deferred objects have methods that let you register callbacks for two of their states: *fulfilled* and *rejected*. You are going to start by updating **RemoteDataStore** so that it returns the Deferreds produced by jQuery's Ajax methods. Later, you will modify your other modules to register callbacks with the Deferreds.

Returning Deferred

Take advantage of the Deferred objects returned by jQuery's **$.ajax** methods. In remotedatastore.js, update the prototype methods so that they return the result of calling **$.get**, **$.post**, and **$.ajax**.

```
...
  RemoteDataStore.prototype.add = function (key, val) {
    return $.post(this.serverUrl, val, function (serverResponse) {
      console.log(serverResponse);
    });
  };

  RemoteDataStore.prototype.getAll = function (cb) {
    return $.get(this.serverUrl, function (serverResponse) {
      console.log(serverResponse);
      cb(serverResponse);
    });
  };

  RemoteDataStore.prototype.get = function (key, cb) {
    return $.get(this.serverUrl + '/' + key, function (serverResponse) {
      console.log(serverResponse);
      cb(serverResponse);
    });
  };

  RemoteDataStore.prototype.remove = function (key) {
    return $.ajax(this.serverUrl + '/' + key, {
      type: 'DELETE'
    });
  };
...
```

Because they now return the **Deferred** produced by jQuery's Ajax methods, it is not absolutely necessary for **get** and **getAll** to accept callbacks. To account for the possibility of no callback, add an if statement to check that cb was passed in before invoking it.

```
...
  RemoteDataStore.prototype.getAll = function (cb) {
    return $.get(this.serverUrl, function (serverResponse) {
      if (cb) {
        console.log(serverResponse);
        cb(serverResponse);
      }
    });
  };

  RemoteDataStore.prototype.get = function (key, cb) {
    return $.get(this.serverUrl + '/' + key, function (serverResponse) {
      if (cb) {
        console.log(serverResponse);
        cb(serverResponse);
      }
    });
  };
...
```

Save remotedatastore.js. Since the **RemoteDataStore** methods return Deferreds, you will need to update the **Truck** methods to do the same. For now, you will focus on **createOrder** and **deliverOrder**.

Open truck.js and add a return to these two methods where you call them on this.db.

```
...
  Truck.prototype.createOrder = function (order) {
    console.log('Adding order for ' + order.emailAddress);
    return this.db.add(order.emailAddress, order);
  };

  Truck.prototype.deliverOrder = function (customerId) {
    console.log('Delivering order for ' + customerId);
    return this.db.remove(customerId);
  };
...
```

Save truck.js. **Truck** now returns the Deferreds that **RemoteDataStore** produces. When using Promises and Deferreds, it is a best practice to return them from your functions. Returning them lets any object that calls **createOrder** or **deliverOrder** register callbacks that are triggered when the asynchronous work is finished.

In the next section, you will do just that.

Registering Callbacks with then

$.ajax returns a Deferred, which has a **then** method. The **then** method registers a callback that is run when the Deferred is resolved. When the callback is invoked, it is passed the value sent back in the server response (Figure 14.3).

Figure 14.3 Deferred object invokes callbacks registered with **then**

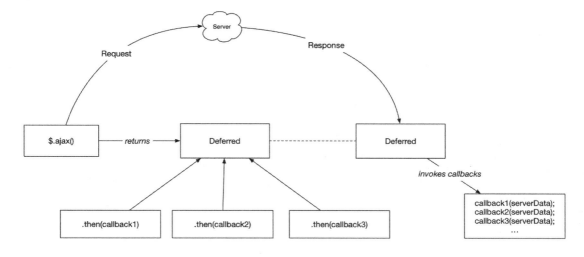

Start with a simple usage of **then**. In main.js, your submit handler calls **createOrder** and **addRow**. Change this so that **addRow** is registered as a callback of **createOrder**.

Open main.js and update the call to **formHandler.addSubmitHandler**. Chain a **.then** to the invocation of **createOrder**. Pass it a callback that runs **checkList.addRow**.

```
...
  formHandler.addSubmitHandler(function (data) {
    myTruck.createOrder.call(myTruck, data)+
      .then(function () {
        checkList.addRow.call(checkList, data);
      });
  });
...
```

Instead of invoking **addRow** immediately after **createOrder**, you are making **addRow** dependent on **createOrder** completing without errors or exceptions.

Handling Failures with then

then accepts a second argument, which is invoked when the Deferred shifts to the rejected state. To see this in action, add a second function argument (making sure to add a comma between the two function arguments) to **formHandler.addSubmitHandler** in main.js. Inside of this function, show an alert with a simple error message.

```
...
  formHandler.addSubmitHandler(function (data) {
    myTruck.createOrder.call(myTruck, data)
      .then(function () {
        checkList.addRow.call(checkList, data);
      },
      function () {
        alert('Server unreachable. Try again later.');
      }
      );
  });
...
```

At the top of main.js, misspell the server name so that Ajax requests fail. (This change will only be temporary, so you may want to simply cut a section out of the URL that you can paste back in later.)

```
(function (window) {
  'use strict';
  var FORM_SELECTOR = '[data-coffee-order="form"]';
  var CHECKLIST_SELECTOR = '[data-coffee-order="checklist"]';
  var SERVER_URL = 'http://coffeerun-v2-rest-api.herokuapp.com/api/coffeeorders/';
  var App = window.App;
...
```

Save your changes, make sure browser-sync is running, and open CoffeeRun in the browser. Fill out the form. You should see an alert pop up when you submit it (Figure 14.4).

Figure 14.4 Alert shown when Ajax call fails

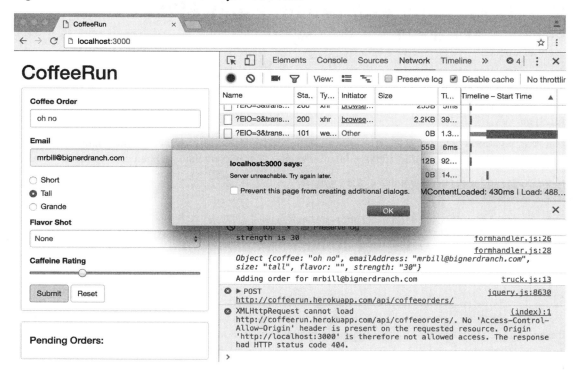

Restore the SERVER_URL to http://coffeerun-v2-rest-api.herokuapp.com/api/coffeeorders/. You can also delete the function argument that shows the **alert**.

```
(function (window) {
  'use strict';
  var FORM_SELECTOR = '[data-coffee-order="form"]';
  var CHECKLIST_SELECTOR = '[data-coffee-order="checklist"]';
  var SERVER_URL = 'http://coffeerun-v2-rest-api.herokuapp.com/api/coffeeorders/';

  ...

  formHandler.addSubmitHandler(function (data) {
    myTruck.createOrder.call(myTruck, data)
      .then(function () {
        checkList.addRow.call(checkList, data);
      },
      function () {
        alert('Server unreachable. Try again later.');
      }
      );
  });
  ...
```

Using **then** to register callbacks maps onto the way `Promises` work. If the `Promise` changes state to fulfilled, one set of callbacks is run. If the `Promise` changes state to rejected, the other set of callbacks is run.

Using Deferreds with Callback-Only APIs

Sometimes you will need to coordinate your `Deferred`-based code with callback-only APIs, such as event listeners.

Currently, **formHandler.addSubmitHandler** resets the form and focuses on the first element – no matter what happens with the Ajax request. However, you only want those things to happen if the Ajax request is successful. Put another way, you only want those things to happen if the `Deferred` is fulfilled.

How can you know whether the `Deferred` is fulfilled? Your function argument to **addSubmitHandler** can return the `Deferred`, and inside of **addSubmitHandler** you can chain a **.then** call to the `Deferred`.

In `main.js`, add a `return` keyword to the callback.

```
...
  formHandler.addSubmitHandler(function (data) {
    return myTruck.createOrder.call(myTruck, data)
      .then(function () {
        checkList.addRow.call(checkList, data);
      });
  });
...
```

Save `main.js`. Next, open `formhandler.js`, find the **addSubmitHandler** method, and locate the call to the anonymous function, `fn`. Because that anonymous function now returns a `Deferred`, you can chain a call to **.then** on the end of it. Use **.then** to register a callback that resets the form and focuses on the first element.

```
...
  FormHandler.prototype.addSubmitHandler = function (fn) {
    console.log('Setting submit handler for form');
    this.$formElement.on('submit', function (event) {
      event.preventDefault();

      var data = {};
      $(this).serializeArray().forEach(function (item) {
        data[item.name] = item.value;
        console.log(item.name + ' is ' + item.value);
      });
      console.log(data);
      fn(data)+
      .then(function () {
        this.reset();
        this.elements[0].focus();
      });
    });
  };
...
```

Before, you had three sequential statements: invoke the callback, reset the form, and focus on the first form element. Now, you have one statement that depends on the result of the previous statement. You invoke the callback and – *if* the promised work finishes execution normally, without encountering an exception – *then* you reset the form and focus on the first form element.

There is just one concern. When you register a callback function with **.then**, that callback function has a new scope. You need to **.bind** that anonymous function so that the value of this is set to the **FormHandler** instance.

Make this change in formhandler.js.

```
...
  FormHandler.prototype.addSubmitHandler = function (fn) {
    ...
      fn(data)
        .then(function () {
          this.reset();
          this.elements[0].focus();
        }.bind(this));
    });
  };
...
```

Save formhandler.js.

Similarly, you only want to remove an item from the checklist if the call to **Truck.prototype.deliverOrder** is successful.

Chain a call to **.then** off the function passed to **addClickHandler** in checklist.js. Remember to **.bind** the value of this for the anonymous function.

```
...
  CheckList.prototype.addClickHandler = function (fn) {
    this.$element.on('click', 'input', function (event) {
      var email = event.target.value;
      this.removeRow(email);
      fn(email)
        .then(function () {
          this.removeRow(email);
        }.bind(this));
    }.bind(this));
  };
...
```

Save checklist.js. Recall that you invoke **addClickHandler** in main.js:

checkList.addClickHandler(myTruck.deliverOrder.bind(myTruck);

There is no need to make any changes to this method call. Because **Truck.prototype.deliverOrder** is returning the Deferred, **addClickHandler** will work as written.

All of your data is remote, which means you need to load it and draw checklist items for each coffee order. You can use the **Truck.prototype.printOrders** method along with the **CheckList.prototype.addRow** method to do this.

You will make two changes to **printOrders**. First, you will update **printOrders** to work with Deferreds. Then, you will add a function argument to **printOrders** which it will call as it iterates through the data to print.

In truck.js, your code for **Truck.prototype.printOrders** currently looks like this:

```
...
  Truck.prototype.printOrders = function () {
    var customerIdArray = Object.keys(this.db.getAll());

    console.log('Truck #' + this.truckId + ' has pending orders:');
    customerIdArray.forEach(function (id) {
      console.log(this.db.get(id));
    }.bind(this));
  };
...
```

Update this implementation to call and return **this.db.getAll**, chaining a **.then** to it. Pass an anonymous function to **.then** and set its this keyword using **.bind**:

```
...
  Truck.prototype.printOrders = function () {
    return this.db.getAll()
      .then(function (orders) {
        var customerIdArray = Object.keys(this.db.getAll());

        console.log('Truck #' + this.truckId + ' has pending orders:');
        customerIdArray.forEach(function (id) {
          console.log(this.db.get(id));
        }.bind(this));
      }.bind(this));
  };
...
```

Your anonymous function expects to receive an object containing all of the coffee order data retrieved from the server. Extract the keys from that object and assign them to the variable named customerIdArray.

```
...
  Truck.prototype.printOrders = function () {
    return this.db.getAll()
      .then(function (orders) {
        var customerIdArray = Object.keys(this.db.getAll(), orders);

        console.log('Truck #' + this.truckId + ' has pending orders:');
        customerIdArray.forEach(function (id) {
          console.log(this.db.get(id));
        }.bind(this));
      }.bind(this));
  };
...
```

Likewise, change the **console.log** statement so that it does not call this.db.get(id). It should use the allData object, which already has all of the coffee orders. You should not make an extra Ajax call for each item that needs to be printed.

```
...
  Truck.prototype.printOrders = function () {
    return this.db.getAll()
      .then(function (orders) {
        var customerIdArray = Object.keys(orders);

        console.log('Truck #' + this.truckId + ' has pending orders:');
        customerIdArray.forEach(function (id) {
          console.log(this.db.get(id)), orders[id]);
        }.bind(this));
      }.bind(this));
  };
...
```

printOrders should take an optional function argument. You need to check whether it was passed in and, if it was, invoke it. When you invoke it, you will pass it the current coffee order allData[id].

```
...
  Truck.prototype.printOrders = function (printFn) {
    return this.db.getAll()
      .then(function (orders) {
        var customerIdArray = Object.keys(orders);

        console.log('Truck #' + this.truckId + ' has pending orders:');
        customerIdArray.forEach(function (id) {
          console.log(orders[id]);
          if (printFn) {
            printFn(orders[id]);
          }
        }.bind(this));
      }.bind(this));
  };
...
```

Save truck.js. In main.js, invoke **printOrders** and pass it **checkList.addRow**. Make sure that **addRow** is bound to the **CheckList** instance.

```
...
  formHandler.addInputHandler(Validation.isCompanyEmail);

  myTruck.printOrders(checkList.addRow.bind(checkList));

  webshim.polyfill('forms forms-ext');
  webshim.setOptions('forms', { addValidators: true, lazyCustomMessages: true });

})(window);
```

Save and return to the browser. CoffeeRun should show the existing coffee orders in the checklist. Manually reload to confirm that the checklist is repopulated each time. Inspect the network panel and see that Ajax requests are taking place (Figure 14.5).

Figure 14.5 Drawing orders on page load

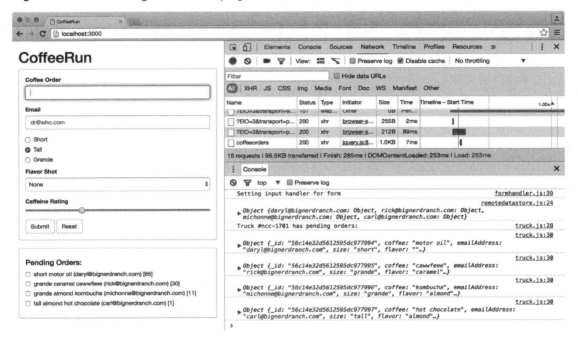

Giving DataStore a Promise

By returning **Deferred**s from **RemoteDataStore**'s methods, you have a flexible way to use the data sent back from the server.

But you may have noticed that **RemoteDataStore**'s methods now stray far away from how **DataStore**'s methods work. If you were to swap a regular **DataStore** back in, you would see that it no longer works with your application (Figure 14.6).

Figure 14.6 Uh oh. DataStore is no longer compatible

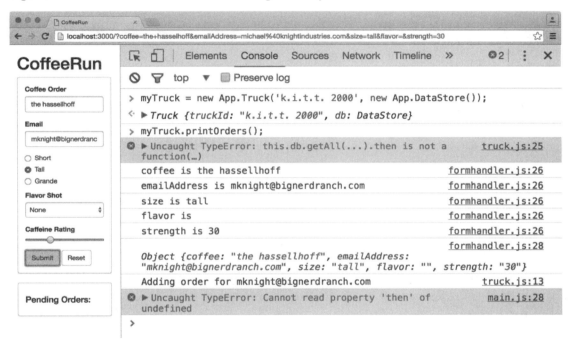

In Figure 14.6, you can see that instantiating a **Truck** with a regular **DataStore** throws errors and fails to work correctly with the UI. CoffeeRun expects a `Promise`-based **DataStore** in order to function correctly.

To remedy this situation, you are going to change **DataStore**'s four methods so that they return `Promises`.

jQuery's `Deferred` objects have treated you well. However, because **DataStore** is not using the jQuery **$.ajax** methods you have been using to access `Deferreds`, you will need to use the native **Promise** constructor to create and return `Promises`.

Creating and returning Promises

In datastore.js, you are going to update the **add** method. But first, create a Promise variable and assign it the value window.Promise. While not absolutely necessary, it is a good idea to continue this pattern of importing anything from the global scope that you will need inside of your module.

Inside the **add** method, create a new variable called promise. Assign it a new instance of **Promise**. Make sure to return the promise variable at the end of **add**.

```
(function (window) {
  'use strict';
  var App = window.App || {};
  var Promise = window.Promise;

  function DataStore() {
    this.data = {};
  }

  DataStore.prototype.add = function (key, val) {
    this.data[key] = val;
    var promise = new Promise();

    return promise;
  };
...
```

The **Promise** constructor needs a function argument. Pass it an anonymous function that accepts two function arguments, resolve and reject.

```
...
  DataStore.prototype.add = function (key, val) {
    this.data[key] = val;
    var promise = new Promise(function (resolve, reject) {
    });

    return promise;
  };
...
```

When the **Promise** does its work, it will invoke the anonymous function argument and pass it two values: resolve and reject. The resolve function is invoked to change the state of the Promise object to fulfilled. The reject function is invoked to change the state of the Promise object to rejected.

Next, move the data storage line (this.data[key] = val;) down into the body of the anonymous function. To make sure that this.data correctly refers to the **DataStore**'s data instance variable, **bind** the anonymous function to this.

```
...
  DataStore.prototype.add = function (key, val) {
    this.data[key] = val;
    var promise = new Promise(function (resolve, reject) {
      this.data[key] = val;
    }.bind(this));

    return promise;
  };
...
```

Resolving a Promise

At the very end of the anonymous function, invoke `resolve` with no argument.

```
...
  DataStore.prototype.add = function (key, val) {
    var promise = new Promise(function (resolve, reject) {
      this.data[key] = val;
      resolve(null);
    }.bind(this));

    return promise;
  };
...
```

Why use `null` as the argument? **add**ing a value to the **DataStore** does not produce a value, so there is nothing for it to **resolve** to. When you need to explicitly return a non-value you should use `null`. (You could also use `resolve(val)` to give the next function in the chain access to the freshly stored value. For **CoffeeRun**, this is not necessary, and therefore not included as part of the example.)

Promise-ifying the other DataStore methods

You could manually update the other three methods using this same pattern of code. But instead of retyping all that code, create a helper function called **promiseResolvedWith** to create a **Promise**, resolve it, and return it. Update **DataStore.prototype.add** to use this helper.

```
...
  function DataStore() {
    this.data = {};
  }

  function promiseResolvedWith(value) {
    var promise = new Promise(function (resolve, reject) {
      resolve(value);
    });
    return promise;
  }

  DataStore.prototype.add = function (key, val) {
    var promise = new Promise(function (resolve, reject) {
      this.data[key] = val;
      resolve(null);
    }.bind(this));

    return promise;
    return promiseResolvedWith(null);
  };
...
```

promiseResolvedWith is a reusable form of the `Promise` code you wrote in the **add** method. It accepts a parameter called `value`, creates a new variable named `promise`, and assigns it to a new instance of **Promise**. It passes an anonymous function to the **Promise** constructor that accepts two arguments: `resolve` and `reject`. Inside the anonymous function, you invoke `resolve` and pass it the `value` argument.

In **promiseResolvedWith**, you do not need to **bind** the function argument to this, as there are no references to this that need to be maintained.

Update the other methods to use **promiseResolvedWith**. Pass **get** and **getAll** the value you were returning in the non-Promise version. Pass null to **remove**.

```
...
  DataStore.prototype.get = function (key) {
    return this.data[key];
    return promiseResolvedWith(this.data[key]);
  };

  DataStore.prototype.getAll = function () {
    return this.data;
    return promiseResolvedWith(this.data);
  };

  DataStore.prototype.remove = function (key) {
    delete this.data[key];
    return promiseResolvedWith(null);
  };
...
```

Finally, update main.js to use a **DataStore** instead of a **RemoteDataStore**.

```
...
  var remoteDS = new RemoteDataStore(SERVER_URL);
  var webshim = window.webshim;
  var myTruck = new Truck('ncc-1701', remoteDS), new DataStore());
  window.myTruck = myTruck;
...
```

After making these changes, save your code and take CoffeeRun for another spin. You should see that it works correctly using **DataStore**, but makes no Ajax requests (Figure 14.7).

Figure 14.7 CoffeeRun is done!

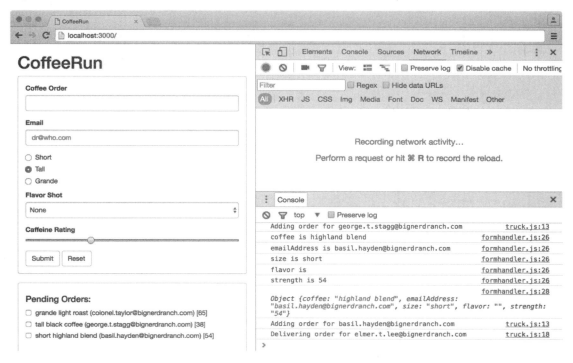

CoffeeRun has taken you on quite a journey! Along the way, you wrote some pretty serious JavaScript using IIFEs, callbacks, and `Promises`. You also got a taste of jQuery, which you used to manipulate DOM elements and communicate with a RESTful web service.

It is time to part ways with CoffeeRun and move on. The next app, Chattrbox, is a *full-stack* chat application. You will not only create the front-end code but also write the server. Do not worry if this is your first server application. You will still be using JavaScript, just not for the browser. Get ready to work with Node.js!

Silver Challenge: Fallback to DataStore

If you are lucky, you have a nice, stable network connection all the time. But you should be prepared in case your connection goes down while using CoffeeRun.

Update CoffeeRun so that it uses a **DataStore** when its Ajax requests cannot reach the server.

To make sure that this is working, turn off your computer's network connection while loading and saving coffee orders.

Part III
Real-Time Data

15

Introduction to Node.js

Node.js is an open-source project that lets you write JavaScript that runs outside the browser.

When you write JavaScript for the browser, your code is given access to global objects like the document and window, as well as other APIs and libraries. With Node, your code can access the hard drive, databases, and the network (Figure 15.1).

Figure 15.1 JavaScript running in browser vs via Node

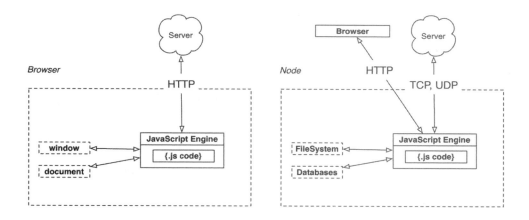

Using Node, you can create anything from command-line tools to web servers. Over the next four chapters, you will use Node to help create a real-time chat application called Chattrbox (Figure 15.2).

Figure 15.2 Chattrbox: strictly for important conversations

Chattrbox will consist of two parts: a Node.js server and a JavaScript app running in the browser. The browser will connect to the Node server and receive the HTML, CSS, and JavaScript files. At that point, the JavaScript app in the browser will begin handling real-time communication over WebSockets. This process is diagrammed in Figure 15.3.

Figure 15.3 Network diagram of the Chattrbox application

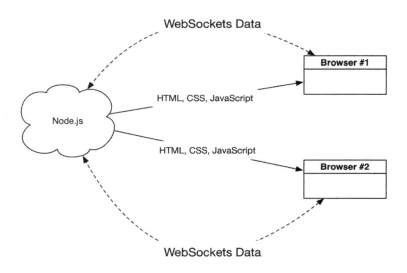

You will learn about WebSockets in the next chapter. This chapter focuses on getting you familiar with Node.

Node and npm

When you installed Node.js in Chapter 1, you got access to two command-line programs: node and the Node package manager, npm. You may recall that npm allows you to install open-source development tools, like browser-sync. The node program does the work of running programs written in JavaScript.

Most of your work will be with npm in this chapter. The npm command-line tool can perform a variety of tasks, like installing third-party code that you can incorporate into your project and managing your project's workflow and external dependencies. In this chapter, you will be using npm to:

- create the package.json file, using npm init

- add third-party modules, using npm install --save

- run frequently used tools saved in package.json's scripts section

Node is much more than the node and npm commands. It also includes a number of useful modules that provide constructors to help you do things like work with files and folders, communicate over a network, and handle events. Also, when writing JavaScript for Node you will have access to utility functions that facilitate JavaScript's interaction with the Node module ecosystem. For example, Node provides a much simpler module pattern than the IIFEs you used for CoffeeRun.

The package.json file mentioned above is a file that acts as your Node project's manifest. It holds your project's name, version number, description, and other information. More important, it is where you can store configuration settings and commands for npm to use when testing and building your application.

You could create this file by hand, but it is much easier to let npm do it for you.

npm init

Create a directory in your projects folder named chattrbox. In your terminal program, change to that directory and run npm init to have npm create package.json.

npm will prompt you for information about the project. It will also offer default answers, which are fine for now. Press the Return key to accept the defaults (Figure 15.4).

Figure 15.4 Running `npm init`

```
● ● ●                    chattrbox — bash — 80×39
$ npm init
This utility will walk you through creating a package.json file.
It only covers the most common items, and tries to guess sensible defaults.

See `npm help json` for definitive documentation on these fields
and exactly what they do.

Use `npm install <pkg> --save` afterwards to install a package and
save it as a dependency in the package.json file.

Press ^C at any time to quit.
name: (chattrbox)
version: (1.0.0)
description:
entry point: (index.js)
test command:
git repository:
keywords:
author:
license: (ISC)
About to write to /Users/chrisaquino/Projects/chattrbox/package.json:

{
  "name": "chattrbox",
  "version": "1.0.0",
  "description": "",
  "main": "index.js",
  "scripts": {
    "test": "echo \"Error: no test specified\" && exit 1"
  },
  "author": "",
  "license": "ISC"
}


Is this ok? (yes)
$ █
```

Open the chattrbox project folder in Atom. You will see that the package.json file was indeed created for you (Figure 15.5).

Figure 15.5 `package.json` contents after `npm init`

npm scripts

In package.json, notice the section labeled "scripts". This is for commands that you might need to run again and again while working on your project.

As you build Chattrbox, you will add to the "scripts" section of package.json to make your development workflow more efficient. Create your first npm workflow script by adding a "start" script (note that you must add a comma to the end of the "test" line):

```
...
  "scripts": {
    "test": "echo \"Error: no test specified\" && exit 1",
    "start": "node index.js"
  },
...
```

This lets you start your Node server by running npm start from the command line.

Hello, World

To introduce you to the world of writing JavaScript outside the browser, you are going to start with a classic Hello, World program. Create a new file named index.js within your chattrbox folder and type the following, which we will explain after you have entered it:

```
var http = require('http');

var server = http.createServer(function (req, res) {
  console.log('Responding to a request.');
  res.end('<h1>Hello, World</h1>');
});
server.listen(3000);
```

On the first line, you used Node's built-in **require** function to access the http module included with Node. This module provides a number of tools for working with HTTP requests and responses, such as the **http.createServer** function.

http.createServer takes in one argument, a function. This function is called for every HTTP request. You may recognize this as the callback pattern you used with browser events – except that in this case it is a server-side event (receiving an HTTP request) that triggers the callback.

In your callback, you log a message to the console and write some HTML text to the response. In Node, it is common to use req and res as the variable names for HTTP request and response objects.

Finally, you tell the server to listen on port 3000 using **server.listen**. This is commonly referred to as "binding to a port."

Save your files. To see your Node server in action, run the command npm start. The terminal results are shown in Figure 15.6.

Figure 15.6 Running index.js via npm `start`

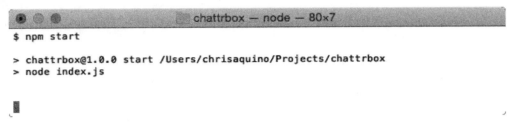

```
$ npm start

> chattrbox@1.0.0 start /Users/chrisaquino/Projects/chattrbox
> node index.js
```

Next, open your browser to `http://localhost:3000`. Your results will look like Figure 15.7. (Note that in some browsers other than Chrome, you may see your HTML as plain text. These browsers are expecting either a `doctype` or an extra piece of metadata in the response declaring that the response should be interpreted as HTML. You will address this as one of the challenges at the end of the chapter.)

Figure 15.7 Accessing your Node server in a browser

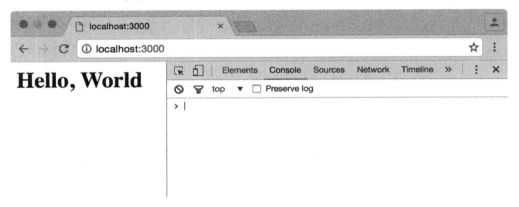

Unlike when you ran Ottergram and CoffeeRun, there is no JavaScript to see in the browser. By the time you see this page, your JavaScript code has already done its work on the server.

Return to your terminal. You should see that **console.log** printed `Responding to a request` when the request was received (Figure 15.8).

Figure 15.8 **console.log** when request arrives

```
$ npm start

> chattrbox@1.0.0 start /Users/chrisaquino/Projects/chattrbox
> node index.js

Responding to a request.
```

Adding an npm Script

In addition to letting you write command-line JavaScript programs, Node gives you a way to orchestrate your workflow as you develop these programs. It is a powerful feature that you should take advantage of. To see how this works, you will add a bit of automation to your project.

Take running your server, for example. Every time you want to try something new in your code, you have to repeat a few steps:

- make the change to the code in your editor

- switch to your terminal

- press Control-C to stop the program

- run npm start to start your program again

You could write a program to automate the work of restarting your service. You are in luck, though – someone has already written it for you, in a module called nodemon. Integrating nodemon into your workflow early on will make writing your program a much smoother experience.

In the terminal, stop your program and run the following command to install the nodemon module:

```
npm install --save-dev nodemon
```

You will see the lines below, in which npm is warning you about some blank fields in your package.json file. Do not be alarmed – just be aware that npm is a stickler for details.

```
npm WARN chattrbox@1.0.0 No description
npm WARN chattrbox@1.0.0 No repository field.
```

Notice the --save-dev option that you used in this npm install command. It tells npm to help you keep a list of any third-party modules your application depends on. That list is stored in your package.json file. If necessary, all of the dependencies in that list can be installed by running the npm install command (with no arguments). This means that when you are sharing your code you do not need to include all of the third-party modules as well.

If you look in your package.json file, you will see that npm created a new "devDependencies" section for you, with an entry for nodemon.

```
...
  "author": "",
  "license": "ISC",
  "devDependencies": {
    "nodemon": "^1.9.1"
  }
```

Now, update your package.json to add another item to the "scripts" section:

```
...
"scripts": {
  "test": "echo \"Error: no test specified\" && exit 1",
  "start": "node index.js",
  "dev": "nodemon index.js"
},
...
```

In the terminal, restart your node program via your new npm script using the command npm run dev. Note that the command is not simply npm dev. This differs from npm start in that npm assumes that certain commands (like start) will exist. For custom npm scripts, you must specify that you want to run them.

You should see that nodemon is now managing your node program (Figure 15.9).

Figure 15.9 Running via npm run dev

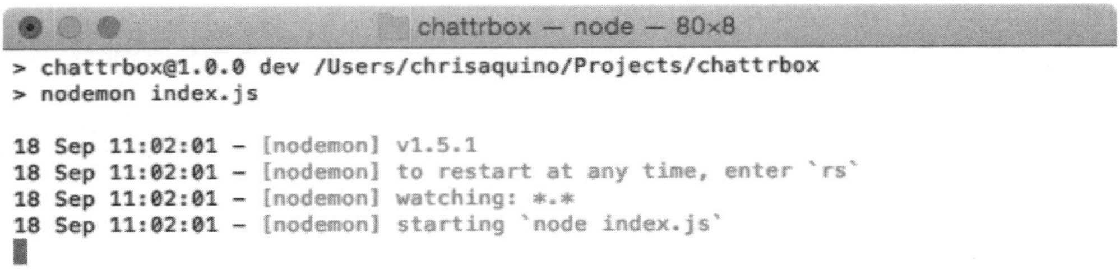

```
● ● ●                         chattrbox — node — 80×8
> chattrbox@1.0.0 dev /Users/chrisaquino/Projects/chattrbox
> nodemon index.js

18 Sep 11:02:01 - [nodemon] v1.5.1
18 Sep 11:02:01 - [nodemon] to restart at any time, enter `rs`
18 Sep 11:02:01 - [nodemon] watching: *.*
18 Sep 11:02:01 - [nodemon] starting `node index.js`
```

In index.js, change "Hello, World" to "Hello, World!!" and save the changes. nodemon notices and restarts your node program automatically (Figure 15.10).

Figure 15.10 nodemon restarts when your code changes

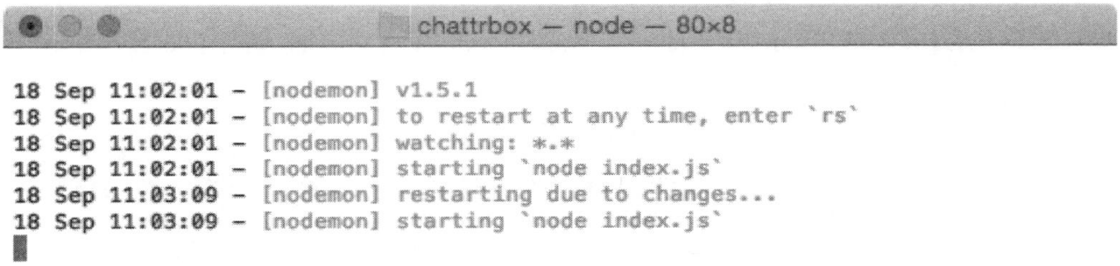

```
● ● ●                         chattrbox — node — 80×8
18 Sep 11:02:01 - [nodemon] v1.5.1
18 Sep 11:02:01 - [nodemon] to restart at any time, enter `rs`
18 Sep 11:02:01 - [nodemon] watching: *.*
18 Sep 11:02:01 - [nodemon] starting `node index.js`
18 Sep 11:03:09 - [nodemon] restarting due to changes...
18 Sep 11:03:09 - [nodemon] starting `node index.js`
```

As you continue to work with node and npm in the following chapters, you will periodically pull in a new module to help out.

Serving from Files

Being able to write and run JavaScript on your server is nice. Most servers will want to vend out and process content living in files, too. Your next job is to make your server read files from a subfolder and send them in a response back to the browser. This is similar to what browser-sync was doing for you in earlier chapters.

Create a new folder named app inside of your chattrbox project folder. In it, create an index.html file with the following text:

```
Hello, File!
```

You do not need any actual HTML in this file – it only needs some content that can be read. Your project folder should look like Figure 15.11.

Figure 15.11 Chattrbox project layout

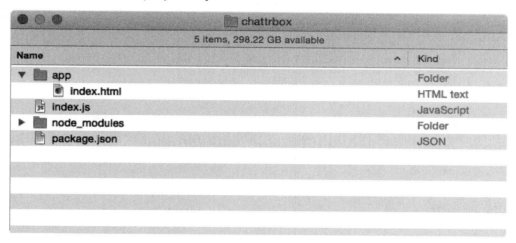

Reading a file with the fs module

In index.js, import the Node.js file system module, fs, and call its **readFile** method.

```
var http = require('http');
var fs = require('fs');

var server = http.createServer(function (req, res) {
  console.log('Responding to a request.');
  res.end('<h1>Hello, World</h1>');
  fs.readFile('app/index.html', function (err, data) {
    res.end(data);
  });
});
server.listen(3000);
```

The **readFile** method takes a file name and a callback. Inside your callback, you sent the contents of the file instead of the HTML text using res.end.

Notice that your callback accepts an err argument as well as the data from reading the file. This is a Node.js programming convention that we will discuss later in this chapter.

nodemon should have restarted your program, so you can go directly to your browser and reload. In your browser, you should see exactly what you wrote in your index.html file:

```
Hello, File!
```

This is a good start, but your chat application will need to do more than serve a single HTML file. That HTML file may request other CSS or JavaScript files. To fulfill those requests, your node program will need to understand what file is being requested and where to look for the requested file. You will work on that next.

Working with the request URL

First, you need to get the URL path from the request object. If the path is just '/', it is best to return the index.html file. This is a common convention from the early days of the web.

Otherwise, you should try to return the file the request object is asking for.

In index.js, update your callback to check what file the browser is requesting.

```
var http = require('http');
var fs = require('fs');

var server = http.createServer(function (req, res) {
  console.log('Responding to a request.');
  var url = req.url;

  var fileName = 'index.html';
  if (url.length > 1) {
    fileName = url.substring(1);
  }
  console.log(fileName);
  fs.readFile('app/index.html', function (err, data) {
    res.end(data);
  });
});
server.listen(3000);
```

Using the request object's url property, you can see whether the browser is asking for the default (index.html) or another file. If it is another file, you call **url.substring(1)** to strip off the first character, which will be a '/'.

For now, you are just logging the filename to the console.

After nodemon restarts your program, try going to `http://localhost:3000/woohoo` or any other path, including the default `'/'` path. The results in your terminal will look something like Figure 15.12.

Figure 15.12 Logging the requested file path

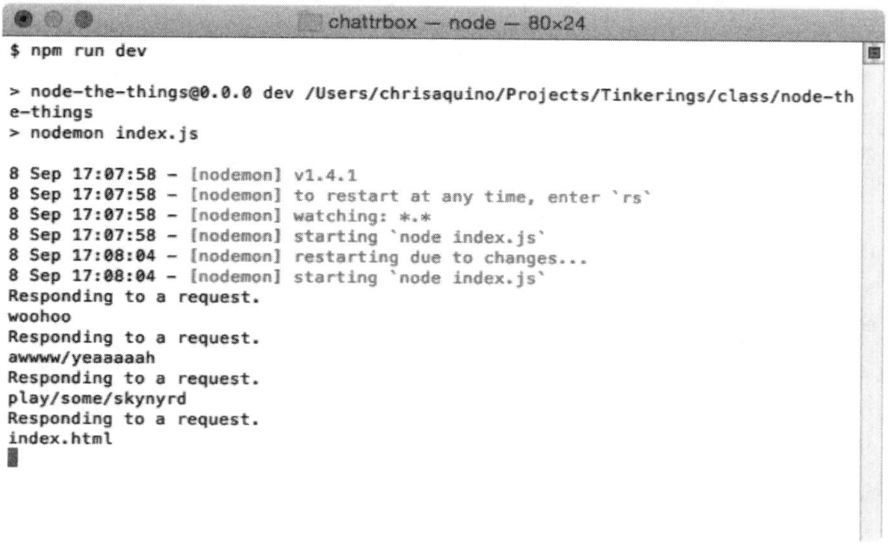

```
$ npm run dev

> node-the-things@0.0.0 dev /Users/chrisaquino/Projects/Tinkerings/class/node-th
e-things
> nodemon index.js

8 Sep 17:07:58 - [nodemon] v1.4.1
8 Sep 17:07:58 - [nodemon] to restart at any time, enter `rs`
8 Sep 17:07:58 - [nodemon] watching: *.*
8 Sep 17:07:58 - [nodemon] starting `node index.js`
8 Sep 17:08:04 - [nodemon] restarting due to changes...
8 Sep 17:08:04 - [nodemon] starting `node index.js`
Responding to a request.
woohoo
Responding to a request.
awwww/yeaaaaah
Responding to a request.
play/some/skynyrd
Responding to a request.
index.html
```

(Recall from Chapter 2 that browsers will automatically ask for a `favicon.ico` file, so you may see a request for it logged to the terminal as well.)

Now it is time to make use of this path information.

Using the path module

You could just pass the fileName to **fs.readFile**, but it is better to use the path module, which has utilities for handling and transforming file paths. One small but important reason for using the module is that some operating systems use a forward slash and some use a backslash. The path module handles these differences with ease.

Update index.js to import the path module and use it to find the file that was requested.

```
var http = require('http');
var fs = require('fs');
var path = require('path');

var server = http.createServer(function (req, res) {
  console.log('Responding to a request.');
  var url = req.url;

  var fileName = 'index.html';
  if (url.length > 1) {
    fileName = url.substring(1);
  }
  console.log(fileName);
  var filePath = path.resolve(__dirname, 'app', fileName);
  fs.readFile('app/index.html'filePath, function (err, data) {
    res.end(data);
  });
});
server.listen(3000);
```

Test a few filepaths in the browser to make sure your application still works the same. The default path should return index.html, and nonexistent paths (like '/woohoo/') should show nothing and log out their filename.

Next, create a test.html file in the app folder. Write the following inside it:

Hola, Node!

Try to access it in the browser. Your node program should return it without any trouble (Figure 15.13).

Figure 15.13 Retrieving test.html

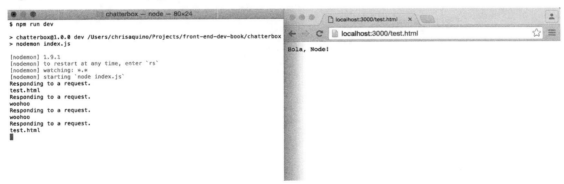

You have added code that successfully serves a specific file based on the URL path. The next thing to do is abstract out that functionality into its own module.

Creating a custom module

Your callback has (at least) two jobs. It figures out what file is being requested, and it reads that file to send back in the response. To make the code a bit more modular and maintainable, one of those responsibilities should be moved to its own module.

In CoffeeRun, you declared modules in an IIFE that assigned a value to a property of the global namespace. Modules in Node programs work differently. You still write your module code in a file by itself, but you do not need the IIFE.

Create a new file called extract.js in the same directory as your index.js (not in the app directory). Add a function called **extractFilePath** that finds the appropriate file. (This code is very similar to what you already wrote in index.js.)

```
var path = require('path');

var extractFilePath = function (url) {
  var filePath;
  var fileName = 'index.html';

  if (url.length > 1) {
    fileName = url.substring(1);
  }
  console.log('The fileName is: ' + fileName);

  filePath = path.resolve(__dirname, 'app', fileName);
  return filePath;
};
```

You have taken much of the code from index.js and placed it in its own function, called **extractFilePath**. Next, make the **extractFilePath** function available so that other modules can import it with **require**. To do this, assign **extractFilePath** to a global variable named module.exports. This is a special variable provided by Node. Whatever value is assigned to it is the value other modules are able to import. Any other variables or functions will not be visible to other modules.

```
...
  filePath = path.resolve(__dirname, 'app', fileName);
  return filePath;
};

module.exports = extractFilePath;
```

This new line tells Node that when you import the extract module by calling require('./extract'), the value returned is the **extractFilePath** function. Do that now in index.js.

Using your custom module

Update index.js to use your new extract module instead of handling those responsibilities.

```
var http = require('http');
var fs = require('fs');
var path = require('path');
var extract = require('./extract');

var server = http.createServer(function (req, res) {
  console.log('Responding to a request.');
  var url = req.url;

  var fileName = 'index.html';
  if (url.length > 1) {
    fileName = url.substring(1);
  }
  console.log(fileName);
  var filePath = path.resolve(__dirname, 'app', fileName);
  var filePath = extract(req.url);
  fs.readFile(filePath, function (err, data) {
    res.end(data);
  });
});
server.listen(3000);
```

You imported your custom module using the **require** function. You assigned the value of the module to the new variable extract. Now you are able to use the **extract** function just as you would the **extractFilePath** function.

After nodemon has reloaded your code, test some URL paths and confirm that the default index.html and test.html still load. Also, make sure that nonexistent paths come up as a blank page and without an error.

Error Handling

One last job remains. When a file cannot be found, it is better to return an error code than to silently pretend that all is well. To do that, you will need to detect when **fs.readFile** returns an error instead of a file.

In JavaScript, it is common to pass callbacks to API methods. The same is true for Node.js, and callbacks typically take in an error as their first argument. Because the error comes before the result, you are forced to at least see the error, whether or not you handle it.

In index.js, check for a file error and write a 404 error code if one is found:

```
var http = require('http');
var fs = require('fs');
var extract = require('./extract');

var handleError = function (err, res) {
  res.writeHead(404);
  res.end();
};

var server = http.createServer(function (req, res) {
  console.log('Responding to a request.');
  var filePath = extract(req.url);
  fs.readFile(filePath, function (err, data) {
    if (err) {
      handleError(err, res);
      return;
    } else {
      res.end(data);
    }
  });
});
server.listen(3000);
```

Save your changes. After nodemon restarts, go to a nonexistent path, such as `http://localhost:3000/woohoo`. Open the network panel in the DevTools, and you should see the error code, as in Figure 15.14.

Figure 15.14 404 Status code in the network panel

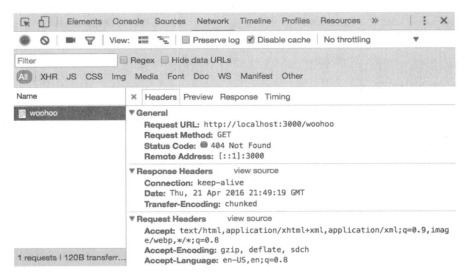

In your callback, the very first thing you do is check whether this `err` argument has a value that is not `null` or `undefined` and do something with it. In this example, you pass the error information along to the function **handleError** and then `return` to exit the anonymous callback.

Errors should never be silently discarded. A simple 404 will do fine for now, which is what **handleError** does.

This pattern – "errors first, return early" – is one of the best practices that is a part of the Node ecosystem. All of the modules that come with Node follow this pattern, as do most open-source modules.

You have built a working web server with just a few dozen lines of JavaScript, using patterns (such as callbacks) that you were already familiar with.

Node provides a rich set of modules for working with networks and files, such as the `http` and `fs` modules you used in this project. Thanks to Node's `require` and `module.exports` keywords, you can modularize your own code very easily.

Over the next three chapters, you will continue to build the Chattrbox server as well as a working front end.

For the More Curious: npm Module Registry

There are a wealth of available packages that can be installed via `npm`. You can search or browse these packages in the Module Registry, `www.npmjs.com`.

Make sure to look at the documentation for npm at docs.npmjs.com. You might also be interested in creating your own modules for others to use. If so, see docs.npmjs.com/getting-started/creating-node-modules.

Bronze Challenge: Creating a Custom Error Page

When you go to a path for a file that does not exist, you currently get a blank browser page and a 404 status code.

For this challenge, create a special error page to display to the user instead of returning the error as a status code.

For the More Curious: MIME Types

Have you ever wondered how a computer knows how to open a movie file with a video player and a PDF with a document viewer? Your computer keeps a table of file types and the programs associated with those file types. It infers a file's type by looking at the file extension (e.g., .html or .pdf).

A browser needs those same associations so that it knows whether to render the response as HTML, use a plug-in to play music, or download a file to the hard drive. But HTTP responses do not have file extensions. Instead, the server must tell the browser what type of information is in the response.

It does this by specifying the *MIME type* or *media type* in the response's Content-Type header. For example, Figure 15.15 shows what you would see in the network panel of the DevTools if you inspected the response for www.bignerdranch.com.

Figure 15.15 Inspecting the Content-Type header on www.bignerdranch.com

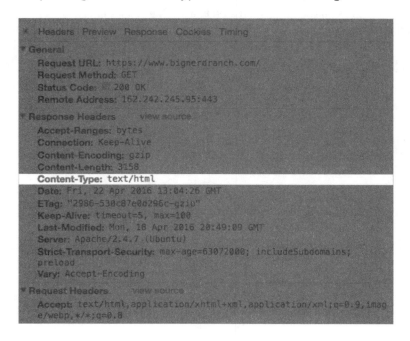

The `Content-Type` header is set to `text/html` – the MIME type for HTML. You can set this header in your projects. This is what that would look like for Chattrbox:

```
...
var server = http.createServer(function (req, res) {
  console.log('Responding to a request.');
  var filePath = extract(req.url);
  fs.readFile(filePath, function (err, data) {
    if (err) {
      handleError(err, res);
      return;
    } else {
      res.setHeader('Content-Type', 'text/html');
      res.end(data);
    }
  });
});
server.listen(3000);
```

(Note that you must set the header before you end the response.)

To find out more about MIME types in general, check out `en.wikipedia.org/wiki/ Media_type`. For more about setting headers in your Node programs, go to `nodejs.org/api/ http.html#http_response_setheader_name_value`.

Silver Challenge: Providing a MIME Type Dynamically

Dynamically provide a MIME type for your responses based on the file type. To help you with this task, install the `mime` module using `npm`. Information and documentation about the `mime` module is available at `github.com/broofa/node-mime`.

Add different files to your app folder, including plain text, PDFs, audio files, and movies. Make sure that your browser is displaying each type correctly.

Gold Challenge: Moving Error Handling to Its Own Module

Take the code that does the file reading and error handling and move it into its own module.

Also, make the module configurable so that when you import it you can specify what base folder the static HTML, CSS, and JavaScript are in.

16

Real-Time Communication with WebSockets

With regular GET and POST requests, your browser has to make a new request and wait for a response for each exchange of data with the server. As you learned in earlier chapters, this is also the case with Ajax requests. While Ajax requests do not cause page reloads, they do generate just as much network traffic, with each request and response requiring a little bit of overhead to produce and process.

WebSockets, on the other hand, provides a two-way communication protocol over HTTP. It creates a single connection and keeps it open for real-time communication (Figure 16.1).

Figure 16.1 Multiple Ajax requests vs a single WebSockets connection

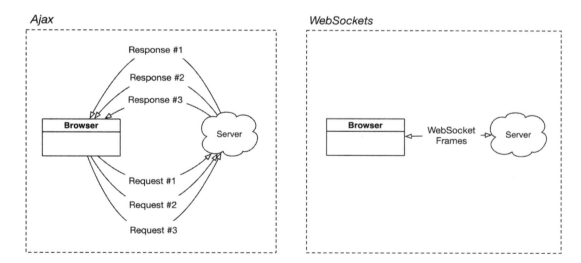

With WebSockets, web applications can go beyond saving and loading remote data. Push notifications, collaborative document editing, and real-time chat are just the beginning. WebSockets makes it possible for servers to handle the load of the Internet of Things (e.g., smart lights, smart locks, smart cars). Traditional techniques like Ajax polling are ineffective at coordinating such intense traffic.

In this chapter, you will build a chat client and server. If you were to use Ajax to build this, you would have to juggle at least two connections – one to poll for new messages and a second to send messages. Using WebSockets, you can accomplish the same thing with a single connection.

When you reach the end of the chapter, Chattrbox will be able to handle multiple, simultaneous chat clients, sending new messages along to each client (Figure 16.2).

Figure 16.2 Pirate chat-arr

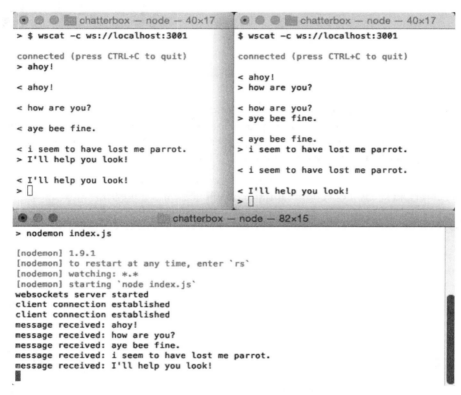

Setting Up WebSockets

To set Chattrbox up with WebSockets, you are going to:

1. install the ws module

2. create a WebSockets server

3. add chat functionality to the server

4. accommodate new users by having the server send them the message history

Begin at the beginning.

The `http` module that comes with Node.js gives you a simple way to start an HTTP server so that browsers can talk to the server.

Similarly, the `ws` module gives your Node.js programs an easy way to communicate via WebSockets. There are several modules that implement WebSockets for Node.js, but `ws` is the standard implementation and performs well.

Begin by installing the `ws` WebSockets module in your Chattrbox directory. (Do not be alarmed if you see warnings from `npm` about a missing description or repository field for your project.)

```
npm install --save ws
```

Next, create a file in Chattrbox's root folder named `websockets-server.js`. Add the following code to import the `ws` module and start listening.

```
var WebSocket = require('ws');
var WebSocketServer = WebSocket.Server;
var port = 3001;
var ws = new WebSocketServer({
    port: port
});

console.log('websockets server started');
```

You imported the `ws` module with the `require` statement. The module contains a `Server` property that you will need in order to create a working WebSockets server.

The code `var ws = new WebSocketServer(/*...*/);` does just that. When this runs, the WebSockets server is established and bound to the specified port (here, `3001`).

Unlike the module you created in `extract.js`, you will not need a `module.exports` assignment. The code in `websockets-server.js` will run when it is imported. It handles all initialization and events related to the WebSocket.

Now that you have a WebSockets server, the first thing you will do with it is handle connections. In `websockets-server.js`, establish a callback for any `connection` events for your WebSockets server:

```
var WebSocket = require('ws');
var WebSocketServer = WebSocket.Server;
var port = 3001;
var ws = new WebSocketServer({
    port: port
});

console.log('websockets server started');

ws.on('connection', function (socket) {
  console.log('client connection established');
});
```

The event-handling syntax is similar to jQuery's. You will notice that many JavaScript libraries (in Node and in the browser) use this style.

Your event-handler callback accepts a single argument named `socket`. When a client makes a connection to your WebSockets server, you have access to that connection via this `socket` object.

Before you write the chat server code, you will set up your server to repeat any messages sent to it. This is commonly known as an *echo server*.

Add the echo functionality in `websockets-server.js` by registering a callback for any `message` events generated by the client connection.

```
...
console.log('websockets server started');

ws.on('connection', function (socket) {
  console.log('client connection established');

  socket.on('message', function (data) {
    console.log('message received: ' + data);
    socket.send(data);
  });
});
```

You registered the event handler directly on the `socket` object. Your `message` event callback is passed any information sent by the client. For now, you are simply sending it back to the same socket connection.

You will see this in action in just a moment.

You could run your WebSockets server by itself with the command `node websockets-server.js`, but it is just as easy to connect it to `index.js`. This has the benefit of taking advantage of `nodemon` to automatically reload your code when you make changes to either `websockets-server.js` or `index.js`.

At the top of `index.js`, add a `require` statement to import the `websockets-server` module.

```
var http = require('http');
var fs = require('fs');
var extract = require('./extract');
var wss = require('./websockets-server');
...
```

Save your file and `nodemon` will reload your code, making it ready for you to try out.

Testing Your WebSockets Server

One way to easily test your server is to use the `wscat` npm module. `wscat` is a tool for connecting to and communicating with a WebSockets server. The module provides a command-line program that you will use as a chat client.

Open a second terminal window and install `wscat` globally. You may need to run this command with administrator privileges. (If you need a refresher, refer to Chapter 1.)

```
npm install -g wscat
```

When `wscat` is installed, you are ready to connect to your WebSockets server.

In the second terminal window, run the command `wscat -c ws://localhost:3001`. You should see the message `connected (press CTRL+C to quit)` in the second terminal window and `'client connection established'` in the first window.

In the second terminal window, enter some text at the prompt. Each time you type some text and press the Return key, your text will be repeated by the WebSockets server, as shown in Figure 16.3.

Figure 16.3 Testing the server with `wscat`

```
$ npm run dev

> chatterbox@1.0.0 dev /Users/chrisaquino/Projects/
ont-end-dev-book/chatterbox
> nodemon index.js

[nodemon] 1.9.1
[nodemon] to restart at any time, enter `rs`
[nodemon] watching: *.*
[nodemon] starting `node index.js`
websockets server started
client connection established
message received: hello
message received: Kumustá
message received: bonjour
message received: 你好
```

```
> $ wscat -c ws://localhost:3001

connected (press CTRL+C to quit)
> hello

< hello
> Kumustá

< Kumustá
> bonjour

< bonjour
> 你好

< 你好
>
```

Now that you have confirmed that you are able to communicate with your server via WebSockets, it is time to add the real functionality that will power Chattrbox's chat system.

Creating the Chat Server Functionality

With your WebSockets server up and running, you are now ready to build out your chat server. Your chat server needs to do a few things:

- keep a log of the messages sent so far to the server

- broadcast older messages to new people joining the chat

- broadcast new messages to all clients

Keeping a log of messages as your users send them is necessary in order to send the message history to new users, so you will tackle that first.

In `websockets-server.js`, create an array to hold on to messages.

```
var WebSocket = require('ws');
var WebSocketServer = WebSocket.Server;
var port = 3001;
var ws = new WebSocketServer({
    port: port
});
var messages = [];

console.log('websockets server started');
...
```

If you were creating a more robust chat system, you might store your messages in a database. For now, a simple array is fine.

Next, call **messages.push(data)** to add each new message to your array as it arrives.

```
...
ws.on('connection', function (socket) {
  console.log('client connection established');

  socket.on('message', function (data) {
    console.log('message received: ' + data);
    messages.push(data);
    socket.send(data);
  });
});
```

Just like that, you have an array of all the messages that have been received by your chat server.

The next step is to allow new users to see all the previous messages. Update the connection event handler in websockets-server.js to send out all the old messages to each new connection as it arrives.

```
...
ws.on('connection', function (socket) {
  console.log('client connection established');

  messages.forEach(function (msg) {
    socket.send(msg);
  });

  socket.on('message', function (data) {
    console.log('message received: ' + data);
    messages.push(data);
    socket.send(data);
  });
});
```

As soon as a connection is made, the server iterates through the messages and sends each one to the new connection.

The last job is to send new messages to all the users as each new message comes in. WebSockets keeps track of your connected users for you. Use this mechanism in websockets-server.js to rebroadcast your received messages.

```
...
ws.on('connection', function (socket) {
  console.log('client connection established');

  messages.forEach(function (msg) {
    socket.send(msg);
  });

  socket.on('message', function (data) {
    console.log('message received: ' + data);
    messages.push(data);
    ws.clients.forEach(function (clientSocket) {
      clientSocket.send(data)
    });

    socket.send(data);
  });
});
```

The ws object keeps track of all connections via its clients property. It is an array that you can iterate through. In your iterator callback, you only need to send the message data.

Finally, because you end up sending your message to your own socket when you iterate over all the sockets, you no longer need the call to **socket.send(data)**. Deleting it cleans things up nicely.

First Chat!

Let's test the new functionality. Make sure that nodemon has reloaded your code. (If you need to, you can manually stop nodemon with Control-C and restart it with npm run dev.)

Open a third terminal window and run the command wscat -c http://localhost:3001. (You should have one terminal running nodemon and two running wscat.) Enter some chat messages in the two windows connected to the server.

After you have chatted with yourself for a bit, open a fourth terminal and run wscat -c http://localhost:3001. This chat client should be sent all the previous messages.

If everything went well, you should see something like Figure 16.4.

Figure 16.4 Chatting with some friends

Congratulations! You have written a fully functional chat server using WebSockets – and it took less than two dozen lines of JavaScript.

For the More Curious: socket.io WebSockets Library

The ws npm module is a perfectly fine WebSockets implementation. But, admittedly, it is lacking in a few ways. For example, WebSockets connections sometimes get dropped, but the ws module provides no way to automatically reconnect.

Another problem is that ws lives in Node.js. That means that it is only available on the server. In your client-side JavaScript, you would need to learn a totally different library that accomplishes essentially the same task.

On top of that, on the client side you may have additional challenges: What if your browser is old and does not support WebSockets? You would need to provide a fallback mechanism of some kind.

socket.io (socket.io) provides a solution to these problems. For browsers, it provides backward-compatible fallbacks, including a Flash implementation. In addition, it has been ported to a number of other platforms, including iOS and Android.

For the More Curious: WebSockets as a Service

If you are interested in a real-time platform as a service, you may want to look into firebase (www.firebase.com). If socket.io tries to make writing your server simpler, firebase goes one step further: It provides the entire server for you, including mechanisms for clients to share and synchronize data. firebase provides solutions for web, iOS, and Android.

Bronze Challenge: Am I Repeating Myself?

Update your `message` handler so that every message received is sent twice to each user.

Test it out using `wscat` and confirm that each message is repeated.

For a really interesting effect, increment the number of repetitions by one each time a new message is sent.

Silver Challenge: Speakeasy

In the United States, it was illegal to produce or sell alcohol during the 1920s. In response, "speakeasies" were created: secret establishments that sold alcoholic beverages and required a password before patrons were allowed to enter.

Create a speakeasy version of your chat program – but without the alcohol. Hide all messages from a user until they enter a secret password. ("Swordfish" is a good one, for historical reasons.)

When users enter the password, send them all previous messages and allow them to see new messages.

Gold Challenge: Chat Bot

You used the `WebSocket.Server` property to create the chat server. You can also programmatically create a chat client by using `WebSocket` as a constructor.

The following line is an example:

```
var chatClient = new WebSocket('http://localhost:3001');
```

The documentation at `github.com/websockets/ws` has a simple example of sending and receiving text data.

Create a chat bot that automatically connects to the chat server. It should greet each new user but otherwise remain silent unless directly spoken to. For example, if your chat bot responds to the name "Jinx," you could type "Jinx, put Max in space," and your chat bot would respond appropriately. (The appropriate response is up to you.)

Make sure that the code for your chat bot is in a separate module, not built directly into the chat server code.

17

Using ES6 with Babel

The JavaScript language was created in 1994, received a few updates in 1999, but went unchanged from 1999 to 2009. A set of small changes was introduced in 2009, resulting in the version of JavaScript known as ES5, or the fifth edition of the standard.

In 2015, a number of language improvements were added as the sixth edition of the standard. Many of these new language features were influenced by languages like Ruby and Python. Technically, this sixth edition is named ES2015, but it is more commonly known as ES6.

ES6 is well supported by Google Chrome, Mozilla Firefox, and Microsoft Edge. These are *evergreen* browsers, meaning that they self-update without the user needing to manually download and install the latest version. As Google, Mozilla, and Microsoft have added more and more ES6 compatibility to their browsers, they have been able to roll out these enhancements quickly to their users.

However, non-evergreen and most mobile browsers have poor support for ES6. Figure 17.1 shows the percentage of ES6 features supported by recent versions of desktop and mobile browsers. (In the figure, IE = Internet Explorer, FF = Mozilla Firefox, CH = Google Chrome, SF = Safari, KQ = Konqueror, and AN = Android.)

Figure 17.1 ES6 feature support as of spring 2016

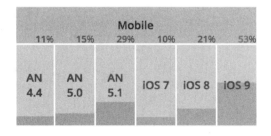

If you would like a closer or up-to-date look at browser support for ES6, go to kangax.github.io/compat-table/es6/ to check out the latest information. The table's creator, Juriy Zaytsev, updates the data frequently.

Support may be spotty among older browsers, but we love, love, love ES6. It is a beautiful thing, and it is worth the effort to switch over as soon as possible rather than waiting until support is universal.

In this chapter, you will begin working on the user-facing portion of Chattrbox, which you will write using a number of ES6 features. To make sure your application works on all browsers, you will use the open-source tool Babel to take care of compatibility.

There is one item of housekeeping to take care of before you begin. So that you can focus on learning ES6 and using Babel, the index.html and stylesheets/styles.css files for Chattrbox are provided for you at www.bignerdranch.com/downloads/front-end-dev-resources.zip. Download the .zip file and extract the contents (including the entire stylesheets/ folder) into your chattrbox/app directory. (index.html will replace your existing copy of index.html.)

Also, one note: While working through the code in this chapter, you may see a warning in the console about the MIME type of your CSS files. It is safe to ignore this warning.

Onward and upward! By the end of this chapter, Chattrbox will communicate over WebSockets with your chat server (Figure 17.2).

Figure 17.2 Chattrbox at the end of this chapter

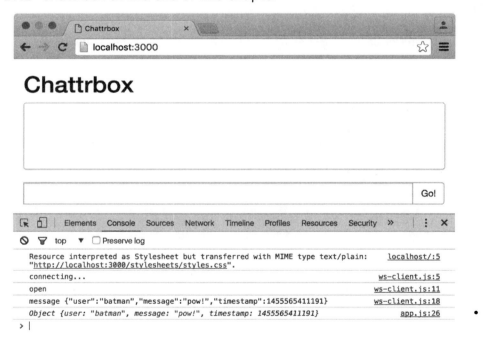

Tools for Compiling JavaScript

Babel is a compiler. Its job is to translate ES6 syntax into the equivalent ES5 code to be run by a browser's JavaScript engine (Figure 17.3).

Figure 17.3 Building ES5 code from ES6 files

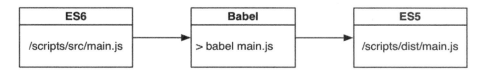

To use Babel effectively, you will need to install a few npm modules to create an automated build process. You will use Babel to compile your ES6 code to ES5, Browserify to bundle your modules together into a single file, and Babelify to make the two work together. Additionally, you will use Watchify to trigger the build process any time you save changes to your code (Figure 17.4).

Figure 17.4 Compilation workflow

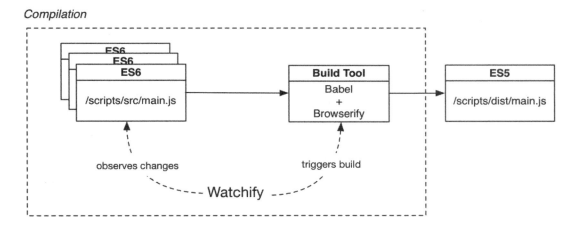

First, you need to install Babel. It has a few different moving parts, depending on your needs. In your case, you will need the ability to compile in two ways: from the command line and programmatically. The tools babel-cli and babel-core, respectively, will address these needs. You will also need to install a Babel configuration suitable for compiling the ES6 standard, which is called babel-preset-es2015.

Run the following npm commands in your chattrbox directory to install the appropriate Babel tooling. (If you need a refresher on how to run npm install -g with administrator privileges, refer to Chapter 1.)

```
npm install -g babel-cli
npm install --save-dev babel-core
npm install --save-dev babel-preset-es2015
```

Now you need to configure Babel to compile using the es2015 preset you installed. Create a file called .babelrc in your root chattrbox folder and add the following configuration information to it:

```
{
  "presets": [
    "es2015"
  ],
  "plugins": []
}
```

Finally, install Babelify, Browserify, and Watchify to the chattrbox/node_modules/ directory:

```
npm install --save-dev browserify babelify watchify
```

You will be using these three tools later in this chapter, after you have Babel up and running.

The Chattrbox Client Application

You already built the Chattrbox server, which serves out the static files and handles communication over WebSockets. The client application will send and receive messages to and from the server over WebSockets. It will define a format for individual messages. The user will be able to view the messages in a list as well as create new messages by entering text into a form.

Those responsibilities will be handled by three modules:

- the ws-client module will manage the WebSockets communication for the client

- the dom module will display data to the UI and handle form submissions

- the app module will define the structure of messages and pass messages between ws-client and dom

Figure 17.5 diagrams the relationships among the three modules.

Figure 17.5 Chattrbox application modules

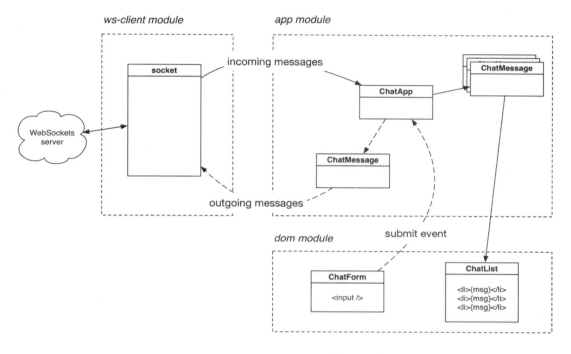

In your chattrbox/app folder, create scripts, scripts/dist, and scripts/src subfolders, as shown in Figure 17.6.

Figure 17.6 chattrbox/app folder structure

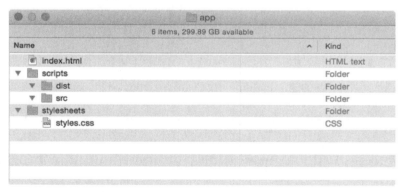

Now, create four JavaScript files in `scripts/src`:

- `app.js`
- `dom.js`
- `main.js`
- `ws-client.js`

Your file structure should look like Figure 17.7.

Figure 17.7 `chattrbox/app`

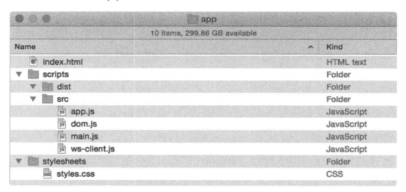

`app.js`, `dom.js`, and `ws-client.js` correspond to the modules shown in Figure 17.5. The `main.js` file will contain the code that initializes your application.

First Steps with Babel

Now that you have your tools installed and your files in place, it is time to get started with ES6.

For the moment, you will use Babel from the command line. Later, you will add it to your npm scripts so that compilation happens automatically. That way, as you work with new ES6 features you can focus on the new syntax without worrying about running extra commands in the terminal.

Class syntax

The first ES6 feature you will use for building the Chattrbox client is the `class` keyword. It is important to keep in mind that the ES6 `class` keyword does not work exactly like classes in other programming languages. Instead, ES6 classes merely provide a shorter syntax for constructor functions and `prototype` methods.

Open `app.js` and define a new class called **ChatApp**.

```
class ChatApp {
}
```

In this chapter, **ChatApp** will not do much. Ultimately, though, **ChatApp** will be responsible for most of your application logic.

The definition of the class is currently empty. Add a **constructor** method with a **console.log** statement:

```
class ChatApp {
  constructor() {
    console.log('Hello ES6!');
  }
}
```

constructor is a method that is run any time you create a new instance of a class. Usually, the constructor will set values for properties belonging to the instance.

Next, create an instance of **ChatApp** in app.js, right after the class declaration:

```
class ChatApp {
  constructor() {
    console.log('Hello ES6!');
  }
}
new ChatApp();
```

Let's give your code a test run. Open a second terminal window and switch to Chattrbox's root directory, where package.json, index.js, and app/ live. You will use this window to run your build commands and keep the other one open for running your server.

To test your code, use Babel to compile app/scripts/src/app.js and output the result to app/scripts/dist/main.js:

```
babel app/scripts/src/app.js -o app/scripts/dist/main.js
```

If you do not see anything happen in your terminal, that is normal – and good news. Babel will not report anything on the command line unless there is an error (Figure 17.8).

Figure 17.8 Babel works quietly

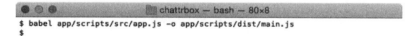

Make sure your Node server is running in your other terminal (with npm run dev), and open your browser to http://localhost:3000. Now you will see your results (Figure 17.9).

Figure 17.9 Hello, ES6!

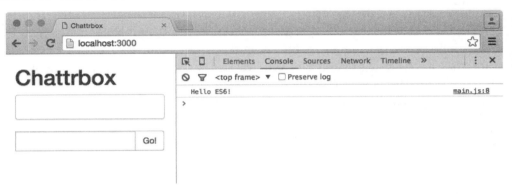

Your app/index.html sources the main.js you generated from app.js. And because app.js creates a new **ChatApp**, the code in **ChatApp**'s constructor is run, logging out "Hello ES6!"

Now that you have confirmed that Babel is working with a single JavaScript file, it is time to start working with multiple modules.

Using Browserify for Packaging Modules

One thing that ES5 does not have is a built-in module system. When you built CoffeeRun, you used a workaround that let you write modular code – but depended on modifying a global variable.

ES6 provides true modules, like those in many other programming languages. Babel understands ES6 module syntax, but there is no equivalent ES5 code for it to convert to. That is why Browserify is necessary.

Figure 17.10 shows how Browserify and Babel will work together.

Figure 17.10 Converting from ES6 modules to ES5 modules with Babel and Browserify

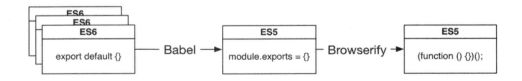

By default, Babel converts ES6 module syntax into the equivalent Node.js-style `require` and `module.exports` syntax. Browserify then converts Node.js module code into ES5-friendly functions.

Open `package.json` and add a configuration section for Browserify:

```
...
  "scripts": {
    "test": "echo \"Error: no test specified\" &&
    exit 1",
    "start": "node index.js",
    "dev": "nodemon index.js",
  },
  "browserify": {
    "transform": [
      ["babelify", {"presets": ["es2015"], "sourceMap": true}]
    ]
  },
...
```

This tells Browserify to use Babelify as a plug-in. It passes two options to Babelify: First, it activates the ES2015 compiler option. It also turns on the `sourceMap` option, which helps with debugging. You will learn how to debug with source maps as you build the rest of Chattrbox.

You will also want to write some scripts for common Browserify tasks, as you did for nodemon. Write those in your `"scripts"` section in `package.json`. (Remember to add the comma at the end of `"dev":` `"nodemon index.js"`.)

```
...
  "scripts": {
    "test": "echo \"Error: no test specified\" && exit 1",
    "start": "node index.js",
    "dev": "nodemon index.js",
    "build": "browserify -d app/scripts/src/main.js -o app/scripts/dist/main.js",
    "watch": "watchify -v -d app/scripts/src/main.js -o app/scripts/dist/main.js"
  },
  "browserify": {
    "transform": [
      ["babelify", {"presets": ["es2015"], "sourceMap": true}]
    ]
  },
...
```

The first script, `build`, uses the `browserify` command directly. The second script, `watch`, uses `watchify` to rerun `browserify` whenever your code changes. (It serves a similar purpose to `nodemon`.)

Now to use the ES6 module system. In ES6 modules, you must explicitly export the pieces of your module you want others to use. Update `app.js` to export your **ChatApp** class rather than simply creating an instance.

```
class ChatApp {
  constructor() {
    console.log('Hello ES6!');
  }
}
new ChatApp();
export default ChatApp;
```

331

You specified that **ChatApp** is the default value available from the app module. Some of your other modules will export multiple values. When you only need to export a single value, it is best to use `export default`.

In `main.js`, import the **ChatApp** class and create a new instance of it.

```
import ChatApp from './app';
new ChatApp();
```

`main.js` is importing the **ChatApp** class that `app.js` exported. After the import, you create a new instance of the **ChatApp** class.

One important note here: The name **ChatApp** is not significant in `main.js`. Because **ChatApp** is the default export from `app.js`, writing `import MyChatApp from './app'`, for example, would assign the default export value to the local **MyChatApp** name. Naming it **ChatApp** is a best practice, however, because that is its name inside `app.js`.

Running the build process

Next, go to your terminal and run your build script:

```
npm run build
```

npm will run your `build` command, which will then run `browserify`. As it runs each command, it will show you what it is doing. Browserify itself will be silent, though, unless there is an error (Figure 17.11).

Figure 17.11 Running Browserify via `npm run build`

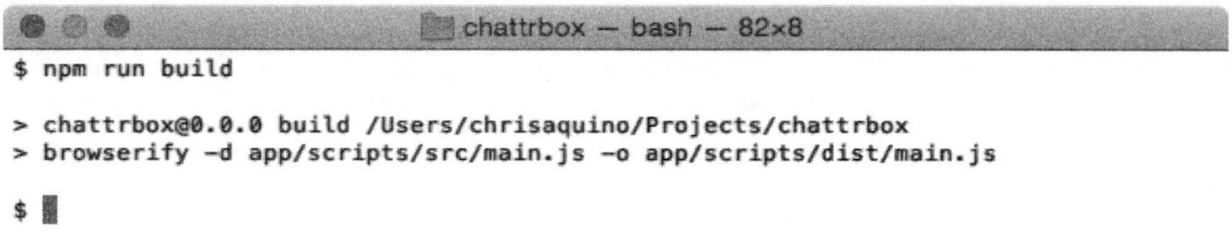

```
$ npm run build

> chattrbox@0.0.0 build /Users/chrisaquino/Projects/chattrbox
> browserify -d app/scripts/src/main.js -o app/scripts/dist/main.js

$
```

When Browserify is successful, it will package your en-Babeled `main.js` in your `app/dist/` folder, just as you did earlier by hand.

Now to reload your browser and see the output. You added no new functionality, other than restructuring where the call to **ChatApp**'s constructor lives. So you should see the same message in the console that you saw earlier (Figure 17.12).

Figure 17.12 Hello again!

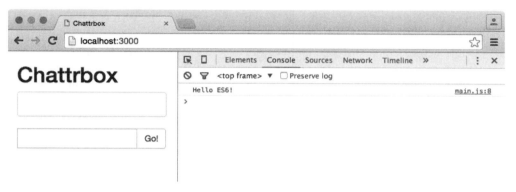

The next piece to integrate is Watchify. Watchify will do the same thing for running your Browserify build that nodemon did for running your Node.js server: It will automatically trigger a rebuild every time you modify one of your source files.

Start Watchify to kick off the build process any time you make a change to your code:

```
npm run watch
```

Watchify will confirm that it is running (Figure 17.13).

Figure 17.13 Running Watchify via npm run watch

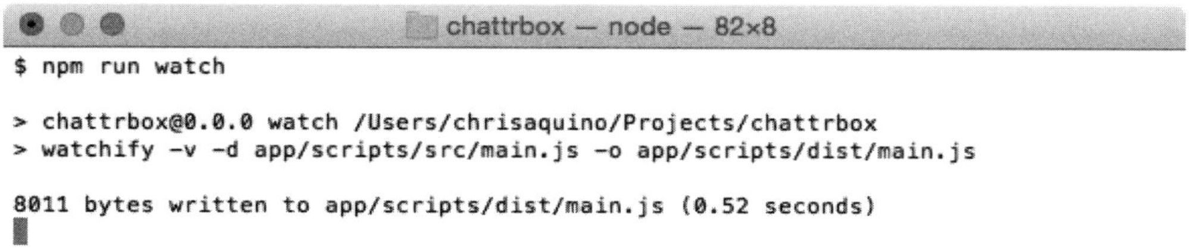

```
● ● ●                      chattrbox — node — 82×8
$ npm run watch

> chattrbox@0.0.0 watch /Users/chrisaquino/Projects/chattrbox
> watchify -v -d app/scripts/src/main.js -o app/scripts/dist/main.js

8011 bytes written to app/scripts/dist/main.js (0.52 seconds)
```

Watchify is a bit chattier than Browserify. Every time it runs Browserify, it tells you how many bytes it wrote to the file. That is not terribly interesting, but it does tell you when the output changes. Leave Watchify running in one of your terminals as you continue to work on Chattrbox. (Your server should still be running in the other terminal.)

Adding the ChatMessage Class

Chatting between two terminals is fun (and makes you look cool at the coffee shop), but it is time to upgrade to sending messages from browser to browser. You will write a helper class that handles constructing and formatting message data.

There are three pieces of information you will want to track for each message. You need to know the text of the message, who sent it, and at what time.

JavaScript Object Notation – more commonly known as JSON (pronounced "Jason," per creator Douglas Crockford) – is a lightweight data-interchange format. You have already been using JSON for your package.json file. It is human readable and language independent, and it is ideal for sending and receiving the kind of data you want to exchange with Chattrbox.

Here is a sample message formatted as JSON:

```
{
  "message": "I'm Batman",
  "user": "batman",
  "timestamp": 614653200000
}
```

Chattrbox message data will come from two different sources. One source is in the client, when the user fills out the form. The other source is the server, when the message is sent over a WebSocket connection to other clients.

When message data comes from the form, you will need to add the username and timestamp before sending it to the server. When the data comes from the server, all three pieces of information should be included. How should you handle this discrepancy? There are a number of options. Let's briefly look at a few of them, including some that take advantage of some handy ES6 features.

Create a class to represent individual chat messages in app.js.

```
class ChatApp {
  constructor() {
    console.log('Hello ES6!');
  }
}

class ChatMessage {
  constructor(data) {
  }
}

export default ChatApp;
```

The first way to approach the problem is a simple constructor that accepts the message text, username, and timestamp. (Do not make this change in your file. It is only an example.)

```
...
class ChatMessage {
  constructor(message, user, timestamp) {
    this.message = message;
    this.user = user || 'batman';
    this.timestamp = timestamp || (new Date()).getTime();
  }
}
...
```

You have seen this pattern a number of times. You assign the parameter values to instance properties, providing fallbacks for username and timestamp using the || operator.

This is fine, but ES6 gives you a more compact way to write this same pattern using *default arguments*.

```
...
class ChatMessage {
  constructor(message, user='batman', timestamp=(new Date()).getTime()) {
    this.message = message;
    this.user = user;
    this.timestamp = timestamp;
  }
}
...
```

This syntax makes it obvious which values must be passed in and which ones are optional. You can see that only the message argument is mandatory. The others have defaults.

This version of the constructor can handle messages received from the server or created by the form. But it requires that the caller know the order of arguments, which can get cumbersome for functions and methods that have three or more arguments.

An alternative to this is for the constructor to receive a single object as argument, with the key/value pairs specifying the values for message, user, and timestamp. For that, you can use the *destructuring assignment syntax*.

```
...
class ChatMessage {
  constructor({message: m, user: u, timestamp: t}) {
    this.message = m;
    this.user = u;
    this.timestamp = t;
  }
}
...
```

Destructuring may look a little odd, but here is how it works. You call the constructor like this:

```
new ChatMessage({message: 'hello from the outside',
                user='adele25@bignerdranch.com', timestamp=1462399523859});
```

The destructuring syntax looks for the key message in the argument. It finds the value 'hello from the outside' and assigns it to a new local variable m. This variable can then be used inside the body of the constructor. The same thing happens for the username and timestamp properties.

But with this syntax you lose the convenience of the default parameters. Luckily, you can combine the two techniques. This final version of the constructor is the one you should add to app.js:

```
...
class ChatMessage {
  constructor(data){
    message: m,
    user: u='batman',
    timestamp: t=(new Date()).getTime()
}) {
    this.message = m;
    this.user = u;
    this.timestamp = t;
  }
}
...
```

In this version, you are plucking values out of the object that is passed to the constructor. For any values that do not exist, defaults are provided.

While default arguments can only exist as part of a function (or constructor) definition, destructuring can be used as part of an assignment. You might also write the constructor like this:

```
...
class ChatMessage {
  constructor(data) {
    var {message: m, user: u='batman', timestamp: t=(new Date()).getTime()} = data;
    this.message = m;
    this.user = u;
    this.timestamp = t;
  }
}
...
```

OK, the detour is over. Time to get back to building Chattrbox!

Your **ChatMessage** class stores all of the important information as properties, but its instances also inherit **ChatMessage**'s methods and other information. That makes **ChatMessage** instances unsuitable for sending through WebSockets. A stripped-down version of that information is necessary.

Write a **serialize** method in app.js to represent the data in **ChatMessage**'s properties as a plain JavaScript object.

```
...
class ChatMessage {
  constructor({
    message: m,
    user: u='batman',
    timestamp: t=(new Date()).getTime()
  }) {
    this.user = user;
    this.message = message;
    this.timestamp = timestamp;
  }
  serialize() {
    return {
      user: this.user,
      message: this.message,
      timestamp: this.timestamp
    };
  }
}

export default ChatApp;
```

Your **ChatMessage** class is now ready for use. It is time to move on to the next module for Chattrbox.

Creating the ws-client Module

The ws-client.js module will handle communicating with your Node WebSocket server.

It will have four responsibilities:

- connecting to the server

- performing initial setup when the connection is first opened

- forwarding incoming messages to their handlers

- sending outgoing messages

Check out how those responsibilities relate to your other components (Figure 17.14).

Figure 17.14 ws-client's interfaces

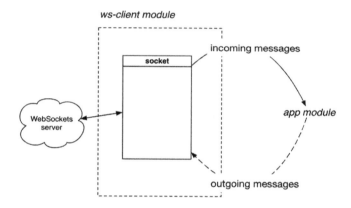

As you build out your client, you will get a tour of some new ES6 features as well.

Connection handling

First, build out your collection handling. Begin by opening ws-client.js and declaring a variable for the WebSocket connection.

```
let socket;
```

This declaration uses a new way of defining variables in ES6 called *let scoping*. If you use let scoping to declare a variable – using the keyword let instead of var – your variable will not be *hoisted*.

Hoisting means that the variable declarations get moved to the top of the function scope in which they are created. This is something that the JavaScript interpreter does behind the scenes. Unfortunately, it can lead to hard-to-find errors.

You will read more about hoisting at the end of the chapter. For now, know that let is a safer way to declare variables in if/else clauses and in the body of loops.

Now, add a method to ws-client.js to initialize your connection.

```
let socket;

function init(url)  {
  socket = new WebSocket(url);
  console.log('connecting...');
}
```

The **init** function connects to the WebSockets server. Next, you want to wire up ws-client.js to **ChatApp** in app.js.

To be a functioning module, ws-client.js needs to specify what it exports. You need to export a single value: an object code with the exported functions as its properties. You are going to use the same export default syntax that you used at the beginning of the chapter – plus an additional bit of ES6 handiness.

Add the export to the end of ws-client.js, as shown.

```
...
function init(url)  {
  socket = new WebSocket(url);
  console.log('connecting...');
}

export default {
  init,
}
```

Notice that you did not have to specify the property names. This syntactic shortcut is the equivalent of:

```
export default {
  init: init
}
```

If the key and value have the same name, ES6 allows you to omit the colon and the value. The key will automatically be the variable name, and the value will automatically be the value associated with that name. This feature of ES6 is the *enhanced object literal* syntax.

Now that you have the ws-client module set up, it is time to import the values it provides in app.js. Begin by adding an import statement to the top of app.js:

```
import socket from './ws-client';

class ChatApp {
  constructor() {
    console.log('Hello ES6!');
  }
}
...
```

socket will be the object you exported from ws-client.js.

Next, in the **ChatApp** constructor, call **socket.init** with the URL of your WebSocket server.

```
import socket from './ws-client';

class ChatApp {
  constructor() {
    console.log('Hello ES6!');
    socket.init('ws://localhost:3001');
  }
}
...
```

Your npm script should rebuild the code for you. (You may need to restart npm run watch and npm run dev in separate windows, if you have let one or both of them stop.) Reload your browser and you should see 'connecting...' logged to the console, as shown in Figure 17.15.

Figure 17.15 Message logged on WebSocket initialization

With that, you have the skeleton of your app up and running.

Handling events and sending messages

When your App module calls **init**, a new **WebSocket** object is instantiated and a connection is made to the server. But your App module needs to know when this process has completed so that it can do something with the connection.

The **WebSocket** object has a set of special properties for handling events. One of these is the onopen property. Any function assigned to this property will be called when the connection to the WebSocket server is made. Inside this function, you can carry out any steps that need to be made upon connecting.

In order for the ws-client module to be flexible and reusable, you will not hardcode the steps that the App module needs to make upon connecting. Instead, you will use the same pattern you used for registering click and submit handlers in CoffeeRun.

Add a function called **registerOpenHandler** to ws-client.js. **registerOpenHandler** will accept a callback, assign a function to onopen, and then invoke the callback inside the onopen function.

```
let socket;

function init(url)  {
  socket = new WebSocket(url);
  console.log('connecting...');
}

function registerOpenHandler(handlerFunction) {
  socket.onopen = () => {
    console.log('open');
    handlerFunction();
  };
}
...
```

This function definition is different from what you have written before. This is a new ES6 syntax called an *arrow function*. Arrow functions are a shorthand for writing anonymous functions. Apart from being a bit easier to write, arrow functions work exactly the same as anonymous functions.

registerOpenHandler takes a function argument (**handlerFunction**) and assigns an anonymous function to the onopen property of the socket connection. Inside of this anonymous function, you call the **handlerFunction** that was passed in.

(Using an anonymous function is more complicated than writing socket.onopen = handlerFunction. This pattern will serve you well when you need to respond to an event but have intermediary steps that must happen before forwarding it on – like writing a log message, as you have done here.)

Next, you need to write an interface for handling messages as they come in over your WebSockets connection. Write a new method called **registerMessageHandler** in ws-client.js. Assign an arrow function to the socket's onmessage property; this arrow function should expect to receive an event argument.

```
...
function registerOpenHandler(handlerFunction) {
  socket.onopen = () => {
    console.log('open');
    handlerFunction();
  };
}

function registerMessageHandler(handlerFunction) {
  socket.onmessage = (e) => {
    console.log('message', e.data);
    let data = JSON.parse(e.data);
    handlerFunction(data);
  };
}
...
```

Arrow function parameters go inside the parentheses, just as they do for regular functions.

The Chattrbox client receives an object from the server in its **onmessage** callback inside **registerMessageHandler**. This object represents the event and has a data property that contains the JSON string from the server. Each time you receive a string, you convert the string to a JavaScript object. You then forward it along to **handlerFunction**.

The last bit is the piece that will actually send the message to your WebSocket. Write this in ws-client.js as a function called **sendMessage**. You will do this in two parts. First, you will turn your message payload (containing the message, the username, and the timestamp) into a JSON string. Then you will send that JSON string to the WebSocket server.

```
...
function registerMessageHandler(handlerFunction) {
  socket.onmessage = (e) => {
    console.log('message', e.data);
    let data = JSON.parse(e.data);
    handlerFunction(data);
  };
}

function sendMessage(payload) {
  socket.send(JSON.stringify(payload));
}
...
```

Finally, add exports for your new methods using the enhanced object literal syntax.

```
...
function sendMessage(payload) {
  socket.send(JSON.stringify(payload));
}

export default {
  init,
  registerOpenHandler,
  registerMessageHandler,
  sendMessage
}
```

With that, ws-client.js has everything it needs to communicate back and forth with the server. Your last job in ws-client.js will be to test it by sending a message.

Sending and echoing a message

Update the **ChatApp** constructor in app.js. After calling **socket.init**, call **registerOpenHandler** and **registerMessageHandler**, passing them arrow functions.

```
import socket from './ws-client';

class ChatApp {
  constructor() {
    socket.init('ws://localhost:3001');
    socket.registerOpenHandler(() => {
      let message = new ChatMessage({ message: 'pow!' });
      socket.sendMessage(message.serialize());
    });
    socket.registerMessageHandler((data) => {
      console.log(data);
    });
  }
}
...
```

When the connection is open, you are immediately sending a dummy message. And when a message is received, you are logging it to the console.

Save your code and reload the browser when the build process finishes. You should see that a message was sent and echoed back (Figure 17.16).

Figure 17.16 Call and response with WebSockets

Excellent work! You have two of the three primary modules for Chattrbox working. You will finish Chattrbox in the next chapter by creating a module that connects your existing modules to the UI. This module will draw new messages to the message list and send messages when the form is submitted.

For the More Curious: Compiling to JavaScript from Other Languages

There are quite a few languages that will compile to JavaScript. Here is a short list:

- CoffeeScript: `coffeescript.org`

- TypeScript: `www.typescriptlang.org`

- C/C++: `kripken.github.io/emscripten-site`

One of the most prominent is CoffeeScript, which provides shorthand syntax for some of the most common patterns (e.g., the arrow syntax for anonymous functions). In fact, CoffeeScript had a significant influence on ES6.

Google, Microsoft, Mozilla, and others are collaborating on a project to standardize an assembly language for JavaScript engines, called WebAssembly. The goal is to create a high-performance, low-level language that can be compiled to from many different languages.

The intention for WebAssembly is to supplement JavaScript – not replace it – and to capitalize on the strengths of multiple languages. JavaScript is good at creating browser-based applications, for example, but not at rendering math-intensive game graphics. C and C++, meanwhile, excel at rendering game code. Rather than porting C++ code over to JavaScript and potentially introducing bugs, it could be compiled to WebAssembly.

The WebAssembly project sprang out of an earlier project called asm.js, which specified a subset of the JavaScript language for writing high-performance code.

For more information about asm.js and WebAssembly, check out this blog post by the creator of JavaScript: `brendaneich.com/2015/06/from-asm-js-to-webassembly`.

Bronze Challenge: Default Import Name

In main.js, your import statement creates a local variable named ChatApp. What happens if you change this to ApplicationForChatting?

Try it (making sure you also change the new statement on the next line) and find out whether it still works. If so, why? If not, why not?

Silver Challenge: Closed Connection Alert

In the ws-client module, add another function called **registerCloseHandler**. It should take a callback that is invoked when the close event is triggered on the socket.

In main.js, use **registerCloseHandler** to alert the user that the connection is closed. Then, test it to make sure it works.

How can you test it? Obviously, you cannot close the browser window. You will need to close the other end of the connection.

For an added bonus, write a function that attempts to reconnect. You can either use a **setTimeout** or you can prompt the user for confirmation (search the MDN for details).

For the More Curious: Hoisting

JavaScript was created so that nonprofessional programmers could create web content with some basic interactivity. Although the language has features intended to make code error-resistant, some of its features end up causing errors in practice. One of these features is hoisting.

When the JavaScript engine interprets your code, it finds all of the variable and function declarations and moves them to the top of the function they are in. (Or, if they are not in a function, they are evaluated before the rest of the code.)

This is best illustrated with an example. When you write this code:

```
function logSomeValues () {
  console.log(myVal);
  var myVal = 5;
  console.log(myVal);
}
```

it is interpreted as though you had written:

```
function logSomeValues () {
  var myVal;
  console.log(myVal);
  myVal = 5;
  console.log(myVal);
}
```

If you called **logSomeValues** the console, you would see this:

```
> logSomeValues();
undefined
5
```

Notice that it is only the *declaration* that is hoisted. The assignment stays in place. Naturally, this can cause confusion, especially if you were to try to declare variables in an if statement or inside of a loop. In other languages, the curly braces denote a *block*, which has its own scope. In JavaScript, curly brace blocks do not create scope. Only functions create scope.

Take a look at another example:

```
var myVal =  11;
function doNotWriteCodeLikeThis() {
  if (myVal > 10) {
    var myVal = 0;
    console.log('myVal was greater than 10; resetting to 0');
  } else {
    console.log('no need to reset.');
  }
  return myVal;
}
```

You might expect that 'myVal was greater than 10; resetting to 0' would be printed to the console and the value 0 returned. Instead, this is what would be printed:

```
> doNotWriteCodeLikeThis();
no need to reset.
undefined
```

The declaration var myVal is moved to the top of the function, so before the if clause is evaluated, myVal has a value of undefined. The assignment stays inside the if block.

Function declarations are also hoisted, but in their entirety. That means that this works just fine:

```
boo();

// Declare after calling:
function boo() {
  console.log('BOO!!');
}
```

JavaScript moves the entire function declaration block to the top, allowing the invocation of **boo** to happen without any problems:

```
> boo();
BOO!!
```

let statements are immune to hoisting. *const* statements, which let you declare variables that cannot be reassigned, are also immune.

For the More Curious: Arrow Functions

We fibbed. Arrow functions do not work *exactly* like anonymous functions. For some situations, they are *better*.

In addition to providing shorter syntax, arrow functions:

- work as though you had written `function () {}.bind(this)`, making `this` work as expected in the body of the arrow function

- allow you to omit the curly braces if you only have one statement

- return the result of the single statement when curly braces are omitted

For example, here is CoffeeRun's **CheckList.prototype.addClickHandler** method:

```
CheckList.prototype.addClickHandler = function(fn) {
  this.$element.on('click', 'input', function (event) {
    var email = event.target.value;
    fn(email)
      .then( function () {
        this.removeRow(email);
      }.bind(this));
  }.bind(this));
};
```

Replacing the anonymous functions with arrow functions makes this code a bit clearer:

```
CheckList.prototype.addClickHandler = (fn) => {
  this.$element.on('click', 'input', (event) => {
    let email = event.target.value;
    fn(email)
      .then(() => this.removeRow(email));
  });
};
```

The work that **addClickHandler** is doing is more apparent without the extra noise of `function` and `.bind(this)`.

18

ES6, the Adventure Continues

Chattrbox is a working application, but right now it focuses on "under the hood" business logic. It connects to the WebSockets server. It defines a message format and is able to send and receive messages.

In this chapter, you will complete Chattrbox by wiring up the UI layer. You will continue to use Node and npm to manage your build process and act as a server, and at the end of the chapter you will have a fully functional web-based chat app (Figure 18.1).

Figure 18.1 The completed Chattrbox

When you built CoffeeRun, you created **FormHandler** and **CheckList** modules that corresponded to the form and the list area. You will use the same pattern with Chattrbox for creating the **ChatForm** and **ChatList** modules.

You will also create a **UserStore** module that will hold information about the current chat user. These will make Chattrbox more robust and make its main modules more reusable.

Installing jQuery as a Node Module

Chattrbox will make use of jQuery for DOM manipulation. But you will not load jQuery from cdnjs.com, as you did for CoffeeRun, nor will you use a `<script>` tag in your HTML, the way you have been integrating client-side dependencies.

With Browserify, this is no longer necessary. Browserify automatically builds your JavaScript dependencies into your application bundle to be used in your browser. So, all you need to do to integrate jQuery is include it via `import`, and Browserify will take care of the rest.

Begin by installing the jQuery library to the node_modules folder:

```
npm install --save-dev jquery
```

Open dom.js to begin writing this module. The dom.js module will use jQuery, so add an `import` statement to include it.

```
import $ from 'jquery';
```

Later in this chapter, you will install and use another third-party library. When you do, you will follow these same steps for installing and importing it.

Creating the ChatForm Class

As you did with CoffeeRun, you will create an object to manage the form element in the DOM. This will be the **ChatForm** class. Using ES6 classes will make your code a bit more readable than your code from CoffeeRun.

Creating a **ChatForm** instance and initializing its event handlers will occur in two separate steps, because a constructor's job should only be to set the properties of an instance. Other work (like attaching event listeners) should be done in other methods.

Define **ChatForm** in dom.js with a constructor that accepts selectors. In the constructor, add properties for the elements the instance will need to track.

```
import $ from 'jquery';

class ChatForm {
  constructor(formSel, inputSel) {
    this.$form = $(formSel);
    this.$input = $(inputSel);
  }
}
```

Next, add an **init** method that will associate a callback with the form's submit event.

```
...
class ChatForm {
  constructor(formSel, inputSel) {
    this.$form = $(formSel);
    this.$input = $(inputSel);
  }

  init(submitCallback) {
    this.$form.submit((event) => {
      event.preventDefault();
      let val = this.$input.val();
      submitCallback(val);
      this.$input.val('');
    });

    this.$form.find('button').on('click', () => this.$form.submit());
  }
}
```

In the **init** method, you used an arrow function for the submit handler. Inside the arrow function, you prevented the default form action, retrieved the value from the input field, and then passed that value to **submitCallback**. Finally, you reset the value of the input.

To make sure the form submits when the button is clicked, you added a click handler that causes the form to fire its submit event. You did this by getting the form element with jQuery and then calling jQuery's **submit** method. You used the single-expression version of the arrow function, allowing you to omit the curly braces.

To make this module useful, you need to export **ChatForm**. In the previous chapter, you used export default for this purpose. This allowed you to export a single value for the module. In some cases, you used a plain JavaScript object to package up multiple values within that single default value.

In this chapter, you will use *named exports* to export multiple named values instead of a single default value.

Export **ChatForm** as a named value to users of this module by adding the export keyword just before the class declaration.

```
...
export class ChatForm {
  constructor(formSel, inputSel) {
    this.$form = $(formSel);
    this.$input = $(inputSel);
  }
  ...
```

Easy enough. Now to import **ChatForm** in app.js.

In Ottergram and CoffeeRun, you used the var keyword for selector strings. In ES6, you can declare constants for this purpose, because the values of the strings will not change. Like let, const is block-scoped, meaning that it is visible to any code inside the same set of curly braces. When it is outside all curly braces (which will be the case here), it is visible to any code in the same file.

In app.js, import the **ChatForm** class and create constants for the form's selector and message input selector. Also, create an instance of **ChatForm** in **ChatApp**'s constructor function.

```
import socket from './ws-client';
import {ChatForm} from './dom';

const FORM_SELECTOR = '[data-chat="chat-form"]';
const INPUT_SELECTOR = '[data-chat="message-input"]';

class ChatApp {
  constructor() {
    this.chatForm = new ChatForm(FORM_SELECTOR, INPUT_SELECTOR);

    socket.init('ws://localhost:3001');
    socket.registerOpenHandler(() => {
      let message = new ChatMessage('pow!');
      socket.sendMessage(message.serialize());
    });
    socket.registerMessageHandler((data) => {
      console.log(data);
    });
  }
}
...
```

When you imported **ChatForm**, you wrapped it in curly braces: {ChatForm}. This signifies a *named import*. The named import for **ChatForm** declares a local variable named ChatForm and binds it to the value from the dom module of the same name.

Connecting ChatForm to the socket

In the last chapter, you sent a dummy message: "pow!". Now you are ready to send real form data from **ChatForm**.

Inside the socket.registerOpenHandler callback, you will initialize the **ChatForm** instance. It is important to do this *after* the socket is open, instead of initializing immediately after creating the instance. By waiting, you prevent your user from entering chat messages before they can actually be sent to the server. (That would be a bad thing.)

Remember that **ChatForm**'s **init** method accepts a callback. This callback will be used to handle form submissions.

In app.js, delete your dummy message code and replace it with a call to ChatForm.init, passing it a callback that sends message data coming from **ChatForm** to your socket.

```
...
class ChatApp {
  constructor() {
    this.chatForm = new ChatForm(FORM_SELECTOR, INPUT_SELECTOR);

    socket.init('ws://localhost:3001');
    socket.registerOpenHandler(() => {
      let message = new ChatMessage('pow!');
      socket.sendMessage(message.serialize());
      this.chatForm.init((data) => {
        let message = new ChatMessage(data);
        socket.sendMessage(message.serialize());
      });
    });
    socket.registerMessageHandler((data) => {
      console.log(data);
    });
  }
}
...
```

Let's look at what **ChatApp** is doing now. First, it opens the socket connection to the server. When the connection is open, **ChatApp** initializes your instance of **ChatForm** with a form submission callback.

Now, when the user submits a message in the form the **ChatForm** instance will take that data and send it to **ChatApp**'s callback, and the callback will then package it up as a **ChatMessage** and send it to the WebSockets server.

Creating the ChatList Class

That takes care of sending outgoing chat messages. Your next job is to display new messages from the server as they come in. To do that, you will create a second class in dom.js representing the list of chat messages the user sees.

ChatList will create DOM elements for each message, which will display the name of the user who sent the message and the message text. In dom.js, create and export a class definition for a new class called **ChatList** to fulfill this role:

```
import $ from 'jquery';

export class ChatForm {
  ...
}

export class ChatList {
  constructor(listSel, username) {
    this.$list = $(listSel);
    this.username = username;
  }
}
```

ChatList accepts the attribute selector and the username. It needs the attribute selector so that it knows where to attach the message list elements it creates. And it needs the username so it can see which messages were sent by your user and which were sent by everyone else. (Your messages will be displayed differently from those sent by other users.)

Now that **ChatList** has a constructor, it also needs to be able to create DOM elements for messages.

Add a **drawMessage** method to **ChatList**. It will expect to receive an object argument, which it will destructure into local variables for the username, timestamp, and text associated with the message. (To make it clearer what the destructuring assignment is doing, single character local variables are used.)

```
...
export class ChatList {
  constructor(listSel, username) {
    this.$list = $(listSel);
    this.username = username;
  }

  drawMessage({user: u, timestamp: t, message: m}) {
    let $messageRow = $('<li>', {
      'class': 'message-row'
    });

    if (this.username === u) {
      $messageRow.addClass('me');
    }

    let $message = $('<p>');

    $message.append($('<span>', {
      'class': 'message-username',
      text: u
    }));

    $message.append($('<span>', {
      'class': 'timestamp',
      'data-time': t,
      text: (new Date(t)).getTime()
    }));

    $message.append($('<span>', {
      'class': 'message-message',
      text: m
    }));

    $messageRow.append($message);
    $(this.listId).append($messageRow);
    $messageRow.get(0).scrollIntoView();
  }
}
```

Your **drawMessage** method creates a row for the message with the username, timestamp, and the message itself displayed. If you are the sender of the message, it adds an extra CSS class for styling. It then appends your message's row to **ChatList**'s list element and scrolls the new message row into view.

With that, **ChatList** is ready to rock. Time to integrate it into **ChatApp**.

In app.js, update the dom import statement so that it also imports **ChatList**. Add a const for the list selector, then instantiate a new **ChatList** in the constructor.

```
import socket from './ws-client';
import {ChatForm, ChatList} from './dom';

const FORM_SELECTOR = '[data-chat="chat-form"]';
const INPUT_SELECTOR = '[data-chat="message-input"]';
const LIST_SELECTOR = '[data-chat="message-list"]';

class ChatApp {
  constructor() {
    this.chatForm = new ChatForm(FORM_SELECTOR, INPUT_SELECTOR);
    this.chatList = new ChatList(LIST_SELECTOR, 'wonderwoman');

    socket.init('ws://localhost:3001');
    ...
```

You are almost up and running. The final step to getting basic chat functionality is to draw new messages as they come in by calling **chatList.drawMessage**. Do this in **registerMessageHandler** in app.js:

```
...
class ChatApp {
  ...
    socket.registerMessageHandler((data) => {
      console.log(data);
      let message = new ChatMessage(data);
      this.chatList.drawMessage(message.serialize());
    });
  }
}
...
```

You create a new **ChatMessage** using the incoming data, then you **serialize** the message. This is a precautionary step to strip away extra metadata that might have been added to the data. Creating a new **ChatMessage** from the socket data gives you your message, and **this.chatList.drawMessage** draws that **serialize** message into your browser.

Time to give it a whirl. If you have not already, start Watchify (with npm run watch) and nodemon (with npm run dev). Open or refresh your browser and type in a message (Figure 18.2).

Figure 18.2 Seeing your own chat message

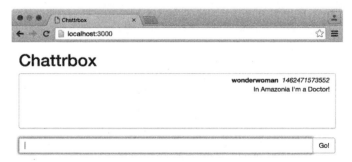

353

Hooray! You now have a working chat application. It just needs a few design touches for some polish.

Using Gravatars

Gravatar is a free service that lets you associate a profile picture with your email address. Gravatar makes each user's profile image available via a specially formatted URL. For example, Figure 18.3 shows the Gravatar of one of our test accounts.

Figure 18.3 Gravatar image example

See the end of the URL? That is a unique identifier generated from the user's email address. This identifier is called a *hash* and is easy to generate with the help of a third-party library called crypto-js.

Add crypto-js to your project using npm:

```
npm install --save-dev crypto-js
```

crypto-js is now installed in your project's local node_modules folder and ready for use.

When you create strings in JavaScript, you often need to concatenate the string with some other value. ES6 provides a better way to create strings that include values from expressions and variables, called *template strings*. You will use this feature to create the URL for accessing Gravatar images.

In dom.js, add another import statement for the md5 submodule of the crypto-js library, using a / to separate the name of the main module and the name of the submodule. Then, write a **createGravatarUrl** function that accepts a username, generates an MD5 hash, and returns the URL for the Gravatar.

```
import $ from 'jquery';
import md5 from 'crypto-js/md5';

function createGravatarUrl(username) {
  let userhash = md5(username);
  return `http://www.gravatar.com/avatar/${userhash.toString()}`;
}
...
```

Take note: In return `http://www.gravatar.com/avatar/${userhash.toString()}`, those are not single quote characters. They are backticks, located just below the Escape key on most US keyboard layouts.

Inside the backticks, you can use the ${userhash.toString()} syntax to include JavaScript expression values directly in your string. Here, you refer to the variable userhash and call its **toString** method, but any expression is valid inside of the curly brackets.

Next, use this function to display the Gravatar in new messages. At the bottom of **ChatList**'s **drawMessage** method (still in dom.js), create a new image element and set its src attribute to the user's Gravatar.

```
...
    $message.append($('<span>', {
      class: 'message-message',
      text: m
    }));

    let $img = $('<img>', {
      src: createGravatarUrl(u),
      title: u
    });

    $messageRow.append($img);
    $messageRow.append($message);
    $(this.listId).append($messageRow);
    $messageRow.get(0).scrollIntoView();
...
```

Run your chat app, and you should see a Gravatar pop up this time (Figure 18.4).

Figure 18.4 Showing a Gravatar

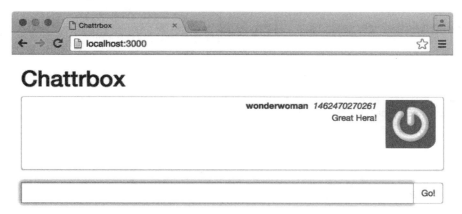

Sadly, there is no Gravatar for the wonderwoman username. As a result, you get the unexciting default Gravatar.

Prompting for Username

It would be really cool to be Wonder Woman. But it is more cool to be a JavaScript developer using Chattrbox. (Especially because real users actually have Gravatars.) In order to know who is using Chattrbox, you will need to prompt users for their usernames.

It is the responsibility of the dom module to interact with the UI, so create a **promptForUsername** function in dom.js. Add it to the exports instead of making it part of **ChatForm** or **ChatList**.

```
...
function createGravatarUrl(username) {
  let userhash = md5(username);
  return `http://www.gravatar.com/avatar/${userhash.toString()}`;
}

export function promptForUsername() {
  let username = prompt('Enter a username');
  return username.toLowerCase();
}
...
```

In the **promptForUsername** function, you created a let variable to hold the text entered by the user. (The **prompt** function is built into the browser and returns a string.) Then you returned a lowercase version of that text.

Next, you will need to update app.js to use this new function. Update the import statement for the dom module and call the **promptForUsername** function to get a value for the username variable:

```
import socket from './ws-client';
import {ChatForm, ChatList, promptForUsername} from './dom';

const FORM_SELECTOR = '[data-chat="chat-form"]';
const INPUT_SELECTOR = '[data-chat="message-input"]';
const LIST_SELECTOR = '[data-chat="message-list"]';

let username = '';
username = promptForUsername();

class ChatApp {
  ...
```

Now, update **ChatMessage** to use that username as the default. Remember, only messages received from the server have a data.user value.

```
...
class ChatMessage {
  constructor({
    message: m,
    user: u=~~batman~~, username,
    timestamp: t=(new Date()).getTime()
...
```

Finally, pass the username to the **ChatList** constructor:

```
...
class ChatApp {
  constructor() {
    this.chatForm = new ChatForm(FORM_SELECTOR, INPUT_SELECTOR);
    this.chatList = new ChatList(LIST_SELECTOR, ~~wonderwoman~~ username);
    ...
```

After the build process completes, reload your browser and enter a username in the prompt (Figure 18.5).

Figure 18.5 Prompting for a username

Now, try sending messages. You should see your selected username echoed back at you, as well as the Gravatar associated with that username (Figure 18.6).

Figure 18.6 Your user's name

Gravatars are assigned using email addresses. If you do not have one associated with your email address, try diana.prince@bignerdranch.com or clark.kent@bignerdranch.com.

User Session Storage

Typing the username each time you reload the page gets tedious. It would be better to store that username in the browser. For simple storage, the browser provides two APIs for storing key/value pairs (with one limitation – the value must be a string). These are *localStorage* and *sessionStorage*. The data stored in localStorage and sessionStorage is associated with your web application's server address. Code from different sites cannot access each other's data.

Using localStorage would work. But you might only want to keep the username until you close the tab or the window, so in this case you will use the sessionStorage API. It is just like localStorage, but the data is erased when the browsing session ends (either by closing the browser tab or the window).

You will create a new set of classes to manage your sessionStorage information.

Create a new file named storage.js in the app/scripts/src folder and add a class definition:

```
class Store {
  constructor(storageApi) {
    this.api = storageApi;
  }
  get() {
    return this.api.getItem(this.key);
  }

  set(value) {
    this.api.setItem(this.key, value);
  }
}
```

Your new **Store** class is generic and can be used with either localStorage or sessionStorage. It is a thin wrapper around the Web Storage APIs. You specify which storage API you want to use when you instantiate one.

Notice that there are references to this.key, which is *not* set in the constructor. This implementation of **Store** is not intended to be used on its own. Instead, you use it by building a subclass that defines the key property.

Create a subclass, using the extends keyword, that you can use for storing the username in sessionStorage:

```
class Store {
  constructor(storageApi) {
    this.api = storageApi;
  }
  get() {
    return this.api.getItem(this.key);
  }

  set(value) {
    this.api.setItem(this.key, value);
  }
}

export class UserStore extends Store {
  constructor(key) {
    super(sessionStorage);
    this.key = key;
  }
}
```

UserStore only defines a constructor, which performs two actions. First, it calls **super**, which invokes the **Store**'s constructor, passing it a reference to sessionStorage. Second, it sets the value of this.key.

Now the value of api is set for the **Store**, and the value of key is set for the **UserStore** instance. This means that all the pieces are in place for a **UserStore** instance to invoke the **get** and **set** methods.

UserStore will be what app.js will use, so that is what you export here.

Now to use your new **UserStore**. Import **UserStore** into app.js, create an instance, and use it to stash the username:

```
import socket from './ws-client';
import {UserStore} from './storage';
import {ChatForm, ChatList, promptForUsername} from './dom';

const FORM_SELECTOR = '[data-chat="chat-form"]';
const INPUT_SELECTOR = '[data-chat="message-input"]';
const LIST_SELECTOR = '[data-chat="message-list"]';

let username = '';
let userStore = new UserStore('x-chattrbox/u');
let username = userStore.get();
if (!username) {
  username = promptForUsername();
  userStore.set(username);
}

class ChatApp {
  ...
```

Run Chattrbox one more time in your browser. This time, you should only be prompted for your username when you initially load the page. Subsequent reloads should have the same username you initially entered.

To confirm that your username is being stored in sessionStorage, you can use the resources panel in the DevTools. After you click to activate the resources panel, you will see a list on the left. Click the ▶ next to the Session Storage item in the list, revealing http://localhost:3000. Click this URL to reveal the data being stored by **UserStore** (Figure 18.7).

Figure 18.7 The resources panel in the DevTools

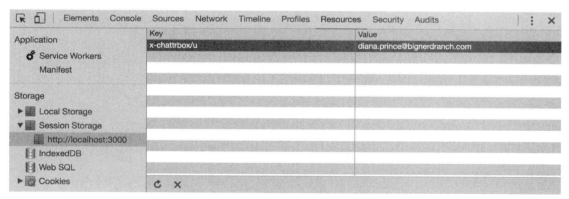

At the bottom of this list of key value pairs, there are buttons for refreshing the list and for deleting items from the list. You can use these if you need to manually modify the stored data.

Formatting and Updating Message Timestamps

Your messages have timestamps that are not very human-friendly. (Seriously, who tells time by the number of milliseconds since January 1, 1970?) To provide nicer timestamps (such as "10 minutes ago"), you will add a module called moment. Install it using npm and save it as a development dependency:

```
npm install --save-dev moment
```

Each of your messages stores its timestamp as a data attribute. Write an **init** method for **ChatList** that calls the built-in function **setInterval**, which takes two arguments: a function to run and how often that function should be run. Your function will update each message with a human-readable timestamp.

To set the timestamp string, use jQuery in dom.js to find all elements with a data-time attribute whose value is the numerical timestamp. Create a new **Date** object using that numerical timestamp and pass the object to **moment**. Then call the **fromNow** method to produce the final timestamp string and set that string as the element's HTML text.

```
...
  drawMessage({user: u, timestamp: t, message: m}) {
    ...
  }

  init() {
    this.timer = setInterval(() => {
      $('[data-time]').each((idx, element) => {
        let $element = $(element);
        let timestamp = new Date().setTime($element.attr('data-time'));
        let ago = moment(timestamp).fromNow();
        $element.html(ago);
      });
    }, 1000);
  }
}
```

You are running this function every 1,000 milliseconds. To make sure a human-readable timestamp appears immediately, update **drawMessage**. Use **moment** to create a formatted timestamp string when the message is first drawn to the chat list.

```
...
  drawMessage({user: u, timestamp: t, message: m}) {
    ...
    $message.append($('<span>', {
      'class': 'timestamp',
      'data-time': t,
      text: (new Date(t)).getTime()
      text: moment(t).fromNow()
    }));
    ...
```

Finally, update app.js, adding a call to this.chatList.init inside the socket.registerOpenHandler callback:

```
...
class ChatApp {
  constructor () {
    this.chatForm = new ChatForm(FORM_SELECTOR, INPUT_SELECTOR);
    this.chatList = new ChatList(LIST_SELECTOR, username);

    socket.init('ws://localhost:3001');
    socket.registerOpenHandler(() => {
      this.chatForm.init((text) => {
        let message = new ChatMessage({message: text});
        socket.sendMessage(message.serialize());
      });
      this.chatList.init();
    });
    ...
```

Save and let your npm scripts compile your changes. Refresh the browser and start chatting. You should see your new timestamps appear with your message text. After a couple of minutes, you will notice that the message timestamps update (Figure 18.8).

Figure 18.8 Not-so-secret identities

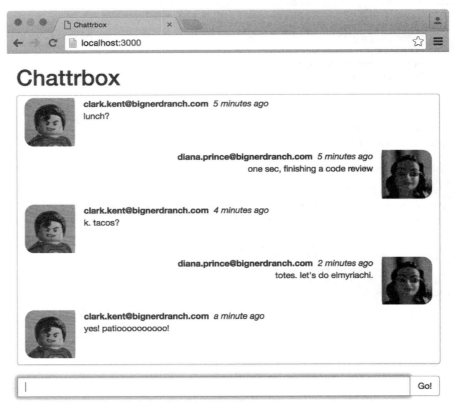

You have come to the end of the road with Chattrbox. Though it only spanned a few chapters, it had quite a few moving parts. You learned how to write two kinds of servers in Node.js: a basic web server and a WebSocket server. You built the client application using ES6, utilizing Babel and Browserify to compile your code to ES5 so that Chattrbox can be used in older browsers, and you automated your workflow with npm scripts.

Chattrbox is the culmination of the techniques you have learned so far. The next application, Tracker, will introduce you to Ember.js, a framework for building large applications. It will build on your hard-won knowledge of modularity, asynchronous programming, and workflow tools.

Bronze Challenge: Adding Visual Effects to Messages

Give new messages a visual effect. You can fade them in or have them slide in. (Check jQuery's *Effects* documentation for options.)

For an added challenge, apply this effect only to truly new messages – not to messages already in the chat that are loaded by the app when users first sign on or refresh their browser.

How can you tell which messages are old and which are new? Each message has a data attribute that can help you tell whether it is more than a second or two old.

Silver Challenge: Caching Messages

If you are in the middle of a chat and need to reload the browser, all of your messages disappear. It is nice that your **UserStore** remembers your username – but it would be better if you also had a similar mechanism for caching chat messages.

Create a **MessageStore** that subclasses **Store**. It should store messages as they come in, making sure not to store the same message more than once.

When the page loads, Chattrbox should get any cached messages from **MessageStore**. Decide if you would like messages to persist even if the browser tab is closed and re-opened. (If so, what alternative to sessionStorage would you use?)

Gold Challenge: Separate Chat Rooms

This challenge will require you to modify both the server and client applications.

Add separate chat rooms for your users. After they enter their username, prompt them to enter the name of the chat room they would like to use.

When users are logged in to a chat room, they should only receive messages for that room over the WebSocket connection. You might need to change how you store messages on the server, how you send messages to the client, or both.

For an added challenge, show a dropdown of available chat rooms in the client UI so that users can switch from room to room. When changing to another room, make sure that any new messages are received from the server and displayed in the chat list.

Part IV
Application Architecture

19

Introduction to MVC and Ember

Model-View-Controller (MVC) is an extremely useful software design pattern. It works well in web applications, allowing you to build structure in separate layers. This chapter introduces the MVC pattern and walks you through installing and setting up Ember, a framework for MVC. The next few chapters focus on individual pieces of the pattern as you create a new application layer by layer.

There are many interpretations of MVC, especially in the front-end world. Figure 19.1 shows the interpretation we will use.

Figure 19.1 The Model-View-Controller pattern

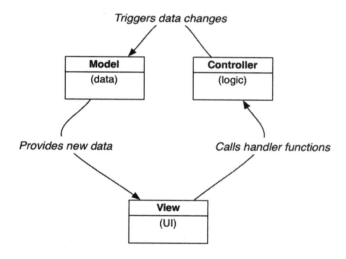

Here is a breakdown of what each layer does:

- *Models* manage data. When data changes, the model tells anyone who is listening.

- *Views* manage the user interface. They handle the presentation of models and listen for any changes. Also, when UI events fire in response to user input, they call handler functions in the controller.

- *Controllers* hold application logic. They retrieve model instances and give them to views. They also contain handler functions that make changes to model instances.

If this seems circular, it is. The three pieces work together. Application data flows from the models to the view. Event data flows from the view to the controller. Controllers trigger data changes in the model based on UI events.

You may be wondering how, then, you get into the circular pattern of MVC. In Chapter 8, you created the CoffeeRun application and enclosed all the functionality you needed in the `Window.App` object. Each added module had a specific role in the application and was named for its functionality. The MVC pattern needs an initial set-up function, like creating a new **Truck**, to load controllers. Controllers, in turn, load models and views.

Your next application, called Tracker, will load an initial DOM state in an HTML file as only an empty <body> tag. The scripts to initialize your application will be loaded from this HTML file as well. In the MVC pattern, views (HTML content) are dynamically rendered depending on the route and state of the data (models).

The application you are going to build will require more than CoffeeRun's seven modules. The MVC pattern helps you break up modules into functionality-specific files and maintain consistent organization – whether you have a dozen modules or a hundred.

Tracker

Your Tracker application will include *URL routing*, one of the best features of web applications. It will have models to define the data, controllers to handle user actions, templates to define the UI, and routes to assign the models to the templates. As you build the application, you will pick up some new patterns and techniques that will make your code lightweight and elegant.

Your customer for the Tracker application is a cryptozoologist, traveling the world in search of animals like Bigfoot, chupacabras, the Loch Ness Monster, and unicorns. This client wants an app for tracking these mysterious creatures and recording information about any sightings. The requirements may change (and they usually do), but to begin with the user should be able to:

- list existing sightings

- add new sightings

- link creatures to sightings

- see the latest sightings via flash messages

Each sighting should have the following model data and associations:

Sighting model attribute	Attribute type
date creature was seen	date object
location	string
creature	creature model key
witness(es)	array of witness keys

Each creature should have the following model data: ·

Creature model attribute	Attribute type
name	string
type	string
image path	string

And each witness should have the following model data and associations:

Witness model attribute	Attribute type
first name	string
last name	string
full name	string: concatenation of first name and last name
email	string
sighting(s)	array of sighting keys

Building Tracker will be slightly different than building the previous applications in this book. It will more closely resemble real-world application development. There will be more code in sections and less instant feedback. However, you will get a realistic sense of app development and will build a satisfyingly complex app (Figure 19.2).

Figure 19.2 Finished Tracker app

Ember: An MVC Framework

As you build Tracker, you will learn the basic pattern of web application development using Ember, one of the leading MVC frameworks. Ember incorporates concepts and naming conventions that allow for rapid development. As you build your application, you will learn the Ember fundamentals.

As described on Ember's homepage (emberjs.com), Ember is "a framework for building ambitious web applications." In contrast to a library like jQuery, a framework like Ember informs your app's structure and often includes *scaffolding tools*, which are scripts to create boilerplate files in the correct directories. Since its inception in 2011, the Ember community has been building a diverse ecosystem of libraries and tooling to accelerate development.

You will start your Ember journey with Ember CLI, Ember's tool for scaffolding, development, testing, and building. If you are not familiar with the term *CLI*, it stands for "command-line interface." You will create a new project, load dependencies, generate your Ember objects, and build and run your Tracker application from this tool.

Installing Ember

To get started, you will need to install some tools.

First, make sure you are using the latest version of Node.js (>0.12.0). You can check your version with the terminal command node --version. At the time of this writing, Node is at version 5.5.0. (Yeah, that is a large difference from the minimum requirement of 0.12.0. For more on the history of when and why Node jumped from version 0.12.0 to 4.0.0, check out Wikipedia's article at en.wikipedia.org/wiki/Node.js.)

If necessary, download an updated version of Node.js from `nodejs.org`.

Once Node is up to date, you are ready to install Ember CLI using the following terminal command:

```
npm install -g ember-cli@2.4
```

The installation may take a few minutes. If you get this error: `Please try running this command again as root/Administrator`, then there is an issue with owner permissions. **Do not rerun** the install command with `sudo`, as `npm` and `sudo` do not play well together. Instead, run this command: `sudo chown -R $USER /usr/local`. Then rerun the original install command (without sudo).

You may get other errors when you install Ember CLI that have to do with incompatibility with your existing system. Most errors have instructions for repairing the install process. Some install errors will require basic internet searches to update existing programs running on your computer. If you need more information, the Ember CLI website has a page for common issues at `ember-cli.com/user-guide/#commonissues`.

Next, install Bower, another asset management tool.

```
npm install -g bower
```

Bower and `npm` are required to create an Ember application.

Next, install the Ember Inspector plug-in for Chrome. To do this, open Chrome and, in the address bar, enter `chrome://extensions/`. At the bottom of the extension page, click Get more extensions. Search for "Ember Inspector" (Figure 19.3), click Add to Chrome, and follow the prompts to install the extension.

Figure 19.3 Installing the Ember Inspector extension for Chrome

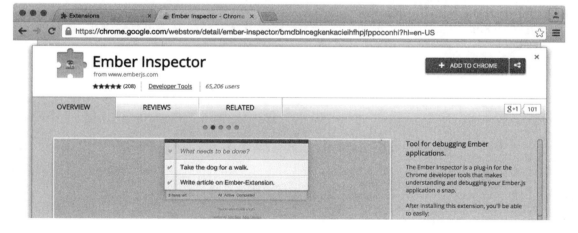

Ember CLI uses a program called Watchman when it is running. Watchman is a command-line tool that integrates with browsers to enable live reload of applications.

On a Mac, you can install Watchman via Homebrew. Homebrew, a package manager for OS X, can be downloaded using a terminal command you can copy from its website, brew.sh. Once Homebrew is installed, install Watchman (version 3.0.0 or greater) with this terminal command:

```
brew install watchman
```

Instructions for installing Watchman on Windows can be found at facebook.github.io/watchman/docs/install.html

With that, you have the tools you need to begin your Ember project, Tracker.

Creating an Ember application

Ember's emphasis on conventions and patterns allows you to create an application with minimal code. The framework does a lot of the work behind the scenes, generating a number of objects and events when your application starts. As you build out more of the Tracker app, you will use your own objects in place of the ones Ember created for you.

In the terminal, navigate to your projects folder. The command ember new [project name] will create a directory and will scaffold all the necessary files to start developing.

Create a new Ember app called tracker:

```
ember new tracker
```

Creating a new Ember application may take a few minutes. As you can see from the terminal output, some of which is shown below, the ember new command creates the base project files and directory structure. Also, it uses npm and Bower to load external library assets. These libraries are essential to running an Ember application and also to running the server to compile, build, and test your application.

```
installing app
  create .bowerrc
  create .editorconfig
  create .ember-cli
  create .jshintrc
  create .travis.yml
  create .watchmanconfig
  create README.md
  create app/app.js
  create app/components/.gitkeep
  create app/controllers/.gitkeep
  create app/helpers/.gitkeep
  create app/index.html
  create app/models/.gitkeep
  create app/router.js
  create app/routes/.gitkeep
  create app/styles/app.css
  create app/templates/application.hbs
  . . .
Successfully initialized git.
Installed packages for tooling via npm.
Installed browser packages via Bower.
```

When Ember has finished setting up the Tracker app, verify that everything is working by starting a local server.

Starting up the server

In a moment, you are going to use the command ember server (or ember s, for those looking to save a few keystrokes) to build your application and start a server so that you can access it locally. As a convenience, ember server watches your files for changes and restarts the build/serve/watch process to make sure you only see the latest code in the browser (much like the browser-sync tool you used in Ottergram and CoffeeRun).

Ember CLI uses the Broccoli program for compilation. If you have programmed in languages like Java or Objective-C, you may think of "compilation" a bit differently than what it means in JavaScript. In this case, Broccoli combines all of the JavaScript files needed to run your application, while ensuring that all dependencies are met.

It is time to *fight for the user*. Change directories into the Tracker folder and start up the server:

```
cd tracker
ember server
```

In Chrome, open a new browser window and go to http://localhost:4200 to see your new Ember app in action (Figure 19.4). You will also want to open the Ember tab in the DevTools, as shown.

Figure 19.4 Ember server

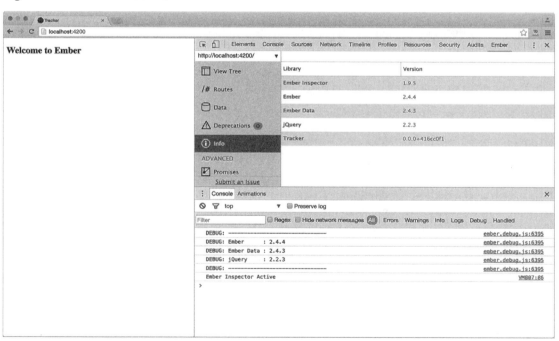

As mentioned above, Ember CLI will reload the browser page when you make changes to the application files. This is called Livereload, and you will see it mentioned in the terminal output as:

```
Livereload server on http://localhost:49152
```

In Figure 19.4, notice that both the console and Ember Inspector list various components that were generated for you, along with their versions. This book uses version 2.4 of both Ember and Ember Data. At the time of publication, Ember CLI generates a 2.x Ember application, as you can see by the version numbers in the figure. If you see version numbers starting with 1.x.x, you may have skipped the step to install or update Ember-CLI.

(Note that the Version you see after starting a server in the terminal is the version of Ember CLI, not the version of the actual Ember app you are launching.)

External Libraries and Addons

Ember CLI is set up to offer developers speed in many ways, including adding code from the open-source community. In previous chapters, you added node modules to your local environment via npm. Earlier in this chapter we discussed loading external libraries via Bower, another package manager.

Ember CLI works well with both of these package managers. Installing libraries or tools is done with simple commands like:

```
npm install [package name] --save-dev
npm install [package name] --save
bower install [package name] --save
```

When using external libraries, these command-line tools load files to the directories bower_components and node_modules.

You used Bootstrap for CoffeeRun, and you are going to start Tracker with it as well. To add Bootstrap with Bower, enter the following command in the terminal:

```
bower install bootstrap-sass --save
```

You have now loaded the Bootstrap library locally, with all its JavaScript and style files. You will roll this library into the Ember CLI build process so that you can ship your application with the Bootstrap assets your application needs.

The modern web workflow for developing scripts and styles includes compilation. You are going to add a tool to help reduce the complexity of compilation: ember-cli-sass will handle converting SCSS stylesheets to CSS during the Ember CLI build process. SCSS, commonly referred to as "Sass," adds many familiar programmatic constructs to your stylesheets like variables, functions, loops, and key/value pairs – without losing the CSS syntax you know and love.

Install ember-cli-sass from the terminal:

```
ember install ember-cli-sass
```

ember-cli-sass is an example of an Ember addon. Addons (www.emberaddons.com) are projects that have added external libraries or configuration code, created helpers or components, or done some other type of heavy lifting for you. Ember CLI makes it easy to add these existing projects to your project with the ember install command.

Note that Ember CLI is a relatively new tool, and addons can be out of sync. If you run into problems with a particular addon, visit the issues page at the addon's GitHub repository.

You have just added the ability to compile SCSS files. Now you need to change the app/styles/ app.css to be a .scss file. Rename app/styles/app.css to app/styles/app.scss. Restart the Ember server when you are done so the new CLI tools initialize.

To test the new CLI tool, you are going to add a SCSS variable to your stylesheet. With a $ as a prefix, create a name/value pair to test the SCSS compilation in app/styles/app.scss:

```
$bg-color: coral;
html {
  background: $bg-color;
}
```

Check your browser. Your page now displays a background color (Figure 19.5).

Figure 19.5 Compiling SCSS: test

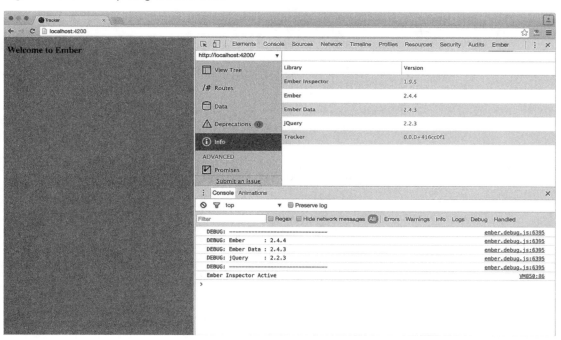

Next, you will add Bootstrap styles and scripts to your project. Earlier you added the SCSS version of Bootstrap via bower install bootstrap-sass. To add the library to your stylesheet, you will need to import the style library into your file and configure Ember CLI to build your application with those assets.

Configuration

Broccoli, the compilation engine we mentioned earlier, requires some configuration when adding new JavaScript and stylesheet assets.

Ember-CLI generates a configuration file named `ember-cli-build.js`. This file is where you can inject dependencies and configure the output structure of your application. For Tracker, you will only be adding external libraries and settings for SCSS compilation.

Open `ember-cli-build.js`, assign a variable to the directory path to `bootstrap`, and add Bootstrap's `stylesheets` directory to the key `includePaths` in the `sassOptions`:

```
...
var EmberApp = require('ember-cli/lib/broccoli/ember-app');

module.exports = function(defaults) {

  var bootstrapPath = 'bower_components/bootstrap-sass/assets/';

  var app = new EmberApp(defaults, {
    // Add options here
    sassOptions: {
      includePaths: [
        bootstrapPath + 'stylesheets'
      ]
    }
  });

  // ... Template comments ...

  // Create paths to bootstrap assets
  // Add assets to app with import
  app.import(bootstrapPath + 'javascripts/bootstrap.js');

  return app.toTree();
};
```

You have added a configuration for Ember CLI to look for *.scss files in the bower_components/bootstrap-sass/assets/stylesheets directory. Save your file and restart the Ember server so the new configuration can load with the application.

You can now use the @import directive in your app.scss file to import Bootstrap's styles:

```
$bg color: coral;
html {
  background: $bg color;
}

// ----------------------------
// bootstrap variable overrides
// ----------------------------

// end bootstrap variable overrides
@import 'bootstrap';
```

The @import directive adds the contents of bootstrap.scss to app.scss, which will be created by the Ember CLI build process. Bootstrap's file is found in the directory bower_components/bootstrap-sass/assets/stylesheets/.

In ember-cli-build.js, you added Bootstrap's JavaScript components to the application build process with app.import(bootstrapPath + 'javascripts/bootstrap.js');. An import in the CLI build configuration adds the file to the list of assets to be concatenated into a single dist/assets/vendor.js file. Bootstrap's bootstrap.js has individual JavaScript modules for collapsing DOM elements, modals, tabs, dropdowns, and many others all in a single file. Adding all the JavaScript components is probably overkill, but in the future you can tweak your ember-cli-build.js configuration to only add the specific components you need.

After you add assets, you should always make sure they are working before you move forward. In the app directory, there is an index.html file – but this is not the place to test your new Bootstrap code. This file is mainly for the build process.

Instead, all of your HTML elements will be added to application *templates*, in the app/templates directory. You will learn about templates in greater detail in Chapter 23.

For now, add a Bootstrap `NavBar` component to `app/templates/application.hbs`:

```
<h2 id="title">Welcome to Ember</h2>

{{outlet}}
<header>
  <nav class="navbar navbar-default">
    <div class="container-fluid">
      <!-- Brand and toggle get grouped for better mobile display -->
      <div class="navbar-header">
        <button type="button" class="navbar-toggle collapsed"
          data-toggle="collapse" data-target="#top-navbar-collapse">
          <span class="sr-only">Toggle navigation</span>
          <span class="icon-bar"></span>
          <span class="icon-bar"></span>
          <span class="icon-bar"></span>
        </button>
        <a class="navbar-brand">Tracker</a>
      </div>

      <!-- Collect the nav links, forms, and other content for toggling -->
      <div class="collapse navbar-collapse" id="top-navbar-collapse">
        <ul class="nav navbar-nav">
          <li>
            <a href="#">Test Link</a>
          </li>
          <li>
            <a href="#">Test Link</a>
          </li>
        </ul>
      </div><!-- /.navbar-collapse -->
    </div><!-- /.container-fluid -->
  </nav>
</header>
<div class="container">
  {{outlet}}
</div>
```

You have added Bootstrap's `NavBar` component with specific HTML attributes: IDs, class names, and data attributes. Also, the existing {{outlet}} has been moved from the main containing element to inside a <div> element. This piece of code is how templates nest child templates. You will learn more about the {{outlet}} in the next chapter.

The result of your code is shown in Figure 19.6.

Figure 19.6 Bootstrap NavBar

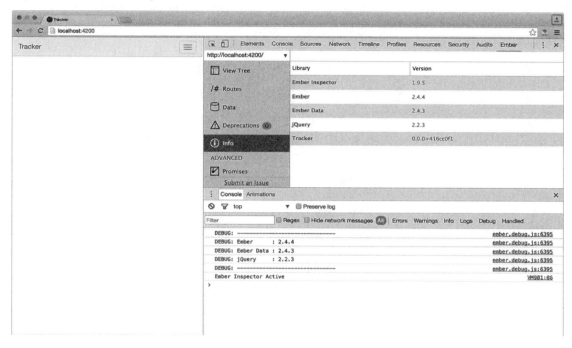

The NavBar component is responsive and shows a collapse button when the browser window is less than 768px wide. This button responds to click events by opening and closing the list of links (Figure 19.7). The event listener setup for the collapse feature is the code written in the bootstrap.js file.

Figure 19.7 Testing Bootstrap NavBar's collapse component

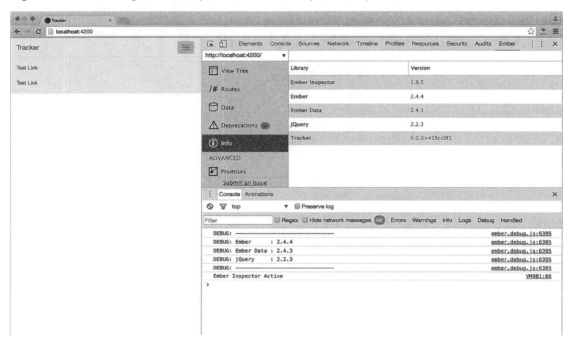

Congratulations – you have an Ember app up and running! You installed tools to generate code, compile assets, load dependencies, and serve the app. You now have a solid starting point for building the rest of your app in upcoming chapters.

For the More Curious: npm and Bower Install

The options --save-dev and --save at the end of the commands npm install and bower install add key/value pairs of library names and versions to a JSON for each tool. In the case of Bower, the JSON is bower.json; for npm – as you saw in Chattrbox – it is package.json.

For example, in bower.json the key/value pairs added in this chapter were:

```
{
  "name": "tracker",
  "dependencies": {
    "ember": "~2.4.3",
  }
}
```

The file bower.json lists the dependency ember.js with its minimum version number. The libraries and assets listed will not be saved to your development project repository or version control system, only the bower.json file. A developer who checks out the code can run bower install and npm install to create a local environment for development.

Bronze Challenge: Limiting Imports

Change ember-cli-build.js to only import the collapse.js and transition.js files. When you do this, your vendor.js will be smaller in size and your NavBar component will still work.

Before you make any changes, find dist/assets/vendor.js and note the number of lines of code (or file size). Make the change and compare the new file size.

Silver Challenge: Adding Font Awesome

Font Awesome is a UI library for adding commonly used icons to your project. The icons can be scaled, just like a font. Add Font Awesome with Ember CLI addons and add an icon to app/templates/application.hbs. Check out the addon's GitHub repository for more information.

Gold Challenge: Customizing the NavBar

Bootstrap is written in SCSS and makes liberal use of variables and functions. When you use the SCSS version in your project, you can control how the library compiles its style rules. You can even create Bootstrap themes to modify the default variables.

Change the background-color, border-radius, and padding value of the NavBar by only adding or changing variables in your app/stylesheets/app.scss.

20

Routing, Routes, and Models

At this point, you have the shell for your Tracker application. Now you need to decide what pages – or *routes* – your application will contain.

Routing is like a traffic cop: When a user pulls up a specific URL, routing directs the user to the data that makes up that page. In earlier projects, you built event listeners for form submission and button clicks. Routing is like an event listener, but it watches for changes to the current URL.

Every website uses some form of routing. For example, if you go to www.bignerdranch.com/we-teach/, the server maps the route /we-teach/ to the HTML files in a folder on the server named we-teach. Other servers may do it differently: Instead of retrieving static HTML files, they may run a function that outputs some HTML.

An Ember app can do the same thing, but without asking a server for the HTML. When your app needs to go to a different screen, it will update the URL with a new route name. The Router, which is a child of the main application object, has event listeners and handlers for URL changes. Using the new route, it does a lookup in its routing table and finds an Ember.Route object. The Router then calls a series of methods from this route object, which starts the process of getting the data needed for the next screen. This process of callbacks is called *route lifecycle hooks*.

Creating routes is fundamental to Ember development. Ember's naming conventions assume you will be creating associated controllers and templates with names that match your routes. So, for example, when you create a route called sightings, the router will map a request for /sightings to SightingsRoute, which in turn sets up a SightingsController and, finally, renders a app/templates/sightings.hbs template.

In this chapter, you will learn about Ember application constructs and use Ember CLI to create Tracker's route module files and templates. Routes are the key to an Ember application, and work in this chapter will set you up to develop your app over the next five chapters.

Figure 20.1 shows Tracker at the end of this chapter.

Figure 20.1 Tracker app

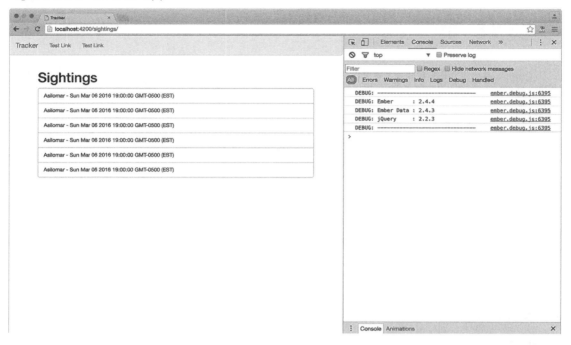

ember generate

Ember CLI provides a scaffolding tool called generate that can be useful while you are learning Ember's conventions and naming patterns. You will use ember generate, or ember g for short, to create files and add boilerplate code to your project.

Recall that Tracker's purpose is to record sightings of cryptids – creatures like the Sasquatch. It will track information about sighting events, cryptids, and witnesses. It will need quite a few routes:

Route	Route path	Route data
index	/index	no data – redirects to sightings
sightings	/sightings	list of sightings
cryptids	/cryptids	list of cryptids
witnesses	/witnesses	list of witnesses
sighting	/sighting	individual sighting details
cryptid	/cryptid	individual cryptid details
witness	/witness	individual witness details
sightings index	/sightings/index	landing page for sightings list
sightings new	/sightings/new	form to create new sighting
sighting index	/sighting/:sighting_id/index	landing page for individual sighting
sighting edit	/sighting/:sighting_id/edit	form to edit individual sighting

You will create all of these with ember generate. Open the terminal and navigate to your tracker directory. Run the following commands, one line at a time, to generate your routes:

```
ember g route index
ember g route sightings
ember g route sightings/index
ember g route sightings/new
ember g route sighting
ember g route sighting/index
ember g route sighting/edit
ember g route cryptids
ember g route cryptid
ember g route witnesses
ember g route witness
```

This will look something like Figure 20.2.

Figure 20.2 Generating routes

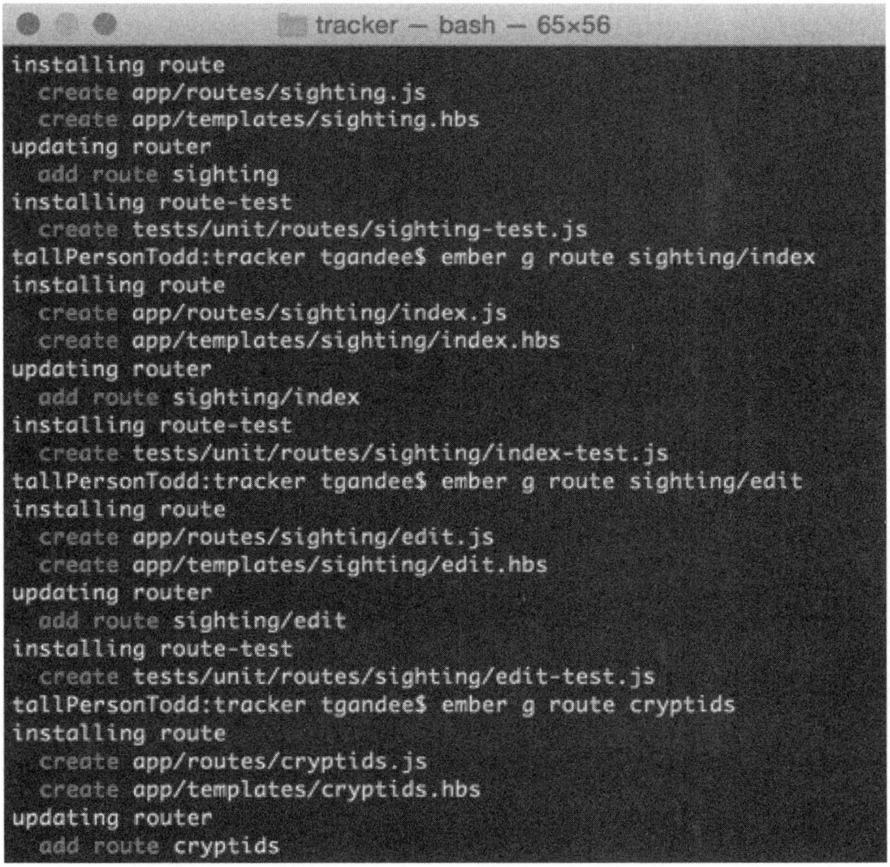

Now, take a look at what ember g created for you. You should have new files under the routes/ and templates/ directories.

Open app/routes/index.js and notice that the module imports Ember and exports an Ember.Route:

```
import Ember from 'ember';

export default Ember.Route.extend({
});
```

The method **.extend** creates a new subclass of an Ember.Route and accepts a JavaScript object as its argument. Using the ES6 module syntax, you can create individual modules for each route.

Ember CLI will automatically find the Ember.Route module you just created and import it into your app – whether you use the generate command, as you did here, or create modules manually. generate is convenient because it adds some boilerplate code to the file.

Open app/templates/index.hbs, which Ember CLI also generated for you. This template will be used for the IndexRoute. It has a single line in it: {{outlet}}.

You probably remember this bit of code from the last chapter, when you were editing the templates/application.hbs file. This helper allows templates to nest content between routes. You will learn more about the {{outlet}} helper shortly.

For now, leave this line in app/templates/index.hbs alone and add an HTML <h1> element above it:

```
<h1>Index Route</h1>
{{outlet}}
```

Now start up the app with ember server. Leave the server running while working on your project. If you need to interact with the Ember CLI (for example, to generate more modules), just open a second terminal window. The server will load the new modules into your Ember app and reload your browser.

In Chrome, navigate to http://localhost:4200. Your app should look like Figure 20.3.

Figure 20.3 Index route

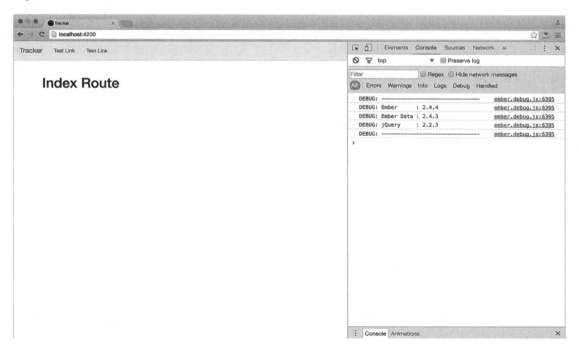

You should see the NavBar elements from app/templates/application.hbs and the <h1> element from app/templates/index.hbs. How did this element get here?

When you created your application, a number of files were generated for you, including app.js and router.js. The app.js file is the starting point for your application, and it handles things like initialization. It has functions to create a new Ember app, much like creating a new **Truck** in CoffeeRun.

In particular, the Ember app will instantiate a Router object and an ApplicationRoute object when the application is loaded or restarted. These two Ember objects control your application.

In your router.js file, you will register routes to associate URLs with specific pages. Each route can be configured with a few options. You can even create nested routes. This powerful feature of Ember lets you reuse content and logic on different screens.

Open router.js and take a look at the method that registers your routes:

```
import Ember from 'ember';
import config from './config/environment';

const Router = Ember.Router.extend({
  location: config.locationType
});

Router.map(function() {
  this.route('sightings', function() {
    this.route('new');
  });
  this.route('sighting', function() {
    this.route('edit');
  });
  this.route('cryptids');
  this.route('cryptid');
  this.route('witnesses');
  this.route('witness');
});

export default Router;
```

Router.map is being passed a callback. Inside this callback, the **route** method registers your routes. This method also takes callbacks. Ember converts these nested callbacks into a hierarchy of routes. At the top of this hierarchy is the ApplicationRoute.

When you visit the URL for a nested route, Ember uses the HTML from the parent template. Inside that parent template, it will look for an {{outlet}} helper, which indicates "This is where you should put the HTML from the child template."

Let's see how this works in your app.

Ember renders the content of the ApplicationRoute with the content of the IndexRoute nested inside. Behind the scenes, Ember is checking for a file called index.js in the routes/ folder of your project. You can create a landing page for any route by creating an index.js in the corresponding folder. In fact, this is a common practice that you should use in your own Ember apps.

You may have noticed that there are no references to index routes in router.js. Ember autogenerates the index route for all parent routes with nested child routes, just as though they appeared in router.js:

```
...
Router.map(function() {
  this.route('index');
  this.route('sightings', function() {
    this.route('index');
    this.route('new');
  });
  this.route('sighting', function() {
    this.route('index');
    this.route('edit');
  });
  this.route('cryptids');
  this.route('cryptid');
  this.route('witnesses');
  this.route('witness');
});
...
```

Nesting Routes

Routes allow you to structure data in views. Like folders, nested routes group together related routes under a base URL. It is helpful to think of parent routes as representing nouns and child routes as representing verbs or adjectives:

```
// Parent route is noun
this.route('sightings', function() {
  // Child route is verb or adjective
  this.route('new');
});
```

`sightings` is a parent route representing *sightings*, which are things (nouns), and `new` is a nested route representing the action of *creating* a sighting (a verb). **this.route** is used to build up the URL including the parent and child.

With template nesting, parts of your site can be rendered on all routes (such as navigation), while others will only show on more specific routes (like `IndexRoute` on the root URL). You will instruct each route on how to retrieve its data using callback functions.

Now, you are going to edit some of the template files you generated along with your routes and navigate to different pages of your application. The code you are adding in this section is temporary, but it will allow you to see the relationship between your routes.

To begin, open the `app/templates/sightings.hbs` template file and add an `<h1>` element above the existing `{{outlet}}` helper.

```
<h1>Sightings</h1>
{{outlet}}
```

Next, edit the `app/templates/sightings/index.hbs` template. Add another `<h1>` element, and this time delete the `{{outlet}}` helper. Parent templates use `{{outlet}}` to nest child views. `app/templates/sightings/index.hbs` is a child template without any nested route, so it does not need an `{{outlet}}` helper.

```
{{outlet}}
<h1>Index Route</h1>
```

Save your files and point your browser to `http://localhost:4200/sightings/` to see the results (Figure 20.4).

Figure 20.4 Sightings: nested routes

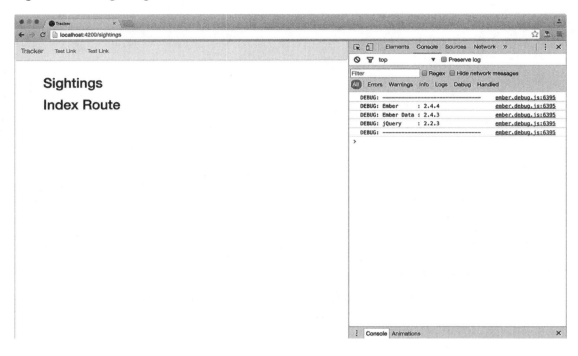

Next, edit app/templates/sightings/new.hbs. This route tree also ends with this child route, so delete {{outlet}} and add an <h1> element.

```
{{outlet}}
<h1>New Route</h1>
```

Now, change the URL in your browser to http://localhost:4200/sightings/new (Figure 20.5).

Figure 20.5 Sightings: new route

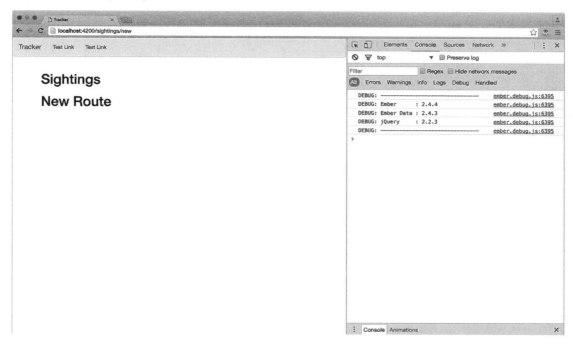

Your Tracker app now has nested routes rendering a template for the parent `app/templates/`
`sightings.hbs` file and for each child: `app/templates/sightings/index.hbs` and `app/templates/`
`sightings/new.hbs`. The parent template uses {{outlet}} to nest the views.

Ember Inspector

The Ember Inspector gives you an easy way to see all of your application's routes. Click the Routes menu item in the Ember Inspector to see them (Figure 20.6).

Figure 20.6 Route structure

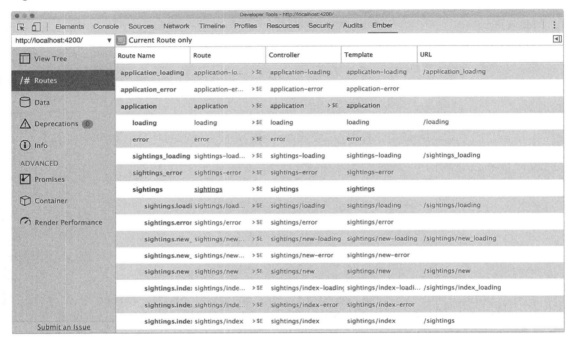

That is a lot of routes! Even more than you generated. Notice that there are numerous routes ending in loading and error. These are autogenerated routes for the lifecycle states of loading data in routes. Like index routes, these objects are created by Ember to fill gaps to get from one route state to another route state.

Assigning Models

The next step is to get data to each route using the route's model callback. Each Ember.Route has a method to assign a model (which, remember, is the data backing the template) to a controller. This method, called **model**, returns data as a Promise.

Under the hood, the Ember app initializes the Route object when the URL changes. This Route object has four *hooks* to set itself up: **beforeModel**, **model**, **afterModel**, and **setupController**.

We will focus on the **model** callback for now.

Add some dummy data in the **model** callback in the SightingsRoute, app/routes/sightings.js:

```
import Ember from 'ember';

export default Ember.Route.extend({
  model(){
    return [
      {
        id: 1,
        location: 'Asilomar',
        sightedAt: new Date('2016-03-07')
      },
      {
        id: 2,
        location: 'Asilomar',
        sightedAt: new Date('2016-03-07')
      },
      {
        id: 3,
        location: 'Asilomar',
        sightedAt: new Date('2016-03-07')
      },
      {
        id: 4,
        location: 'Asilomar',
        sightedAt: new Date('2016-03-07')
      },
      {
        id: 5,
        location: 'Asilomar',
        sightedAt: new Date('2016-03-07')
      },
      {
        id: 6,
        location: 'Asilomar',
        sightedAt: new Date('2016-03-07')
      }
    ];
  }
});
```

Notice the syntax of the **model** hook:

```
model() {
  [your code goes here]
}
```

This is ES6 shorthand for:

```
model: function() {
  [your code goes here]
}
```

Throughout the next chapters you will be using this syntax to define your object methods in Ember.

The **model** callback is a place to retrieve data needed to render a template. The route lifecycle methods in an Ember.Route return objects for each hook. The **model** hook will eventually return data to a **setupController** hook, which sets a property named model on SightingsController. You can access this data in your templates: app/templates/sightings.hbs and app/templates/sightings/index.hbs.

Edit app/templates/sightings/index.hbs as shown. We will explain the code after you enter it.

```
<h1>Index Route</h1>
<div class="panel panel-default">
  <ul class="list-group">
    {{#each model as |sighting|}}
      <li class="list-group-item">
        {{sighting.location}} - {{sighting.sightedAt}}
      </li>
    {{/each}}
  </ul>
</div>
```

This code might look strange if you have never used template languages. The words in the double curlies ({{ }}) are essentially JavaScript functions disguised as statements. In English, these lines say, "For each sighting in the model property (which is expected to be an array), render an <li> element with the sighting's location and sightedAt date."

You will learn about {{ }} syntax in general and {{#each}} in particular in Chapter 23.

Switch to http://localhost:4200/sightings in your browser, where your app should look like Figure 20.7.

Figure 20.7 Index model listing

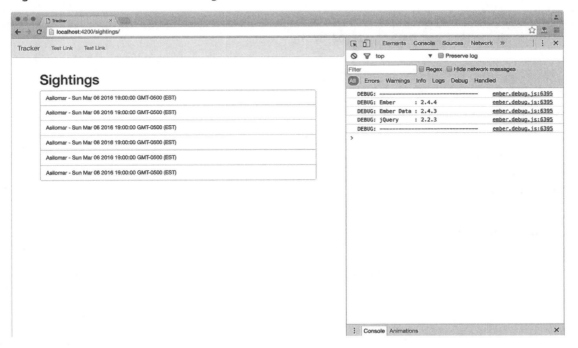

You have now completed the first half of the route cycle by passing data to the template for it to display. In the next chapter, you will explore the Handlebars templating language. This language allows you represent the state of your application with properties from a controller, rendering only necessary DOM elements as the state of the application changes.

beforeModel

As described above, the route object calls a sequence of functions, starting with **beforeModel**. This function is a good place to check the state of the application before retrieving data. It is also a good place to reroute a user who cannot be on a page, such as to check for user authentication.

You will use **beforeModel** to unconditionally transition the user to a new page. The IndexRoute is a good place to do this. You may want to add a dashboard in the future, but for now the landing page will be sightings.

In app/routes/index.js, add a **beforeModel** callback:

```
import Ember from 'ember';

export default Ember.Route.extend({
  beforeModel(){
    this.transitionTo('sightings');
  }
});
```

Now, when you navigate to http://localhost:4200/ the URL changes to http://localhost:4200/sightings, and you should see the sightings list from app/templates/sightings/index.hbs.

The last two routing hooks, **afterModel** and **setupController**, will not be used in Tracker. When creating a route file, you are cloning the Ember.Route object and overwriting the method, much like an interface in languages like Java. The **setupController** hook will run by default to set the **model** property on the route object's controller.

At this point, your application has some basic routes that outline its functionality: a landing page, a list of sightings, and a route for adding a new sighting. You created templates for your routes and added model data to the sightings route. You rerouted the index route to the sightings index. You are off to a great start!

In the next chapter, you will learn about Ember.Models, adapters, computed properties, and storage mechanisms.

For the More Curious: setupController and afterModel

The hook **setupController** is for setting properties on a controller that will render those properties. It is possible to run the default behavior of setting the controller's model property while setting other active controller properties with this._super:

```
setupController(controller, model) {
  this._super(controller, model);
  // this.controllerFor('[other controller]').set("[property name]", [value]);
}
```

The hook **afterModel** is run after the **model** hook (which is a Promise) is resolved. Note that there are special cases where the **model** hook would not be called because the Promise has already been resolved. In these cases, **afterModel** is called before **setupController** and can be used as a method to test the integrity of the model data before passing it to the controller.

21

Models and Data Binding

For the next part of the Tracker app, you will focus only on the data layer.

You have already worked quite a bit with data in the form of object literals. You have created and modified objects and their properties, and you have created functions to quickly make objects with default values. You know how to store data in `localStorage` and `sessionStorage`.

In Tracker, you are going to work with data in the form of models. Models are essentially functions that create objects with specific properties and methods. They are the architecture of data flowing through your application.

Ember has an object class that can take care of your initial need to define your app's data architecture: **Ember.Object**. All Ember classes inherit from this class. With a simple definition and naming pattern, Ember gives you the power to create, retrieve, update, and destroy model instances while the app is running.

However, for your modern application you need more than what **Ember.Object** provides. Your models need to be able to persist themselves when business logic asks them to retrieve or save data from a data source.

Enter *Ember Data*, a JavaScript library built on top of **Ember.Object**, which will help you add model-specific functionality. Ember Data adds classes built on **Ember.Object** that abstract the complexity of working with various data sources: `RESTful APIs`, `localStorage`, and even static fixture data.

Ember Data also adds an in-memory store for data. The data store is where you create, retrieve, update, and delete your model instances.

Model Definitions

Ember CLI has already loaded the Ember Data library, so you are ready to build your models.

In the last chapter, you used `ember g route [route name]` to make Ember CLI create route files for you. You can also use `ember generate` to create a model file with the command `ember g model [model name]`.

Create the model files you will need to back your routes for cryptids, sightings, and witnesses:

```
ember g model cryptid
ember g model sighting
ember g model witness
```

Cryptids will have a model definition in the file `app/models/cryptid.js`. Open this file and add attributes for name, cryptid type (species), profile image, and sightings to the `cryptid` model:

```
import DS from 'ember-data';

export default DS.Model.extend({
  name: DS.attr('string'),
  cryptidType: DS.attr('string'),
  profileImg: DS.attr('string'),
  sightings: DS.hasMany('sighting')

});
```

Ember Data, referenced here as `DS` (for "data store"), has an **attr** method that is used to specify model attributes. When data is parsed from the source, **attr** returns the value. If you give **attr** an attribute type, it will be coerced to that type. If you do not set the attribute type, your data will be passed through to the appropriate key unchanged.

There are a few attribute types built in: `string`, `number`, `boolean`, and `date`. You can also create custom model attributes using `transforms`, which you will learn about in Chapter 22.

attr can also take a second argument to specify default values. This optional argument is a hash with a single key: `defaultValue`. Here are some examples:

```
name: DS.attr('string', {defaultValue: 'Bob'}),
isNew: DS.attr('boolean', {defaultValue: true}),
createdAt: DS.attr('date', {defaultValue: new Date()}),
numOfChildren: DS.attr('number', {defaultValue: 1})
```

In the cryptid definition, you used the `string` attribute type for the `name`, `cryptidType`, and `profileImg` attributes. (Why a `string` type for `profileImg`? It will reference the image path, not the image itself.)

The `sightings` attribute uses a different method to define its data: **hasMany**. This method is part of Ember Data's relationship methods. When you query a `RESTful API` for a cryptid, it will have associated sightings. That association will be returned as an array of sighting `ids` referencing an instance of a sighting model.

Ember Data has methods to handle one-to-one, one-to-many, and many-to-many relationship types:

Relationship	"Owning" model	"Owned" model
one-to-one	`DS.hasOne`	`DS.belongsTo`
one-to-many	`DS.hasMany`	`DS.belongsTo`
many-to-many	`DS.hasMany`	`DS.hasMany`

The first argument is the model to associate. In your app, a cryptid will have many `sighting` instances (you would be surprised how often people see these creatures). The second argument is an optional hash which, similar to **attr**'s second argument, is a configuration object to set values when evaluating the function. It contains an `async` key and a value (with a default of `true`).

Model relationships could require requests to a server to retrieve other model data. For cryptids, a request to `sightings` is needed to display sighting data for each cryptid. The same is true for the inverse relationship of sightings *belonging to* a cryptid. The default value, `async: true`, requires a separate request and API endpoint to retrieve the linked data.

If your API has the ability to send all the data together, you can set the `async` value to `false`. For the Tracker app, leave the value as the default, `true`.

Next, open the model for witnesses in `app/models/witness.js` and add attributes for a witness's first and last name, email address, and recorded sightings:

```
import DS from 'ember-data';

export default DS.Model.extend({
  fName: DS.attr('string'),
  lName: DS.attr('string'),
  email: DS.attr('string'),
  sightings: DS.hasMany('sighting')
});
```

You defined a witness to be an object that contains a first name (`fName`), a last name (`lName`), an email address (`email`), and a many-to-many relationship to sightings (`sightings`).

Finally, open your third model file: `app/models/sighting.js`. Add attributes to your `sightings` model for the who, what, where, and when of the sighting as well as the date the sighting was recorded:

```
import DS from 'ember-data';

export default DS.Model.extend({
  location: DS.attr('string'),
  createdAt: DS.attr('date'),
  sightedAt: DS.attr('date'),
  cryptid: DS.belongsTo('cryptid'),
  witnesses: DS.hasMany('witness')
});
```

Sightings are defined much like witnesses and cryptids, with basic properties defined as strings. The `location` is a value the user will input in the app, while `createdAt` and `sightedAt` will be added server-side when the sighting has been added to the database.

The relationship for the property `cryptid` is something new, **DS.belongsTo('cryptid')**. This method is a one-to-many relationship linking a `cryptid` instance to the `sighting` instance – one-to-many because each cryptid will have many sightings.

createRecord

When the application initializes, Ember Data creates store, a local store object. this.store is the object that will create, retrieve, update, and delete all of the Tracker app's model records. Ember injects the store object in all Routes, Controllers, and Components. In the scope of route methods, you have access to the store from this.

To create a record, you will call **this.store.createRecord**. This method expects two arguments: a model name, as a string, and record data, as an object.

Open app/routes/sightings.js. Delete your dummy sightings and create three new sighting records, each with a location value as a string and a sightedAt value as a **new Date**:

```
import Ember from 'ember';

export default Ember.Route.extend({
  model() {
    return [
      {
        id: 1,
        location: 'Asilomar',
        sighted_at: new Date('2016-03-07')
      },
      ...
      {
        id: 6,
        location: 'Asilomar',
        sightedAt: new Date('2016-03-07')
      }
    ];
    let record1 = this.store.createRecord('sighting', {
      location: 'Atlanta',
      sightedAt: new Date('2016-02-09')
    });

    let record2 = this.store.createRecord('sighting', {
      location: 'Calloway',
      sightedAt: new Date('2016-03-14')
    });

    let record3 = this.store.createRecord('sighting', {
      location: 'Asilomar',
      sightedAt: new Date('2016-03-21')
    });

    return [record1, record2, record3];
  }
});
```

In Chapter 20, the sightings route model returned an array. Instead of returning JavaScript objects, you have created three sighting records and returned these records in an array. Run ember server, if it is not running already, to see your new records on the sightings route, http://localhost:4200/sightings (Figure 21.1).

Figure 21.1 **create** sightings

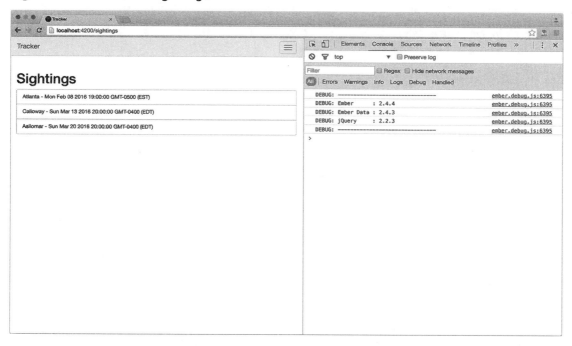

This example shows that creating Ember Data models is very similar to creating JavaScript objects. The advantage to having Ember Data model objects is all the methods these objects give you. Let's start with **get** and **set**.

get and set

At the core of Ember Data's model records is an **Ember.Object**. This object definition contains the methods **get** and **set**. Unlike most languages, JavaScript does not force the use of getters and setters on object instances. Ember applies the concepts of getters and setters with these methods to force a function to be run when changing an object property. This allows Ember to add event triggers to **set** and make programmers be intentional when getting properties.

The **get** method takes a single argument, the property name, to retrieve the property value. Try it out in the app/routes/sightings.js model callback.

```
import Ember from 'ember';

export default Ember.Route.extend({
  model() {
    let record1 = this.store.createRecord('sighting', {
      location: 'Atlanta',
      sightedAt: new Date('2016-02-09')
    });
    console.log("Record 1 location: "  +  record1.get('location') );
    ...
    return [record1, record2, record3];
  }
});
```

Reload your browser. Make sure the DevTools are open and select the JavaScript console tab. You should see the log notes from Ember, ending with the line: "Record 1 location: Atlanta."

Next, back in app/routes/sightings.js, **set** the value of record1's location after creating the record and before you log the property.

```
import Ember from 'ember';

export default Ember.Route.extend({
  model() {
    let record1 = this.store.createRecord('sighting', {
      location: 'Atlanta',
      sightedAt: new Date('2016-02-09')
    });
    record1.set('location', 'Paris, France');
    console.log("Record 1 location: " + record1.get('location'));
    ...
    return [record1, record2, record3];
  }
});
```

Reload the browser and you will see that the console reflects the **set** value: "Record 1 location: Paris, France" (Figure 21.2).

Figure 21.2 **set** location

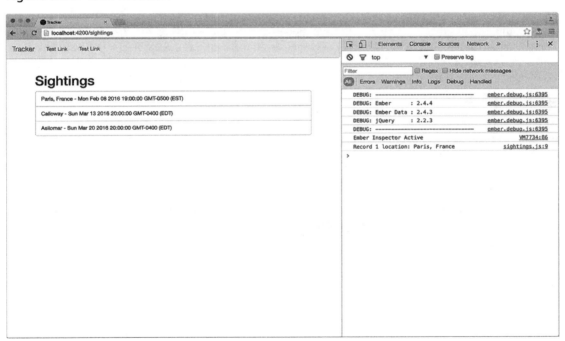

These are basic examples of **get** and **set**. When setting a property on a model record, you can also assign other model records to the record property in order to create a relationship between two model records for properties that were defined with **hasMany** or **belongsTo**.

Computed Properties

Computed properties are a huge part of managing model properties for your templates and components. **Ember.computed** is a method that takes the values of scoped properties and returns a value when the method ends. Invoking the following, for example, would give you a computed property with the object's first_name property changed to lowercase:

```
Ember.computed('first_name', function(){
  return this.get('first_name').toLowerCase();
});
```

In this example, **Ember.computed** is acting as an event listener for changes to first_name. You do not have to change the **set** method to trigger an event, you do not have to add an event listener, and you do not have to change the first_name property. All you do is create a new property that returns the value you want.

The use of computed properties is fairly global in Ember. You will also be creating computed properties for components in Chapter 25. A computed property is used either as a *decorator* for a view or component, like the example above, or to retrieve specific data embedded deep in the model object.

"Decorating" data means formatting it a certain way – such as making a string lowercase. Data from an API is not always formatted the way you want it. Decorators are functions that input arguments and output objects or arrays to be used specifically for the view layer of an application. The formatting or construction of new decorated data generally does not return to the database. For this reason, decorators are generally added to a controller, unless every page is rendering data from a model that is not formatted in the database.

Add a computed property for a fullName to your witness model in app/models/witness.js.

```
import DS from 'ember-data';

export default DS.Model.extend({
  fName: DS.attr('string'),
  lName: DS.attr('string'),
  email: DS.attr('string'),
  sightings: DS.hasMany('sighting'),
  fullName:  Ember.computed('fName', 'lName', function(){
    return this.get('fName') + ' ' + this.get('lName');
  })
});
```

(If the autorestarting server complains, be sure you added the trailing comma to the sightings property declaration. It is an easy one to miss.)

The property you added to the witness model is a function that will be invoked every time fName and lName change. Computed properties can take any number of arguments as observed properties with the final argument being the function to return a value. Each argument that is a property will trigger the function argument to be invoked.

Open app/routes/witnesses.js and create a new witness record to test the computed property of the witness model:

```
import Ember from 'ember';

export default Ember.Route.extend({
  model() {
    let witnessRecord = this.store.createRecord('witness', {
      fName: "Todd",
      lName: "Gandee",
      email: "fake@bignerdranch.com"
    });
    return [witnessRecord];
  }
});
```

To get your witness data onscreen, edit app/templates/witnesses.hbs to use the same {{#each}} iterator used in app/templates/sightings/index.hbs:

```
{{outlet}}
<h1>Witnesses</h1>
<div class="row">
  {{#each model as |witness|}}
    <div class="col-xs-12 col-sm-6 col-md-4">
      <div class="well">
        <div class="thumbnail">
          <div class="caption">
            <h3>{{witness.fullName}}</h3>
            <div class="panel panel-danger">
              <div class="panel-heading">Sightings</div>
            </div>
          </div>
        </div>
      </div>
    </div>
  {{/each}}
</div>
```

Navigate to http://localhost:4200/witnesses and check out the results (Figure 21.3).

Figure 21.3 Witnesses listing

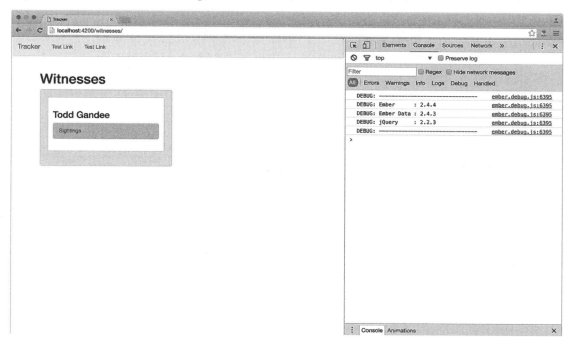

In this view, you added the listing of witnesses (which, at the moment, includes just one witness) and used a computed property to display the witness's `fullName` property. This property was generated from the values you added when creating the witness record. With **witnessRecord.set**, you can supply a different first name or last name before the model callback returns the record to see the property change.

You have come pretty far in these first few chapters on Ember! You can now define your data models, create records, create computed properties, and get and set property values. In a moment, you will read about retrieving, updating, and destroying records using an API.

In the next chapter, you will learn about using adapters, serializers, and transforms to link your data models with data on the web.

For the More Curious: Retrieving Data

As mentioned above, the data store manages model data and knows how to retrieve it. In the previous chapter, you returned data in the SightingRoute model callback with an array. In Chapter 22, you will retrieve model data in this route and return data as a Promise using **this.store.findAll** and other data retrieval methods.

Below is a table of methods Ember Data's store object has at its disposal for retrieving data from an API, storing it in memory, and returning it to the requester.

Request type	Retrieve all records	Retrieve a single record
find persisted and local records	`findAll`	`findRecord`
find local records only	`peekAll`	`peekRecord`
find filtered records	`query`	`queryRecord`

Retrieval methods come in several flavors: persisted and local, local only, and filtered persisted and local. Most use cases call for **findAll** and **findRecord**. The arguments for each match closely to the API endpoints that Ember Data will create to request the data from the API.

For **findAll**, the only required argument is the model name. For example, a request for all the witnesses would be **findAll('witness')**. Notice the singular name? Remember, this argument is the model name. Ember Data will make sure the request has a plural name when it builds the Ajax URL /witnesses/.

For **findRecord**, an additional argument is needed to indicate a specific record. This argument is the identifier, usually the id of the record, such as this.store.findRecord('witness', 5). When called, findRecord('witness', 5) will create a request for data at /witnesses/5.

For **peekAll** and **peekRecord**, the same arguments are needed to retrieve data. Invoking these methods will return the data immediately, not as a Promise.

Querying your API for data is another way to form requests. If your API supports query parameters, or *params*, for individual endpoints, Ember Data's **query** and **queryRecord** are great options. Like the other store methods, these methods take the model name as their first argument. The last argument is the query object, whose key/value pairs are converted into query string values. For **query**, the request will find all records filtered by keys and values. **queryRecord** is used when you know the request will return a single record.

For example, calling

```
this.store.query('user',{fName: "todd"})
```

would produce this request: /users/?f_name=todd. Alternatively,

```
this.store.queryRecord('user', {email: 'me@test.com'})
```

would produce this request: /users?email=me@test.com.

All of these store methods leverage adapters, which you will read about in the next chapter.

For the More Curious: Saving and Destroying Data

Updating (i.e., saving) and destroying records are the next logical steps after creating and retrieving. (There is a mnemonic for this: CRUD, which stands for "create, read, update, destroy.") The methods **save** and **destroyRecord** are available directly on model instances. These methods trigger requests through the adapter to update the data store. They return Promise objects, so you can chain callbacks with .then to do something with the returned data.

As you saw in this chapter, **set** is the way to change property values on your model records. If you change a value locally in the app, the data will be different from the persisted source. Therefore, after you change a value with **set**, you should save your data. You can do this with **modelRecord.save**. Saving a model will tell the store to make a request to the API with a POST or PUT, depending on the state of the record.

Although this was not mentioned above, when retrieving data the store will make **get** requests for data. When saving data, requests are sent with a type POST when the data does not exist in the persisted source and PUT when the data does exist and is being updated.

When you call **createRecord**, as noted earlier, you are not saving the data to the database. You are merely making an in-memory object. Calling **save** is for creation and updating.

Destroying records is the last step. Like the methods for retrieving and updating records, **modelRecord.destroyRecord** uses a request method – in this case DELETE – to remove a record from the persisted source. The store then removes the record from memory. Like **save**, **destroyRecord** is actually two function calls in one, **deleteRecord** and **save**, because **deleteRecord** only deletes the record locally. **destroyRecord** is more commonly used because it combines these steps into a single action.

Bronze Challenge: Changing the Computed Property

The fullName computed property currently uses fName and lName. Change the bound properties to be email and fName to create a fullName that displays as Todd – tgandee@bignerdranch.com.

Silver Challenge: Flagging New Sightings

Add a new Boolean attribute to sightings, isNew. Give this attribute a defaultValue of false. Add this property to one of your created records and set it to true. Navigate to the sightings route and use the Ember Inspector in Chrome to review the data for the route. Only one sighting instance should have an isNew property set to true.

Gold Challenge: Adding Titles

The witnesses need a proper title, such as *Mr.* Gandee. Add a title property to the model, then set it for each witness record except one. Add an object argument with a defaultValue. Pick an interesting default title for instances without a specified title. After creating the title property and supplying your created record with some new data, add a computed property to display the titleName.

Have fun with your default title. Wikipedia has a nice list of titles (en.wikipedia.org/wiki/Title). "Mahatma Gandee" sounds pretty good...

22

Data – Adapters, Serializers, and Transforms

Applications require data going in and out of the interface. Connecting to a data source is an important aspect of developing an application. Otherwise, you have a complex system of forms, events, and listings with no data to display.

In this chapter, you will learn some of the basics of wiring up a data source in Ember. You will use an API created for this book and create an adapter for your application.

This chapter is a little different from the other chapters in the book. It has more information and less coding. However, this chapter will give you an important real-world view of application development with a server and database that may not be under your control. In the next chapter you will return to your regularly scheduled coding.

As mentioned in Chapter 21, adapters are the translators of your application. When you communicate with a data source, your application will need to request and send data in a variety of ways. Ember Data comes with built-in adapter objects to handle some of the most common data scenarios: JSONAPI and generic "RESTful" APIs.

You are going to use the JSONAPIAdapter object to connect to a data source and return JSONAPI-formatted data. The RESTAdapter object is set of methods to work with data formatted from APIs generated from Rails and ActiveRecord plug-ins for Rails.

The JSONAPI spec was created to give API consumers a predictable and scalable pattern for sending and receiving data from servers. While there are numerous server languages – and API object pattern conventions for each – JSONAPI set out to be a pattern any language could use so that front-end applications were not affected by a change in server technology. You can find out more about JSONAPI at its website, jsonapi.org.

In this chapter, you will also learn about security issues as well as *serializers*, which are the translation layer in the adapter flow. Finally, you will be introduced to *transforms*, the tool to coerce your data into the types your models expect. Adapters, serializers, and transforms work together as shown in Figure 22.1.

Figure 22.1 Adapter, serializers, and transforms

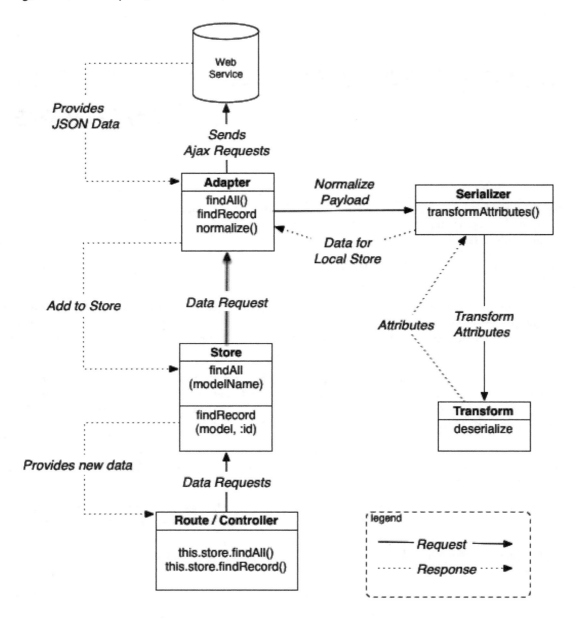

At the end of this chapter, Tracker will look like Figure 22.2.

Figure 22.2 Tracker at the end of this chapter

Adapters

The Ember team has built their framework with specific conventions in mind. Adapters are a large part of those conventions. The JSONAPIAdapter will communicate with a REST API for all requests originating from the store. Each request will add the model name and appropriate attribute data to a relative path of the domain.

To generate a specific URL for Ajax requests, the adapter needs the properties host and namespace. The adapter makes Ajax requests and expects the JSON responses to be formed with a particular structure. For example, the JSONAPIAdapter would expect a response for witnesses on a GET request to look like this:

```
{
"links": {
  "self": "http://bnr-tracker-api.herokuapp.com/api/witnesses"
},
"data": [
  {
    "id": "5556013e89ad2a030066f6e0",
    "type": "witnesses",
    "attributes": {
      "lname": "Gandee",
      "fname": "Todd"
    },
    "links": {
      "self": "/api/witnesses/5556013e89ad2a030066f6e0"
    },
    "relationships": {
      "sightings": {
      "data": [],
      "links": {
        "self":
        "/api/witnesses/5556013e89ad2a030066f6e0/relationships/sightings"
        }
      }
    }
  }
]
}
```

With each response, for example, the `type` of each object is expected to be the model name requested, in order to resolve all records for that model type. Also, an `id` is expected to be the primary key for each individual model object.

Begin by generating an application adapter:

```
ember g adapter application
```

Your application will be making requests to the Big Nerd Ranch Tracker API. As we have said, the `JSONAPIAdapter` property values require a host URL and a namespace, which is added to the end of the host when making an Ajax request for model data. Open `app/adapters/application.js` and declare the host and namespace.

```
import JSONAPIAdapter from 'ember-data/adapters/json-api';

export default DS.JSONAPIAdapter.extend({
  host: 'https://bnr-tracker-api.herokuapp.com',
  namespace: 'api'
});
```

Like other Ember classes, naming patterns also apply to adapters – and adapters can be created to customize any model's API needs. Irregularities in the data structure on the server can be contained in a single adapter rather than forcing all models to conform to edge cases.

What you have added to `app/adapters/application.js` is a global setting for all data requests. This is all you need for Tracker, because the API is sending all JSON responses from the same host and namespace. But if the witness model, for example, needed a different namespace or host, you could create an `app/adapters/witness.js` file and configure that particular adapter for witness requests.

Next, you need to retrieve your data from the API via the `store`. The API has cryptids and witnesses ready to go.

Open `app/routes/witnesses.js`. Delete the dummy data and replace it with a call to the retrieval method you learned in Chapter 21.

```
...
  model(){
    let witnessRecord = this.store.createRecord('witness', {
      fname: "Todd",
      lname: "Gandee",
      email: "fake@bignerdranch.com"
    });
    return [witnessRecord];
    return this.store.findAll('witness');
  }
});
```

Now, restart your application from the terminal with `ember server` and point your browser to `http://localhost:4200/witnesses` (Figure 22.3).

Figure 22.3 Witnesses listing

Like most lifecycle flows in Ember, adapters have a number of methods that get your data from the API to the `store` and to your routes, controllers, and templates. The purpose of a specific adapter, like the `JSONAPIAdapter`, is to handle a broad pattern and deal with an expected input/output for each model. Our example uses a Node.js server backed by a MongoDB database using a `json-api node` module to have API endpoints that work with `JSONAPI`-spec'd data.

Working with an API that has a specific pattern to follow (with minor edge cases of irregularity) makes for a happy programmer. You also might need to handle some extra data in your request, like authentication or request headers. Adapters can be customized to deal with any scenario.

Ember previously had built-in adapters for other data source scenarios, like `localStorage` and fixture data. These adapters, and others, are now addons. They can be added via Ember CLI when your model data needs to sync with other sources.

If you find that you have to hack together an adapter, dive into the documentation to find your answers. Some methods and properties of note are: **ajaxOptions**, **ajaxError**, **handleResponse**, and `headers`.

At this point, your app is making requests to a server to receive a collection of witnesses. Before you move on to reading about the content security policy, serializers, and transforms, you will use the same method, **this.store.findAll**, to retrieve all the `cryptid` records from the API. Because there is no view template for `cryptids`, you will examine the returned records with the Ember Inspector.

Add the method call to `app/routes/cryptids.js`:

```
import Ember from 'ember';

export default Ember.Route.extend({
  model(){
    return this.store.findAll('cryptid');
  }
});
```

Now that you have the data returning, reload the app in the browser and navigate to `http://localhost:4200/cryptids`. Use the Ember Inspector to examine the returning data: In the DevTools, select the Ember tab and click Data, then cryptid(4) (Figure 22.4).

Figure 22.4 Cryptid data

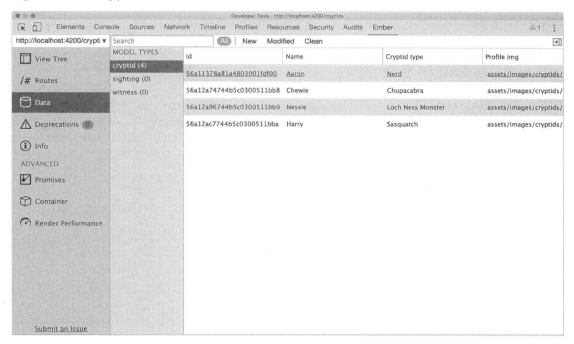

Up to this point, there has not been a need to use the Ember Inspector in depth. It is used here to show you how to examine in-memory data. Ember retrieves the data from the API and populates the store with the correct model data. When debugging issues with model data, tracing the path of the request can be tedious. The Ember Inspector should be the first place to look when you have this problem.

Content Security Policy

Ember makes use of a new security layer in JavaScript for detecting cross-origin requests before they hit your server. The working standard is called `Content Security Policy`. Ember CLI has a `contentSecurityPolicy` object to add the appropriate information. The defaults are fairly strict when it comes to requesting data, scripts, images, styles, and other file types outside of your app's domain.

There is an addon to set some defaults and integrate the security policy into your app: ember-cli-content-security-policy. You do not need it for Tracker, but it is good to know about. This addon makes it easier to add environment variables to set the security policy. The security policy object will work with the browser specification `content-security-policy`. This browser spec, available in some newer browsers, is a standard introduced to prevent cross-site scripting and other code injection attacks resulting from execution of malicious content in the application.

Here is an example of the `contentSecurityPolicy` object:

```
module.exports = function(environment) {
  ...
  // config/environment.js
  ENV.contentSecurityPolicy = {
    'default-src': "",
    'script-src': "",
    'font-src': "",
    'connect-src': "",
    'img-src': "",
    'style-src': "",
    'media-src': null
  }
  ...
}
```

Each line of the security policy creates a *whitelist* – a set of safe paths – for each type of request. `default-src` is a catch-all setting and is originally set to `null` to force programmers to whitelist the settings they need. Other settings, like `script-src` and `connect-src`, are for requests external to the application domain, like `https://bnr-tracker-api.herokuapp.com`.

For more information, see the MDN *Content Security Policy* page and the GitHub repository for the Ember CLI addon.

Serializers

When data comes in and goes out, the JSON structure is serialized and deserialized. The adapter uses the serializer to get the data in and out of the store to build and resolve request/response data.

You can create a serializer with `ember g serializer [application or model name]`, which will create a serializer file with boilerplate code, like this:

```
import DS from 'ember-data';

export default DS.JSONAPISerializer.extend({
});
```

The serializer is an object assigned to the `serializer` property in the adapter. Without a specific serializer file in your application, Ember will use a default adapter and serializer, the `JSONAPIAdapter` and `JSONAPISerializer`.

When you include a new serializer for the application, that serializer will be used as the `defaultSerializer` for the corresponding `app/adapters/application.js` file. Using the model's name as the command option in `ember g serializer` allows you customize serialization of data for a specific model.

As with the `JSONAPIAdapter`, the configuration should only be changed if your API does not conform to the `JSONAPI` specification or if you have strange edge cases. If, in your own project, you were to need changes to request or response data, here are some methods to investigate in the Ember Data documentation: **keyForAttribute**, **keyForRelationship**, **modelNameFromPayloadKey**, and **serialize**.

keyForAttribute is a method to transform attribute names from the model to a keyname sent in the request. This method expects three arguments: `key`, `typeClass`, and `method`. For the `JSONAPISerializer`, this method returns the key *dasherized*, meaning that any underscores or camelcasing in the keyname will be converted to dashes. For example, if a model has a property `first_name`, the request object will have a key of `first-name`. If your API expects `first_name`, you will need to make a change to your the **keyForAttribute** method to resolve the naming issue.

keyForRelationship follows the same process, only for relationship keys. If your model names contain underscores you will need to edit this method for `JSONAPISerializer` when you have linked models with **belongsTo** or **hasMany** relationships. Some APIs expect relationships to add a suffix of `_id` or `_ids` for these relationships. This is the method to make that change.

The `bnr-tracker-api` you are using for Tracker uses the appropriate `JSONAPI` key names with dashes, such as `cryptid-type`. You will not need to add a serializer in your app. However, for illustration, here is an example of using the Ember utility method **Ember.String.underscore** to change the attribute keys of the incoming and outgoing JSON data.

```
import Ember from 'ember';
import DS from 'ember-data';
var underscore = Ember.String.underscore;
export default DS.JSONAPISerializer.extend({
  keyForAttribute(attr) {
    return underscore(attr);
  },
  keyForRelationship(rawKey) {
    return underscore(rawKey);
  }
});
```

Ember provides a number of string manipulation methods on the `Ember.String` object. **Ember.String.underscore** converts a string with dashes or camelcase to use an underscore to separate words.

The serializer methods are called during the lifecycle of a request for data, such as `this.store.findAll('witness')`. One way to examine the callback flow of a data request would be to add a `debugger` statement in this code to see what comes in and what goes out of the method.

Here is an example:

```
import Ember from 'ember';
import DS from 'ember-data';

var underscore = Ember.String.underscore;

export default DS.JSONAPISerializer.extend({
  keyForAttribute(attr) {
    let returnValue = underscore(rawKey);
    debugger;
    return returnValue;
    return underscore(rawKey);
  },
  keyForRelationship(rawKey) {
    return underscore(rawKey);
  }
});
```

When working with a new API, this style of debugging comes in handy. You have access to the Ember.String object for when you need to manipulate the attr argument to serialize your key names. Thankfully, Ember and the Ember community build adapters and serializers for numerous API patterns.

Transforms

Ember Data gives you the ability to transform data from your API to fit the needs of your application. You have already seen in Chapter 21 that Ember Data has built-in transforms – the methods **DS.attr('string')**, **DS.attr('boolean')**, **DS.attr('number')**, and **DS.attr('date')**.

When you add a transform to your application, you can call **DS.attr** with your target attribute type. Transforms are like JavaScript coercion – they take a value and return the value in a specified type.

Here is an example of a basic **DS.attr('object')** transform:

```
export default DS.Transform.extend({
  deserialize(value) {
    if (!Ember.$.isPlainObject(value)) {
      return {};
    } else {
      return value;
    }
  },
  serialize(value) {
    if (!Ember.$.isPlainObject(value)) {
      return {};
    } else {
      return value;
    }
  }
});
```

The transform has two methods: **deserialize** and **serialize**. The first, **deserialize**, tests whether the incoming data is an object and returns it. Otherwise, it returns an empty object. The second, **serialize**, returns the outgoing data if it is an object, and otherwise returns an empty object. The transforms guarantee that the data returning from the API and going out to the API are the type defined in the model.

For the More Curious: Ember CLI Mirage

One the most common blockers for front-end application development is the API. A number of problems can come up: the API might not have been created, the API might be in development, or the API might be behind a firewall while you are developing.

The easiest solution to an inaccessible API is using static text or fixture data. But this solution might introduce a number of other issues, like changing the application logic to suit the inaccessible data, changing the requests to this.store, or changing the adapter or serializer.

Ember CLI Mirage is an addon that will proxy the requests to specific API routes. You can set up models to establish relationships, set up factories to seed data, create fixture data for specific responses, and define CRUD routes to intercept specific requests to the API. Once these are set up, you can develop as though the API were in place.

While Mirage is enabled, all requests will be diverted to the local Mirage setup.

At the time of printing, ember-cli-mirage is in version 0.2.0-beta.8. You are going to explore Mirage in just a moment as part of a challenge. To find out more about Ember CLI Mirage, visit www.ember-cli-mirage.com.

In the next chapter, you will bring together the concepts of the last three chapters and create a working application that routes requests and displays data. In Chapter 24, you will create, edit, and delete content. You will see the power of Ember Data, adapters, and serializers when you can call **save** and **destroyRecord** on models and your data is sent to the API without much heartache.

Silver Challenge: Content Security

Adding layers of security in an application is always important. As mentioned above, there is a new browser API for Content Security Policy, and Ember has an environment object to handle configuring your application's whitelist policy. Install the addon and follow the console errors to make sure your application's external request endpoints are added to the policy.

Gold Challenge: Mirage

Ember CLI Mirage is a great addition to your development arsenal. It allows you to develop your application's API needs before the back-end team finishes their stack.

Install ember-cli-mirage from your terminal to start using it:

```
ember install ember-cli-mirage
```

Next, to turn Mirage on and off, add an environment variable to config/environment.js:

```
if (environment === 'development') {
  // ENV.APP.LOG_RESOLVER = true;
  // ENV.APP.LOG_ACTIVE_GENERATION = true;
  // ENV.APP.LOG_TRANSITIONS = true;
  // ENV.APP.LOG_TRANSITIONS_INTERNAL = true;
  // ENV.APP.LOG_VIEW_LOOKUPS = true;
  ENV['ember-cli-mirage'] = {
    enabled: true
  }
}
```

Finally, add fake data in the form of *factories* for your witness and cryptid endpoints.

To work with your Tracker app, you can retrieve a configured `app/mirage` directory from the supplied example assets in `Tracker/Data_Chapter/mirage-example`. We will keep the example up to date for current releases of the addon.

23

Views and Templates

The V in MVC is for *views*. In Tracker, the views will be templates. Templates are processed with JavaScript to create HTML elements. This allows you to change the DOM without firing off a new request to the server.

In this chapter, you will be creating template files and adding the data retrieved in the route **model** hook. The template language and helper functions built into Ember will allow you to create templates with minimal effort beyond regular HTML syntax.

By the end of this chapter, you will have created listings like Figure 23.1.

Figure 23.1 Sightings listing

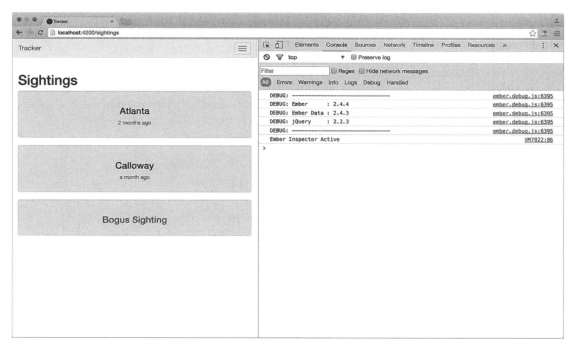

Handlebars

You will be using Handlebars, a powerful language for creating dynamic templates. It is similar to server-side templating languages like PHP, JSP, ASP, and ERB. It includes HTML element tags and delimiters to process data objects.

In Handlebars, the delimiters are double curly braces, like {{}}. Inside the "double curlies," you can render strings of data and execute limited logic using helper methods. You have seen two helper methods like this already: {{outlet}} and {{#each}}.

Ember's implementation of Handlebars recently transitioned to a new mechanism, nicknamed "HTMLBars." Some of the details of the language in this chapter are from HTMLBars, but are applicable to older versions of Ember (at least back to version 1.13.x) as well.

Models

In Ember, templates are always backed by models. This means that an object (or array of objects) will be passed as an argument when the template is rendered to a string of HTML and appended to the DOM.

The model object can have properties with strings, arrays, or other objects. When writing templates with Ember and Handlebars, you access this object with the double curlies.

When you want to display the value of a model property, you write {{model.name}}, where name is a property on the model object. The dot syntax should feel familiar, but do not be fooled into thinking any JavaScript code can go within the curlies.

Helpers

Handlebars templates are strings interpolated by JavaScript functions. When the function comes across double curlies, it tries to resolve the instance of the delimiter with an object property or invoke a nested function to return a string. These nested functions are called *helpers* and are created in the application. There are a few helpers built into the Handlebars library, and Ember adds some of its own.

Helpers can take two forms. The first are inline helpers, which use the syntax {{[helper name] [arguments]}}. The arguments can include a hash of options, such as:

```
{{input type="text" value=firstName disabled=entryNotAllowed size="50"}}
```

More complex helpers use a block syntax:

```
{{#[helper name] [arguments]}}
  [block content]
{{/[helper name]}}
```

For example, if you wanted to present a sign-in link only to users who were not already logged in, you could use something like the block below:

```
{{#if notSignedIn}}
  <a href="/">Sign In</a>
{{/if}}
```

For block helpers, content can be passed to the block to augment the output with dynamic segments. Handlebars' built-in conditionals, described in the next section, are block helpers.

You are going to use helpers to render sections of your templates for sightings and cryptids as well as the NavBar.

Conditionals

Conditional statements let you introduce basic control flow into Handlebars templates. Their syntax looks like this:

```
{{#if argument}}
  [render block content]
{{else}}
  [render other content]
{{/if}}
```

Or, alternatively, like this:

```
{{#unless argument}}
  [render block content]
{{/unless}}
```

Conditional statements take a single argument that resolves to a truthy or falsy value. (Those are not typos. A *truthy* value is one that evaluates to true in a Boolean context. All values are truthy except those defined as *falsy*: the values false, 0, "", null, undefined, and NaN.)

Time to get to work. Open app/templates/sightings/index.hbs and add a conditional statement so that sighting entries display either the location or, if there is no location data, a polite warning about the missing data.

```
<div class="panel panel default">
  <ul class="list group">
    {{#each model as |sighting|}}
      <li class="list group item">
        {{sighting.location}}   {{sighting.sightedAt}}
      </li>
    {{/each}}
  </ul>
</div>
<div class="row">
  {{#each model as |sighting|}}
    <div class="col-xs-12 col-sm-3 text-center">
      <div class="media well">
        <div class="caption">
          {{#if sighting.location}}
            <h3>{{sighting.location}} - {{sighting.sightedAt}}</h3>
          {{else}}
            <h3 class="text-danger">Bogus Sighting</h3>
          {{/if}}
        </div>
      </div>
    </div>
  {{/each}}
</div>
```

You changed the DOM structure of your sightings template to start outputting sighting information in the form of styled elements using Bootstrap's *wells* style. The use of {{#if}} and {{else}} allows you to render different HTML when the location of the sighting has not been added.

Now you need to change the data sent from the route to the template to see the results of your new conditional. In your sightings route model in app/routes/sightings.js, set the location property of one sighting to the empty string.

```
...
  model(){
    ...
    let record3 = this.store.createRecord('sighting', {
      location: 'Asilomar',
      sightedAt: new Date('2016-03-21')
    });

    return [record1, record2, record3];
  }
});
```

Start your server and point your browser to http://localhost:4200/sightings to see the new list of sightings (Figure 23.2).

Figure 23.2 Bogus sighting

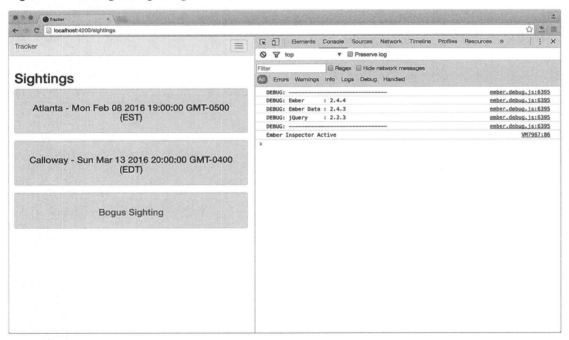

The conditional statement evaluated the truthy value of the empty string for the last sighting instance. Thus, the template rendered the block content with the text "Bogus Sighting."

Loops with {{#each}}

You have already used the {{#each}} block helper in the index template. This helper renders each object in the array as an instance of the content in the block. The argument for {{#each}} is the array as an |instance| contained in the block argument. The block will only render if the argument passed in to {{#each}} is an array with at least one element.

Like the {{#if}} block helper, this helper supports an {{else}} block that will render when the array argument is empty.

Use {{#each}} {{else}} {{/each}} to create a listing of all recorded cryptids – or, if there are none, the text "No Creatures" – in app/templates/cryptids.hbs:

```
{{outlet}}
<div class="row">
  {{#each model as |cryptid|}}
    <div class="col-xs-12 col-sm-3 text-center">
      <div class="media well">
        <div class="caption">
          <h3>{{cryptid.name}}</h3>
        </div>
      </div>
    </div>
  {{else}}
    <div class="jumbotron">
      <h1>No Creatures</h1>
    </div>
  {{/each}}
</div>
```

Similar to sightings, you are listing the cryptids in styled wells. The {{else}} block allows you to include a condition in your template when there are no items in the array you are listing. Your app can render a different element for this conditional of an empty model array.

Navigate to http://localhost:4200/cryptids to see your new cryptid listing (Figure 23.3).

Figure 23.3 Cryptids listing

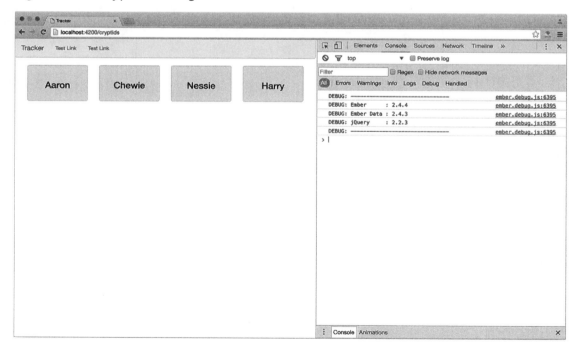

Now, in app/routes/cryptids.js, remove the model callback by commenting out the return statement to exercise the else of your conditional.

```
...
  model(){
    // return this.store.findAll('cryptid');
  }
});
```

Reload http://localhost:4200/cryptids. Your cryptid listing is now blank (Figure 23.4).

Figure 23.4 Empty cryptids listing

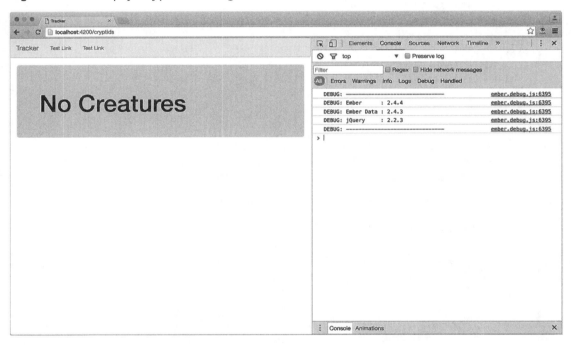

With {{each}} {{else}} {{/each}}, you can have conditional views based on the presence of data and very little conditional logic. Now that you have seen (and tested) the wonders of conditional iterators, return app/routes/cryptids.js to its previous state:

```
...
  model(){
    // return this.store.findAll('cryptid');
  }
});
```

Binding element attributes

Element attribute values can be rendered from controller properties just as element content is rendered between DOM element tags. In earlier versions of Ember, there was a helper to bind attributes called {{bind-attr}}. Now, thanks to HTMLBars, you can you just use {{}} to bind a property to the attribute.

Attribute binding is common with element properties like `class` and `src`. Your cryptids have an image path in their data, so you can dynamically bind their `src` property to a `model` attribute.

Add an image to the cryptid listing in `app/templates/cryptids.hbs`:

```
<div class="row">
  {{#each model as |cryptid|}}
    <div class="col-xs-12 col-sm-3 text-center">
      <div class="media well">
        <img class="media-object thumbnail" src="{{cryptid.profileImg}}"
          alt="{{cryptid.name}}" width="100%" height="100%">
        <div class="caption">
          <h3>{{cryptid.name}}</h3>
        </div>
      </div>
    </div>
  {{else}}
    <div class="jumbotron">
      <h1>No Creatures</h1>
    </div>
  {{/each}}
</div>
```

You will need to add the cryptid images from your course assets to the directory `tracker/public/assets/image/cryptids`. When the Ember server is running, the `public` directory is the root for assets. For a production application you may need to configure these paths, but for development, `public/assets` is a good place to work. These files are copied to the `dist` directory where your application is compiled and served.

When deploying an application to a server and adding images to persisted data you need to be conscious of the path to the actual image file. In our example, we are serving the images from the same directory as our application, and the database stores the relative path of the image to our application.

Before HTMLBars, the {{bind-attr}} helper could be used as an inline ternary operation for assigning properties based on a Boolean property. Now, you can use the inline {{if}} helper. This is common when your UI has styles that represent true and false states of a specific property.

Use the ternary form in `app/templates/cryptids.hbs` to handle missing images:

```
<div class="row">
  {{#each model as |cryptid|}}
    <div class="col-xs-12 col-sm-3 text-center">
      <div class="media well">
        <img class="media-object thumbnail" src="{{cryptid.profileImg}}"
          src="{{if cryptid.profileImg cryptid.profileImg
          'assets/images/cryptids/blank_th.png'}}"
          alt="{{cryptid.name}}" width="100%" height="100%">
        <div class="caption">
          ...
```

Unlike the block {{#if}} helper, the inline {{if}} helper does not yield block content. The inline helper evaluates the first argument as a Boolean and outputs either the second or third argument.

Here, you are evaluating the truthiness of {{cryptid.profileImg}} for the first argument. If it is truthy, the output is the cryptid's image path. Otherwise, a placeholder image is specified.

You can use a dynamic value as an argument to all inline helpers. You can also pass any JavaScript primitive as an argument, such as a string, number, or Boolean.

Before you look at the results of your conditional, create a cryptid without an image path in the **beforeModel** hook in app/routes/cryptids.js:

```
import Ember from 'ember';

export default Ember.Route.extend({
  beforeModel(){
    this.store.createRecord('cryptid', {
      "name": "Charlie",
      "cryptidType": "unicorn"
    });
  },
  model(){
    return this.store.findAll('cryptid');
  }
});
```

Now reload http://localhost:4200/cryptids and check out your new images (Figure 23.5).

Figure 23.5 Cryptids listing with images

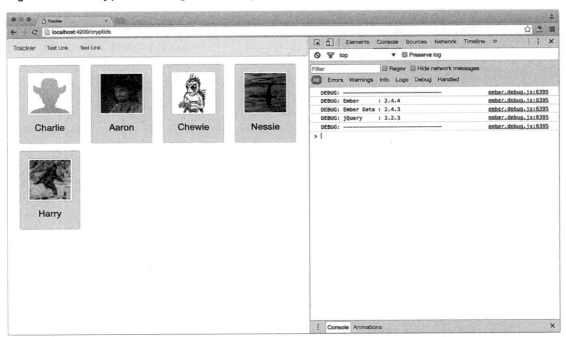

Links

As discussed in Chapter 20, routing is unique to browser-based applications. Ember listens to a couple of event hooks to manage routing in your application. For this reason, you should create links with {{#link-to}} block helpers. This helper takes the route (represented by a string) as the first argument to create an anchor element. For example, {{#link-to 'index'}}Home{{/link-to}} creates a link to the root index page.

To see how this works, you are going to update your main navigation with links using {{#link-to}} helpers.

Begin in app/templates/application.hbs. Replace the NavBar's test links with links to your sightings, cryptids, and witnesses:

```
...
    <div class="collapse navbar-collapse" id="top-navbar-collapse">
      <ul class="nav navbar-nav">
        <li>
          <a href="#">Test Link</a>
        </li>
        <li>
          <a href="#">Test Link</a>
        </li>
        <li>
          {{#link-to 'sightings'}}Sightings{{/link-to}}
        </li>
        <li>
          {{#link-to 'cryptids'}}Cryptids{{/link-to}}
        </li>
        <li>
          {{#link-to 'witnesses'}}Witnesses{{/link-to}}
        </li>
      </ul>
    </div><!-- /.navbar-collapse -->
```

Now that you have links to your listing pages, reload your app and test them. Click around. Hit the back button. You have a working web app! Take a moment to celebrate.

Your next task is to make the images on the cryptids page link to an individual page for each creature. To do this, you will take advantage of the fact that the {{#link-to}} helper can take multiple arguments to customize the link. In app/templates/cryptids.hbs, wrap the <img> tag with a link to a specific cryptid using cryptid.id as the second argument:

```
...
  <div class="media well">
    {{#link-to 'cryptid' cryptid.id}}
      <img class="media-object thumbnail"
      src="{{if cryptid.profileImg cryptid.profileImg
      'assets/images/cryptids/blank_th.png'}}"
      alt="{{cryptid.name}}" width="100%" height="100%">
    {{/link-to}}
    <div class="caption">
      <h3>{{cryptid.name}}</h3>
    </div>
  </div>
...
```

Now that you have links to the `cryptid` route and the anchor has a path to `cryptids/[cryptid_id]`, you will need to edit `router.js` so the `CryptidRoute` knows to expect a dynamic value.

```
...
Router.map(function() {
  this.route('sightings', function() {
    this.route('new');
  });
  this.route('sighting', function() {
    this.route('edit');
  });
  this.route('cryptids');
  this.route('cryptid', {path: 'cryptids/:cryptid_id'});
  this.route('witnesses');
  this.route('witness');
});
...
```

Try it out. You should see a blank page after clicking one of the cryptid images. This is good. Your app is routing you to the `CryptidRoute`, which is rendering the `app/templates/cryptid.hbs`, singular. That file is currently blank.

If you clicked on Charlie the unicorn's image, you probably got an error. Recall that his record was created in the **beforeModel** hook and does not have an id. That means that the value it tries to pass to the `{{#link-to}}` helper is `null`.

This is a good time to remove that **beforeModel** hook. Creation should be reserved for pages creating new cryptids, which we will cover in Chapter 24.

Remove the hook from app/routes/cryptids.js.

```
...
  ~~beforeModel(){~~
    ~~this.store.createRecord('cryptid', {~~
      ~~"name": "Charlie",~~
      ~~"cryptidType": "unicorn"~~
    ~~})~~
  ~~},~~
  model(){
    return this.store.findAll('cryptid');
  }
...
```

Next, add the request for cryptid data in the app/routes/cryptid.js (singular).

```
import Ember from 'ember';

export default Ember.Route.extend({
  model(params){
    return this.store.findRecord('cryptid', params.cryptid_id);
  }
});
```

The `cryptid_id` dynamic route parameter is passed to the route's `model` hook as an argument. You use this parameter to call the `store`'s **findRecord** method.

Now, edit the template for an individual cryptid, `app/templates/cryptid.hbs`, to show the cryptid's image and name.

```
{{outlet}}
<div class="container text-center">
  <img class="img-rounded" src="{{model.profileImg}}" alt="{{model.type}}">
  <h3>{{model.name}}</h3>
</div>
```

The `model` passed to this template is a single object, not an array of objects to iterate over. The **`this.store.findRecord`** method returns a single `cryptid` instance. In the template, the `model` is this instance and the properties are retrieved using `{{model.[property-name]}}`.

In the browser, use your `NavBar` to navigate to Cryptids and then click one of the cryptid images to view its detail page (Figure 23.6).

Figure 23.6 Cryptid detail page

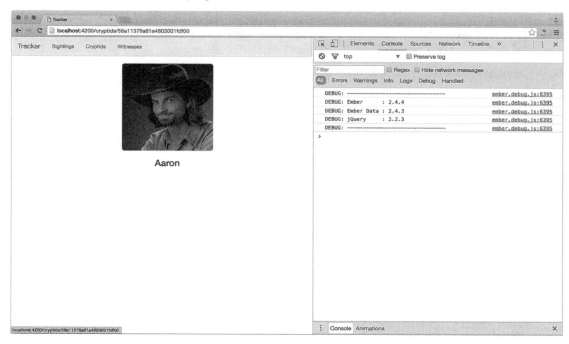

You will explore `{{#link-to}}` more in future chapters. Remember, helpers are functions that are invoked when the template is rendered. Ember comes with its own, but you are not limited to the built-in helpers.

Custom Helpers

The sighting's `sightedAt` date property is displayed as an ugly raw date string. To format your dates more nicely, you are going to use the same `moment` library you used in Chattrbox.

Add `moment` from the terminal:

```
bower install moment --save
```

Then, use `app.import` to add `moment` to your vendor assets in `ember-cli-build.js`:

```
...
  // Add assets to app with import
  app.import(bootstrapPath + 'javascripts/bootstrap.js');
  app.import('bower_components/moment/moment.js');

  return app.toTree();
};
```

Changes to your server configurations require a restart, so after you change the `ember-cli-build.js`, stop your Ember server (Control+C) and start it back up (`ember server`).

Now you need to generate the helper module from the terminal:

```
ember g helper moment-from
```

From here, you will create a function that will return HTML as a string. The function will have a date as an argument, and it will process the date with the `moment.js` library. You will surround the date with an HTML `<span>` tag and apply a Bootstrap text utility to the element.

Open the generated file, `app/helpers/moment-from.js`, and create this new function:

```
import Ember from 'ember';

export function momentFrom(params/*, hash*/) {
  return params;
}
export function momentFrom(params) {
  var time = window.moment(...params);
  var formatted = time.fromNow();
  return new Ember.Handlebars.SafeString(
    '<span class="text-primary">'
    + formatted + '</span>'
  );
}

export default Ember.Helper.helper(momentFrom);
```

Now that you have created the helper, use it in your `app/templates/sightings/index.hbs` template:

```
...
        {{#if sighting.location}}
          <h3>{{sighting.location}}  {{sighting.sightedAt}}</h3>
          <p>{{moment-from sighting.sightedAt}}</p>
        {{else}}
...
```

The `moment-from` helper takes a single argument and returns the formatted date as a string of HTML. When you use a custom helper to render HTML elements, Ember provides the **`Ember.Handlebars.SafeString`** method to output clean markup.

Check out your newly formatted dates (Figure 23.7).

Figure 23.7 Sightings `moment.js` date

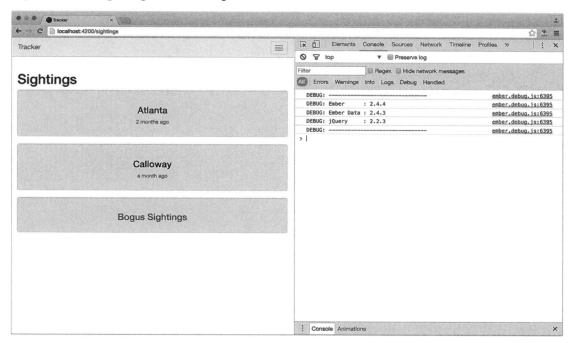

The `moment.js` library takes the date object and formats it as something like "2 months ago." That looks much better than "Tue Feb 9 2016 19:00:00 GMT-0500 (EST)"! (There are many options in `moment.js` for formatting dates – explore momentjs.com to find out more.)

By creating a helper to output the specific text, you can remove some logic from the template. Custom helpers allow you to cut down on repetition and centralize UI formatting. This is the first step to abstracting your code into Ember Components, which you will learn about in Chapter 25.

In this chapter, you learned to display basic model properties and customize your templates with conditionals and loops. You bound HTML element attributes to properties and created new routes with dynamic attributes to load individual records as the model backing the template. Finally, you used helpers for linking to pages and rounded out your understanding of helpers by building your own helper to format dates.

In the next chapter, you will complete the application lifecycle by creating and editing data with controllers. You will learn about actions, retrieve multiple collections from your data store, and create decorators.

Bronze Challenge: Adding Link Rollovers

The links you created need some rollover content. To achieve this, add a title attribute to your {{#link-to}} helpers. The title should be the sighting's cryptid name.

Silver Challenge: Changing the Date Format

The {{moment-from}} helper has made the date less clunky, but now it is not as informative as it should be. Review the moment documentation and change the output of the helper to format the date as "Sunday May 31, 2016."

Gold Challenge: Creating a Custom Thumbnail Helper

The markup for the cryptid thumbnails seems a bit long. Create a custom helper to display cryptid thumbnails by passing the image path to the helper. Clean up your code by using the helper in all the places the cryptid images appear.

24

Controllers

Controllers are the last piece of the MVC pattern. As you learned in Chapter 19, controllers hold application logic, retrieve model instances and give them to views, and contain handler functions that make changes to model instances.

The controllers you will build in this chapter will not be particularly large pieces of code. That is the idea behind MVC: distributing the complexity of an application to the places it belongs. Managing the data is the job of the models, and handling the UI is the province of the views. The controller only needs to, well, *control* the models and views.

Without your knowledge, Ember has been adding controller objects to your application when it is running. Controllers are a proxy between the route object and the template, passing the model through. When you do not add a controller object, Ember knows that the model data is sufficient to pass to the template, and it does that for you.

Creating a controller in Ember allows you to define the events or actions to listen for when the route is active. It also allows you to define decorator properties to augment model data you want to display without persisting it.

One of the goals of the Tracker application is for the user to be able to create new sightings. For this goal, you will need to create a route, a controller, controller properties, and controller actions.

You have already created the new sighting route, `app/routes/sightings/new.js`. For this page, you are you going to create a new sighting record and load the collections of cryptids and witnesses. Each new sighting will need the relationships of belonging to a cryptid and having one or many witnesses. The form you will create will look like Figure 24.1.

Figure 24.1 Tracker's New Sighting form

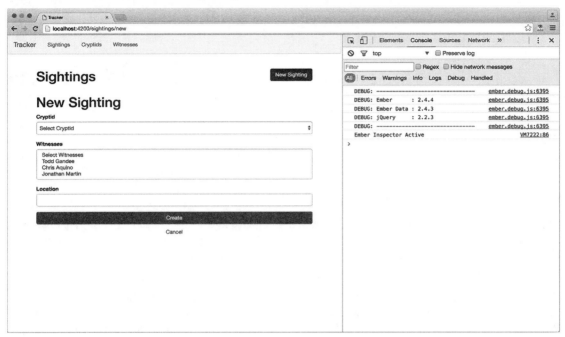

When you have all of that set up, you will create a controller to manage events from the new sighting form. You will also expand on your work to allow existing sightings to be edited and deleted.

New Sightings

The SightingsRoute's model that you have set up returns all the sightings. For the new sightings model, you will return the result of creating a single new, empty sighting. Also, you will return a set of Promises for the cryptids and witnesses. To do this you will return Ember.RSVP.hash({}).

Let's get started. Open app/routes/sightings/new.js and add a model hook to return a collection of Promises as an **Ember.RSVP.hash**:

```
...
export default Ember.Route.extend({
  model() {
    return Ember.RSVP.hash({
      sighting: this.store.createRecord('sighting')
    });
  }
});
```

When this route is active, a new record of a sighting is returned. If you were to return to the sightings, you would see a blank entry, because you created a new record. You will handle the *dirty records* (model data that has been changed but not saved to the persisted source) toward the end of this chapter. For now, know that **createRecord** has added a new sighting to the local collection.

When creating a new sighting, you will need the list of cryptids and witnesses. Here, Ember.RSVP.hash({}) is used to say you are returning a hash of Promises. The only key is sighting, which means that your `model` reference in the template will need to do a look-up on `model.sighting` to reference the sighting record you created.

Add the retrieval methods for cryptids and witnesses to this hash (do not neglect the comma after `this.store.createRecord('sighting')`).

```
...
export default Ember.Route.extend({
  model() {
    return Ember.RSVP.hash({
      sighting: this.store.createRecord('sighting'),
      cryptids: this.store.findAll('cryptid'),
      witnesses: this.store.findAll('witness')
    });
  }
}
```

Next, you are going to use `<select>` tags in your new sightings template to present the lists of cryptids and witnesses to the user. But before you set up your template with the new model data, you will need an Ember CLI plug-in that makes it easy to use `<select>` tags with bound properties.

From the command line, install emberx-select:

```
ember install emberx-select
```

You will use this component, usually called x-select, in your template. This saves you from writing onchange actions for each `<select>` tag.

Restart `ember server` before using the x-select component.

With all the model data set up, you can now edit the template, `app/templates/sightings/new.hbs`, to create the new sighting form:

```
<h1>New Route</h1>
<h1>New Sighting</h1>
<form>
  <div class="form-group">
    <label for="name">Cryptid</label>
    {{#x-select value=model.sighting.cryptid class="form-control"}}
      {{#x-option}}Select Cryptid{{/x-option}}
      {{#each model.cryptids as |cryptid|}}
        {{#x-option value=cryptid}}{{cryptid.name}}{{/x-option}}
      {{/each}}
    {{/x-select}}
  </div>
  <div class="form-group">
    <label>Witnesses</label>
    {{#x-select value=model.sighting.witnesses multiple=true class="form-control"}}
      {{#x-option}}Select Witnesses{{/x-option}}
      {{#each model.witnesses as |witness|}}
        {{#x-option value=witness}}{{witness.fullName}}{{/x-option}}
      {{/each}}
    {{/x-select}}
  </div>
  <div class="form-group">
    <label for="location">Location</label> {{input value=model.sighting.location
      type="text" class="form-control" name="location" required=true}}
  </div>
</form>
```

Wow! That has got everything you have been working on – and more. The route is using a new
Ember.RSVP method, the template is using helpers, and the new {{x-select}} and {{x-option}}
components are used.

The {{x-select}} component is built to use the <select> element to assign a value to a property. It
is designed to work just like a <select> element in the Ember data-binding environment. You assign
the value to the sightings model's cryptid property and the component will handle the onchange event
when a new option is selected. This works because the cryptid property needs a cryptid model record
as its value.

For the witnesses, there is an extra attribute, multiple=true, which will allow your users to select
multiple witnesses for a sighting. Multiple selections will translate into a collection of **hasMany**
witnesses.

Before you go any further, you will need to add a link to the sightings route template so you have a
way to get to the sightings.new route. Open app/templates/sightings.hbs and take care of that.

```
<h1>Sightings</h1>
<div class="row">
  <div class="col-xs-6">
    <h1>Sightings</h1>
  </div>
  <div class="col-xs-6 h1">
    {{#link-to "sightings.new" class="pull-right btn btn-primary"}}
      New Sighting
    {{/link-to}}
  </div>
</div>
{{outlet}}
```

Your link takes advantage of the simplicity of **Bootstrap** formatting to create a button. Load http://
localhost:4200/sightings to see it (Figure 24.2).

Figure 24.2 New Sighting button

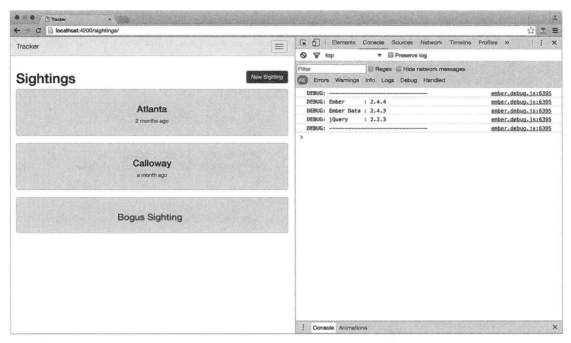

Now you have the ability to navigate to the `sightings.new` route. The new button adds a link to create a new sighting from anywhere in the sightings route tree structure.

Also, notice that when you are on the `sightings.new` route, the button is active. Ember has thought of it all, giving an active class to a link even when the current route is the link's route. Having an active state on a button or link signifies the current route in the form of UI cues.

Actions are the key to handling form events – or any other events in your app. The `actions` property is a hash where you assign functions to keys. The keys will be used in the templates to trigger the callback.

You are ready to create the controller for the `sightings.new` route, using this terminal command:

```
ember g controller sightings/new
```

Ember creates the `app/controllers/sightings/new.js` file. Open it and add the `create` and `cancel` actions you will need to create sightings:

```
import Ember from 'ember';

export default Ember.Controller.extend({
  actions: {
    create() {
    },
    cancel() {
    }
  }
});
```

When creating a form element, the action attribute usually has a URL to which you submit the form. With Ember, the form element only needs the name of a function to run.

In app/templates/sightings/new.hbs, have the form element set the action for submit. Also, add Create and Cancel buttons:

```
<h1>New Sighting</h1>
<form {{action "create" on="submit"}}>
...
  <div class="form-group">
    <label for="location">Location</label> {{input value=model.location
      type="text" class="form-control" name="location" required=true}}
  </div>
  <button type="submit" class="btn btn-primary btn-block">Create</button>
  <button {{action 'cancel'}} class="btn btn-link btn-block">Cancel</button>
</form>
```

Atom may complain about the syntax of the lines with the {{action}} helpers. You can ignore its complaints. (You can also install Language-Mustache and enable it in Atom's preferences so that Atom recognizes this syntax. The package can be found at atom.io/packages/language-mustache.)

The two {{action}} helpers have string arguments matching the actions you created in app/controllers/sightings/new.js. Actions are bound to event handlers. The {{action}} helper accepts an argument, on, to which the action is assigned. A click event listener is assigned to the action if you do not add the on argument to the helper.

In the new sightings form, you added on="submit" to specify that the create action will be called on submit. You did not give an on argument to the cancel button, on the other hand, so the event bound with the action will be a click.

Your form now works to submit and cancel using controller actions, but those actions need some code. Start with the create action. Update app/controllers/sightings/new.js to complete the sighting, save it, and return to the sightings listing.

```
...
  actions: {
    create() {
      var self = this;
      this.get('model.sighting').save().then(function() {
        self.transitionToRoute('sightings');
      });
    },
    cancel() {
    }
  }
});
```

When the form is submitted, **create** is called. First, you set a reference to the controller with self. Next, you get the sighting model and call **save**.

The last step is saving to the persistent source. There is a flag on the model for hasDirtyAttributes that is set to false when a model is saved.

Saving a model returns a Promise. You chained that Promise with then, which takes a function to be called when the model has been saved successfully. Finally, you return to the sightings listing with **transitionToRoute**.

Check out your form at http://localhost:4200/sightings/new (Figure 24.3).

Figure 24.3 New Sighting form

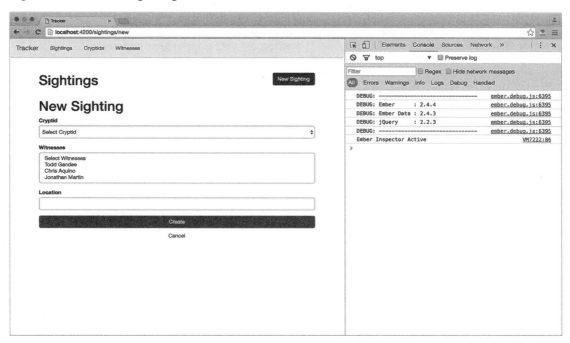

Fill in the form and click Create. Although you successfully added a new sighting, your sightings list route model is still returning the records created inline. Open app/routes/sightings.js, delete the dummy data, and replace it with a call to the store to retrieve the sightings.

```
import Ember from 'ember';

export default Ember.Route.extend({
  model() {
    let record1 = this.store.createRecord('sighting', {
      location: 'Atlanta',
      sightedAt: new Date('2016-02-09')
    });
    record1.set('location', 'Paris, France');
    console.log("Record 1 location: " + record1.get('location'));

    let record2 = this.store.createRecord('sighting', {
      location: 'Calloway',
      sightedAt: new Date('2016-03-14')
    });

    let record3 = this.store.createRecord('sighting', {
      location: '',
      sightedAt: new Date('2016-03-21')
    });

    return [record1, record2, record3];
    return this.store.findAll('sighting', {reload: true});
  }
});
```

Now your app has creation and retrieval.

Notice the second argument of **findAll**, the object literal with the single key reload. This argument tells the store to request fresh data from the API each time the route model is called. Adding this argument makes it explicit that you always want the freshest data each time you view the list.

Next, the cancel action needs to delete the in-memory, dirty sighting instance. You will use **model.deleteRecord**, as you did in Chapter 21. Add it to app/controllers/sightings/new.js.

```
...
  actions: {
    create() {
      var self = this;
      this.get('model.sighting').save().then(function() {
        self.transitionToRoute('sightings');
      });
    },
    cancel() {
      this.get('model.sighting').deleteRecord();
      this.transitionToRoute('sightings');
    }
  }
...
```

After deleting the record, the user will be returned to the listing. This scenario works when the user clicks the cancel button, but what happens when the top navigation is used to go back to the listing or another route?

If you do not destroy the dirty record, it will stay in memory while the user's session is active. To destroy the record you will use an action in the route.

In the lifecycle of a route, there are actions called at different states and transitions. You can override these actions to customize callbacks for different stages of your route transition.

Open app/routes/sightings/new.js and override the willTransition action to ensure that dirty records are deleted:

```
...
  model(){
    return Ember.RSVP.hash({
      sighting: this.store.createRecord('sighting'),
      cryptids: this.store.findAll('cryptid'),
      witnesses: this.store.findAll('witness')
    });
  },
  actions: {
    willTransition() {
      var sighting = this.get('controller.model.sighting');
      if(sighting.get('hasDirtyAttributes')){
        sighting.deleteRecord();
      }
    }
  }
});
```

The action willTransition will fire when the route changes. Using **deleteRecord** will destroy the model object, but only when the model property hasDirtyAttributes is true.

You have now covered your bases with a dirty record on creation. You are also set up to save to a persistent data source with minimal changes to the controller.

Editing a Sighting

After creating and reading data, CRUD tells us that updating is the next step. You have an edit route for a sighting, but you need to put it to use by updating the sighting listing with a button to navigate to the edit route. You also need to add a form with sighting fields to the edit template; have the edit route's **model** retrieve witnesses, cryptids, and the sighting; and add route parameters to the edit route object in app/router.js. Finally, you need to create a controller to add actions for the edit form.

Let's start with adding an Edit button in app/templates/sightings/index.hbs. To give more context to the list, add the name and image of the cryptid that was sighted as well.

```
...
    <div class="media well">
      <img class="media-object thumbnail" src="{{if sighting.cryptid.profileImg
        sighting.cryptid.profileImg 'assets/images/cryptids/blank_th.png'}}"
        alt="{{sighting.cryptid.name}}" width="100%" height="100%">
      <div class="caption">
        <h3>{{sighting.cryptid.name}}</h3>
        {{#if sighting.location}}
          <h3>{{sighting.location}}</h3>
          <p>{{moment-from sighting.sightedAt}}</p>
        {{else}}
          <h3 class="text-danger">Bogus Sighting</h3>
        {{/if}}
      </div>
      {{#link-to 'sighting.edit' sighting.id tagName="button"
        class="btn btn-success btn-block"}}
        Edit
      {{/link-to}}
    </div>
...
```

Load `http://localhost:4200/sightings` and check out your new Edit button (Figure 24.4).

Figure 24.4 Sightings list with Edit button

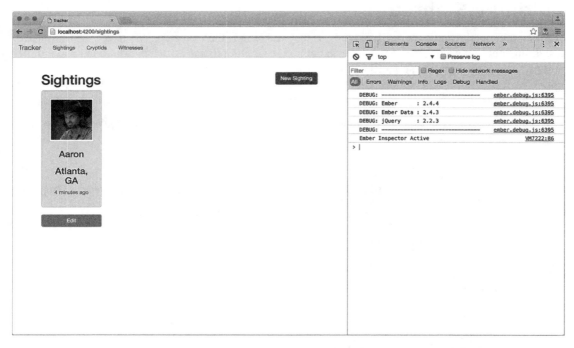

Now add the dynamic parameters to the edit route in `router.js`.

```
...
  this.route('sighting', function() {
    this.route('edit', {path: "sightings/:sighting_id/edit"});
  });
...
```

Add the retrieval methods for sightings, cryptids, and witnesses to the route in `app/routes/sighting/edit.js`:

```
...
export default Ember.Route.extend({
  model(params) {
    return Ember.RSVP.hash({
      sighting: this.store.findRecord('sighting', params.sighting_id),
      cryptids: this.store.findAll('cryptid'),
      witnesses: this.store.findAll('witness')
    });
  }
});
```

Next, add the form elements to `app/templates/sighting/edit.hbs`, as you did when creating a new sighting.

```
{{outlet}}
<h1>Edit Sighting:
  <small>
    {{model.sighting.location}} -
    {{moment-from model.sightin.sightedAt}}
  </small>
</h1>
<form {{action "update" model on="submit"}}>
  <div class="form-group">
    <label for="name">Cryptid</label>
    {{input value=model.sighting.cryptid.name type="text" class="form-control"
      name="location" disabled=true}}
  </div>
  <div class="form-group">
    <label>Witnesses</label>
    {{#each model.sighting.witnesses as |witness|}}
      {{input value=witness.fullName type="text" class="form-control"
        name="location" disabled=true}}
    {{/each}}
  </div>
  <div class="form-group">
    <label for="location">Location</label>
    {{input value=model.sighting.location type="text" class="form-control"
      name="location" required=true}}
  </div>
  <button type="submit" class="btn btn-info btn-block">Update</button>
  <button {{action 'cancel'}} class="btn btn-block">Cancel</button>
</form>
```

You are almost there; the controller is the final step. You need to set the form {{action}} to update. Also, because Tracker is only going to allow location changes at this point, you will render the cryptid and witnesses in disabled input fields.

Create the controller:

```
ember g controller sighting/edit
```

Open app/controllers/sighting/edit.js and add the update and cancel actions:

```
import Ember from 'ember';

export default Ember.Controller.extend({
  sighting: Ember.computed.alias('model.sighting'),
  actions: {
    update() {
      if(this.get('sighting').get('hasDirtyAttributes')){
        this.get('sighting').save().then(() => {
          this.transitionToRoute('sightings');
        });
      }
    },
    cancel() {
      if(this.get('sighting').get('hasDirtyAttributes')){
        this.get('sighting').rollbackAttributes();
      }
      this.transitionToRoute('sightings');
    }
  }
});
```

Similar to creating model records, updating is as easy as calling **save**. You only want to call the API when your record has changed, hence `sighting.get('hasDirtyAttributes')`. Ember has thought of it all!

Notice the use of `Ember.computed.alias`. This is a computed property assigned so you do not have to type as much when calling on the active `sighting`. You can alias any property to get quick access, especially if the properties are nested.

Deleting a Sighting

Every so often a reported cryptid sighting turns out to be a hoax. While this may be rare, you do need a way to delete old or debunked data. Recall from Chapter 21 that destroying records is achieved by calling **record.destroyRecord**. Simple enough.

Make it so: Add a delete button to your template in `app/templates/sighting/edit.hbs`.

```
  <button type="submit" class="btn btn-info btn-block">Update</button>
  <button {{action 'cancel'}} class="btn btn-block">Cancel</button>
</form>

<hr>
<button {{action 'delete'}} class="btn btn-block btn-danger">
  Delete
</button>
```

In addition to the new button, you added a horizontal rule (a simple line) between the form elements to separate the Update and Cancel buttons from the new Delete button. The <hr> is a UI tool you are using to indicate that deleting a sighting is a separate process from editing a sighting.

Next, add the `delete` action to your controller, `app/controllers/sighting/edit.js`:

```
...
    cancel() {
      if(this.get('sighting').get('hasDirtyAttributes')){
        this.get('sighting').rollbackAttributes();
      }
      this.transitionToRoute('sightings');
    },
    delete() {
      var self = this;
      if (window.confirm("Are you sure you want to delete this sighting?")) {
        this.get('sighting').destroyRecord().then(() => {
          self.transitionToRoute('sightings');
        });
      }
    }
  }
});
```

The `delete` action adds a `window.confirm` to get the user's confirmation. Aside from the conditional, this action is like the others: get the model, call a method, and add an async `then` to call when the API request is done.

Now navigate to `http://localhost:4200/sightings` and click the Edit button for one of your sightings to view the `app/templates/sightings/edit.hbs` and its new Delete button (Figure 24.5).

Figure 24.5 Edit Sighting form

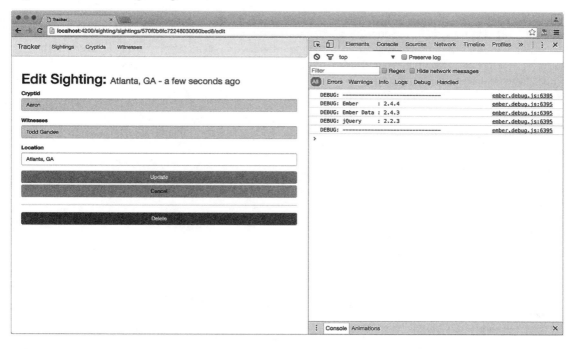

The cycle is now complete: creation to destruction.

Route Actions

Actions are not just for controllers. Routes can declare the actions for templates and override lifecycle actions. When an action is called, it bubbles up from the template to the controller to the route and to parent routes.

A route can therefore act as the controller when a controller definition is not needed. This might seem contradictory after all our talk about separating the application concerns, but Ember really split the controller's job into two units: route information and controller logic. Sometimes the route file has more logic and sometimes the controller has more logic. The file separation allows for small digestible chunks of code when the other file has numerous actions or decorators.

To see how this works, you are going to move the `create` and `cancel` actions from `app/controllers/sightings/new.js` to `app/routes/sightings/new.js`. Making this change will also broaden your perspective on methods and objects passed between these files – and it will be good practice for when you only want a route file and components controlling an application view. (You will learn about components in the next chapter.)

First, add the actions to `app/routes/sightings/new.js`:

```
import Ember from 'ember';

export default Ember.Route.extend({
  model() {
    ...
  },
  sighting: Ember.computed.alias('controller.model.sighting'),
  actions: {
    willTransition() {
      var sighting = this.get('controller.model.sighting');
      if(sighting.get('hasDirtyAttributes')) {
        sighting.deleteRecord();
      }
    },
    create() {
      var self = this;
      this.get('sighting').save().then(function(data) {
        self.transitionTo('sightings');
      });
    },
    cancel() {
      this.get('sighting').deleteRecord();
      this.transitionToRoute('sightings');
    }
  }
});
```

You also created an `Ember.computed.alias` for the sighting object in the route. The major difference in accessing the controller's `model.sighting` object from the route is where that object lives. The `model` on the "new" route is not the same as the model on the "new" controller. To access the `sighting` object you use `get('controller.model.sighting')`. Creating an alias to this object will save you from typing that out each time.

Now, delete the actions from app/controllers/sightings/new.js:

```
import Ember from 'ember';

export default Ember.Controller.extend({
  actions: {
    create() {
      var self = this;
      this.get('model.sighting').save().then(function() {
        self.transitionToRoute('sightings');
      });
    },
    cancel() {
      this.get('model.sighting').deleteRecord();
      this.transitionToRoute('sightings');
    }
  }
});
```

Make sure your application has reloaded (or restart ember server). Navigate to http://localhost:4200/sightings/new and create a new sighting to make sure you can still run the route actions.

At this point, app/controllers/sightings/new.js is irrelevant. You can delete this file. Ember will still create the controller object while the app is running, but you do not need the empty file cluttering up the app directory.

This chapter focused on Ember controllers to show you how to create actions and properties for your templates, transition to new routes after saving data, and destroy records on cancel or a route change. Actions allow you to change the model data backing your application with a simple callback. The controller properties allow you to have page-specific properties before adding relationships to the model data. Last, you have completed the basic CRUD actions of updating and deleting records from an edit route.

Ember allows rapid development by making the creation of controllers optional for when you need these specific details for your routes. Beyond these features, controllers allow you to fine-tune your views and have control over your model data. Actions are the key to user interaction. Furthermore, actions can live on routes, controllers, and components – which are the subject of the next (and final) chapter.

Bronze Challenge: Sighting Detail Page

Create a sighting detail page with app/templates/sighting/index.hbs and app/routes/
sighting.js to display the cryptid image, location, and list of witnesses. Add an Edit button for good
measure. (Hint: You can add your actions on the route.)

Silver Challenge: Sighting Date

When creating and editing a sighting, add a sightingDate property to the controller and an input that
is bound to that property. Use either a basic text input or input[type="date"] to capture the sighting
date. Convert the date to an ISO8601 string using moment and set the sighting property sightingAt
with that date string.

Gold Challenge: Adding and Removing Witnesses

When creating a new sighting, build a list of witnesses from a select onchange action. Create a new
property for the list of witnesses. On create, add the objects to the sightings property witnesses.

While on the page, make the collection of selected witnesses render as a list with a Remove button.
Use the select element as a way to add to the list while removing the options from the select
element. You will need two actions: addWitness and removeWitness.

25

Components

Components are objects that hold the properties of controllers and views in Ember. The concept behind components is to have reusable DOM elements that have their own context or scope. Components accept attributes to customize the content rendered inside their templates. Also, components can allow actions to be assigned to properties from a parent controller or parent route (Figure 25.1).

Figure 25.1 Component property

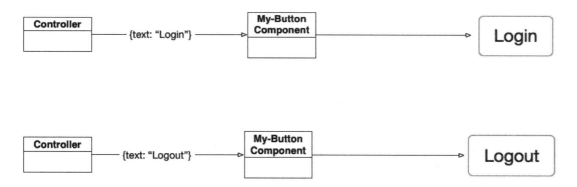

As you assess the architecture of your application, you will start to see elements grouped together with minor differences throughout many routes and templates. If a grouping of elements can be removed from the template and described with variables depicting the elements' state, it is a prime candidate to become a component.

This chapter will show you relatively simple examples of wrapping DOM elements in JavaScript objects to be used across multiple routes. Much like the helpers you saw in Chapter 23, components take arguments in the form of attributes to produce HTML. They also have the added feature of having their own actions and scoped properties to update themselves upon user interaction.

This chapter will only show you the tip of the iceberg of scalable application development. Ember applications in production rely heavily on components to create consistent user interfaces and maintainable code bases that sometimes span hundreds of routes. However, the examples you see here will provide a foundation of understanding for future projects where you want to turn your route templates into reusable pages or single elements.

Iterator Items as Components

An example of grouped elements that can often become a component is elements rendered in {{#each}} iterators. There may be a `<div>` container element with a particular `className` based on the iterator object, a title, an image path, a button with an action, and/or styles based on the object's property states. To make these easily reusable, you can wrap all the DOM code in a component template and create a component JavaScript file to handle the decorators and actions that a controller would normally handle.

Your sightings list is built with an {{#each}} iterator, and you are going to create your first component to represent a sighting list item. Start by generating a component via Ember CLI in the terminal:

```
ember g component listing-item
```

This creates three files: `app/components/listing-item.js`, `app/templates/components/listing-item.hbs`, and the test file `tests/integration/components/listing-item-test.js`.

Now that the component is created, you need to find the code you want the component to replace. Open `app/templates/sightings/index.hbs` and locate this block of code. You will be moving part of this code to the component in a moment. For now, just take a look at it.

```
<div class="row">
  {{#each model as |sighting|}}
    <div class="col-xs-12 col-sm-3 text-center">
      <div class="media well">
        <img class="media-object thumbnail" src="{{if sighting.cryptid.profileImg
          sighting.cryptid.profileImg 'assets/images/cryptids/blank_th.png'}}"
          alt="{{sighting.cryptid.name}}" width="100%" height="100%">
        <div class="caption">
          <h3>{{sighting.cryptid.name}}</h3>
          {{#if sighting.location}}
            <h3>{{sighting.location}}</h3>
            <p>{{moment-from sighting.sightedAt}}</p>
          {{else}}
            <h3 class="text-danger">Bogus Sighting</h3>
          {{/if}}
        </div>
        {{#link-to 'sighting.edit' sighting.id tagName="button"
          class="btn btn-success btn-block"}}
          Edit
        {{/link-to}}
      </div>
    </div>
  {{/each}}
</div>
```

The container `<div>` with the `col-xs-12` class (that is, the shaded `<div>`) needs to be on this specific page. It is a visual container for the layout, specifying the size of its content. If you were to add this container to your sightings list component, the container size would be fixed for every instance of the component across the site.

However, the `<div class="media well">` container and its contents can be moved to a component. This component can then be added to any size of container while holding the characteristics of a single item in a list. The component will contain the major elements of the item being listed – mainly the media container and the image, title, and Edit button.

Open `app/templates/components/listing-item.hbs` and begin by adding the image and cryptid name:

```
<img class="media-object thumbnail" src="{{imagePath}}" alt="{{name}}"
  width="100%" height="100%">
<div class="caption">
  <h3>{{name}}</h3>
  {{yield}}
</div>
```

A component represents a single DOM element. Everything in the component template, then, is a child of that DOM element. By default, Ember's HTMLBars uses JavaScript to create `<div>` elements and renders the component template inside them.

The code you just wrote adds an image and a caption with a name to the `<div>` element created by a `{{#listing-item}}` component. Just like other templates, the component has dynamic portions that are variables you will pass in. (We will discuss the `{{yield}}` in a moment.)

When you add this component to the route template, it will render this:

```
<div>
  <img class="media-object thumbnail" src="[cryptid's imagePath string]"
    alt="[cryptid's name string]" width="100%" height="100%">
  <div class="caption">
    <h3>[cryptid's name string]</h3>
    {{yield}}
  </div>
</div>
```

The dynamic portions of the template, `{{name}}` and `{{imagePath}}`, will be attributes provided to the component. The `{{yield}}` is where you can pass child elements to the component to render in a specific location of the DOM node structure. The component template file acts a layout or master set of elements, and the `{{yield}}` is for elements you need to add with each instance of the component. You will use it later in the chapter.

While this is not exactly the markup you are replacing in `app/templates/sightings/index.hbs`, it is a good starting point.

Replace your existing code in `app/templates/sightings/index.hbs` with the component.

```
<div class="row">
  {{#each model as |sighting|}}
    <div class="col-xs-12 col-sm-3 text-center">
      <div class="media well">
        <img class="media-object thumbnail" src="{{if sighting.cryptid.profileImg
          sighting.cryptid.profileImg 'assets/images/cryptids/blank_th.png'}}"
          alt="{{sighting.cryptid.name}}" width="100%" height="100%">
        <div class="caption">
          <h3>{{sighting.cryptid.name}}</h3>
          {{#if sighting.location}}
            <h3>{{sighting.location}}</h3>
            <p>{{moment from sighting.sightedAt}}</p>
          {{else}}
            <h3 class="text-danger">Bogus Sighting</h3>
          {{/if}}
        </div>
        {{#link to 'sighting.edit' sighting.id tagName="button"
          class="btn btn-success btn-block"}}
          Edit
        {{/link to}}
      </div>
      {{#listing-item imagePath=sighting.cryptid.profileImg
        name=sighting.cryptid.name}}
      {{/listing-item}}
    </div>
  {{/each}}
</div>
```

You have replaced a lot of code with a single line. Some functionality was removed in the process, but you will fix that soon. The next step is adding the container styles back on the component element. It is missing the `"media"` and `"well"` Bootstrap styles.

Open `app/components/listing-item.js` and add a `classNames` property to the `listing-item` component:

```
import Ember from 'ember';

export default Ember.Component.extend({
  classNames: ["media", "well"]
});
```

The property `classNames` passes its value to the `classNames` attribute of the `<div>` element created by the component.

Now the rendered component looks like this:

```
<div class="media well">
  <img class="media-object thumbnail" src="[imagePath string]" alt="[name string]"
    width="100%" height="100%">
  <div class="caption">
    <h3>[name string]</h3>
    {{yield}}
  </div>
</div>
```

Next, you will add elements to the {{yield}} section of the component template to make the implementation of this component instance unique to the sightings route. First, in app/templates/sightings/index.hbs, add the component's contextual content that will render in the {{yield}}:

```
...
    {{#listing-item imagePath=sighting.cryptid.profileImg
      name=sighting.cryptid.name}}
      {{#if sighting.location}}
        <h3>{{sighting.location}}</h3>
          <p>{{moment-from sighting.sightedAt}}</p>
      {{else}}
        <h3 class="text-danger">Bogus Sighting</h3>
      {{/if}}
      {{#link-to 'sighting.edit' sighting.id tagName="button"
        class="btn btn-success btn-block"}}
        Edit
      {{/link-to}}
    {{/listing-item}}
```

This code, which should look familiar, reinstates the sighting location and time as well as the Edit button.

Components for DRY Code

Time to DRY up your code.

Say what? DRY is a programming principle that stands for "don't repeat yourself." In other words, if you write something down, write it down in just one place.

Both the listings for sightings and cryptids use an element with `class="media well"` with images and titles. So this is some code that can be DRYed up. The component does not match exactly to the cryptid listing item, but that is where the `{{yield}}` comes in.

Add the new `{{#listing-item}}` component to the cryptids listing. In `app/templates/cryptids.hbs`, replace the `<div class="media well">` element and its child elements:

```
<div class="row">
  {{#each model as |cryptid|}}
    <div class="col-xs-12 col-sm-3 text-center">
      <div class="media well">
        {{#link-to 'cryptid' cryptid.id}}
          <img class="media object thumbnail"
            src="{{if cryptid.profileImg cryptid.profileImg
            'assets/images/cryptids/blank_th.png'}}"
            alt="{{cryptid.name}}" width="100%" height="100%">
        {{/link-to}}
        <div class="caption">
          <h3>{{cryptid.name}}</h3>
        </div>
      </div>
      {{#link-to 'cryptid' cryptid.id}}
        {{listing-item imagePath=cryptid.profileImg name=cryptid.name}}
      {{/link-to}}
    </div>
  {{else}}
    <div class="jumbotron">
      <h1>No Creatures</h1>
    </div>
  {{/each}}
</div>
```

Did you notice that there is a difference between the way you referenced your component in the two templates? The sightings iterator uses the `{{yield}}` to add elements inside the `<div class="caption">` and the cryptids template does not. When you want a component to only use the code in the component template file, you can use an *inline component*, written without the hash (#) – `{{listing-item}}` – as you did here. With this syntax, there is no closing HTMLBars element (`{{/listing-item}}`).

To add a link to the component, you wrapped the component with a `{{#link-to}}`. In the old iterated elements, only the image linked to the cryptid detail page. Now the entire element links to the cryptid detail. This example shows the flexibility of components to conform to the context of different route templates while rendering similar content. You could also add more attributes to the component to account for the need for a link inside the component template.

Data Down, Actions Up

Next, you will add a component to be controlled by a state change in the application. Specifically, you will create a flash alert to display a message when you create a new listing.

One of the tenets of components is "data (or state) down and actions up." Unlike controllers, components should not change the state of an application; they should pass changes up through actions. The state of a component, on the other hand, should be passed in from a parent template – data down (Figure 25.2).

Figure 25.2 Component Data Down Actions Up

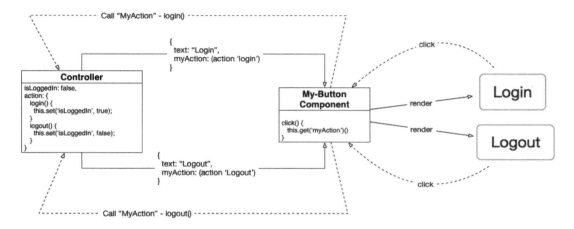

A component could easily replace a controller by passing a route's model directly to the component without the need for a controller's decorators or actions.

You will create a new component and actions and add the component to the `app/templates/application.hbs` file to render a global message when a new sighting is created.

First, generate the new component in the terminal:

```
ember g component flash-alert
```

The `{{flash-alert}}` component will be a container element for a `<strong>` alert title and a text message.

Open and edit `app/templates/components/flash-alert.hbs` to make it so:

```
{{yield}}
<strong>{{typeTitle}}!</strong> {{message}}
```

Edit the component file `app/components/flash-alert.js` and add `classNames`:

```
import Ember from 'ember';

export default Ember.Component.extend({
  classNames: ["alert"]
});
```

Now the component will render the following elements:

```
<div class="alert">
  <strong>{{typeTitle}}!</strong> {{message}}
</div>
```

Class Name Bindings

This container gives the impression that it will display the correct message, but the styling will not give you context to its alert type. Bootstrap has state-variant styles for alert components: "alert-success", "alert-info", "alert-warning", and "alert-danger".

In order to set the correct alert type, you will add one of these classes with a computed property and class name binding.

Start with the computed property in app/components/flash-alert.js:

```
...
export default Ember.Component.extend({
  classNames: ["alert"],
  typeClass: Ember.computed('alertType', function() {
    return "alert-" + this.get('alertType');
  })
});
```

Here, you added a computed property for typeClass, which will be used to add a className to the component's <div> element. The computed property expects a property called alertType, which you will add later, and returns a string with "alert-" prefixing the "alertType". This allows you to pass in a property with a value of "success", "info", "warning", or "danger" to supply the context of the alert. You will be using this same alertType property for another computed property.

Finally, add the className bindings in the app/components/flash-alert.js file for classNames bound to component properties:

```
...
export default Ember.Component.extend({
  classNames: ["alert"],
  classNameBindings: ['typeClass'],
  typeClass: Ember.computed('alertType', function() {
    return "alert-" + this.get('alertType');
  })
});
```

This adds a className to the classNames array from the value of the computed property typeClass. When you set the alertType property, the style changes on the component.

Using classNameBindings is specific to the classNames attribute on an element. There is a complementary Ember component property for the other attributes: attributeBindings. You can bind component properties to the attributes of the component's element. A basic example is setting the href of a link to a computedProperty. For example:

```
export default Ember.Component.extend({
  attributeBindings: ['href', 'customHREF:href'],
  href: "http://www.mydomain.com",
  customHREF: "http://www.mydomain.com"
});
```

With attribute bindings you can set all the component's attributes with the state data passed into the component. To explore this further, check out the Ember documentation online.

Next, add a computed property to display the alert type as a string. The component template is expecting a property `typeTitle`, so you have to add this computed property to `app/components/flash-alert.js`:

```
import Ember from 'ember';

export default Ember.Component.extend({
  ...
  typeClass: Ember.computed('alertType', function() {
    return "alert-" + this.get('alertType');
  }),
  typeTitle: Ember.computed('alertType', function() {
    return Ember.String.capitalize(this.get('alertType'));
  })
});
```

Now you have a string in the message bound to the alert type that is capitalized and is a `<strong>` element in the template. You have bound a class name and a decorated property to the component by computing the value of each from data passed into the component via the `alertType` property.

Next you need to add your component to your page in `app/templates/application.hbs`:

```
<header>
  ...
</header>
<div class="container">
  {{flash-alert}}
  {{outlet}}
</div>
```

This component is an inline component, meaning there will be no elements to render in the `{{yield}}` and the component template does not need a `{{yield}}`.

Data Down

At this point the alert does not have any state data to render content and classNames, only containers. Pass in the state of the component in app/templates/application.hbs:

```
...
  {{flash-alert message="This is the Alert Message" alertType="success"}}
  {{outlet}}
</div>
```

Start the server and open your browser to http://localhost:4200/sightings to see the {{flash-alert}} component rendered with the inline data you supplied (Figure 25.3).

Figure 25.3 Flash alert

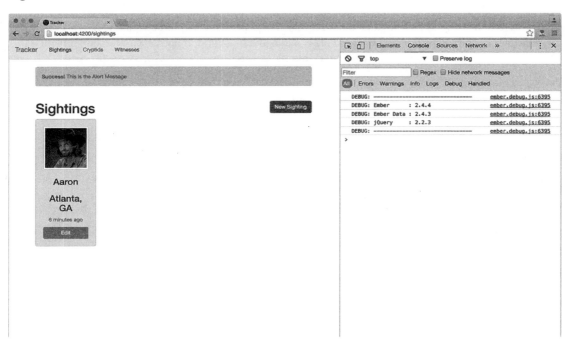

Now that the alert is on the screen, you want to set the properties of message and alertType dynamically. You will need an application controller to achieve this. Using the Ember CLI generator, add the controller:

```
ember g controller application
```

The application controller will maintain the dynamic state of the {{flash-alert}} component. The controller will need properties to maintain the state of the alert. Add the following property to app/controllers/application.js:

```
import Ember from 'ember';

export default Ember.Controller.extend({
  alertMessage: null,
  alertType: null,
  isAlertShowing: false
});
```

You added properties that will be set by an action. Now you have controller properties to pass to the flash-alert component in app/templates/application.hbs:

```
...
</header>
<div class="container">
  {{#if isAlertShowing}}
    {{flash-alert message="This is the Alert Message" alertType="success"}}
                   alertMessage alertType=alertType}}
  {{/if}}
  {{outlet}}
</div>
```

The controller's properties can now be set from an action. The application only needs to render the component when the isAlertShowing property is set to true and when the other properties have values. The action to set these properties will be coming from controllers all over the application. How do you bubble these actions up? Ember does it for you (Figure 25.4).

Figure 25.4 Flash alert process

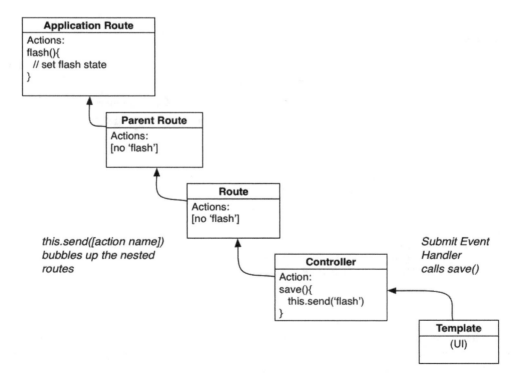

461

You have to add an action to a route. You can call an action from a controller, and it will hit the current controller, then the current route, the parent routes, then the application route.

Because your flash-alert is in the app/templates/application.hbs, you need an application route. Create one:

```
ember g route application
```

You will see this message returned in the command line:

```
[?] Overwrite app/templates/application.hbs?
```

Enter n or no to continue. You do not want to overwrite the template file you just created. You only want to add the JavaScript file app/routes/application.js.

Next you will need to edit the route in app/routes/application.js:

```
import Ember from 'ember';

export default Ember.Route.extend({
  actions: {
    flash(data){
      this.controller.set('alertMessage', data.message);
      this.controller.set('alertType', data.alertType);
      this.controller.set('isAlertShowing', true);
    }
  }
});
```

Actions Up

Now you have an action to set the flash-alert to display the appropriate message. You just need to pass the action some data. That data will be an object with keys for alertType and message.

The alertType will be a part of both the message and the style with Bootstrap alert variants: "success", "warning", "info", or "danger". Calling the action from a controller will look like this:

```
this.send('flash', {alertType: "success", message: "You Did It! Hooray!"});
```

You will be adding the call to the application action after creating a new sighting. In app/routes/sightings/new.js, add the following:

```
...
  create() {
    var self = this;
    this.get('sighting').save().then(function(data){
      self.send('flash', {alertType: "success", message: "New sighting."});
      self.transitionTo('sightings');
    });
...
```

Now navigate to create a new sighting by clicking the New Sighting button. Select a cryptid and a witness, type a new location, and click Save. Once the sighting is saved in the database, the app will route you to the list of sightings with a new flash message at the top of the list (Figure 25.5).

Figure 25.5 Flash alert – new sighting

The last step is adding the action and event that will remove the alert from the screen. You only want to show the flash-alert after you have created a new message, so you need to flip the switch to hide the alert when you remove it.

In app/controllers/application.js, add an action called removeAlert:

```
...
export default Ember.Controller.extend({

  alertMessage: null,
  alertType: null,
  isAlertShowing: false,
  actions: {
    removeAlert(){
      this.set('alertMessage', "");
      this.set('alertType', "success");
      this.set('isAlertShowing', false);
    }
  }
});
```

This will set isAlertShowing to false, set the alertMessage to an empty string, and set the alertType to "success".

Next, send the `removeAlert` action to the component. Add the following to app/templates/
application.hbs:

```
...
</header>
<div class="container">
  {{#if isAlertShowing}}
    {{flash-alert message=alertMessage alertType=alertType}}
      close=(action "removeAlert")}}
  {{/if}}
  {{outlet}}
</div>
```

The syntax `close=(action "removeAlert")` probably looks weird. This is new to Ember 2.0 and is
called a *closure action*. The function literal is passed through to be called from the component as an
attribute named `close`, much like an alias.

Older versions of Ember had a more complex version of this flow. Closure actions are more than
just functions passed from an object as an argument under the hood. To find out more about closure
actions, visit the EmberJS blog post about the features for version 1.13 and 2.0 at emberjs.com/
blog/2015/06/12/ember-1-13-0-released.html.

Next, you need to call this action from the component. Components are instances of DOM elements;
thus, they have key/value pairs representing DOM element events. You can add a declaration of a
`click` event listener and Ember will add the listener to the `<div>` element wrapping the template. Add
the following to app/components/flash-alert.js:

```
import Ember from 'ember';

export default Ember.Component.extend({
  ...
  typeTitle: Ember.computed('alertType', function() {
    return Ember.String.capitalize(this.get('alertType'));
  }),
  click() {
    this.get('close')();
  }
});
```

The property `close`, when called, will invoke the action `"removeAlert"` defined on the application
controller. By using a closure action, you have assigned a component's property to a function defined
in the parent controller and tied the component's functionality to the scope of its parent. You can add a
`flash-alert` at any level and assign different functionality to `close` based on its context.

You have added a component that responds to data going down to customize the component and to
actions going up to set the external state of the component from the parent controller. This the lifecycle
of a component: data down, actions up. Keep this pattern in mind when creating components.

Throughout the Application Architecture chapters you have learned about the structure of modern
applications built with Ember. You have learned about the patterns of MVC and how this framework
helps you separate concerns with pre-built JavaScript objects. It also helps you maintain sanity with
naming patterns, scaffolding, build tools, and conventions. From here you can feel confident creating
a new app with ember new. You can dive straight into your application needs modeling data, creating
routes, and building components.

The Ember community maintains this wonderful framework and continues to build in efficiencies as JavaScript matures. This framework is built by people who have struggled with the same challenges you will face as you hone your JavaScript skills. Remember to ask questions when something does not work, help fix bugs when you find something that is broken, and give back when you can. You are now part of the greater JavaScript community.

Bronze Challenge: Customizing the Alert Message

The {{flash-alert}} you trigger when adding a sighting is generic. Add the sighting location and date to the message.

Silver Challenge: Making the NavBar a Component

Make the NavBar in the application template a component. Add a property state to show two versions of the navigation. Add conditional statements in the NavBar component for showing specific links.

Gold Challenge: Array of Alerts

Restructure the flash-alert component to accept an array of alerts with different alert types and messages. You may need to have multiple warnings on the screen at the same time. Use an Ember.ArrayProxy in place of the individual properties setting the alert. Add to the array with the message, type, and a new index property so that you can remove the item from the array when you click it.

26

Afterword

Congratulations! You are at the end of this guide. Not everyone has the discipline to do what you have done and learn what you have learned. Take a quick moment to give yourself a pat on the back.

Your hard work has paid off: You are now a front-end developer.

The Final Challenge

We have one last challenge for you: Become a *good* front-end developer. Good developers are good in their own ways, so you must find your own path from here on out.

Where might you start? Here are some ideas:

Write code. Now. You will quickly forget what you have learned here if you do not apply your knowledge. Contribute to a project or write a simple application of your own. Whatever you do, waste no time: Write code.

Learn. You have learned a little bit about a lot of things in this book. Did any of them spark your imagination? Write some code to play around with your favorite thing. Find and read more documentation about it – or an entire book, if there is one. Also, check out the JavaScript Jabber podcast for some thoughtful and entertaining discussion about the latest developments in front-end development (devchat.tv/js-jabber).

Meet people. Local meetups are a good place to meet like-minded developers. Lots of top-notch front-end developers are active on Twitter. And you can attend front-end conferences to meet other developers (maybe even us!).

Explore the open source community. Front-end development is exploding on www.github.com. When you find a cool library, check out other projects from its contributors. Share your own code, too – you never know who will find it useful or interesting. We find the WDRL (Web Development Reading List) mailing list to be a great way to see what is happening in the front-end community (wdrl.info).

Shameless Plugs

You can find us on Twitter. Chris is @radishmouse and Todd is @tgandee.

If you enjoyed this book, check out the other Big Nerd Ranch Guides at www.bignerdranch.com/books. We also have a broad selection of week-long courses for developers, where we make it easy to learn a book's worth of stuff in only a week. And of course, if you just need someone to write great code, we do contract programming, too. For more info, go to www.bignerdranch.com.

Thank You

Without readers like you, our work would not exist. Thank you for buying and reading our book.

Index

Symbols

+= (concatenation operator), 232
. (dot operator), 111, 114
:focus pseudo-class, 254
:hover pseudo-class, 150
:invalid pseudo-class, 253
:required pseudo-class, 254
`<a>` tag, 25
`<body>` tag, 21
`<div>` tag
    about, 67, 200
    for styling with Bootstrap, 201
`<form>` tag, 200
`<h1>` tag, 21
`<head>` tag, 21
`<hr>` tag, 446
`<img>` tag, 25
`<input>` tag
    for checkboxes, 230
    for radio buttons, 205
    for range sliders, 207
    for reset buttons, 208
    for submit buttons, 208
    for text input, 201
    linking to `<label>` tag, 202, 205
`<label>` tag
    about, 202
    linking to `<input>` tag, 202, 205
`<link>` tag, 23
`<meta>` tag, 21
`<option>` tag, 206
`<script>` tag, 105
`<section>` tag, 200
`<select>` tag, 206
`<span>` tag, 24
`<style>` tag, 253
`<title>` tag, 20
`<ul>` tag, 23
= (assignment operator), 107
== (loose equality operator), 145
=== (strict equality operator), 145
@font-face declaration, 60
@import directive, 377
@media declaration, 96

{{#each}} helper, 424
{{#if}} helper, 423
{{#link-to}} helper, 429
{{action}} helper, 440
{{if}} helper, 427
{{outlet}} helper, 388, 389
{{x-select}} component, 438
{{yield}} helper, 453
|| (default/logical or operator), 171

A

`<a>` tag, 25
absolute positioning, 86
{{action}} helper, 440
actual viewport (see layout viewport)
add method, 142
addEventListener method, 123, 124
afterModel method, 396
Ajax
    about, 258
    and jQuery, 258
    XMLHttpRequest API, 258
align-items flexbox property, 84
alt attribute, 25
anchor tags (see `<a>` tag)
anonymous functions
    about, 124
    vs named functions in callbacks, 133
arguments, 118
arrow functions
    about, 340
    vs anonymous functions, 346
assignment operator (=), 107
asynchronous communication
    about, 258
    in callbacks, 268
Atom
    autocompletion with emmet, 20, 23
    copying the project path, 26
    creating a file, 18
    creating a folder, 19
    finding and replacing text, 102
    installing, 4
    opening a project, 18
    plug-ins, 4-7
    snippets, 61
atomic styling